J.M.N. Jeffries

Colin Andersen

Balfour in the Dock

J.M.N. Jeffries & the
Case for the Prosecution

SKYSCRAPER

SKYSCRAPER PUBLICATIONS

"Really there is no canon, no axiom of justice, no propriety which has not been violated in the endeavour to install the Jewish National Home."

J.M.N. Jeffries,
Palestine: The Reality, 1939, p 190

"It is intolerable when those who bring evidence find that it is passed over and that they are treated as though they uttered empty and unsupported allegations."

J.M.N. Jeffries,
letter to the Catholic Herald, 9 June, 1939

"What is needed to settle the imbroglio in [Palestine], as far as it can be settled, is a Royal Commission upon Mr. Lloyd George. Lord Balfour would be included, of course, in the terms of reference."

J.M.N. Jeffries,
Palestine, Arab or Jew: A Criticism of the Palestine Report, The Tablet, 17 July, 1937

First published 2017 by Skyscraper Publications
20 Crab Tree Close, Bloxham, Oxon OX15 4SE, U.K.
www.skyscraperpublications.com

First published 2017

A CIP catalogue record for this book is available
from the British Library.
ISBN-13: 978-1-911072-22-5

Portrait drawings by
Lilly Platt-Hepworth

Cover concept and design by
Chandler Book Design

Designed and typeset by
Chandler Book Design

Printed in the United Kingdom
by Latitude Press

DEDICATION

To my inspirations, Siri and Hala. To Paul and Peter for their unstinting help. To Karl for the idea. To Lilly for the artwork. To anyone who has ever raised a voice in support of justice and freedom in Palestine.

CONTENTS

Introduction: Searching for J.M.N. Jeffries

In the lead-up to the August 2014 centenary of the start of World War I, the UK's *Daily Mail* delved deep into its archives for a feature on a once popular column called *Soldiers' Letters*. The column's appeal at the time was obvious; it published letters written by British troops to their loved ones back home. It was, however, relatively short-lived – 1914–15 – and fell victim to the demands of wartime censorship.

The writer of the feature, *Letters from hell soaked in blood*, commented that:

> Its passing did not go unnoticed. On 15 July [1915], the *Mail* published a letter from a Mr. J.M.N. Jeffries. 'One misses the soldiers' letters in the paper,' he wrote. 'I suppose they died suddenly on a dark night, strangled by military exigencies, and we shall never see their like again till after the war. They were wonderful letters, plucky, anomalous, witty things, telling of bright incidents from the fields of gore, homely trench struggles, neighbourly grenade throwings, exclusive little hand-to-hands. They certainly illuminated the school-report style of the official news.'[1]

It is clear from the above that the journalist concerned, Tony Rennell, was unaware that, at the time, J.M.N. Jeffries was not only

---

1. *Letters from hell soaked in blood: At the outbreak of war, the Daily Mail invited readers to send in letters for publication, the response was overwhelming*, Tony Rennell, *Daily Mail*, 12/7/14

one of the *Daily Mail*'s war correspondents, but one, moreover, who would go on to become one of its best known foreign correspondents. If the *Daily Mail* could not remember one of its own, it is perhaps understandable that the name J.M.N. Jeffries means virtually nothing to the rest of us today. Understandable, but most unfortunate, because Jeffries was so much more than just another name in the annals of British journalism.

To begin with, Joseph Mary Nagle Jeffries was one of the most brilliant investigative journalists of the interwar period. It was Jeffries, for example, who published, in 1923, a translation from the Arabic of the text of a *suppressed* British wartime pledge to the Arabs, promising support for Arab independence "*in all the regions lying within the territories included in the... boundaries proposed by the Shareef of Mecca*" in return for an alliance aimed at ousting the Ottoman Turks from the Middle East. The pledge came in the form of an exchange of letters, known as the Hussein-McMahon Correspondence, between the Sharif of Mecca, Hussein ibn Ali al-Hashemi, and Britain's High Commissioner in Egypt, Sir Henry McMahon. This took place from July 1915 to January 1916, and ignited the Arab Revolt of 1916–18, best remembered today for the exploits of T.E. Lawrence, or 'Lawrence of Arabia' as he came to be known. The McMahon pledge, of course, was the first of three British wartime pledges concerning the Middle East. It was followed by the Sykes-Picot Agreement of 1916, which divided the area into British and French spheres of influence, and the Balfour Declaration of 1917, which promised the nascent Zionist movement "*a national home for the Jewish people*" in Palestine.

But Jeffries' 'scoop' did not end there. His revelation of the Hussein-McMahon Correspondence was just one part, albeit the most important, of an exhaustive exposé of British policy in Palestine, which ran from 8 January to 8 February, 1923, in the pages of the *Daily Mail*. Based on an investigation he had conducted in Palestine in 1922, it provided the vital ammunition needed by a group of concerned British politicians to mount a concerted challenge to Britain's policy of support for a Jewish national home in Palestine.

In addition, as his letter of 1915 indicates, and as will become abundantly clear during the course of this narrative, Jeffries can write – so exquisitely, in fact, that 'every sentence should be carved in stone or engraved on bronze.'[2]

But Jeffries' *real* claim on the attention of posterity lies, ultimately, neither in his journalistic prowess nor in his fine prose, but in the fact that he has written the most passionate and forensic account in English of how the British went about turning innocent, unsuspecting, prewar Palestine into today's 'Palestine problem.' Published in 1939, *Palestine: The Reality* is at once a masterwork of history and a scathing indictment of British policy in Palestine from 1914 to1938. Those responsible for its formulation, namely Prime Minister David Lloyd George and Foreign Secretary Arthur James Balfour, are, as it were, indicted for crimes against the Palestinian people, tried, and judged accordingly:

> Readers will see that I have not dealt tenderly with certain statesmen and certain Governments of ours. There is no reason, to my mind, for euphemism, for saying that these men and these Cabinets were mistaken or ill-advised or pursued mere erroneous policy in Palestine, or foolishly accepted an unworkable Mandate. They did nothing of the kind. They pursued a policy involving fraud and perfidy. They tyrannously withdrew from the Arabs the Arabs' natural and inherent rights over their native land. They broke Britain's word to the Arabs. To suit their aims in Palestine they gerrymandered as far as they could the Covenant of the League of Nations, and where they could gerrymander it no further they broke it. They falsified the Mandate. Later Governments have been less guilty. But they have committed their own sins of omission by not reconsidering the acts of their predecessors, and by continuing with a policy into the antecedents of which they have not inquired. These charges have to be made. The evidence which justifies them accompanies them.[3]

(Note that the term 'mandate' here refers to the authority vested in Britain by the League of Nations to administer Palestine. Britain's Palestine Mandate lasted from 1923–48.)

---

2. To borrow the words of a fellow British journalist of his day, Philip Gibbs.
3. *Palestine: The Reality*, p XVI (Hereinafter: PTR)

Despite the book's great significance, however, it is all but impossible to find an *original* copy today. In terms of library copies in the UK, the *British Writers in Support of Palestine* blog estimates only '21 possible copies' in existence. Any attempt to procure a copy online is invariably greeted by the message 'Currently unobtainable.' *Palestine: The Reality*, therefore, tends to be known, if at all, largely by reputation. (Fortunately, however, this long eclipse is now over; *Palestine: The Reality* has been republished this year, by Skyscraper Publications in the United Kingdom and Olive Branch Press in the United States.)

Compounding the mystery of the book's 'disappearance,' all record of Jeffries himself is inexplicably missing from biographical dictionaries and Wikipedia alike.

Needless to say, the dust jacket of the original *Palestine: The Reality* is even harder to come by than the book itself. Yet it contains an invaluable explanation of just what it was that Jeffries and/or his publisher hoped a reader of the time would find in the book. The first thing a browser would have read on the front cover, under the author's name, and the book's title, is this:

> Here is the Arab case; the fullest and most authoritative account of the Palestine question ever written. Many vital documents are made public for the first time and an entirely new light is shed on the Arab claims. It is not too much to say that, if its evidence and arguments are accepted, this book alters everything in respect of Palestine and its publication is a political event of high importance.

The statement that 'this book alters everything in respect of Palestine and its publication is a political event of high importance,' like the title, speaks to the revelatory nature of the book.

Turning to the jacket's inside flaps, we read that,

> This is a book of the highest importance, both as an essential document in the present critical phase of the Palestine question and as a contribution to the history of British policy in the Near East since the outbreak of the War.
>
> It brings to light a mass of unpublished documents in support of the Arab case and should profoundly affect our whole outlook on it. Every chapter of the forty tells something which has not

been told before – or puts a new construction on circumstances hitherto differently reported.

For the first time in this country documents are quoted showing how the Allies were connected with the Arab National Movement even before the War. The rise of Zionism is studied afresh from rare Zionist and official documents. Details of secret proposals of peace with Turkey are produced for the first time, likewise many new facts connected with the McMahon-Hussein treaty. For the first time the full story of the drafting of the Balfour Declaration is told – and the discovery of the original source of the cardinal sentence is entirely new. The story of the assumption of the British Mandate has never been disclosed before. There are startling disclosures concerning the immixture of American Zionists in British Government affairs and of the manipulation of the Covenant of the League [of Nations] in the interests of Zionism. The author even supplies evidence of the Zionists' share in drafting the Mandate.

Mr. Lloyd George and Lord Balfour are very severely handled for their action in the Holy Land. The most surprising charge against the former, very fully documented, is that in the interests of the [Jewish] "National Home" he set up an Administration in Palestine which governed for three years without any valid authority. Since many of the statutes governing Zionist immigration and other primary matters were issued during these three years, the charge is of considerable consequence.

Perhaps the most important point for the future of Palestine made by Mr Jeffries is that no solution of the present situation is just unless it predicates the bestowal of independence upon the population of the country. The schemes mooted for making a Crown Colony or Dominion of Palestine are held to be illegitimate.

In all its great length Mr Jeffries's book has not a dull page. He writes brilliantly and he hits hard, and there are flashes throughout of that wit which served him so well in *Front Everywhere*, the account of his experiences as a foreign correspondent during the War and after.

In short, this is a book for those interested in the inside story of how and why Britain came to be involved in Palestinian affairs.

George Antonius' *Arab Awakening*

Only one other book on the modern Middle East from the interwar period matches *Palestine: The Reality* in stature, George Antonius' *The Arab Awakening* (1938). Antonius' book, while covering some of the ground covered by Jeffries, is, as the eminent Palestinian-American scholar Edward Said has pointed out, 'the classic and foundational book on Arab nationalism.'[4] As such, it lacks the detailed focus on Palestine of Jeffries' book, which, to borrow Said's phrasing, may be characterised as 'the classic and foundational book on the creation of the Palestine problem.'

We do not know for certain whether Antonius and Jeffries ever met, although, with Antonius acting as secretary general to an Arab delegation attending the February 1939 London Conference on Palestine, and Jeffries as a leading member of a London information office known as the Arab Centre, which hosted receptions for the Arab delegates, it is inconceivable that they did not. We do know, however, that the two exchanged letters on the subject of Balfour in 1936.[5]

Jeffries had this to say of Antonius and his book in a footnote in *Palestine: The Reality*:

> Since this book has been completed Mr. George Antonius has included the McMahon-Hussein Correspondence in his *The Arab Awakening*. Equally a scholar in English and in Arabic, he has made his own translation of the text, and the reader will find interest in comparing it with the literal version given to me in 1922. Mr. Antonius writes a full account of the rise of the Arab [nationalist] societies, which should be read to supplement my brief summary. The same may be said of his account of the Arab revolt. I have had the benefit of Mr. Antonius's wide knowledge and erudition when preparing Chapter XV of the present work, and the reader will find elucidation and confirmation of various details in that and in adjoining chapters in Mr. Antonius's admirable book.[6]

It is equally inconceivable that Antonius, who remained in London until the end of April, before departing for Egypt, did not take a copy of *Palestine: The Reality* with him.

---

4. Edward Said, *The Question of Palestine*, Vintage Books, New York, 1979/1992, p 245

5. See Susan Silsby Boyle, *Betrayal of Palestine: The Story of George Antonius*, Westview Press, Boulder, 2001, p 129. Typically, *Palestine: The Reality* is not to be found in Boyles' bibliography.

6. PTR, p 87

Of particular interest here, though, is how the two books fared down the years. While *The Arab Awakening*, published in November 1938, made it to a second impression as soon as December 1938, and has never been out of print since, *Palestine: The Reality*, published in March 1939, never got that far. (I will examine possible reasons for the incredible scarcity of Jeffries' book later in this narrative.)

One factor, in particular, helps explain the initial success of Antonius' book. Published, as it was, in time for the aforementioned conference, 'British officials,' explains Antonius' biographer, 'hastened to purchase it in order to study the little-known and hitherto unpublished documents pertaining to Palestinian claims to independence... Because of the documents and force of Antonius's analysis and arguments, British officials in the foreign and colonial offices were forced to restructure entirely their arguments for the denial of Palestinian independence.'[7]

In fact, not only was Antonius' book taken up by British officials, it was, according to another source, actively *promoted* by the Foreign Office:

> In addition to its immediate impact in London, *The Arab Awakening* received official attention in British and US diplomatic circles. During the early 1940s the Foreign Office provided copies of *The Arab Awakening* to all British consuls in the Arab world with instructions that they read the book.[8]

Consider, too, these (post-war) references to the book by (pro-Zionist) British Labour MP Richard Crossman:

> On the *Queen Mary* I had read George Antonius's *The Arab Awakening*, a brilliant survey of Arab history, far superior as a piece of writing to any Zionist publication I had read.[9]
>
> After dinner at the King David [Hotel], I went out to a party in the Mufti's villa, given by Mrs. Antonius, the widow of George Antonius. By the way, his book, *The Arab Awakening*, has been

---

7. Susan Silsby Boyle, p 3

8. William L. Cleveland, *The Arab Nationalism of George Antonius Reconsidered*, in *Rethinking Nationalism in the Arab Middle East*, edited by James P. Jankowski & Israel Gershoni, Columbia University Press, 1997, p 84

9. Richard Crossman, *Palestine Mission*, Hamish Hamilton, London, 1946, pp 49-50

standard reading for the British members of the Committee, but we found in Washington that the State Department had not got a copy.[10]

Quotations & Citations

In addition to being virtually unobtainable on the second-hand book market, *Palestine: The Reality* is conspicuous by its absence in relevant scholarly works, whether in the form of quotations, citations, or bibliographical listings. This, of course, is not the case with *The Arab Awakening*. To cite but two examples of the phenomenon, neither Elizabeth Monroe's influential *Britain's Moment in the Middle East: 1914–1956* (1963), nor the extensive 'Bibliographical Note' appended to Edward Said's seminal work, *The Question of Palestine* (1979) include any reference to Jeffries' book.

Only a handful of works defy this trend. These include: Frances P. Newton, *Fifty Years in Palestine: The Case for the Arabs* (1948); Christopher Sykes, *Cross Roads to Israel* (1965); Robert John & Sami Hadawi, *The Palestine Diary* (1970); Izzat Tannous, *The Palestinians: Eyewitness History of Palestine Under British Mandate* (1988); Karl Sabbagh, *Palestine: A Personal History* (2007); Adel Safty, *Might Over Right: How the Zionists Took Over Palestine* (2009); and Alison Weir, *Against Our Better Judgment: How the US Was Used to Create Israel* (2014).

Jeffries' incisive analysis of the Balfour Declaration (Chapter 11 of *Palestine: The Reality*), has, however, helped keep his name alive, even if only just. It was singled out in 1967 by the Institute for Palestine Studies for republication in its Monographs Series (No. 7) under the title, *The Balfour Declaration*, and included by the Palestinian historian Walid Khalidi in his monumental 1971 anthology, *From Haven to Conquest: Readings in Zionism & the Palestine Problem Until 1948*, with later anthologies by Ian S. Lustick (1994) and Michael Dumper (2009) following suit.

---

10. Richard Crossman, p 132. Antonius died in 1942. The Committee referred to is the 1946 Anglo-American Committee of Enquiry regarding the problems of European Jewry and Palestine.

Zionist References

As for contemporary Zionist writers, I have been able to find only two (predictably negative) references to Jeffries.

British academic Rory Miller refers to him as 'the author of two of the central pieces of English anti-Zionist propaganda before the Second World War: *The Palestine Deception: A Daily Mail Enquiry on the Spot* (1923) and *Palestine, the Reality* (1939).' (Of course, whether Miller has read either is a moot point.) His assessment, however, raises the question of why such 'central pieces' have all but disappeared.[11]

Michael J Cohen's *Britain's Moment in Palestine: Retrospect & Perspectives, 1917-1948* (2014), mentions Jeffries, but only in relation to quotations found in Frances Newton's aforementioned book. Cohen writes that Jeffries' book, 'which has been called the most comprehensive statement of the Palestine problem from the Arab view, went through several editions.' (Needless to say, he is wrong on the matter of 'several editions.') Curiously, despite acknowledging *Palestine: The Reality* as the 'most comprehensive statement of the Palestine problem from the Arab view,' Cohen blithely dismisses its author as a 'fringe figure of marginal importance.'[12]

How extraordinary then, that a book described as 'the central piece of English anti-Zionist propaganda' (Miller), and 'the most comprehensive statement of the Palestine problem from the Arab view' (Cohen), has languished in obscurity for the past 77 years.

11. Rory Miller, *The Other Side of the Coin: Arab Propaganda and the Battle against Zionism in London, 1937-48*, in *Israel: The First Hundred Years, Vol 1 Israel's Transition from Community to State*, ed. By Efraim Karsh, Frank Cass, London, 2000, p 201

12. Michael J. Cohen, *Britain's Moment in Palestine: Retrospect & Perspectives*, 1917-1948, Routledge, Oxon, 2014. Cohen also accuses Jeffries of portraying the 1921 Zionist Rutenberg concessions in Palestine as 'part of an international Jewish conspiracy, whereby Jewish capital would be used to industrialise and control the world,' this being the erroneous construction he places on the following sentence of Jeffries: 'The devisers [of the Rutenberg scheme] meant to make of Palestine a land of industrialism, linked with the centres of industrialism about the globe.'

The Tide is Turning

Thankfully, though, the tide has begun to turn. In addition to this year's republication of *Palestine: The Reality*, the Institute for Palestine Studies has republished Jeffries'1923 *Daily Mail* expose under the title *The Palestine Deception 1915-1923: The McMahon-Hussein Correspondence, the Balfour Declaration, and the Jewish National Home* (2014). (Tellingly, the editor refers only in passing to *Palestine: The Reality*, and cites only an Internet source for its fourth chapter. One can only assume that he did not have access to a copy of the book.)

My Aims

I have three major objectives in writing this book. The first is simply to pay tribute to Jeffries and to rescue him from Orwell's 'memory hole,' into which he has all but disappeared. The second is to take the reader back in Palestinian time, before the *Naksa* (Setback) of 1967 and the occupation of the Palestinian territories (1967– 2017) which followed it, and before the *Nakba* (Catastrophe) of 1948, which led to the birth of the Palestinian refugee problem (1948–2017), to the deep settler-colonial roots of the Palestine problem. And the third is to arm the reader against the tsunami of propaganda that is sure to accompany this year's commemoration of the centenary of the Balfour Declaration.

First, the tribute. I have read hundreds of fine scholarly and personal works on the subject of Palestine over many decades, and each, in its way, has contributed something to my understanding of the issue. I salute their authors, and stand in awe of their efforts to tell the truth about one aspect or another of the epic, century-long, struggle of the Palestinian people for the most basic of human rights. No single work on the subject, however, has educated me, and moved me, as profoundly as *Palestine: The Reality*. The best I can do to explain its impact on me is to cite Keats' famous sonnet *On First Looking into Chapman's Homer*. For Chapman, think Jeffries. For Chapman's *Homer*, think *Palestine: The Reality*:

> Much have I travell'd in the realms of gold,
> And many goodly states and kingdoms seen;
> Round many western islands have I been
> Which bards in fealty to Apollo hold.
> Oft of one wide expanse had I been told
> That deep-browed Homer ruled as his demesne;
> Yet did I never breathe its pure serene
> Till I heard Chapman speak out loud and bold:
> Then felt I like some watcher of the skies
> When a new planet swims into his ken;
> Or like stout Cortez when with eagle eyes
> He star'd at the Pacific – and all his men
> Look'd at each other with a wild surmise –
> Silent, upon a peak in Darien.

This book, then, is the very least I can do for the man who led me to Darien.

Second, the roots of the Palestine problem. For many today, the Palestine problem begins and ends with the current Israeli occupation and colonisation of the West Bank, and the Israeli blockade of Gaza. Those who dig deeper into Palestinian history, of course, will come to the *Nakba* of 1948, but emerge, perhaps, with the mistaken impression that the problem has its origins in the failure of two indigenous Palestinian communities, Jews and Arabs, to simply 'get along.' That is, that what happened in 1948 was a kind of obscure civil/ tribal/ religious war from which the Jews emerged as the victors.

The fact of the matter, however, is that the Palestine problem is fundamentally a *settler-colonial* problem, the roots of which lie in imperial Britain's fateful embrace, during World War I, of the *European* Jewish settler-colonial movement known as Zionism, and its consequent decision to open *non-European* Arab Palestine to immigration and colonisation by Zionist settlers, despite the implacable, and completely understandable, opposition of the country's *indigenous* Arab inhabitants. Only if we grasp this simple truth will we be in a position to see Israel for what it really is, a late-flowering but particularly toxic form of European settler-colonialism of the kind which has pitted armed, land-grabbing European colonists against vulnerable, indigenous populations, and led to the creation of such settler-colonial entities as the United States of America, Canada, Australia, French Algeria, and apartheid South Africa. Long before Maxime Rodinson wrote his seminal work *Israel: A Colonial-Settler State?* (1973), Jefferies was writing about the formation of the phenomenon in real time:

> On that Mediterranean shore, so near the highway to India, we especially have deep concern. We shall have to seek accommodation for our interests there. The more these interests are pondered, the more wildly foolish does our present policy appear. Into a plain issue between the Arabs and ourselves, which might have been determined by motives of friendship, we insert a foreign factor. We banish friendship, we introduce the Zionists and go on introducing them, we levy an army and call reservists to the colours and ship troops and lose our soldiers' lives so that Zionists may continue to be introduced. We, as it were, plant brambles everywhere, and defend with rifle and gun the international tangle which ensues. The problems of the future which should have been simple enough become ravelled and complex and even perhaps beyond our untwisting.[13]

Those words were written as the fires of the 1936–39 Palestinian Revolt against British rule (described by one historian as 'the most significant anticolonial insurgency in the Arab East during the interwar period') were raging. To crush it the British were forced to deploy '20,000 troops, RAF aircraft, superior firepower, armed Zionist auxiliaries, and the classical savagery of colonial counterinsurgency.' The Palestinians suffered an estimated 20,000 casualties.[14]

Jeffries' 'international tangle' is, of course, today's Gordian Knot. Variously referred to as the Palestine Problem, the Question of Palestine, the Arab-Israeli Conflict, or the Israeli-Palestinian Conflict, it has become a byword for political intractability. If truth be told it should be recognised for what it is - the worst and most enduring crime of British colonialism.

Third, this book is for those who desire an in-depth understanding of the Balfour Declaration in the year of its centenary.

---

13. PTR, p 21
14. See Ted Swedenburg, *Memories of Revolt: The 1936-1939 Rebellion & the Palestinian National Past*, The University of Arkansas Press, 2003, pp xix-xxi

One of the earliest indications that Britain's Zionists were preparing to celebrate the Declaration's centenary emerged in the context of the British Labour Party's search for a new leader following the resignation of Ed Miliband in May 2015. At a panel discussion organised by *The Jewish Chronicle* in July 2015, featuring the four leadership contenders, Jeremy Corbyn, Andy Burnham, Yvette Cooper and Liz Kendall, a member of the audience asked the panellists the following question: 'With the 100-year anniversary of the Balfour Declaration fast approaching, what do you candidates feel is an appropriate way to mark the occasion and should we feel proud of our role in helping to form the state of Israel?' The panellists' answers, with one exception, indicated an abysmal ignorance of the issue, a state of affairs that, I imagine, extends across the British political spectrum. The Palestine-literate Corbyn, despite minor errors of fact and emphasis, proved, unsurprisingly, to be the exception. He responded,

> I think it should be marked by a serious study of the history of the whole region because it also came on the back of the Sykes-Picot Agreement which didn't become public, I think, until 1922 or 1923... The Balfour Declaration was an extremely confused document. It did not enjoy universal support in the cabinet at the time and was indeed opposed by some of the Jewish members of the cabinet because of its confusion. What it said was, it supported a Jewish homeland for Jewish people in Israel but at the same time it would protect the rights of the existing population and guarantee them similar rights and opportunities. It's obvious that the rights and opportunities are hardly similar across the whole piece. Levels of living, of opportunity, and of power were very, very different. Britain then became the Mandate power under the Versailles Agreement, and later with the League of Nations, and finally, with the establishment of the state of Israel in 1948, which again was a pretty brutal and confused process, and also led to the expulsion of very large numbers of Palestinians which is... the problems are still there. You have to address the rights of everybody if there is to be peace across the region. Surely this is something we can all agree on and strive for?

For purposes of comparison, here are the responses of Cooper, Burnham and Kendall:

- Cooper (a former shadow foreign secretary, no less) 'strongly disagreed' with Corbyn. 'We have to see it,' she went on, 'as an immensely important historic document that was actually ahead of its time in recognising the importance of a Jewish state and Jewish homeland, and also the fact that it recognises the rights of people right across the Middle East, and so it was at its heart about a two-state solution, so I think, of course, we have to recognise the important role, the pioneering role that Britain played in recognition of the rights of the Jewish people to a homeland, but probably the best way to mark it is if we could give more impetus again to the peace process and the two-state solution.'

- Burnham, alluding to then prime minister David Cameron's campaign to have 'British values' taught in UK schools, cited the Declaration as 'an example of British values in action.' He went on to say that, although it 'didn't solve all the problems in the region,' the centenary should be 'a moment to see Britain renewing herself with renewed energy and vigour in pursuit of the two-state solution.'

- Kendall disclosed that she was 'proud' of the Declaration, and said, 'we must remember some of the principles in the [Israeli] constitution that we share as members of the Labour Party: a belief in social and economic equality regardless of race and religion, and to be proudly speaking up for a state where there is equality for women, where the rights of lesbians, gays and transsexuals are championed and celebrated, where there's a free and unfettered media, where trade unions are strong, where education is important – education, which is the beating heart of our Labour Party... We should point out what we share in common as members of the Labour Party in that deeply, deeply troubled region, that Israel is not just a democratic state but has strong principles and values of social democracy which we share.'

With the coming commemoration in mind, the *Guardian*'s Middle East editor, Ian Black, noted in December 2015 that,

These First World War agreements cooked up in London and Paris in the dying days of the Ottoman empire paved the way for new Arab nation states, the creation of Israel and the continuing plight of the Palestinians. And if their memory has faded in the west as their centenaries approach, they are still widely blamed for the problems of the region at an unusually violent and troubled time. 'This is history that the Arab peoples will never forget because they see it as directly relevant to problems they face today,' argues Oxford University's Eugene Rogan, author of several influential works on modern Middle Eastern history... Looking ahead, officials in the UK Foreign Office are brainstorming anxiously about how to mark these agreements. It is far harder than remembering the first world war's military anniversaries – Flanders, Gallipoli, the Somme – because while British and allied sacrifices and heroism can be celebrated and honoured, these were political acts that have left a toxic residue of resentment and conflict. Pro-Palestinian campaigners have demanded that Britain apologise for Balfour's pledge – but that seems unlikely given that it was made in very different circumstances from today and cannot be undone. It and the other wartime agreements are likely to feature in statements and public diplomacy designed to generate 'a more nuanced understanding' of the UK's controversial historical role.[15]

On the Palestinian side, the UK's Palestinian Return Centre (PRC) initiated a *Britain, It's Time to Apologise – 1917–2017 – A Century of Palestinian Suffering* campaign in 2012, and on October 23, 2016, officially launched a *Balfour Apology Campaign* in the House of Lords. Then in 2014, came *The Balfour Project*, which invited 'the government and people of the UK' to mark the centenary of the Balfour Declaration by 'learning what [it] means for both Jews and Arabs; acknowledging that whilst a homeland for the Jewish people has been achieved, the promise to protect the rights of the Palestinian people has not yet been fulfilled; and urging the people and elected representatives of the UK to take effective action to promote justice, security and peace for both peoples.'

On the Zionist side, in November 2016, a 'UK Christian coalition' website, *Balfour 100 – Christians Celebrating the*

---

15. *Middle East still rocking from first world war pacts made 100 years ago,* theguardian.com.uk, 30/12/15

Balfour Declaration of November 2 1917, appeared, dedicated to the 'commemoration' of the centenary, with a particular focus on 'the part played by evangelical Christian beliefs of the time in the events that led up to the letter being written,' and Christians United for Israel – UK launched a petition calling on the UK Government to 'stand with Israel and the Jewish people and to honour the Balfour Declaration without apology.' Further, as a riposte to the launch of the PRC's *Balfour Apology Campaign* in the House of Lords in October 2016, the Henry Jackson Society, a pro-Zionist, neoconservative think tank held a meeting in the House of Commons on 29 November, 2016, at which Dore Gold, a former director-general of Israel's Foreign Ministry, denounced the PRC for 'seeking an apology for past colonial crimes,' and claimed that Israel was not a colonialist entity, but had been 'restored as a Jewish commonwealth after it had been destroyed.'

On the party political side, a lacklustre House of Commons debate was held in Westminster Hall on 16 November, 2016. With one or two exceptions (in particular, George Kerevan, the SNP MP for Balfour's seat of East Lothian, who stated that the Balfour Declaration was 'unfinished business,' and described it as 'a studiously ambivalent document... because Britain and France had decided to exclude the Ottoman Empire from the Wilson[ian] principle of self-determination'), the majority of MPs present used the opportunity to display their limited understanding of the conflict and/or declare their allegiance to Israel. The Minister for the Middle East, Tobias Ellwood MP, however, set out the government's position on the centenary, declaring that,

> The Balfour Declaration had its flaws. It called [however] for the protection of the 'civil and religious rights of existing non-Jewish communities in Palestine'. It should have protected their political rights too, most especially their right to self-determination: a right that underpins the British commitment to a two-state solution to the Israeli-Palestinian conflict. We will mark the centenary of the Balfour Declaration next year. Planning is still at an early stage, but I want to make it clear that we will neither celebrate nor apologise.

Ellwood's neither-one-nor-the-other position, however, was contradicted mere days later, at a Conservative Friends of Israel function on 25 November, by Prime Minister Theresa May when she promised to mark the centenary of the Declaration with 'pride.'

The May government's official response to the PRC's 'Balfour Apology Campaign,' which had garnered 13,637 signatures on a petition, came on May 3, 1917:

> The Balfour Declaration is an historic statement for which His Majesty's Government does not intend to apologise. We are proud of our role in creating the State of Israel. The task now is to encourage moves towards peace. The Declaration was written in a world of competing imperial powers, in the midst of the First World War and in the twilight of the Ottoman Empire. In that context, establishing a homeland for the Jewish people in the land to which they had such strong historical and religious ties was the right and moral thing to do, particularly against the background of centuries of persecution. Of course, a full assessment of the Declaration and what followed from it can only be made by historians. Much has happened since 1917. We recognise that the Declaration should have called for the protection of political rights of the non-Jewish communities in Palestine, particularly their right to self-determination.

The statement goes on, predictably, to trot out the familiar nostrum of a 'two-state solution ... based on the 1967 borders with agreed land swaps,' and dismisses the Palestinian right of return with a reference to a 'realistic settlement for refugees.'

Jeffries would have turned in his grave at the government's statement, particularly at the brazen recycling, 100 years on, of the Declaration's wholesale dismissal of the Palestinian Arabs (who constituted, by his reckoning, 91% of the population of Palestine at the time) as 'the non-Jewish communities in Palestine' - a wording he condemned as 'fraudulent' and designed merely 'to conceal the true ratio between Arabs and Jews, and thereby to make easier the supersession of the former.'

A Word on Sources

Given that this is the story of a largely forgotten book by a largely forgotten scholar, it will come as no great surprise to learn that it is necessarily based on limited sources. The main source for

Jeffries' life from birth to retirement in the early 30s, the pre-*Reality* years, if you will, is his 1935 memoir, *Front Everywhere: The Reminiscences of the Famous Special Correspondent*. The main source of information relating to his circumstances while writing and publishing *Palestine: The Reality* is another memoir, Izzat Tannous' *The Palestinians: Eyewitness History of Palestine Under the Mandate: The Origins of the Palestinian-Israeli Conflict* (1988). For the remaining period of his life, from 1939 to 1960, I have had to rely on only the odd reference or rare personal letter. Editorial letters and opinion pieces by Jeffries from the 30s, and reviews of *Palestine: The Reality*, are reproduced here, all retrieved, to borrow Jeffries' words, from various 'out-of-the-way nooks of print.' Anything, in short, which has enabled me to add another layer of flesh to the bare bones of his story. The reader will note, too, that, at various points, where I have felt this helpful, I have supplemented Jeffries' words with those of George Antonius and the great Palestinian scholar, A.L. Tibawi, whose meticulous research, based on British Cabinet and Foreign Office documents, informs his groundbreaking study, *Anglo-Arab Relations & the Question of Palestine 1914–1921* (1977).

Finally, I have included two appendices by way of illustrating, *vis-à-vis* Jeffries, Antonius and Tibawi, just how bad – it has to be said – too many of today's 'scholarly' treatments of the Hussein-McMahon Correspondence and the Balfour Declaration really are. The examples given in these appendices underscore the pressing need for the works of Jeffries, Antonius and Tibawi, in particular, to be more widely read, and for their findings and perspectives to be incorporated into contemporary historical scholarship on the modern Middle East.

A Word on Structure

This book is overwhelmingly a political biography. Jeffries' analyses of the Arab nationalist and Zionist movements, the Hussein-McMahon Correspondence, the Sykes-Picot Agreement, the Balfour Declaration, the Paris Peace Conference, the San Remo Conference, Britain's Palestine Mandate and related political matters dominate the narrative. Any reader hoping for more of a balance between the personal and the political will, therefore, be disappointed. Jeffries is a man, after all, who neither married nor, at least that we know of, fathered children. His entire adult life was given over, in the first instance, to the relentless coverage of momentous events, and in the second, to an all-consuming passion for justice in Palestine.

In acknowledging the contribution of his fellow British activists in the cause of Palestine in the late thirties, Jeffries wrote that,

> Two motives have maintained their courage, when hope seemed farthest away. One was that a small country should never be downtrodden if they could help it. The other was that their own country should be true to her vows and to herself.[16]

He was, of course, writing as much about himself as his fellow activists. Such dedication to the cause, needless to say, would have left little time for a more personal life.

I have, throughout this narrative, given preference to full, often extended, quotations over paraphrases, preferring to let my sources speak for themselves rather than through me. Note that the original punctuation, spelling and italics have been retained throughout in these.

Where Jeffries is concerned, my aim is to showcase his unique and authoritative voice, and to facilitate, rather than impede, the flow of his analysis. Nor do I have any wish to scissor his elegant and witty prose, or in any way confine what a reviewer of *Front Everywhere* referred to as 'the lovely errant phrase that wanders from the point to make the story literature.' To do so in Jeffries' case, it seems to me, would be tantamount to sacrilege.

As for the other, complementary, voices drawn on here, particularly those of Antonius and Tibawi, I have tended to accord them a similar latitude.

---

16. PTR, p xviii

1

From Stonyhurst
to Belgium

'An accurate estimator of values'

It is symptomatic of just how elusive Jeffries is that he fails to mention the date and place of his birth in his 1935 memoir, *Front Everywhere*. For someone as profoundly cosmopolitan as Jeffries, however, such details hardly seem to matter. Be that as it may, a photograph in the book of an *Ordre de Laisser-Passer*, issued to him by Belgium's Ministry of War in August 1914, gives his place of birth as Cork, and his date of birth as October 16, 1888. The year, however, may be incorrect. For example, his *Times* obituary records his age at death as 80. If so, his birth year would, in fact, be 1880. Certainly, 1880 is more compatible with the years of his senior schooling (1891–98). (To add to the confusion, another source, the *Catholic Who's Who & Year Book 1930* gives 1885 as his birth year.) For the purpose of this narrative, where, at any point, I mention Jeffries' age, it will rest on the assumption that 1880 is the year of his birth.

Jeffries says of his ancestral history:

> I come of that Anglo-Irish stock which nowadays is dwindling away, as the produce of all small workshops dwindles in the modern world... My family entered Ireland in the days of Charles I, in the King's army... They remained aloof from the Irish for a full century and a half, and then my great grandfather married one of them. As a result he was dropped from his

grandfather's will. He died young and his widow brought her children up in her faith and changed their name from Gifford or Jefford – both forms being used in papers – to Jeffries... My paternal grandfather brought the family back to England... I was already in the world then, but very young, and my first memories are of Durham, where my father went for some while. Then came London and other places. Clear and continuous recollection begins for me in a house we had on the outskirts of Bournemouth.[1]

His father was a doctor, 'a man of lofty mind, of infinite kindness, unsparing to himself, an accurate estimator of values, a lover of the humble (he joined the Third Order or lay branch of the Franciscans), most deeply affectionate.'[2] Jeffries might correctly be described as a chip off the old block. Curiously, there is scant reference in his memoir to his mother, but this is more than made up for by the book's dedication: 'To MY MOTHER loving and loved beyond all.' His only siblings were two sisters, Marie and Clare.

From 1891 to 1898, Jeffries attended the Jesuit's Stonyhurst College in Lancashire. He remembers it as a happy and fruitful experience:

> Its name is familiar to all. Stonyhurst is a beacon of the North. Its gardens and avenues, its eagle-crowned towers and its many-windowed courts, the treasures of its sacristies and its libraries annually draw crowds of sightseers. I have been able to visit my old school too rarely, but I have left my thoughts behind there to atone for my truant body. My education was extremely classical, and extremely useful. It seems to be the fashion to-day to decry one's education, to treat it as something no more lasting than the teens during which it is conferred. But mine, besides giving me my life's background, has kept popping in and out of its foreground, helping me in emergencies, and like the hour-notes of the B.B.C., recalling me at intervals to safe and certain realities amidst the babble of views which besets the ears of a newspaper correspondent.[3]

Fortunately, Jeffries has left us with a more detailed account of his years at Stonyhurst, written much later in life for the *The Stonyhurst*

---

1. *Front Everywhere*, p12 (Hereinafter: FE)
2. FE, pp 15-16
3. FE, p 13

Magazine of January 1955. *Stonyhurst in My Time* is a light-hearted reminiscence about his youth, a perfect illustration of Wordsworth's line about the child being the father of the man. There is evidence in it, for example, of the wit who would one day dub David Lloyd George and Arthur James Balfour 'Acetone and accessory,' much to the annoyance of a certain Zionist reviewer in *The Times*:

> One thing strikes me about our comradeship which probably differentiates us from the boys of to-day. Friends as we were, we never called each other by our Christian names. It was indeed uncommon for boys to use Christian names for each other. Nicknames, however, were frequently used, and might be as derisive as you liked and the victim didn't. "Biddy" Irwin, "Scraggs" Monteith and "Pheasant" Partridge are nicknames that come back to me. "Biddy" simply because Irwin came from Roscommon, and "Scraggs" because Monteith was abnormally thin. Poor old Frank Partridge, who was of a fiery nature, always resented his obvious moniker, and subsequently had to endure all manner of variants, from "Thrush" to "Birdie."[4]

It is important to note that while Jeffries was always a believer, he wore his Catholic faith lightly. The paternal influence of a certain Father Cassidy, 'whose solicitude encircled us day and night,' seems to have contributed to this:

> It is not surprising that where I see him again now with the eyes of the spirit should be in the refectory, and in the chapel. The essentials to which he devoted himself were *the* essentials, the soul and the body: he had a gift for discarding the secondary. As for our faith, he imbued us with it – that is the word. Under his guidance it came to us unlectured, unforced, never screwed into us, as it were, but rising gradually on us and warming us like the sun.[5]

Finally, we have Stonyhurst to thank for helping hone his literary skills:

> And I wonder, are Poets still obliged to be poets? In our Augustan era they were. In Poetry, on some formal afternoons, during the Spring Term, I think, when there was a supposedly better chance

---

4. *Stonyhurst In My Time*, January 1955, p 47
5. *Stonyhurst*, p 46

of boyish imaginations sprouting into the written equivalents of daffodils and of primroses, everybody had to try his hand at some form of versification. Or at least he had to learn the workings of the mystic gears in Apollo's car, by unscrambling some famous lines of a great poem which had been given out with all the words higgledy-piggledy. Or he had to dissect the frame of a sonnet. On these lyrical occasions First Sixers got a vast deal of snobbish fun out of the efforts of the prosaic rearguard. I believe that it was from one such séance in Poetry classroom that I recall X's patriotic ode which began, 'Our gracious Queen, I ween...' but never got any further.

A modern generation may find such doings eccentric and useless. Yet I am not so sure that they were. They were the survival of that 17th and 18th century all-roundedness which required from all who were educated some measure of acquaintance with poetry. Poetry was firmly indicated as a universal factor of life, instead of being regarded as a reserve of experts of a curious breed, as the frail technical accomplishment of the untechnical, which is rather the line taken towards poetry to-day. We had great encouragements, too, to persevere in our poetic efforts, and not only in English. But perhaps these are still continued: I should like to think that a glittering calf-bound prize is still to be had for writing voluntarily a thousand Latin verses in the course of the year. These were chiefly Latin renderings of English originals, and I remember that when I had done Whittier's "Barbara Fritchie," I felt that I had earned an immediate reward on the field of battle, so to speak.[6]

'Alone, resourceless, in a foreign country'

After leaving Stonyhurst, Jeffries spent a year at the Pontifical University of Rome, training for the priesthood, only to find that he had 'as much calling to the clerical state as to plumbing or to bee-keeping.'[7] Rome was followed by some years spent in France where he taught English and perfected his French. These he describes as: 'Pleasant years, fruitful in Gallic experience and in the gathering power of living Europeanly...'[8] As we shall see, living 'Europeanly' was always Jeffries' preferred mode.

---

6. *Stonyhurst*, p 49
7. FE, p 14
8. FE, p 14

Returning to England in 1913, he finally found his calling as a journalist for the *Daily Mail*, then owned by the famous press baron Lord Northcliffe, perhaps best remembered today for his observation that 'News is what somebody somewhere wants to suppress, all the rest is advertising.' Jeffries would, in fact, go on to spend much of his life battling both government censorship and Zionist advertising.

The onset of war in Europe cut Jeffries' apprenticeship short, and by 3 August, 1914, he found himself, at the age of 34, in Brussels, charged with reporting on the imminent German invasion of Belgium. The moment is memorably described:

> Presently came Brussels, the confusion of the station, the crowd agog in the square, the room booked for me in the Palace Hotel just across. I had an appointment fixed with Rousseaux, our local correspondent, for early next morning. I read the papers and marked them for possible points. It was getting on for midnight by then and the wisest thing was to turn in quickly. But as I was about to do so, a wave of doubt flooded me all at once, or rather I should say that I became acutely conscious. I woke up out of the stupor of the headlong day, and realised to what I was engaged. I sat down by my bedside, and gazed blankly over the smallish hotel-room. The narrow bed, the barren cupboard, the telephone stark on its hook – these were the sum of my equipment. I had been barely ten months in a newspaper office. I had little habit of realities; no experience of emergencies. That morning I had been walking my daily beat in London, with friends beside me. Now at nightfall I sat alone, resourceless, in a foreign country, with none to direct me. Every moment in prospect was a dilemma, every thought to come a perplexity: war was in front of me, immense war, and millions of people for whom on the instant I must interpret chaos. That was a difficult moment. But I brushed the panic aside. *Deus providebit*, I thought, and got comfortably to sleep.[9]

The Germans had hoped to advance unopposed through a neutral Belgium in order to attack France. Brussels, however, refused to cooperate, and the consequent heroic, but ultimately doomed, Belgian resistance to the German military juggernaut

---

9. FE, pp 68-69

(described by Germany's ambassador in Brussels as akin to 'putting a baby on the line to stop an express') provided Jeffries with the inspiration for some of his finest passages in *Front Everywhere*. Here, for one, is his description of the carnage wrought by German artillery on the Belgian forts which were supposed to protect the approaches to Antwerp:

> While I was in Termonde the fort of Lierre had been unroofed by the "Big Berthas" which had been brought from Maubeuge. Like a number of the forts Lierre was in the very first stages of reconstruction. Its defenders had no electric light and no telephones. Now, next morning, Dorpveld was destroyed. Under the terrific weight of a bombardment to which it could make no reply the men of its garrison had stayed at their place of duty, dead and dying and living all together in corners of the convulsed fort, "without air, without drinking-water, without latrines, without any kind of medical aid whatsoever."
>
> In Lierre the conditions were of the same kind. To call the defenders of these forts defenders was almost a mockery. They could do nothing in the end in Lierre but await the arrival of the monstrous shells pounding their fort to pieces. "*Nous étions reduits*" – has testified its commander, "*à croiser les bras et à attendre que la mort voulut bien de nous*" – "we reached a stage in which there was nothing for us to do but to fold our arms and to wait for the moment when death should think it worthwhile to take us."
>
> That same afternoon Koningshoyct (where there had been no lighting system and the commander had had to improvise one with hurricane-lamps and motor-car headlights) in its turn blew up. Eventually – I look ahead a little – Lierre and Waelhem were abandoned by those of the garrison who could escape from their ruins. In Waelhem the horrors of the bombardment were worst of all perhaps. It was under continuous bombardment for three days and three nights. Two of these nights had been spent in darkness. Punctually every seven minutes an avalanche of explosives from the 305- and 420-mm. Austro-German siege guns landed upon it. (A number of the soldiers manning the fort, be it observed, had already experienced the routine of destruction in the forts of Liege and of Namur.)
>
> One discharge of the enemy's projectiles fell with peculiar effect right in the midst of a large section of the garrison. Those who were not killed outright were maimed and shockingly burned, and such of them as could move ran screaming, bleeding and

blackened hither and thither, up and down, without stop, without sense of their actions. Their presence made even the simulacrum of defence impossible. Their unhappy comrades had to remove them to some other part of the wrecked structure, and in doing so and afterwards returning to their posts seem to me to have reached the extreme of human endurance and bravery. Their commanding officer spoke of the utter devotion of "*ceux qui ont debarassé le fort du spectacle horrifiant de ces fantomes a moitie carbonises*," a description as well left without translation. He or one of his officers had the unusual sight, though in the circumstances it may not altogether have been so much a surprise, of seeing a body of his men draw round in a circle to commit suicide together, from which project by his brave exhortations he dissuaded them.[10]

Jeffries' description of the civilian exodus from Antwerp as the Germans close in on the city is appropriately titled, *I Witness Exodus*:

After we had gone past the accumulated quays and docks, our procession turned rightward over the railway bridges of Merxem. A view of the whole prospect now was offered to us. From here Antwerp presents its side like a gigantic wall, but most of it was obliterated by a rolling, tangled ocean of smoke, out of which the pinnacles of the city emerged as from storm. From the fired oil-tanks in the harbour (set alight to prevent the enemy from using the fuel) the breath of flames bore down upon us, and scraps and ashes of burning materials floated and wavered everywhere into the dust which the shuffling passage of so many of us raised high from the roads.

Away before us a stream of fugitives stretched to the village of Eeckeren, three miles beyond. To the right over more bare country flowed another great stream of mankind. Seen from afar this was so sombre and moved so little that it had the likeness of something cut deep into the soil, of some vast drain. From where we stood I could judge the hours which must pass before we ourselves made junction with it. The day would be growing dark before our united ooze of forlorn mankind could gain the woods next to Eeckeren, whence I could perceive even now a further deadwater of flight stretching to the region which lay about the frontier.

The number of those departing was so great that I gave no thought to estimating it. If huge crowds had fled the city, I might

---

10. FE, pp 162-163

have tried to reckon how many they were. But what I perceived now was not a mere escape or withdrawal of huge crowds. Departure was universal. Antwerp was like a box which had been opened, and its population had fallen out of it. Alexander Powell, the American correspondent, who saw the German entry into the abandoned city, describes that extraordinary scene, taken as from legend, with the regiments tramping in step and the bands playing through streets where there was no one left to watch or to listen, and the glass from the broken windows lay on the deserted footways. Another writer at the time declared that only five thousand persons were left in Antwerp. Suppose he exaggerated and ten times that remained, what were they out of three hundred thousand?

The composition of the long array of fugitives, in the middle-distance, as I watched, where the outlines could just be distinguished of men and women, of laden vehicles and of animals, gave it the appearance of a nation upon the move. That appearance, too, answered to fact. The continual shrinking of Belgian territory because of the advance of the foe had forced the population from town to town, till in Antwerp to its own inhabitants there had come an influx drawn from all the sources of that small but thickly settled land. These were mostly those peasants and humble townsfolk who are their country's fundamental stock, and all unknowingly hold the recipe of its character. In Antwerp, more than in Brussels, the race had taken refuge. Now it was driven forth again and with its primitive belongings was plodding into exile. No wonder then that the unbroken press before me, wherein old-style chariots and improvised litters and herds were all mingled, made me think of the Israelites and of Exodus.[11]

---

11. FE, pp 182-183

2

From Egypt to Egypt

'I seem to have broken out of a cocoon into open air'

When Ottoman Turkey entered the war on the side of the Central Powers, in October 1914, Jeffries was sent to Egypt (then a British protectorate) to cover an expected Turkish attack on the Suez Canal. The experience transformed him:

> I landed at Port Said on the second of December, an unforgettable date for me, since it marks my first step into the Near East. I do not care how paltry may be Port Said, how gimcrack the whole edifice of the Near East; I acknowledge that I felt transfigured as I stood by the Lesseps monument in the African sunlight for the first time. I seemed to have broken out of a cocoon into open air. True, it was but a December forenoon of North Egypt, which judged by standards of authentic sunshine is nothing so much, and I was to learn more in time to come of true daylight, and to purify my understanding of it. I had had some training already in summers of Provence and of Italy, but that morning at Port Said remains a landmark for me. Perhaps not altogether a fortunate one, as I see now. It was the beginning of some years spent in the South, which have deprived me of content in the shores of home.[1]

---

1. FE, p 216

As the assault on the Canal did not occur until 3 February, 1915, Jeffries explored the various foreign communities then living in Egypt. In particular, he made the acquaintance of certain 'Syrians,' that is, people originating in one part or another of 'Greater Syria,' an area encompassing today's Lebanon, Syria, Palestine and Jordan. These Syrians were, of course, Arab nationalists, who had sought refuge in Egypt from Ottoman Turkish repression in Greater Syria. Jeffries was suitably impressed:

> Our then correspondent in Cairo was Selim Makarius of the Arabic newspaper, *Al Mokattam*. Makarius was a Syrian, a Christian, as were the proprietor of the paper, Dr. Nimr, and its editor Tabit Bey. No one could have been kinder to me than were Dr. Nimr and Makarius. Makarius used to buzz like a brotherly bee the moment I came in sight. All his honey was put at my disposition. Tabit was as good a journalist as I have ever met. He knew what was happening in Cairo; by all the gods of Egypt he did.
>
> Through Tabit I made a number of acquaintances in the Syrian community. The Syrians are an interesting, intelligent, widely-travelled nation, containing a full modicum of educated persons. It is true that in practice they have not been allowed to become a nation for reasons in connection with policy which Mr. Lloyd George will or will not disclose if he be sent a stamped-addressed envelope. But nation they are, and the only people for whom after the war the Allied Powers concerted a scheme of National Homelessness, in the composition of which scheme the witty benevolence of Lord Balfour showed at its best.[2]

---

2. FE, pp 221-222. Jeffries would go on to write in *Palestine: The Reality* that 'The average Briton thinks of the Arab as a bearded man in flowing robes who gallops about firing rifles at nothing (except perhaps latterly in Palestine). He lives in a tent and is ruled by sheikhs with burning eyes and a tendency to abduction. This concept is nonsensical. Still, it is widely held. One of the Arab delegates who have come so regularly, and so vainly, to England for so many years, to plead the cause of their people with successive occupants of Whitehall, told me of an incident which shows this well. He and his fellow-delegates were paying a visit to the House of Commons. They waited in the lobby for a Member to come out and see them. Presently he emerged, cast his eyes over them and over others waiting, and then looked round at a loss. He did not conceive that the quiet men dressed in clothes like his own could be an Arab delegation. His gaze searched the lobbies for banditti in burnouses, girt by dangling scimitars, with cords binding their head-dresses. The grave disadvantage of this preconception is that it makes those who entertain it fall in only too readily with the notion, so valuable to Zionists, that the Arabs are a semi-barbaric block of Easterns, who need direction at all points from educated Western governors.' (pp 17-18)

Because his new-found Syrian friends were anti-Turkish, they tended to be pro-British. As Jeffries later put it, 'Their idea of government for Palestine was that we should govern it; the idea was pure bliss to them. It never occurred to them that the destiny of Palestine was being settled by political spade-work in London.' The reference, of course, was to the Zionist movement's cultivation of leading members of the Liberal/Conservative government of Prime Minister David Lloyd George and Foreign Secretary Arthur James Balfour (December 1916–22), which would bear spectacular fruit, on 2 December, 1917, in the form of a promise of British support for a 'national home for the Jewish people' in Palestine.[3]

We do not know exactly when it was, or in what circumstances, Jeffries first became aware of the Zionist movement and its designs on Palestine. There is nothing in *Front Everywhere* to indicate whether his Syrian contacts raised the subject with him. Their overwhelming preoccupation at this time, understandably, was the liberation of Syria from the Turks.

Certainly, while in Egypt, Jeffries encountered displaced Jews from Palestine. 'The Jewish colonies in Palestine had been treated with shameful injustice by the Turks,' he wrote. 'Quantities of these innocent poor people, who did not claim ownership of Palestine nor in any way meddle in politics, were driven from their homes, their belongings stolen and most of them left penniless.'[4]

Suffice it to say that, at some point, if not in Egypt in 1914, then possibly as a result of his next two trips to Palestine, in 1920 and 1922, Jeffries had reached the following conclusion:

> The Arab possession [of Palestine] began five thousand years ago and has never ceased. It has been the most thorough-going possession of all possessions, one which had its own share of conquest, and its lengthy dominion where the Israelite power came and glittered and buzzed for a gnat's span and was gone, but it has been above all possession by uncounted generations of peasants. The passing centuries have given them different names, as one strain after another was absorbed into them, but Amorite,

---

3. J.M.N. Jeffries, *The Palestine Deception 1915-1923: The McMahon-Hussein Correspondence, the Balfour Declaration, & the Jewish National Home*, Edited by William M. Mathew, Institute for Palestine Studies, 2014, p 35
4. FE, p 231

Canaanite, Philistine, Arab, it has been the labouring stock of each and of all which has held the soil, and by that tenure, their present representatives, the Arabs, claim Palestine to-day [...] That a possession so ephemeral and so broken as the Israelite should give them a valid right to oust the Arabs in any degree, eighteen centuries after the last shadow of the Israelite flicker of power faded, is a thesis too fantastic to be taken seriously. If, though, the historic connections of far-vanished eras are to be used as a charter to-day, then at least let it be historic connection. If extravagant claims drawn upon dim antiquity provide title-deeds in Palestine, then it is the Arabs who have the really extravagant and wholly ancient claim, and their right to these strange title-deeds is as unquestionable as their right to the true deeds, proceeding from their current thirteen centuries of occupation.[5]

As for an understanding of the Arab nationalist movement, Makarius, Nimr and Thabit could almost certainly be credited with sowing and watering the seeds that would later bear fruit in the following declaration:

One of the axioms upon which the Palestine Question too often is based is that there has been in that country of late but a single political movement, which is Zionism. Zionism, according to this theory, impinged upon a population which mentally was motionless, and any vigour, or political activity which that population may have showed since has been nothing but a reaction to the intense Jewish effort.

This is a wicked perversion of fact. The Zionist movement, as far as it took shape within Palestine in these later years, followed upon an Arab movement, so genuine and so strong that in the end men were to lay down their lives for it. The Zionist movement sprang... from outside the country: The Arab one was a native one comparable to the irredentist cause in the parts of Italy which were under Austrian rule[6], or in Alsace-Lorraine or in Poland. Like these causes, it aimed at the restoration or completion of

---

5. PTR, p 12
6. See Italian Front (World War I), Wikipedia: '... a radical nationalist political movement, called Unredeemed Italy (Italia irredenta), founded in the 1880s, started claiming the Italian-inhabited territories of Austria Hungary, especially in the Austrian Littoral and in the County of Tyrol. By the 1910s, the expansionist ideas of this movement were taken up by a significant part of the Italian elite. The annexation of those Austrian territories that were inhabited by Italians, became the main Italian war goal, assuming a similar function as the issue of Alsace-Lorraine had for the French.'

an old sovereignty, and would without doubt have developed as they have done into fully restored nationhood if it had not been for the unexpected introduction of the Mandatory system.

Therefore, Zionism, which as a political reality was only created by the terms of the [British] Mandate, far from being the sole force which has stirred Palestine, was a secondary force arbitrarily introduced from outside which did nothing but retard the native, previous and primary force of Arabism.[7]

Be that as it may, however, Jeffries' concerns in Egypt at this time were more immediate. In particular (and in common with many war correspondents of the time), he chafed at the constraints of military censorship. As he explained later in *Front Everywhere*,

Because of [the censorship] I could never fully get an account through of the exploit of the *Doris* at Alexandretta,[8] though I heard all the facts. Eventually, these and other contemporaneous happenings were published in England from roundabout sources, not in full, and in out-of-the-way nooks of print. They deserve to be known better, because they present a perfect picture of old-time Turkish rule and manners, which seem to me, I confess, a loss to the world of Art not compensated by the picture of the Ghazi Mustapha Kemal wearing a tweed-cap.

Turkish commanders, who at sight of a British cruiser instantly became afflicted with household forms of dysentery and until she had steamed away remained in straitened retreats beyond reach of their subordinates; Turkish commanders who, on the approach of a French seaplane, emptied their revolvers at it, and, when this discharge failed to bring it down, ordered all witnesses of the event to be confined in the police station; Turkish commanders of this kind certainly were men who belonged to the realms of Art.

As regards *H.M.S. Doris*, she appeared off Alexandretta and sent a landing-party ashore in charge of a lieutenant-commander. The Turkish Governor had the harbourmaster thrown into the shallows of the harbour for permitting the British cruiser to approach, and then opened negotiations with the landing-party. The officer in charge of this "reported" to him, as it were, said he was awfully sorry, but there were two engines of the Bagdad railway in the station which were being used for military purposes, and under the circumstances of war, these really had to

---

7. PTR, p 22
8. Today's Iskanderun.

be destroyed. The captain of the cruiser would deeply regret were he obliged to open fire with his guns upon the railway-station, as this might well cause damage to property and casualties amidst the innocent population. The best thing would be for the Turkish Governor to have the locomotives blown up himself, in the presence of the British delegation (as I trust the N.O. called it).

Great humming and hawing followed however amid the Turks after this intimation, not so much that the Governor resented complying with the British request, as that he would not take the responsibility of ordering the destruction of two fine German engines, "about which," as he said, "these Germans are sure to enquire." Nor would any subordinate take the onus of carrying out the British suggestion. Moreover, as the Governor continued, the requisite explosives for the business of blowing-up the engines were not to be had anywhere in Alexandretta.

Let the Governor on no account consider that an impediment, retorted the lieutenant-commander. He was quite sure that the *Doris* would oblige with the necessary explosives. He sent his boat back to the cruiser with a message and the boat returned bearing a full supply of gun-cotton, which he at once placed at the Governor's disposition. The latter expressed his thanks for the courtesy, but the touching-off of the engines still, in every sense, hung fire. No one would shoulder this duty.

The British officer regretfully introduced the question of a time-limit, at the end of which he must return to the *Doris*, whereon undoubtedly Alexandretta would be bombarded. The Turks consulted anxiously and out of their deliberations came the solution. Would not the British party themselves oblige still further by blowing-up the locomotives? Certainly they would. But the Governor had not finished. There was a further difficulty. It was not possible officially to have rolling-stock at this important station destroyed by the enemy without retaliation on the part of the Ottoman troops. At least a thousand of these, by the way, were present round the harbour, looking on. But would the lieutenant-commander not agree to accept honorary rank in the Turkish forces for the occasion?

The Turkish Governor would willingly confer it upon him, and so the destruction of the locomotives would be the work of a Turkish officer, anxious to prevent them from being captured. In this manner the question of resistance to the enemy would not arise. The officer in command of the landing-party (trust him!) agreed instantly. He was made a temporary *kaimakam* or something of the sort on the spot, and after his men had laid the charges, he retired with the Turkish official group to safe distance, detonated the gun-cotton, and the two German engines went skyward, everybody, British and Turkish, standing to attention and saluting everybody else. The landing-party re-embarked almost regretfully, with the feeling that an enjoyable day had been had by all. Would that all war were like this.[9]

The much-anticipated Turkish attack on the Suez Canal came on 3 February, 1915. In the event it was something of an anti-climax. 'The strange thing,' writes Jeffries, 'is that an expedition so carefully prepared should have retired so soon. Five months were spent in minute, elaborate organisation for a campaign, and it was abandoned after twelve hours.'[10]

'A slender stripling with brains'

Following the failure of the Turkish assault on the Suez Canal, Jeffries went to Bulgaria to 'await there the fall of Constantinople and to try and reach the city overland as it tottered. But it soon became evident that Constantinople was firm on its feet. Allied ships were being put out of action by mines.'[11]

By May 2015, he was in Italy as it 'entered the war against [the Austro-Hungarians] and, all-careless of its terrors, entered it singing and declaiming.'[12] This was the first of two stints on the Italian front.

Fortunately for us, Julius M. Price, of the *Illustrated London News*, was there to document his presence:

> The English Press was also well to the fore... J.M.N. Jeffries the *Daily Mail* young man, a slender stripling with brains, and bubbling over with a sort of languid interest in his work, but who, in his immaculate grey flannels and irreproachable ties, somehow gave the impression of just going on or coming off the river rather than starting on a warlike expedition...[13]

9. FE, pp 229-230
10. FE, p 250
11. FE, p 258
12. FE, p 270
13. Julius M. Price, *Six Months on the Italian Front*, E.P. Dutton & Co, New York, 1917, p 65

'In 1916,' Jeffries writes, 'I left war for the shadow of it, for the endless stratagems and intrigues of Athens. I wrote of spies and of spy-destroyers, spread the name of [German spy master] Baron Schenck about the world.'[14] An extract from one of his reports at the time shows just how he accomplished this:

> The whole of the city is given over to evil propaganda; four hundred individuals have within a month taken on some sort of connection with the secret police, promising lads are already being brought up to the information business, and in any casual gathering of ten score persons, in for example, any of the larger cafes, when they are full at the report hour, there is probably present the following percentage of craft: sixteen professional spies, five spy-destroyers, four agents-provocateurs, six doggers, miscellaneous watchers, and loiterers, a mysterious woman or two, and half a dozen masculine oddments whose fortunes have been told by Baron von Schenck.[15]

It was in this hotbed of intrigue that Jeffries formed a friendship with the Baron's opposite number, the British writer and memoirist, Compton Mackenzie. He wrote admiringly of him:

> I saw Compton Mackenzie become the Warwick of Greece, rise from having a pair of helpers and one incompetent spy upon his actions (if you photographed him the man left his post to report this) to be the master of an annexe to our legation, the controller of I do not know how many agents, and the quarry of scores of counter-agents all as incompetent as the vexed original. I saw him triumph over his own ill health, the mistakes and misdeeds of his men, the excesses of allies, the omnipotent social machine which worked every coil and every secret spring against him, in London more even than in Athens, saw him win the victory, and Greece at last ranged on our side. He transmuted a junior job of intelligence work into a new instrument, a service which pervaded Greece and forced it from evasiveness into a facing of issues.[16]

The admiration was mutual. Mackenzie would go on, in 1929, to publish a novel set in wartime Greece, *The Three Couriers*,

---

14. FE, p 271

15. *Kataskopopolis: The City of Spies*. My text comes from New Zealand's *Marlborough Express*, 5/5/16

16. FE, p 272

in which Jeffries featured as the character Carteret. In his 1967 autobiography, Mackenzie explained,

In *The Three Couriers* I had drawn a portrait of J.M.N. Jeffries as Carteret the correspondent of the *Daily Mail* in Athens: '... of the many correspondents with whom one side of his work had brought him into touch Waterlow had always found Carteret the most straightforward, the most intelligent, and the most sympathetic. Carteret himself did not look at all like a correspondent. He looked like some delicate gentle creature out of the pages of Lewis Carroll, as diffident and as timorous as the fawn that accompanied Alice across one of the squares on the other side of the looking-glass. He talked like some shy and intellectual undergraduate who had been brought up with a quantity of sisters. And of all the many correspondents in that white blazing city he was almost the only one who never tried to serve himself or his paper, the *Daily Mail*, at the expense of other people, and who by some strange freak of poetic justice never failed to supply his paper with the best authentic news available and who never ran away even from the ugliest situation.'

I was tremendously pleased to get a letter from Jeffries less than a month after the publication of *The Three Couriers* because I knew then that the book had recaptured the life of those hectic years in Greece and the Aegean. He wrote from Port-of-Spain in the West Indies:

'Thank you for 'the portrait of a gentleman'. You were always kindly to me; I never knew you depart from kindliness even when heat and hate and Greece had pointed every human soul against its neighbour in that feverish summer of 1916. I marvel at your understanding. You understand silence, I see, and other kindred ways. It has been a luxury to read you: how great a luxury I doubt if even you know...

'Your book brings back so much to me... I don't know why it should particularly but one minor memory obtrudes itself – you calling in the extremes of exasperation to Tucker, Macartney, etc from the steps of the Hermopolis wharf when they twice fouled the gig of the S.N.O...

'Do you remember your revolution as privately owned by you as any deer-park? What days! What times!'

J.M.N. Jeffries was a sad loss to good journalism. R.I.P. Stonyhurst can be proud of an *alumnus*.[17]

17. Compton Mackenzie, *My Life & Times Octave 6 1923-1930*, 1967, Chatto & Windus, London, pp 175-176

Compton Mackenzie reprised his 1929 portrait of Jeffries in the 1931 memoir, *First Athenian Memories*, thus:

> The British Press correspondent with whom I came into contact most was J.M.N. Jeffries of the *Daily Mail* who, besides serving his paper better than any other English paper was served, contrived to be of great use to our Bureau on many occasions. He did not accord with any preconceived notion of a war correspondent, for he talked like some shy and intellectual undergraduate who has been brought up with a quantity of sisters, and he looked like some delicate and gentle creature out of the pages of Lewis Carroll, as diffident and timorous as the fawn that accompanied Alice across one of the squares on the other side of the looking-glass. Yet, his willowy, his almost lily-like languor of air and ridiculous nervous giggle and absurd mannerism of ending every remark with a chanted 'what?' concealed a bravery that was almost reckless and an energy that was almost incredible in a man of such delicate health and physique.[18]

Returning to the novel, *The Three Couriers*, the following vignette of Carteret/Jeffries is simply too good to omit:

> Carteret was sitting in the middle of the restaurant, reading to himself the poems of Crashaw and looking as lily-like as ever, more so indeed, because in his delicate detachment from the screaming diners and yelling waiters and clatter of plates he was like a flower which had fallen from the table decorations on to one of the chairs and there been left unheeded.[19]

'Shreds of sky were torn like skin'

Jeffries returned to the Italian front in 1917 and remained there until the collapse of the Austro-Hungarian forces in October 1918. Like the Western front, the Italian was characterised by trench warfare – only high up, in the Alps:

> There was a height available which projected towards the river, from which I could look down and see what few ever can, a theoretical battle, see the moves and counter-moves being worked

---

18. Compton Mackenzie, *First Athenian Memories*, Cassell, London, 1931, pp 303-304
19. Compton Mackenzie, *The Three Couriers*, Cassell, London, 1929, p 272

out in military material as the designs left the commanders' heads. Yet, at the same time, I was party to it on the sentient, living and dying human scale, and could watch the soldier waiting for the onset, in perhaps his last bit of shelter on earth, in some recess or cave-mouth or hollow on the slopes of San Gabriele. For some odd reason the Austrians paid little or no attention to this height, though sometimes one had to crawl and run along its flanks to get into an observation post which the Italians had dug and carved until it was something like a small ship's bridge.

There the roar of artillery came from all points and was devastating. Guns fired from above, from below, from behind and away into the distance from either side of the post. Shells crossed in blasts; yowling when sometimes they twisted or overturned or whatever it was; detonating beyond with a continual fracas of rocks and earth. All the mountain echoes exploded and cast echo against echo with the rocks, till the very air seemed broken and scattered as the soil, and shreds of sky were torn like skin.[20]

In October 1918, Jeffries made his way to Vienna, then Warsaw, and on into the wilds of post-revolutionary Russia:

My comrade Hiatt, of the great Associated Press of America, and I went into chaos and into misery. We saw fugitive rulers and pitiful little states which existed a month or two, fragments of pogroms, herds of fugitives trickling over the plains of the Ukraine. We had forlorn icy days in wretched towns where the people were dying on every side with typhus. We occupied rooms corpses had just vacated. We spent days in windowless, seatless trains, clanking from morn till night through the endless snow in zero air, to bournes which never seemed to grow nearer. The people stared like bullocks at us; some murmured with hostility. Our clothes wore out; my knees were through my only pair of breeches. We laboured over the country in peasants' carts constructed like mangers, lying on straw in the angle between the bars. A sheepskin coat, lent to me by a great Polish friend, proved my one life-saver.

There were times when I thought that I should never get away, but must pay the penalty of my rashness and succumb obscurely in a frowsty bed in some corner of Volhynia. We had long lost all contact with Poland, itself then almost severed from contact with the Western world. No one in Europe knew where I had gone: since 1916 practically I had directed my own movements,

---

20. FE, pp 274-275

and now I could no longer send letters or messages anywhere. I tried to store in my memory what I witnessed, and was satisfied to survive each day, emptying entire packets of ersatz insect-powder down the collar of my shirt. I had reached the depths: even the insect-powder was base.[21]

In Spring 1919, he was in Hungary, then under the rule of 'the Red dictator,' Bela Kun:

I was glad to quit Buda-Pesth. We were treated fairly there, and I do not think that my movements were overlooked. But there was something dreadful in a regime which broke with Christianity. Christianity illumines politics little enough in any country, but in Hungary then it was excluded deliberately, and behind boarded windows men lived by the electrical bulbs of humanitarianism. That was putting things at their best, taking no account of the secret inhumanitarian and inhuman terror which pervaded the city. Passers-by under its influence walked according to their politics either with apprehension or with exaltation in their eyes. The worst thing in Buda-Pesth, indeed, was the absence in the public's eyes of the humdrum, fallow look which in a normal country most people wear. After all, it is the sign of their freedom.[22]

As may be inferred from this passage, Jeffries' political outlook, never in any sense 'party political,' was informed both by his Catholic faith, and, one imagines, by direct exposure to the rigours of Communist rule in post-revolutionary Russia and Hungary. This emerges most clearly in a book review he wrote in 1937, touching, in part, on the subject of the Spanish Civil War of 1936–39:

Over Spain, though, Mr. Slocombe comes to grief. Mr. Slocombe, as I know from having met him once, has leftward sympathies. He belongs to the humane Left. Now there is a curious character appertaining to all members of the humane Left... They will not admit that there is an inhumane Left, a murdering blood-red Left. I suppose I belong myself to the humane Right. But I acknowledge that there is a Right which morally or actually, by legislation or by butchery, would like to cow all workmen, all the poor, all who entertain a democratic idea. But the humane Left will never admit that there is any such section on their side of politics. No one on

---

21. FE: p 277
22. FE, pp 278-279

the Left, if you believe them, wishes to cow the free expression of ideas or to butcher individuality or to reduce to silence all constitutional opposition. The humane Left draws pictures of Russia and of red Spain in half-tones.[23]

Jeffries' career as a war correspondent for the *Daily Mail* concluded with his coverage of Russia. In summing up the all-consuming nature of his work, he remarked in *Front Everywhere* that,

> Leave does not enter into the outlook of a war correspondent. Between the late July of 1914 and early July of 1919, five years, I only spent thirty-seven days at home, free of work. By 1919 I had become a mere tradition in Carmelite House, as Sir Andrew Caird observed when he encountered me that year. In my existence, the more sceptical were coming to disbelieve.[24]

Needless to say, he did not hang up his spurs.

'I joined up with my old Egyptian self and became a complete person again'

If the seeds of Jeffries' interest in the Near East were first sown in Egypt in 1914–15, 1920 was the year in which they began to germinate and take root. By *The Times* reckoning, he would have been 40 years old. As he put it in *Front Everywhere*,

> Mr Marlowe thoughtfully sent me to the Near East. I joined up with my old Egyptian self and became a complete person again. So to Greece once more, to Syria, to the Lebanon, to further if less lengthy exclusion from the West. Feisul was King of Syria in Damascus, warring with the French. Communications with Palestine were thin and infrequent. I visited Bedouins in their black tents, and my belongings were carried about in many-tinted rugs. I saw the Lejja, the Druses' country, a land of ashes, with dark villages behind lava ramparts, like burned-out fires within grates.
>
> In Damascus at the time there will not have been more than a dozen Europeans. One day Rosita Forbes arrived, I fancy upon

---

23. *Politics Political Baedeker, The Catholic Herald*, 12/3/37
24. FE, p 269. Carmelite House was the London headquarters of Lord Northcliffe's *Daily Mail*.

the first of her series of journeys. I had a long interview with King Feisul, much interrupted by swarthy half-brothers and quite possibly not without its listeners-in. Family jealousy, no doubt, accounted for this and an attitude half of pride, half of doubt concerning the man who had assimilated so well the ways and the thoughts of the West. I have an impression that King Feisul in Arab minds held a place corresponding to that held in English minds by Lawrence.

The curious condition of Damascus provided bits of intimate information. I learned how every pilgrim of any consequence to Mecca had our policy in Palestine exposed to him. I came to know, in a sparring-partner sort of way, one of the Moslem sheiks chiefly engaged in this. He had just come from Mecca. I did not care for him; he was a shifty-eyed talkative man, too forthcoming to be true. He was responsible, I had little doubt, for the leaflets distributed to Mecca pilgrims which bore a representation of the Mosque of Omar with either the cross or a Jewish symbol (I forget which) placed at its summit, supposedly, of course, by the British authorities in Jerusalem. I complained of him in Syrian high quarters, conscious the while that our own policy, for all its material accomplishments in the Holy Land, was as shifty as the sheik. It is no good talking of keeping an even balance between two races when you have imported one of them into the home of the other.

We can see here, perhaps, a clue as to *when* it was that the penny finally dropped for Jeffries on the subject of Palestine: '… conscious the while that our policy, for all its material accomplishments in the Holy Land, was as shifty as the sheik.' This is confirmed in the very next paragraph:

A curious memory of those days is a violent quarrel between two Syrians in a hotel in Beyrout. One came from the British and one came from the French mandatory area, and they quarrelled about the conditions of their areas. Each insisted that his own was in a more deplorable state under foreign government. Was it worse to be slain and tyrannized over by French soldiers, or to be made comfortable but disinherited by the more subtle British? The two were yelling and trying to settle the point by fisticuffs when I departed.[25]

---

25. FE, pp 279-280

At this point in his narrative, Jeffries inadvertently conflates his March–April 1920 visit to Syria and Palestine with his later visit to Palestine in October–November 1922. In doing so, he erroneously conveys the impression that his scoop – the publication of 'key sections' of the hitherto secret Hussein-McMahon Correspondence in the *Daily Mail* in 1923 – resulted directly from his interview with King Faisal in 1920. To clear up the confusion stemming from the conflation, we have to turn to *Palestine: The Reality*:

> When King Feisal told me of the [1915 Hussein-McMahon] pact, I confessed my ignorance of it to him, and asked him for some account of it... This he gave me, but never explained that the pact was unpublished. I was content to make mere reference to it, therefore, assuming that when my cable reached London the sub-editors would insert the details of its text... When I returned to England other matters intruded: Feisal's kingdom had been swept away. The interview went quite out of my mind, and it was not till I started going through old papers methodically for the purposes of the present book that I realized the interest of Feisal's revelation of the McMahon pact to me in March of 1920. It might, if I had but realized the situation, have been made known in its essential details during the period of the Turkish Treaty negotiations at Sevres [August 1920] and San Remo [April 1920] and have been brought to the notice of the League of Nations in good time. My short reference to it had failed to awake attention in our London office, in the throes of nearer and resounding crises upon the Continent, though it was noted in Parliament.[26]

We also learn, in *Palestine: The Reality*, that Jeffries had initially been sent to Egypt to cover the proceedings of the Milner Commission on Anglo-Egyptian relations but that, in March, 'the gravity of the state of Syria and the fear that the fighting in the north might spread to Palestine,' prompted him to travel to Haifa, where he entrained to Damascus:

> I remember well that day, the portal of experiences which have influenced me ever since; how between the gorges of the Yarmook the low, black tents of the Bedouin showed at intervals... how we

---

26. PTR, p 326

came out on the great tableland of the Hauran, and skirted the
Lejja, a gloomy fastness which looked the seat of all outlawry.[27]

After a month in Damascus and other parts of Syria, he
returned to Palestine in the wake of the first (4–8 April) anti-
Zionist 'disturbances,' as the British euphemistically called them.
He noted that,

> When I passed through Palestine (having been recalled home so
> that I might be sent to Ireland), all the officers of the Administration
> whom I met complained of their impossible situation.[28]

He was indeed sent to Ireland, remaining there until the end of
the year. The year 1921 saw him, variously, in Greece, Yugoslavia,
Germany, the United States, and, once more, in Ireland, where
he remained into 1922, reporting on the aftermath of its war of
independence.

---

27. PTR, p 321
28. PTR, p 332

3

Hussein-McMahon, Arab Nationalism & Sykes-Picot

'The official text from the Shereefial archives'

As we have seen, Jeffries first heard about the unpublished Hussein-McMahon Correspondence (or 'pact' as he put it) from Faisal, in Damascus, in 1920. However, as he explained in *Palestine: The Reality*, its significance escaped him entirely at the time. In fact, he had even forgotten that Faisal had mentioned it in interview. Certainly, however, at some point in the interval before his next trip, this time solely to Palestine, in 1922, he had been apprised of its existence, and set out to track down a copy in Arabic:

> Fifteen years ago [in 1923] I published the essential passages of this and of the succeeding letters or dispatches which passed between the Shereef and Sir Henry McMahon, in the series of articles I wrote in the *Daily Mail*, but I think it well to give their entire text now [1939]. This text I received... chiefly through the goodwill of the late King Feisal, when I was in the Near East in 1922. It was not proffered to me: I set about obtaining it myself, as it seemed so wrong that – as was being done at the time and has been done since – these papers should be kept unpublished while the pledges contained in them were being denied. The text is the official text, that is to say the English version of it, from the Shereefial archives. It is the accepted first translation from

Emir Feisal

the Arabic, taken very literally from the original. The grammar, occasionally faulty, I have left unaltered.[1]

Typically, while Antonius is invariably credited with being the first to have introduced the Correspondence to an English-speaking audience in 1938, Jeffries' translation of 'the essential passages' for the *Daily Mail* in 1923 is usually overlooked. Be that as it may, it should be remembered that the Correspondence in its entirety was published for the first time by both men in their respective books, which, as we know, appeared within mere months of one another.

Jeffries' journey to Palestine in 1922, and the political impact in London of his findings there, will be dealt with in due course. For now, having told the story of Jeffries' 'discovery' of the Hussein-McMahon Correspondence, I turn to his analysis of the Correspondence in *Palestine: The Reality*. (Commentary by Antonius and A.L. Tibawi, whose meticulous research on this and related matters for the period 1914-21 is based on Foreign Office files, will be drawn on where appropriate.)[2]

---

1. PTR, p 64
2. Tibawi's delineation of the two parties' shortcomings is worth noting: 'Obviously the Sharif lacked diplomatic experience. He placed too much trust in the British side who did not reciprocate it nor give him advice even when he asked for it. His approach suggests a man who would have preferred to settle the great question of Arab independence in the same way his people at the time settled most of their affairs – by mutual trust and the unwritten word of honour. He did not realise he was dealing with men whose political tradition permits, nay demands, that friend and foe alike must be scored whenever possible in any diplomatic manoeuvres. The shortcomings of the British side were more in individual officials than, at this stage, in their government. The foregoing pages would have shown how far [Foreign Secretary Edward] Grey and [War Secretary Lord] Kitchener were in advance of McMahon and [Oriental Secretary Ronald] Storrs in their attitude to the Arab question. It was often plain that the prejudice, and even the ignorance, of the juniors were suffered to direct, and even deflect, the policy of their seniors. Too often was the amateurishness of the juniors allowed to hide behind delays, evasion and obscure language in dealing with the Arabs whose national character and speech are notoriously explicit. Next to [Sir Mark] Sykes, McMahon and Storrs were the 'experts' who bedevilled the first steps in Anglo-Arab relations. Their enthusiasm for empire-building exceeded the limits of their government's policy at the time.' *Anglo-Arab Relations & the Question of Palestine 1914-1921*, Luzac & Company Ltd, London, 1977, pp 73-74

The Appeal

Jeffries describes Hussein's opening letter to McMahon as 'memorable for the Arab race, because it was in its way their Magna Carta, the foundation of their independence [and] one of the great salient events in the history of the [Palestine] question.'[3]

The letter, dated 14 July, 1915, begins thus:

> Whereas the whole of the Arab nation without any exception have decided in these last years to live, and to accomplish their freedom and grasp the reins of their Administration both in theory and in practice: and whereas they have found and felt that it is to the interest of the Government of Great Britain to support them and aid them to the attainment of their firm and lawful intentions (which are based upon the honour and dignity of their life) without any ulterior motives whatsoever unconnected with this object:
>
> And whereas it is to their interest also to prefer the assistance of the Government of Great Britain in consideration of their geographical position and economic interests, and also of the attitude of the above-mentioned Government, which is known to both nations and need not therefore be emphasized:
>
> For these reasons the Arab nation sees fit to limit themselves, as time is short, to asking the Government of Great Britain, if it should think fit, for the approval, through her deputy or representative, of the following fundamental propositions, leaving out all things considered secondary in comparison with these, so that it may prepare all means necessary for attaining this noble purpose, until such time as it finds occasion for making the actual negotiations.[4]

Hussein lists six 'fundamental propositions,' the first – the only one of the six that need concern us here – reads as follows:

> Firstly, England to acknowledge the independence of the Arab countries, bounded on the north by Mersina-Adana up to 37 degrees of latitude, on which degree falls Birijik, Urfa, Mardin, Midiat, Amadia Island, up to the border of Persia; on the east by the borders of Persia up to the Gulf of Basra; on the south by the Indian Ocean, with the exception of the position of Aden to

---

3. PTR, p 63
4. PTR, pp 64-65

remain as it is; on the west by the Red Sea, the Mediterranean Sea up to Mersina. England to approve the proclamation of an Arab Khalifate of Islam.[5]

It is 'a remarkable document,' writes Jeffries, 'couched in the name of the Arab Nation, which thus was formally proclaimed in it as a political entity again in the world after centuries, never of eclipse, but of subordination.'[6]

With respect to the western border of the proposed Arab nation – which would later become a bone of contention between the British and the Arabs – he asserts categorically that 'the Mediterranean coast, the Syrian coast from the junction with Turkey to the junction with Egypt, inevitably was postulated, and Palestine thereby was included in the Arab dominions. It could not have been otherwise. Of all the boundaries of the Arab people the Mediterranean boundary is the most definite and most natural.'[7]

McMahon replied on 31 August, confirming 'the terms of Lord Kitchener's message... in which was stated clearly our desire for the independence of Arabia and its inhabitants, together with our approval of the Arab Caliphate when it should be proclaimed.'

But with regard to the boundaries proposed by Hussein, he pronounced that discussion of these 'in the heat of war' appeared to be 'premature.'

Jeffries dismisses McMahon's reply as 'a thoroughly diplomatic response,' which 'ignores the cardinal proposition' – Arab independence – and sought to replace it with an 'imaginary' one – Arabian independence. It was clear from Hussein's response of 9 September, he claims, that the Sharif considered McMahon's reply 'a piece of temporization,' and that he felt the need to remind the High Commissioner that '[h]e was not speaking for himself [but] for all Arabs, who knew of his demands, and had entrusted him with the making of them.'[8]

---

5. PTR, p 65. Antonius lists the final sentence as a separate proposition. See p 414 of *The Arab Awakening.*
6. PTR, p 65
7. PTR, p 67
8. PTR, pp 68-71

The Sharif stood, says Jeffries, by the terms of his first letter, namely 'the independence of all the Arab peoples within their natural boundaries... It was to Britain the Arabs now made their final appeal... God forbid that Britain should refuse this appeal, and that they should have to turn to the foe for help in securing their aims.'[9]

The Pledge

The fourth letter in the exchange, McMahon's reply of 25 October (Antonius and Tibawi record it as 24, which seems to be the consensus), 1915, was the clincher. Jeffries describes it as 'the crucial document,' the one which contained Britain's pledge to the Arabs. McMahon's salient paragraphs are as follows:

> The districts of Mersina and Alexandretta and portions of Syria lying to the west of the districts of Damascus, Homs, Hama and Aleppo cannot be said to be purely Arab, and should be excluded from the proposed limits and boundaries. With the above modification, and without prejudice to our existing treaties with Arab chiefs, we accept these limits and boundaries, and in regard to those portions of the territories therein in which Great Britain is free to act without detriment to the interests of her ally, France, I am empowered in the name of the Government of Great Britain to give the following assurances ['pledges' in Antonius' translation] ...
>
> Subject to the above modifications, Great Britain is prepared to recognize and support the independence of the Arabs within the territories included in the limits and boundaries proposed by the Shereef of Mecca.[10]

Jeffries' exposition of the letter's content is masterly:

> That was the crucial document. The Shereef had presented his terms and in it they were accepted formally, under the hand of the High Commissioner for Egypt, the appointed representative of His Majesty's Government, who declared himself empowered to act upon that Government's behalf. The whole is as solemn

---

9. PTR, pp 71-72
10. PTR, p 76

and binding an engagement as any into which Great Britain had entered. It accepts the Shereef of Mecca as the accredited spokesman of the Arab peoples and accepts them as a negotiating body... Its terms are as plain as its character. It undertakes to recognize and to support the independence of the Arabs within the frontiers designated by the Shareef. But it makes a couple of provisos to this undertaking. It rejects the Arab claim to Mersina and to Alexandretta, in the northern boundary; and in the western boundary, which in the Shereef's draft was to be constituted by the coasts of the Red Sea and of the Mediterranean in succession, it makes a proviso concerning the extreme northern portion of this. "Portions of Syria lying to the west of the districts of Damascus, Homs, Hama and Aleppo cannot be said to be purely Arab and should be excluded from the proposed limits and boundaries."

The Arabic word here translated as "district" is equivalent to a town and its adjacencies, what we call nowadays "urban district." The four towns or cities specified lie, as a glance at the map shows, pretty much in a straight line, one below the other, in the order from the north of Aleppo, Hama, Homs and Damascus. The country lying to the west of them roughly corresponds to the coastal territory of the present French Mandatory sphere. At the time the document was indicted it corresponded to the sphere of influence which she claimed.

But if there was this reservation placed upon the northern coastal district of Syria, there was no reservation whatsoever mentioned of the southern sphere of the Arab territories, Palestine. For this reason, to-day, more than twenty years after this Anglo-Arab treaty was concluded, the treaty remains of momentous importance to Palestine. It is not indeed the basis of the primal claim which the Arabs make to Palestine, for that is based on their primordial right to their own country, and upon the illegitimacy of any Powers or of the League of Nations or of any governments or institutions disposing of territory that does not belong to them.

But after that claim, this one comes next, that in this document of the 25th of October, 1915, Great Britain pledged herself to grant an independent Arab Government to Palestine. That this is a just claim cannot be denied. The reservation made by Sir Henry McMahon that the territory to the west of the four cities of Damascus, Homs, Hama and Aleppo must be excluded does not affect Palestine which lies, not west of these cities, but well south of them... Palestine is no more west of the French section of Syria than the lower half of this page which the reader has under his eyes is west of its upper half.

Apart too from the inclusion of Palestine being self evident upon the map, the very phrases of the treaty, as it were, asseverate its inclusion. Where we were free to act without detriment to French interests, that is where we accepted the Arab boundaries without question. In the Persian Gulf hinterland there are stipulations about administrative control, and about the acceptance of British advisers or helpers in the new Arab States, but about fundamental Arab independence being reserved anywhere in the section left to Britain, about the Arab flag not flying anywhere in the British section or about any part of the British section not being purely Arab, there is no sentence, no word, no comma... [Furthermore], in October, 1915, there was no thought in responsible quarters of anything in Palestine but of an Arab state under British guidance. There was no question of Palestine being considered a Jewish or part-Jewish country which required a special regime. Palestine was not yet invested with political singularity nor was there any show of inability to treat it, because of a supposed historic Jewish lien upon it, exactly as the other parts of the Arab territories were treated. In October, 1915, the official doctrine of dual ownership of Palestine had not yet been concocted.[11]

It is important here to note Tibawi's finding concerning the origin of McMahon's phrase 'portions of Syria lying to the west of the districts of Damascus, Homs, Hama and Aleppo,' later to be interpreted by the British as excluding Palestine from the McMahon pledge. His perusal of the relevant Foreign Office papers reveals that the names of the four Syrian cities appeared first in a document written by the head of British Intelligence in Cairo, Gilbert Clayton, in which the latter deliberately misrepresented the views of an Arab nationalist informant, Muhammad Sharif al-Faruqi, in order to accommodate the imperial conception of McMahon. The contentious qualifier 'districts,' says Tibawi, was added by McMahon, who, moreover, ignored guidelines for negotiations with the Sharif drawn up by the British Foreign Secretary, Sir Edward Grey, which contained no mention whatever of the four cities.[12] Tibawi states,

The facts are not in doubt. In 1915 Mersina was predominantly Turkish and Alexandretta roughly half Arab and half Turkish,

---

11. PTR, pp 77-78
12. Tibawi, Chapter 3

but there was no doubt that the Syrian littoral to the west of the line of Damascus-Aleppo was purely Arab. It will be recalled that in his authentic statement, Faruqi said that the northern frontiers between Asia Minor and Syria were dictated by strategic, not ethnic, considerations, and that the Arab leaders would be prepared to revise their demand on this side only. The formula to the west of Damascus-Aleppo was Clayton's, not Faruqi's. Now McMahon used it in his official Arabic letter to the Sharif with the qualification 'districts' added and wrongly translated. Several absurdities resulted from this addition and wrong translation. In particular great confusion was caused by the wrong translation, under [Oriental Secretary Ronald] Storrs' supervision, of 'district' as *wilayah* (province) instead of *sanjaq* [district]. Some of the absurdities are nakedly exposed by any reference to the Ottoman administrative divisions at the time. Here they are: There was no province of Mersina or of Alexandretta: there was only the Mediterranean, not 'portions of Syria', to the west of the province of Aleppo; there was no province of either Homs or Hama, the former being a sub-district and the latter a district within the province of Suriya; there was a *sanjaq*, but not a *wilayah* of Damascus.

All of this goes to show that McMahon's mistaken use of 'district' in English and *wilayah* in Arabic could have yielded no logical meaning in 1915. Any attempt to understand his words in relation to actual Ottoman administrative divisions is futile and produces no valid meaning. The only possible construction is to take the phrase with the names of the four towns as referring either to the towns themselves or to their immediate neighbourhoods... Confirmation that this is the only possible meaning is to be found in two communications exchanged between McMahon and Grey within a week after the despatch of the letter to the Sharif. McMahon wrote in a despatch to Grey that 'while recognising the four towns of Damascus, Hama, Homs and Aleppo...' and Grey telegraphed to McMahon that he had alluded, in a conversation with the French Ambassador, to the importance the Arabs attached to 'Aleppo, Hama, Homs and Damascus.'

This interpretation is important because of its relevance to the status of Palestine. The Arab view has always been that it was included in the areas Britain undertook in the 'McMahon Pledge' to recognise and uphold Arab independence. It was not expressly excluded by any mention of its historical, geographical or administrative names. McMahon received no instructions [from Grey] to exclude it in favour of Britain or France or any other power. A judicious interpretation of his phrase excluding certain areas in the north Syrian littoral, confirmed by his own evidence and that of Grey, leaves no doubt that Palestine was not included in these areas. On this reliable and contemporary evidence the Arab view is unchallengeable. The British official view, *formed after the war* to suit a changed political situation, is the opposite of the Arab view. It was ironically based again on an erroneous translation of the word 'district' as meaning province.[13]

The Betrothal

Hussein responded on 5 November. Jeffries notes that while he renounced Mersina and Adana, 'he still lays claim to the provinces of Aleppo [which included Alexandretta] and of Beyrout and their coasts rather than to the urban districts only of Homs, Hama, Aleppo and Damascus. He had been told of the French contention founded upon France's protection of the Christian Arabs in Syria, but gave no heed to it.'[14]

McMahon's reply of 14 December duly sealed the pact. Jeffries declares that,

> By this document, the Shereef received the guarantee he had asked that no separate peace would be concluded by the British Government, and that the liberation of the Arabs would be an essential part of any peace-treaty. The Arabs were in fact made members of the comity of the Allies by it, and with Great Britain in particular it might be called a wedding. The prosecution of the war was now 'our joint cause': Britain and the Arabs were one. Even the gold wedding ring was clasped on, in the final paragraph.[15]

Concerning French interests in the area, McMahon cautioned that 'With regard to the vilayets of Aleppo and Beyrout... as the interests of our ally, France, are involved, the question will require careful consideration, and a further communication will be addressed to you in due course.'[16]

As for Hussein's response of 1 January, 1916, Jeffries points out that 'The Shereef had shown himself accommodating by his

---

13. Tibawi, pp 86-87
14. PTR, p 81
15. PTR, p 84
16. PTR, p 83

willingness to adjourn a settlement in North Syria with the French till the close of the War. He did not accept an iota of the French claims, though.'[17]

Antonius explains Hussein's flexibility on the matter of the north Syrian coast thus:

> Hussein's willingness to postpone the question of the coastal regions of northern Syria may seem inconsistent with his former insistence on a prompt and full acquiescence in his terms in advance. The explanation is a psychological one: it lies in the profound belief he had in British integrity – a belief widely held in the Arab world at the time. In the years he had spent in Constantinople he had watched the moves on the diplomatic chess-board with a detached and critical eye, and had become attracted to the representatives of Great Britain as being the cleanest players in the game... Having secured McMahon's positive assurances on the fundamental question of the area of Arab independence, he was willing to let secondary definitions bide their time; and he had such faith in the strength of the Arab claim to the whole of Syria and in the fairness with which Great Britain would deal with it in due time, that he confidently left the question of France's interests in the coastal regions, together with the arrangements to be made for the administration of Iraq, remain over for future settlement.[18]

Two more letters, dated 30 January and 16 February, 1916, respectively, complete the correspondence, but since the main thrust of the later controversy is contained in the letters I have already referred to, they need not detain us here.

Final Words

Jeffries concludes his analysis of the Correspondence with an affirmation of its treaty status:

> The Hussein-McMahon Correspondence... closed as a political instrument with Great Britain's acceptance of the Shereef of Mecca's final terms. It is a correspondence only in so far as the

---

17. PTR, p 86
18. Antonius, *The Arab Awakening*, Hamish Hamilton, London, 1938, pp 174-175

papers which compose it, owing to the distance between the negotiators, had to be exchanged in the form of letters. But in fact it was as much of a correspondence in the ordinary sense of that word as were the notes which the negotiators of Versailles occasionally pushed across the table to each other.

It constitutes the negotiations of a treaty and the conclusion of a treaty. The pertinent portions of its text enunciate and then ratify the terms. It is a treaty. The Shereef of Mecca described it in his first document as a treaty, and the terms thus enunciated were accepted. Mr. Lloyd George himself as Prime Minister acknowledged, and indeed insisted to the French Government, that it had treaty-force.[19]

To Jeffries' case for Palestine's inclusion in the McMahon pledge, let us include that of Antonius by way of confirmation and reinforcement:

> The obligations incurred by each side with regard to military performance were not explicitly stated... But it was understood all along... that [Hussein] would bring all his power and influence, with all the material resources he could muster, to bear on the task of defeating Turkey; and similarly understood that Great Britain would help him by supplementing his deficient material resources, in arms, equipment and money. On the political side, the Sharif had committed himself to the proclamation of an Arab revolt and to an open denunciation of the Turks as enemies of Islam, while Great Britain had explicitly incurred two distinct obligations; to recognise the Arab caliphate if one were proclaimed; to recognise and uphold Arab independence in a certain area.
>
> How much of the Arab territory was included in that area became a subject of controversy in the years that followed the War, and the controversy became particularly acute in regard to that part of Syria which is now the mandated territory of Palestine. The Arab view is that Palestine did fall within the area of promised Arab independence. The British Government maintain the contrary. The two opposite assertions remain confronted to the present day [1938], and the only way in which a judgment can be arrived at is to examine the McMahon correspondence, now, for the first time, available in English in full.
>
> It should be noticed at the outset that Sir Henry McMahon never defines in his own words the area of Arab independence.

---

19. PTR, pp 86-87

What he does is to accept *en bloc*, save for certain reservations, the frontiers proposed by Sharif Hussein. It follows, therefore, that, unless Palestine or any other part of the area mentioned by the Sharif was specifically mentioned in the reservations, it must be held to have formed part of the territory accepted by Great Britain as the area of Arab independence.

The first point that strikes one is that nowhere in the texts before us is there any mention of Palestine. While certain portions of the Arab area are specifically... singled out as calling for special treatment, no mention is made anywhere of that part of Syria which was known, in Ottoman administrative parlance, as the Sanjaq of Jerusalem. The territory of Palestine in its present frontiers is made up of the former Sanjaq of Jerusalem with the addition of a portion of the former Vilayet of Bairut which was contiguous with it. And the fact that Sir Henry McMahon, who is at pains throughout the correspondence to enumerate by name each of the provinces affected by his reservations, does not mention the Sanjaq of Jerusalem, even indirectly, disposes at once of the legend that the present territory of Palestine was specifically excluded from the area in which Great Britain pledged herself to recognise and uphold an independent Arab government.[20]

The Arab National Movement
'The Arabs... aim at separating themselves from the Ottoman body and forming an independent State'

Having examined the Hussein-McMahon Correspondence in some detail, it is now time to focus on its progenitor, the Arab nationalist movement. This emerged first in the mid nineteenth century, in Greater Syria, that part of the Arab world in closest proximity to Europe, and was reflected in such phenomena as the translation of Western texts into Arabic; the growth of Arabic-language newspapers; the formation of secret societies; and, as the Turks began to get wind of it and banish its leaders, the formation of communities of Arab exiles abroad. Jeffries records that,

> In 1895 [an Arab National Committee in France] issued a document of high importance. It was the prospective charter of

---

20. Antonius, pp 176-177

Arab Independence, which was never to be lost from sight and to re-appear, some 20 years later, under the pen of the Shereef Hussein, in Mecca itself. The essential parts of its explanatory preamble ran, "The Arabs are awakened to their historical, national and ethnographical homogeneousness and aim at separating themselves from the Ottoman body and forming an independent State... Its boundaries will be from the Tigris and the Euphrates to the Suez Canal and from the Mediterranean to the Gulf of Oman... It will be governed by an Arab sultan as a liberal constitutional monarchy."[21]

As with the nascent Zionist movement, with which we shall deal later, the outbreak of war in August 1914 provided a real opportunity for the Arab nationalists to advance their goals. Although they were strongest in Damascus, it was, as Jeffries points out, the more distant Mecca, 'the sacred city and heart of the Islamic world,' located in the east Arabian province of Hijaz, which became the focal point for an eventual Arab revolt against Turkish rule:

Mecca was conspicuous not alone because of its character as a sanctuary and because of the purity of the Arab stock in the Hedjaz, as the district surrounding Mecca was called. It was the part of the Arab world where the Arabs had more power, and much more appearance of it. [...]

The Arab ruler of this nucleus in 1914 was not so much an official ruler as the Controller of the Holy Places, and he held his position because he was or was assumed to be the senior of the Prophet's descendants. The Hedjaz was not a State. In theory it was a province of the Turkish Empire and Turkey exercised suzerainty over it and its semi-ruler, who was termed the Shereef of Mecca. [...] [T]he Shereef, as the custodian of the Holy Places, enjoyed the highest prestige among the Arabs. He became more and more the chief dignitary of their race, and when modern times set in the eyes of the leaders of the Arab movement turned to him. At that date the Shereef of Mecca was Hussein ibn Ali [al-Hashimi].[22]

Fatefully, British eyes also turned to the Sharif of Mecca. As Jeffries explains,

---

21. PTR, pp 25-26
22. PTR, pp 51-52

[Hussein] was in a key situation. The great menace of Turkey's entry into war against the Allies was in the possible effect of this upon the Moslem subjects of Great Britain and of France if the Turks proclaimed a "*jehad*" or "Holy War"... Mecca was the saving point. If the probable Turkish proclamation stayed Turkish and did not become really Islamic, the danger might pass. It would be all very well for the Sultan... to announce a *jehad*, but a summons to battle against infidel Britain and France did not ring very true from the allies of infidel Germany and Austria. The only peril lay in the *jehad* being countersigned by Mecca. If the Shareef accepted it and gave it forth, it would be a cry as from the tomb of the Prophet and would work who knew what havoc for France and for ourselves.[23]

Thus it was that when Turkey declared for Germany and Austria in October 1914, Britain's War Secretary, Herbert Kitchener, reached out to Hussein with the promise that, 'If the Arab nation assist England in this war, England will guarantee that no intervention takes place in Arabia, and will give the Arabs every assistance against external foreign aggression. It may be that an Arab of true race will assume the Caliphate at Mecca or Medina, and so good come by the help of God out of the evil that now is occurring.'[24]

Hussein responded to Kitchener's feeler with a promise not to endorse the Sultan's call for jihad when it came. By way of underscoring the significance of his promise, Jeffries invokes the words of the British military historian Basil Liddell Hart: 'The Shereef rendered Britain a service greater than any that could be expected in the material realm. He drew the sting of the jehad. Outside Turkey now it would have little meaning... Britain had a war with Turkey on her hands, but to all intents she was saved the back-breaking burden of a Holy War.' Jeffries explains that,

I cite these comments to emphasize the great obligations under which we lie to the Arabs, obligations too easily and too conveniently forgotten nowadays. Nor did Hussein merely help us: he took supreme risks for himself. He might quite well have played an easier hand, knowing that had he endorsed the *jehad* we could do little beyond blockading his coasts. We might not

---

23. PTR, p 57
24. PTR, p 58

even have been in a position to enforce a blockade, because of the odium which might have resulted for us throughout the East if we had tried to starve Mecca. Whereas by refusing to endorse the *jehad* he made the Turks furious. He settled his fate at their hands if they came out of the War as victors... They were otherwise occupied at the moment and had no troops to spare, but as soon as they had time and troops he might expect to be plucked from the divan upon which they had placed him.[25]

Following the outbreak of war, Jeffries informs us, the Arab nationalists in Damascus 'formulated a programme for the independence of the Arab regions and for co-operation with the Allies.' This they sent to the Sharif, 'to whom it was left, if he acquiesced in the programme, to negotiate with Great Britain for help in its carrying-out, in return for Arab support in the field against the Turks.'[26] Arab nationalist plans for a military and civilian uprising backed by the French, 'which might have altered the whole Eastern campaign,' were unfortunately scuttled when the Turks dispersed their Arab conscripts from Syria to south eastern European fronts. Nonetheless,

> The emissaries of the Syrian [Nationalist] Societies... who now were represented by a group of councillors in Mecca, still were for action, and the Shereef presently came to share this view. It is true that Feisal had advocated more prudence because of the growing insuccess of [Britain's] Dardanelles expedition. But Hussein feared that this might be the very reason for an extension of Turkish activity into the Hedjaz. So he set all other considerations aside and made a bold and definite offer of revolt if his conditions based on the Damascus programme were met by Great Britain. This offer took the form of a letter which reached the High Commissioner in Egypt early in August.[27]

---

25. PTR, pp 60-61. Recent research by the British Muslim Heritage Centre reveals that the British army at this time kept its Muslim troops under surveillance out of a concern for what it described as 'Islamic fanaticism,' and to prevent defections to the Germans. The same research indicates that at least 885,000 Muslims fought for the Allies during the war, and that some 89,000 are known to have died. See *Britain's forgotten army of Muslims fighting in WWI*, Mary Atkinson, middleeasteye.net, 13/3/16

26. PTR, p 61

27. PTR, pp 62-63

The Turkish Terror
'He began a policy, as near as he could, of destroying the whole population'

The role of Turkish repression in Greater Syria at this time, and of the famine that wracked the area during the war years (in part the result of an Allied naval blockade of the Levant) are an important, but often neglected, part of the story of this time. Following the discovery, in the Spring of 1916, of a cache of French documents containing the names of Arab secret society members, a reign of terror was unleashed by Jamal Pasha, the Turkish commander in Syria:

> He began a policy, as near as he could, of destroying the whole population. Youths under age were rounded up and thrust into the army. Their fathers were sent into banishment, having first surrendered any little holdings of land which they held. These lands (or houses) were then sold over their heads by the military officials, who pocketed most of the proceeds. The evicted Arab householders or husbandmen were told they would receive compensatory allotments in Turkey in Asia. This was but a pretext for deporting them to Sivas or Angora or some worse spot still, where they were left to their fate... The population shrank by something like a third. In Damascus and in Jerusalem there was terrible misery. Men fell down fainting with starvation in the streets of Beyrout.[28]

Although he does not go into details, Jeffries' reference to 'starvation' in Beirut is no exaggeration, as the following description of the situation in Lebanon by Margaret McGilvary, an American Red Cross representative in wartime Beirut, attests:

> The winter of 1916–17 was the worst that I myself experienced in Syria, although I believe that the following year, when I was in Constantinople, was even more ghastly. Disease and starvation spread abroad throughout the land. In [Beirut], refugees from [Mount] Lebanon, driven down to the coast by the hope of there obtaining work, or at least escaping from the bitter winter of the mountains, died in the streets. There were days when on the walk of a mile from our house to the office, Mr. Dana and I would pass as many as ten or twelve people either dead or dying by the roadside; or with death only a few hours distant. During the

---

28. PTR, p 113

winter typhus raged, and in the summer cholera, dysentery, and pernicious malaria swept over the whole country. One passed four or five funerals each day on any route, and the same coffin did service for every corpse in a district until it literally fell to pieces.[29]

The situation in Jerusalem was almost as dire as that in Beirut, as the following December 1915 diary entry by Private Ihsan Turjman, an Arab soldier in the Ottoman army, reveals:

I haven't seen darker days in my life. Flour and bread have basically disappeared since last Saturday. Many people have not eaten bread for days now. As I was going to the Commissariat this morning I saw a throng of men, women, and boys fighting each other to buy flour near Damascus Gate. When I passed this place again in midday, their numbers had multiplied. Most of the newcomers were peasants. I became very depressed and said to myself, "Pity the poor" – and then I said, "No, pity all of us, for we are all poor nowadays."[30]

While Palestine's Jews also suffered at the hands of the Turk, Jeffries points out that they at least 'had a certain safeguard in the presence of Zionist groups in Berlin and Constantinople, and in New York and the chief neutral capitals.'[31] By contrast,

The Arabs were differently placed. Their adhesion to the enemies of the Turks gave another character to their sufferings. The repression which they underwent was horrible in method, and upon a scale which even from a Turkish point of view was unwise. But in principle most of it was logical. They constituted, which the Jewish colonies did not, a present or potential peril to the Turks. Conversely, what they suffered entitled them to the sympathy and the gratitude of the Allied Powers. If it was primarily for their own independence that they died on the scaffold or in exile, it was also in the cause of Britain and of France, who by every creed of honour were called upon to requite them in the hour of victory, let alone to keep the undertakings made to their race.[32]

---

29. Margaret McGilvary, *The Dawn of a New Era in Syria*, Fleming H. Revell Company, New York, 1920, p 204

30. Salim Tamari, *Year of the Locust: A Soldier's Diary & the Erasure of Palestine's Ottoman Past*, 17/12/15, University of California Press, Berkely, 2011, p 142

31. PTR, p 114

32. PTR, p 115

Jeffries' contention that Arab suffering 'entitled them to the sympathy and gratitude of the Allied Powers' is underscored by the following statement of the Emir Faisal, delivered at the Paris Peace Conference of 1919:

> The Turks committed unspeakable atrocities upon our civilian populations, notably at Aouali and in the valley of Yambou. The Turks respected neither the laws of man nor of God and they never will when they have the upper hand. Incredible as it seems they did not even hesitate to despoil and desecrate the Tomb of the Prophet. The horrors of Belgium pale before what happened in Syria. Dr. Bliss of the American College in Beyrouth is here to tell you all about it. It is a conservative estimate, which he will confirm, that counting those who were hanged, those who died before a firing squad, and those who did not survive the deportations to Anatolia, more than three hundred and fifty thousand Syrians perished. In Irak and in Mesopotamia, in the battles of Hilla and at Karbala, at least thirty thousand more fell.[33]

Antonius proffers the following relevant statistics:

> That 300,000 died of starvation in Syria during the War is not open to doubt. The actual figure may be as high as 350,000. Some 3,000 persons were sent into detention or exile, of whom many died under ill-treatment. Taking into account losses due to military service, Syria's contribution to the holocaust of the War must have been not far short of half a million lives out of a total population of considerably under four million – a higher percentage, probably, than that of any other belligerent.[34]

Finally, lest the point be forgotten, Antonius echoes Jeffries when he reminds us that 'The sufferings endured by the population were not unconnected with their political aspirations and, more particularly, with their sympathies with the cause of the Allies.'[35]

---

33. From Faisal's submission to the American delegation at the Paris Peace Conference of 1919, quoted in Stephen Bonsal, *Suitors & Suppliants: The Little Nations at Versailles*, Prentice-Hall Inc., New York, 1946, pp 36-37
34. Antonius, p 241
35. Antonius, p 242

The Arab Revolt, 1916–18
'No military Ride of the Valkyries'

In Western minds today, T.E. Lawrence is generally thought of as the leader of the Arab Revolt, largely because of his own account of it, *Seven Pillars of Wisdom* (1926), and because of the work of such propagators of the 'Lawrence of Arabia' legend as the American journalist Lowell Thomas (*With Lawrence in Arabia*, 1924), and British filmmaker David Lean (*Lawrence of Arabia*, 1962). This is not the case, however, with the Arabs. In the words of Suleiman Moussa,

> Lawrence's resounding fame was viewed by the Arabs with a mixture of amazement and disbelief. This was because they understood the Revolt to be a purely Arab endeavour, carried out by Arabs to achieve Arab objectives. The participation of the two British and French military missions in the Revolt mainly took the form of technical advice and demolition work. The Arabs certainly appreciated the work done by members of these missions and its contribution to the Revolt, but they never expected that its success would be attributed largely to these missions or to any of their officers. It therefore surprises the Arabs that western writers should have described Lawrence as the leader, the genius and the driving force of the Arab Revolt.[36]

Which brings us to the actual leader of the Arab Revolt, Emir Faisal, the third son of Sharif Hussein. It was at Faisal's command that the Arab forces in Mecca rose up on 5 June, 1916, and expelled the Turks from the city, and under his command that they fought their way from Mecca to Damascus, which they entered on 1 October, 1918.

Jeffries reveals just how starved the British public were, at the time, of real information about the Arab Revolt and its antecedents:

> In England, though the rising was acclaimed in the Press, no intimation was given that it was the result of an alliance. [...] Even when the fame of Lawrence had grown and had spread the fame of the Arab revolt far and wide, officialdom kept its details strangely secret. The War was more than a year over before the dispatches concerning the Hedjaz operations were issued.

36. Suleiman Mousa, *T.E. Lawrence: An Arab View*, Oxford University Press, London, 1966, p viii

Lawrence's personal exploits too were to give an atmosphere of derring-do to the Arab war, which has obscured what may be called the legal facts of it, especially the humdrum debit and credit between Britain and the Arabs.

It must be emphasized that from 1916 to 1918 this revolt was not at all a piece of wild music, a sort of military Ride of the Valkyries, heard "off" the stage of the War. On the contrary, it was a definitely contracted part of the operations, developed in a clear-cut way, and crowned with success in every fashion, except in proper full payment for it by those who had contracted for it. Where payment was evaded by the dominant partners was in Syria. In 1936, by the Franco-Syrian treaty of the 9th September, the French at last acknowledged their debt and when the treaty is ratified will have settled with their Arab creditors in their section of that country. We have settled too in Irak, but we continue to default in Palestine.[37]

Although Jefferies ventures no criticism of Lawrence in *Palestine: The Reality*, one cannot help but wonder what he would have made of the following commentary by Lawrence, published anonymously, in the journal *The Round Table* in September 1920:

Two new elements of some interest have just set foot in Asia, coming rather as adventurers by sea – the Greeks in Smyrna, and the Jews in Palestine. Of the two efforts the Greek is frankly an armed occupation – a desire to hold a tit-bit of Asiatic Turkey, for reasons of trade and population, and from it to influence affairs in the interior. It appears to have no constructive possibilities so far as the New Asia is concerned. The Jewish experiment is in another class. It is a conscious effort, on the part of the least European people in Europe, to make head against the drift of the ages, and return once more to the Orient from which they came. The colonists will take back with them to the land which they occupied for some centuries before the Christian era samples of all the knowledge and technique of Europe. They propose to settle down among the existing Arabic-speaking population of the country, a people of kindred origin, but far different social condition. They hope to adjust their mode of life to the climate of Palestine, and by the exercise of their skill and capital to make it as highly organised as a European state. The success of their scheme will involve inevitably the raising of the present Arab population to their own material level, only a little after themselves in point of time, and the consequences might be of the

---

37. PTR, p 122

highest importance for the future of the Arab world. It might well prove a source of technical supply rendering them independent of industrial Europe, and in that case the new confederation might become a formidable element of world power.[38]

It is obvious from the above that, whatever Lawrence's contribution to the success of the Arab Revolt, his understanding of the Zionist project was the polar opposite of Jeffries'. And yet, while a veritable industry serves to perpetuate Lawrence's memory, Jeffries, who saw clearly what the Zionists were about in Palestine, remains an all but forgotten figure.

A revealing insight into how the Arab Revolt resonated in Palestine may be found in the (already cited) diary of Private Turjman. The date of the entry is 10 July, 1916, 35 days after it was launched in Mecca:

> Rebellion. Sherif Hussein Pasha declared rebellion against the state. There were demonstrations in Medina, and some of the Hijazi rail lines were destroyed. But the rebels' numbers were few, and they were dispersed. Could this be the beginning? Every Arab should be pleased about this news. How can we support this state after it killed our best youth? They were hanged in public squares like common criminals and gangsters. They were executed for demanding their rights and for questioning their fate in the general conscription. They died, and not one voice was raised in protest in this miserable Arab nation. Not one Palestinian or Syrian voice. May God bless our Hijazi leader and strengthen his hand. Our government is doing its utmost to hide news of this [rebellion]. Secret police are everywhere to suppress it, but to no avail. News arrived indicating that the English have sent a large contingent of Indian and Egyptian soldiers to Hijaz and that Jeddah and Makka are in Arabian hands. The Arabians in Hijaz have now retreated, but not for long, may God support them […] May God bless the Sherif of Hijaz and strengthen his arm. And may your campaign spread to every corner of the Arab lands, until we get rid of this cursed state. When the barbaric Ottoman state executed the Arab leaders last year, and then again this year, not a word of protest was made. But now their moment [of retribution] has finally arrived.[39]

---

38. From Lawrence's essay, *The Changing East*, included in *T.E. Lawrence in War & Peace: An Anthology of the Military Writings of Lawrence of Arabia*, Edited by Malcolm Brown, Greenhill Books, London, 2005, pp 257-258

39. Tamari, pp 155-161.

The Sharif's campaign did indeed spread. As British forces under General Edmund Allenby pushed into Palestine, capturing Jerusalem in December 1917, the forces of the Arab Revolt (now known as the Northern Army), on their right flank, captured the Red Sea port of Aqaba in July 1917, and by May 1918, were laying siege to the Transjordanian town of Ma'an on the Hejaz railway. Liddell Hart explained this joint Anglo-Arab operation in the following terms:

> If Turkey be pictured as a bent old man, the British, after missing their blow at his head – Constantinople – and omitting to strike at his heart – Alexandretta – had now resigned to swallowing him from the feet upwards, like a python dragging its endless length across the desert. The difficult process of assimilation, however, was assisted by the spreading paralysis of the Turkish strength under the needle-pricks of Lawrence and the Arabs.[40]

With later Zionist propaganda in mind, Jeffries points out that,

> In this first stage of the conquest the Arabs had played their part well, and had played exactly the part which had been assigned to them. This was true both of the forces under Feisal and Lawrence and of the Arabs behind enemy lines in Palestine and the other portions of Syria. It is necessary to emphasize this, for in the interests of Zionism every Arab role has been minimized or left unmentioned, or even discredited. Zionist commentators have a way of contracting all the Arab forces in the field to the single figures of Lawrence and of Feisal, and of belittling even these two.[41]

The Arab contribution to the success of the Battle of Megiddo in September 1918 was crucial. Liddell Hart saw it as 'one of the most completely decisive battles in all history,' writing that 'Within a few days the Turkish armies in Palestine had practically ceased to exist. Whether it should be regarded primarily as a campaign or as a battle completed by a pursuit is a moot question. For it opened with the forces in contact and hence would seem to fall into the category of a battle; but it was achieved mainly by strategic means, with fighting playing a minor part.'[42]

---

40. Basil Liddell Hart, *History of the First World War*, Book Club Associates, London, 1934/1982, p 399

41. PTR, p 209

42. Liddell Hart, p 553

As he explained,

> Allenby had two comparatively novel tools – aircraft and Arabs.
> Feisal's Arabs under the guiding brain of Colonel Lawrence, had
> long been harassing, immobilizing and demoralizing the Turks
> along the main Hejaz railway. Now they were to contribute more
> directly to the final stroke by the British forces. On September
> 16th and 17th, emerging like phantoms from the desert, they
> blew up the railway north, south, and west of Deraa. This had
> the physical effect of shutting off the flow of Turkish supplies
> temporarily – and 'temporarily' was all that mattered here. It
> had the mental effect of persuading the Turkish Command to
> send part of its scanty reserves towards Deraa [...] While the
> Arabs and the Air Force were perhaps the two most vital factors
> in 'unhinging' the enemy preparatory to the actual push, the plan
> had also the wide and purposeful variety of ruses which marks
> the masterpieces of military history.[43]

Jeffries quotes Liddell Hart as follows:

> Deraa was a vital point, for there centred the rail communications
> of all three Turkish armies and the line of retreat of the fourth.
> Only the Arabs could reach it. Upon them much depended if
> the Turkish dispositions were to be paralysed before Allenby's
> stroke descended.
>
> He then adds, 'They took Deraa on the 28th. On the 30th
> September Damascus was captured and the Arabs' flag hoisted
> on their ancient capital. [...] Between that 5th of June in
> 1916, when the Arabs with such wild daring had begun their
> haphazard revolt, to this 30th September in 1918 the Arabs'
> action had steadily increased in importance and in value to the
> Allied cause.'[44]

Jeffries summarises the significance of the Revolt to the Arabs:

> Thus ended the war in Palestine and the Arabs' splendid part
> in the liberation of their territory. They had fulfilled their
> obligations, setting indeed no term to them and all through
> the campaign taking on obligation upon obligation as each
> emprise they were called upon to accomplish came to its end. As
> Lawrence, identifying himself with them, declared, "Our bond

---

43. Liddell Hart, pp 556-557
44. PTR, p 234

had been most heavily honoured." It was now the turn of Great Britain to reward them in conformity with the promises she had made to them. It was not such an extraordinary reward, after all, since it was but to recognise them as masters of the soil which they had occupied for so many centuries.[45]

It is sobering to reflect on just how different the Middle East might look today if only the Arabs had then received their due. It was not to be, however. Instead of an independent and united Arab world, the British, in collaboration with the French, went on to carve up Greater Syria in accordance with the terms of a secret pact known as the Sykes-Picot Agreement.

The Sykes-Picot Agreement (May 1916)
'Not a parchment with a place of pride, amongst the national charters of England'

The second of Britain's wartime undertakings in the Middle East, the Sykes-Picot Agreement of May 1916, is named for its negotiators, Sir Mark Sykes, the Foreign Office's chief adviser on Near East policy, and Francois Georges-Picot, the French foreign minister. Limited Russian input aside, the Agreement was basically a secret *Anglo-French* plan to divide Ottoman Turkey's Arab provinces after the war into French and British spheres of influence. Tellingly, it came *after* the British had committed themselves to Arab independence in the Middle East, on 24 October 1915, and just *before* the launching of the Arab Revolt on 5 June, 1916. In Jeffries words,

> It was a neat plan with great stretches of Asia docketed with letters of the alphabet and tinted with several colours, and all the still unconquered Turkish territory parcelled off into five zones. France and Great Britain had each a zone of administration and also a zone of influence, and there was to be an international zone, corresponding roughly to Palestine. An independent Arab state in Syria was, whimsically, to be composed of the British zone of influence and the French zone of influence. That is to

---

45. PTR, p 235

say, that over a triangular section of territory lying between the zones where Britain and France were to administer directly, there was to be established a native state under an Arab ruler with Damascus as its chief city. But the northern part of it was to be under French influence. Only the French were to supply advisers or foreign officials, and they were to have a priority right upon enterprises and loans. The south was to be under British influence and the character of influence was to be similar.

It is difficult to imagine anything more unworkable than this "Arab" State, of which the fantastic design might have come to its authors at the end of a dinner, from some dish of Neapolitan ice-cream, wherein vanilla and strawberry zones-of-influence were established over independent sweetmeat.

Quite in this order of ideas the fifth zone was coloured chocolate. This was the international zone of Palestine where "was to be established an international administration whose form shall be decided after consultation with Russia, and subsequently in accord with the other Allies and the representatives of the Shereef of Mecca." The two administrative zones gave Cilicia, much of central Anatolia and coastal north Syria to France, while Great Britain was dowered with Mesopotamia and the ports of Haifa and Acre in Syria...

The new treaty made a mockery of the Syrian Arab State, and Palestine was to be withdrawn from its territories. It took away from the Shereef what had been granted to him, and did so secretly, with no reference to him, at the very moment when his sons and his tribesmen were beginning battle to honour his word. On the face of it, therefore, the Sykes-Picot treaty is not a parchment with a place of pride amongst the national charters of England.[46]

Antonius calls the Sykes-Picot Agreement 'a shocking document,' adding that 'It is not only the product of greed at its worst, that is to say, of greed allied to suspicion and so leading to stupidity: it also stands out as a startling piece of double-dealing.'[47] Echoing Jeffries, he writes,

[M]ore serious... than [its] errors of judgment was the breach of faith. The Agreement had been negotiated and concluded without the knowledge of the Sharif Hussein, and it contained

---

46. PTR, p 123
47. Antonius, p 248

provisions which were in direct conflict with the terms of Sir Henry McMahon's compact with him. Worse still, the fact of its conclusion was dishonestly concealed from him because it was realised that, were he to have been apprised of it, he would have unhesitatingly denounced his alliance with Great Britain. He only heard of the existence of the Agreement some eighteen months later...[48]

In his discussion of the Anglo-French negotiations which preceded the Sykes-Picot Agreement (titled *Perfidious Albion?*), Tibawi points out that both the French and the British had designs on the Arab provinces of the Turkish Empire, but speculates intriguingly that if only Foreign Secretary Grey had 'opened the negotiations with the French by a British renunciation of territorial ambitions in Iraq and elsewhere, the moral force of inviting a similar French disclaimer regarding Syria would have been irresistible.' In the absence of such a British renunciation, however, the partitioning of those provinces was, he says, 'inevitable.' Referring to Sykes as 'one of the architects of the formal scheme of partition,' he remarks acidly that his 'recommendation of the declaration of a British protectorate over southern Syria, still firmly in Turkish hands, is too fantastic even from a fantast.'[49]

As to who was ultimately responsibility for the Agreement, Tibawi blames Herbert Asquith, Britain's Liberal Party prime minister from 1908 to December 1916:

> The last word was of course for Asquith. He wondered whether the French were prepared to give 'good terms' to the British, and Sykes would not be himself if he did not assure the Prime Minister... 'We must have a political deal. We must come to terms with the French...' As a noun the word 'deal' means 'a bargain' or 'an underhand transaction.' That was precisely the meaning of what Asquith had just ordered. To strike a bargain with France by obtaining for Britain a good share in a territory under the control of neither and still under the sovereignty of a belligerent, and to resort to this underhand transaction without taking into account the aspiration of the majority of the native population. The liberal statesman had clearly no scruples on

---

48. Antonius, pp 249-250
49. Tibawi, pp 109-110

the one score or the other. Nor was he deterred by his Foreign Secretary's [Grey] repeated disclaimers of any British territorial ambitions in Syria. The only consideration was that France must not to take it all alone. The idea of renunciation by both powers in favour of the native population was worthy of their liberal traditions, but was completely abandoned in pursuit of more colonial expansion.

It is noteworthy that Palestine figures with Syria as one of the centres of the intellectual and organising power of the Arab national movement. It is equally noteworthy that neither Lloyd George nor Balfour, the future Prime Minister and Foreign Secretary respectively who sponsored Zionism, made any mention of it or even of the Jews when the political future of Palestine was under discussion. Nor for that matter did Sykes himself make any such reference to the Jews or Zionism considering his future enthusiasm [for Zionism]. But the most noteworthy aspect in the whole affair was the withdrawal of Grey. He missed the meeting and ceased to mark official papers in his department. Whether his absence was due to ill-health and eye trouble or disgust with the proceedings is not easy to determine. But his department, the Foreign Office, was now to act according to Asquith's instructions.[50]

Tibawi also deplores the choice of Sykes as a negotiator:

To ask a soldier with only amateurish acquaintance with diplomacy and politics to battle with an experienced career diplomatist [Picot] was an ill-advised decision considering its results.[51]

With regard to a Foreign Office memorandum of 5 January, 1916, initialled by Picot and Sykes, 'the embryo of the notorious Sykes-Picot Agreement,' he explains that,

Although the memorandum reckons the Arabs, next to the British and the French, as the third interested party it has no provision for associating them in the discussions or at least consulting them. The reason is not hard to seek. For despite Picot's assertions that the Syrian Arabs loved France, and those of Sykes that they loved Britain and hated France, the Arab

---

50. Tibawi, pp 111-112
51. Tibawi, p 113

national movement in general was determined all along not to substitute British or French or any other foreign control for Turkish rule. What they wanted was national independence for the Arabs in their native lands. But the words independence and sovereignty do not occur in the memorandum. The utmost that it allows is a confederation of Arab states 'protected' by Britain and France, under the 'suzerainty' of an Arab chief. No Arab leader from the Sharif downward would have accepted anything on these lines.

The cynicism of the authors of the memorandum is perhaps less in their scheme of dividing up the Arab homeland between Britain and France than in ascribing the imposition of British and French control, in place of Turkish, to the wishes of the leaders of the Arab national movement. Nothing could be further from the truth. Sykes in particular was not ignorant of the programme of the Arab national movement, submitted again and again by Arab leaders to their British friends, and by none more authoritatively than by the Sharif of Mecca. On two points he never compromised: surrender of Arab territory to foreign control and derogation of Arab sovereignty to the extent of refusing advisers who might go beyond tendering advice.

Picot was an open enemy, but Sykes professed friendship towards the Arabs. Yet he unashamedly signed a document with Picot that accuses the leaders of the Arab national movement of uncharacteristic and unbelievable pronouncements amounting to betrayal of homeland and nation. 'The leaders of this movement', asserts the memorandum, 'recognise that a closely compacted Arab state is neither in harmony with the national genius of the Arabs nor feasible from the point of view of finance and administration'. They preferred 'a confederation of Arabic-speaking states' comprising the Arabian Peninsula and the provinces of Iraq and Syria, but this confederation would let 'its littoral' be under the protection of Britain and France, take 'administrative advisers' only from the subjects of the two protecting powers, and afford both powers 'especial facilities' for economic enterprise and industrial development.

To the authors of the memorandum it was obviously immaterial that their picture was a gross misrepresentation. It provided them with a *raison d'etre* for their preposterous proposals. These follow closely the 'Arab' suggestions, with one exception. Jerusalem, as a decapitated and truncated Palestine, was to be placed under an international administration in deference to 'the conscientious desires' of the three faiths, but the head of the Arab confederation was to have 'equal voice' in the administration of the enclave. This enclave did not include the ports of Acre and Haifa which were to be given to Britain with the right to construct and operate, as the sole owner, a railway to Iraq for commercial and military purposes. Also excluded from the enclave was most of Galilee in the north and all the land south of Hebron-Rafah. Because neither power would leave Palestine to the other or to the Arabs it was dismembered in this fashion.[52]

By contrast, the author of a 1923 biography of Sykes, who died in 1919, Shane Leslie, is more sympathetically disposed towards the man and his Agreement. Leslie portrays Sykes as a man on the horns of a dilemma, having to please both the French... and the Arabs:

> Mark's mind was moving on the lines of Arab revolt and Meccan independence. During 1915 the Sherif, now King, Hussein was angling for British recognition. The French unfortunately opposed Arab hegemony and it fell to Mark to show himself equally pro-Arab and pro-French. How difficult a task this was is shown by the fact that the British Government did not communicate the Sykes-Picot agreement to the Arabs, who learnt its terms later from the Bolshevists.[53]

In keeping with his take on Sykes, Leslie features a most interesting document in his book, which he refers to as 'the official version [of Sykes-Picot], which has been kindly placed at our disposal by experts of the Foreign Office.' It is a masterpiece of spin, obviously released as part of damage control exercise following the Bolshevik's exposure of the text of the Sykes-Picot Agreement not long after the Russian Revolution of November 1917. Although undated, a reference in it to the abortive August 1920 Treaty of Sevres with Turkey (of which the Sykes-Picot Agreement formed the basis), indicates that it was issued at some point after that date. While the Hussein-McMahon Correspondence was kept securely under wraps by the British until 1939 (and blatantly misrepresented whenever the Arabs and their British allies sought to refer to its contents in official circles, as we shall see later in this narrative),

---

52. Tibawi, p 113-114

53. Shane Leslie, *Mark Sykes: His Life & Letters*, Cassell & Company, Ltd, London, 1923, p 245

the British had no alternative, in the event of the outing of the Sykes-Picot Agreement by the Bolsheviks, but to issue a gloss of this kind. One can only speculate on how they might have handled a similar outing of the Hussein-McMahon Correspondence in 1917–18. Since it is an integral part of the story of British mendacity, double-dealing and betrayal at the time, and since I have nowhere seen it referred to in scholarly commentary on the Sykes-Picot Agreement, it is reproduced here in substantial part, with interpolated commentary:

> The Sykes-Picot Agreement... has been the subject of much hostile and uninformed criticism. It was essentially a secret pact. In the nature of things its terms and antecedent conditions could not have been divulged at the time without serious prejudice to the Allied cause...

In other words, the Arab Revolt (launched barely 20 days *after* the conclusion of the Sykes-Picot Agreement) may never have proceeded if word of it had reached the Sharif.

> But this secrecy came untowardly to an end with the accession to power of the Russian Bolsheviks. Anxious to discredit alike the overthrown Tsarist Government and the so called capitalist Governments of the Western Powers, Lenin and Trotsky published the Sykes-Picot papers and other secret treaties then in the archives of Imperial Russia... Criticism... ignorant of the conditioning facts, saw only the terms of the completed agreement, saw only its secrecy, its apparent haste to apportion among the Allies territory not yet in their power, its alleged indifference to the rights of native inhabitants, its seemingly doubtful treatment of the Arab Allies of Great Britain. It became a commonplace of certain sections of the Press that the Sykes-Picot Agreement was 'iniquitous,' 'unjust,' 'nefarious,' and an outstanding example of the methods of the 'old and evil diplomacy.'

Yes, yes, the Agreement may have looked decidedly dodgy, but please bear in mind *'the conditioning facts.'*

> It may be remarked here that the late Sir Mark Sykes himself was fully conscious of the shortcoming of the arrangement. But though an ardent friend and well-wisher of the Arab cause, he

regarded it as containing the best solution of Arab questions which circumstances at the time permitted. It may be remarked, further, that he always took exception to his name being appropriated to the popular title of the Agreement...

And well he might, given that his Agreement flagrantly contradicted the McMahon pledge, particularly with respect to Palestine.

> The complexity of the situation with which the Arrangement sought to deal may be judged from a brief outline of facts. It was necessary to harmonize the territorial ambitions of France and Russia, the vital and traditional interests of Great Britain in the Ottoman hinterland of the Persian Gulf and the Imperial British waterway of the Suez Canal and the Red Sea. It was necessary to do everything possible to maintain concord and unity, not only between European Allies, but between European Allies and Arab Allies. It was necessary to fulfil previous British undertakings to King Hussein of the Hejaz and the Arabs. It was necessary to make some provision for the treatment of Palestine, or at least of Jerusalem, on some other basis than that of unfettered Arab rule. And it should be borne in mind that at the time the clash of interests between France and the Arabs, and therefore between Great Britain and France, threatened to become acute [...]

If, in fact, Sykes had found it 'necessary to make some provisions for the treatment of Palestine... on some other basis than that of unfettered Arab rule,' then this should have been negotiated first with Hussein. It was not, of course, and deliberately so, as he would most likely have called off the Arab Revolt.

> The Sykes-Picot Agreement may be said to have been made necessary by the long and persistent French claim to Syria. France had taken a sentimental interest in the country from the days of the Crusades and the Frank Kingdoms. The Syrian campaign of Napoleon confirmed and added to this interest. From the earliest times France had claimed to be the protector of all Latin Christians in the Ottoman Empire in general and in Syria in particular. Since 1860 France had made the Maronites of the Lebanon her particular care. French schools had become numerous in Syria; French capital there sought and found investment; the French language and French culture, it was claimed, had there struck deep roots. When the Ottoman Empire threw in its lot with the Germanic Powers,

and it seemed probable that the downfall of that Empire would follow, French public opinion, preoccupied though it was by the presence of German armies on the soil of France, yet found itself able to support the eventual claim of France to Syria with remarkable insistence.

Blame it on the 'sentimental' French, who, despite 'the presence of German armies on the soil of France,' could think only of Syria. The unsentimental British, of course, we are supposed to believe, had no designs whatever on the Middle East.

During the year 1915 Great Britain, in prosecution of the war in the East on behalf of herself and her Allies, obtained the support of the Sherif of Mecca and his sons against the Turks. The Sherif had ambitions for independence of Turkish Sovereignty; he aimed at the creation of an Arab State or a Confederation of Arab States which should embrace all the Arab peoples of Syria, Mesopotamia and the greater part of Arabia, with himself as sovereign of the one and perhaps suzerain of the other. In the negotiations which took place between His Majesty's Government and the Sherif, Great Britain, while giving undertakings to support this scheme, expressly reserved, as not coming within the Arab area, those parts of Syria and south-eastern Anatolia in which France had special claims or which were not peopled by an Arab population. These reserved areas were defined as being Syria lying west of the line, Damascus – Hama – Homs – Aleppo and as the Turkish Vilayet of Adana, which includes the towns of Alexandretta, Adana and Mersina. Subject to these reservations, and in consideration of the Sherif of Mecca and his Arabs making an effective rising against the Turks, Great Britain pledged herself to freeing the Arab populations from Turkish rule, and to establishing, not necessarily over the whole Arab area, an independent Arab State. In this guarantee to the Arabs France subsequently joined. Important results were hoped for from this Arab rebellion led by the Sherif... not only in a military sense, but still more for its effect upon the world of Islam, and the disastrous blow it would strike at the prestige of the Caliph in the person of the Turkish Sultan.

Provision for the Arabs to be robbed of Palestine is presumably covered here by the words, 'establishing, not necessarily over the whole Arab area, an independent Arab state.'

But though France assented to and gave her support to the Arab movement for these purposes, she viewed with extreme disfavour, and even with hostility, the prospect of extended Arab military success ensuing from the rising. When the rising seemed certain to take place she pressed her demands for an agreement with Great Britain in regard to Syria...[54]

The French twisted our arm!

4

Zionism & The Evolution
of the Balfour Declaration

Zionism
'They would vanish like the mist
before the sun of Zion'

We turn now to the subject of Zionism, the 'secondary force,' as Jeffries referred to it earlier in this narrative, 'arbitrarily introduced from the outside which did nothing but retard the native, previous and primary force of Arabism.' Jeffries distinguishes clearly between Jews and Zionists:

> Till recent days, till the start of the nineteenth century, say, the cry of the Jewish race for Palestine has been a religious one. That has made it, to begin with, only nominally the cry of the Jewish race, since out of the millions of Jews how many have been bound by the horizons of commerce and humanitarianism, and have seen no further? Those of them who did look beyond... never thought they would occupy Palestine till a time had come when Time would be no more. The Messiah would bring them back to a Palestine transfigured, a stepping-stone to the next world. It was not for a territory, not so much for earth that they prayed as for Heaven. It has been left to an entirely different set of men, not at all their heirs, the Zionists of to-day, to insinuate that they did dream of a delimited country, and to produce atlases to measure their ancestors' transfiguration.[1]

---

1. PTR, pp 33-34

He saw the roots of Zionism in turn-of-the-century European anti-Semitism: first, in the anti-Semitic pogroms of Czarist Russia (1881–84 & 1903–06), which led to an influx of East European Jews into the United States, but also, in far smaller numbers, into Ottoman Palestine; and second, in the singular reaction of Theodor Herzl, a Jewish Austro-Hungarian journalist, to a rise in anti-Semitic sentiment in France, occasioned by the trial of Captain Alfred Dreyfus, a Jewish French army officer, falsely convicted of treason in 1894.

The Dreyfus Affair, as it came to be known, drove Herzl to conclude that European Jews could not be assimilated in the lands of their birth and needed, therefore, a state of their own, a thesis he set out in a seminal manifesto, *Der Judenstaat* (*The Jewish State*), in 1896. The following year he convened the first Zionist Congress in Basel, Switzerland. From it emerged a steering committee, known as the Zionist Organisation, and a political program, known as the Basel Program. 'Zionism,' it read in part, 'seeks to establish a home for the Jewish people in Eretz Israel [Land of Israel] secured under public law.' This was to be achieved by 'the settlement of Jewish farmers, artisans and manufacturers'; 'the organization and unity of the whole of Jewry'; 'the strengthening and fostering of Jewish national sentiment and consciousness'; and the taking of 'preparatory steps toward obtaining the consent of governments... in order to reach the goals of Zionism.'

But where exactly was Eretz Israel to be?

Herzl, it is worth recalling, was somewhat more pragmatic (though no less colonial in his outlook) than his followers:

> Shall we choose Palestine or Argentine? We shall take what is given us, and what is selected by Jewish public opinion. [While] Argentine is one of the most fertile countries in the world, extends over a vast area, [and] has a sparse population and a mild climate, Palestine is our ever-memorable historic home, the very name of [which] would attract our people with a force of marvellous potency. If His Majesty the Sultan were to give us Palestine, we could in return undertake to regulate the whole finances of Turkey. We should there form a portion of a rampart of Europe against Asia, an outpost of civilization as opposed to barbarism.[2]

---

2. Theodor Herzl, *The Jewish State*, pp 95-96

By implication, for Herzl, Palestine's existing, non-European, Arab population were 'barbarians.'

It wasn't, in fact, until 1905, when the Seventh Zionist Congress definitively ruled out a British offer of territory in Uganda, that Palestine became the Zionist Organisation's exclusive focus. And so it was to the Sultan of Turkey, Palestine's ruler, that the Zionists turned. Jeffries writes,

> The Sultan of Turkey had been approached, in the meantime, and there seemed some chance of his granting a charter of occupation in Palestine to the newly formed Zionist Organization... Abdul Hamid himself had been not so disinclined to dispose of Palestine and its people for a return in cash, but the sum which he had asked, ten million pounds, was beyond attainment. He became aware, too, as negotiation went on and grew known, that there was more and much stronger Moslem sentiment against the plan than he had expected, and his willingness for the bargain lessened correspondingly. He indeed gave a promise, in answer to remonstrations from Palestine, that he would impose a check on Jewish immigration, though he did not do much to fulfil it.[3]

Despite the Zionists being only a tiny minority of world Jewry by 1914 – 130,000 out of 13 million, Jeffries reminds us that, for good or ill, it is always the activist minority that gets things done:

> As usual, however, the small group which wanted to go somewhere and to do something had its own way very much. The 130,000 Zionist cavalry charged into the Chancelleries of Europe and America and created an excitement and an impression of overwhelming unity, unaltered by the pedestrian Jewish millions living peaceably at home. The existence of the non-Zionist multitude, though, is a point which, to say the least of it, deserves to be remembered, now and at all times. Whenever a political Zionist declares that Zionism as begun in Palestine was the cause of the Jews, he can always be gently corrected. It was not the cause of the Jews, it was a cause of Jews.[4]

Herzl's manifesto may have been titled *The Jewish State*, but his followers soon realised that this was altogether too frank an

---

3. PTR, p 37
4. PTR, p 38

admission of their goal, given that said state would have to be established on someone else's land and at their expense. A euphemism of some kind was therefore required. As Christopher Sykes, the British writer and historian (and son of Sir Mark Sykes) relates,

> The term [National Home] was invented by... Max Nordau, one of Herzl's earliest associates. He related how, on his advice, this term, rather than that of Judenstaat, was adopted as a description of the Zionist goal at the first Zionist Congress... He gave this account: "I did my best to persuade the claimants of the Jewish state in Palestine that we might find a circumlocution that would express all we meant, but would say it in a way so as to avoid provoking the Turkish rulers of the coveted land. I suggested 'Heimstatte' [Home] as a synonym for 'State'... This is the history of the much commented expression. It was equivocal, but we all understood what it meant. To us it signified 'Judenstaat' then and it signifies the same now."[5]

Jeffries, it goes without saying, was not one to be taken in by such word games:

> Zionism from the start, wherever it was to be installed, stood for sovereignty. The pretences of blended partnership and blended authority in Palestine – themselves indispensable – with which, till in 1937 Partition was frankly proposed, it had been thought to delude the Arabs, never were the aim of the movement.[6]

Jeffries understood exactly what the Zionists wanted in Palestine – a Jews-only state. Such a goal necessarily blinded them, not just to the wishes of Palestine's indigenous majority Arab population, but seemingly to its very existence:

> The point of essential sovereignty is not the only one which emerges from Dr. Herzl's declarations. Reading them, the reader may be conscious of a remarkable anomaly in them. If Herzl's fundamental thesis was that persecuted or unenfranchised Jews should get away from their false environment and found a State where they would be by themselves and so be the equals of any men, if this was what Herzl meant, how then could he come to consider Palestine as a spot where such a State could be founded?

---

5. Christopher Sykes, *Cross Roads to Israel*, Collins, London, 1965, pp 23-24
6. PTR, p 39

It was a territory where the Jews could not be self-secure, for the Arabs were already living there in hundreds of thousands. How could Herzl fix his eyes on Palestine then, where the conditions for his Sinn-Fein "ourselves-alone" State were unobtainable?

The question may well be asked. But it would be difficult for Zionism to provide an answer to it. Nothing is more significant of the character of the Zionist movement than the fact that in those crucial days of last century it never paid the least attention to the Arabs who peopled the country upon which all its efforts were directed. Not a lift of a Zionist eyebrow seems to have been wasted upon an Arab form.

The sincere Mr. [Leonard] Stein is one of the few Zionist writers who seems conscious of this shortcoming. He does what he can to rectify it. "When Herzl," he explains, "had spoken of a Charter" (from the Sultan) "he had not, needless to say, contemplated any eviction of the Arabs of Palestine in favour of the Jews. He was, to judge from his Congress addresses, hardly aware that Palestine had settled inhabitants, and he had, in perfect good faith, omitted the Arabs from his calculations."

Was there ever anything more extraordinary than this? Vast plans are made engaging the destinies of a multitude of people, yet the man who engenders these plans never takes the essential first step of surveying the land where he proposes to carry them out. Nor apparently do any of his associates suggest it to him. There might be no Arabs in the world for all the difference it makes to him or to his associates.

Year by year Zionist congresses are summoned, and from their platforms and in the corridors of the assembly speakers discourse incessantly about themselves, about champions and about opponents of the cause within the ranks of Jewry, about the dovetailing of ill-fitting factors in their programme, about their hopes and their fears of Gentile help, about their own culture and their own need for spiritual expansion. Without doubt these were reasonable and respectable topics. When however were they put aside to consider the existence of inhabitants in the land which the Congress members proposed to acquire? When indeed? Was a single day's session of a single Congress devoted to the discussion of the understanding which must be reached with the people of Palestine? Not one. [...]

I cannot see how it can be held that for six years a great number of admittedly intelligent educated men remained ignorant of the presence of the Arabs. If they did remain so ignorant, theirs was as bad a case of culpable ignorance as can be imagined, and they cannot be allowed to profit by it. But I do not believe in this

ignorance, and I maintain that the half-and-half prolongation of
it which was kept up till the War, and to all intents was resumed
afterwards, (as will be seen when the Balfour Declaration is
analysed) altogether discredits the leaders of the Zionist cause
as well as their friends in our own Cabinet [...]

The only conclusion then... is that if Zionism was unaware of
the Arabs it was because most Zionists perceived an obstacle in the
Arabs and did not want to be aware of them. The Zionist leaders,
and the more prominent of their followers, obsessed with the
absurd notion that Palestine had always been the patrimony of the
Jews, did not intend to be aware of anything which conflicted with
this. To have made approaches to the Arab population, and to have
discussed at any length the bar which that population presented or
might present to the accomplishment of their plans, would have
[been] to disconfess the plea upon which those plans were based.
It would have disclosed to most of the non-Jewish world, and
indeed to a good part of the Jewish world, that there was a factor
in existence which upset the whole formula of Jewish ownership.

I do not say that all of the leading Zionists viewed the matter
quite in this fashion. Some of them will have thought about the
Arabs in a careless, indifferent way. They will have considered
them as nobodies who would disappear presently, decamping
from the soil after a little money had been spent or by some
other almost natural sequence. They would vanish like the mist
before the sun of Zion.[7]

Needless to say, Zionism's wordless wish for the *actual*
disappearance of the Palestinian Arabs harks back to the very
beginnings of the Zionist movement, to Herzl himself, in fact. Even
when the idea of a Jewish state was still only a gleam in the eye of
its founding father (and Palestine only one of several possibilities
for its establishment), he knew what had to be done with the chosen
land's non-Jewish inhabitants.

Herzl's diaries may not have been available to Jeffries at the time
he was writing *Palestine: The Reality*, but had he read the entry
for 12 June, 1895, its profoundly exclusivist sentiment would have
come as no surprise:

When we occupy the land... We must expropriate gently the
private property on the estates assigned to us. We shall try to

---

7. PTR, pp 39-42

spirit the penniless population across the border by procuring employment for it in the transit countries, while denying it any employment in our own country. The property owners will come to our side. Both the process of expropriation and the removal of the poor must be carried out discretely and circumspectly. Let the owners of immovable property believe that they are cheating us, selling us things for more than they are worth. But we are not going to sell them anything back.[8]

Even Herzl's one and only visit to Palestine, in 1898, failed to arouse any doubts in his mind as to the validity of the enterprise, moral or otherwise. He had gone there seeking an audience with the Kaiser, who was on a tour of the country, hoping to win his support for the Zionist cause. Astonishingly, however, even when surrounded by the sights and sounds of Arab Palestine, it was as though he saw and heard... nothing. As the Palestinian historian, Walid Khalidi, has pointed out,

> Herzl's entries on his Palestine visit cover some twenty-six pages in the English edition [of his diaries]. What is most relevant to us in these pages are Herzl's reactions to the existence of Palestinians in the country. And what *were* these reactions? The answer is that there were none. Having landed in Jaffa, the main port of the country, did he evince any interest in its buildings and inhabitants? None at all. What he saw was "poverty and misery and heat in gay colours. Confusion in the streets, at the hotel, not a carriage to be had. I was already on horse to ride to Rishon [le Zion]..." Crossing the main orange belt between Jaffa and Mikveh Israel, did he wonder who planted these groves? He did not. What he noticed was a "countryside neglected in Arab fashion... [t]hick dust on the roads, a bit of greenery." On his visits to the colonies near Mikveh a doctor had told him about the prevalence of fever. He immediately thought of the Arabs: "Such Arabs as are immune to the fever might be used for the work [of drainage]." Awaiting the Kaiser's cavalcade at Mikveh, he did notice "a mixed multitude of Arab beggars, womenfolk, children" lining the highway. These were his only direct or indirect references to the Palestinians before entering Jerusalem. In the exchange of pleasantries with the Kaiser at Mikveh, the Kaiser had said: "Very hot! But the country has a future." And

---

8. Theodor Herzl, *The Complete Diaries of Theodor Herzl*, The Herzl Press & Thomas Yoseloff, London, 1960, p 88

Herzl, who had arrived two days before and seen a tiny portion of it, had promptly replied: "At the moment it is still sick."

In Jerusalem there is not one single mention of Palestinians. But in his 29 October entry he notes: "The streets were crowded with groups of Jews strolling in the moonlight." Otherwise, when he looks out of his hotel window that afternoon, he sees "the Kaiser pass through the triumphal arches…" On the way to the imperial tent for the audience "[a] few Jews in the streets looked up as we passed." He also notices "wild ducks… flying overhead."

What about the visual impact of Jerusalem? "Jerusalem by moon-dust with its grand outlines made a powerful impression on me. Magnificent the silhouette of the fortress of Zion, the citadel of David." He seems unaware that the fortress/citadel is a Muslim structure. And does he notice the *Ottoman* walls and gates? Not confessedly. In the 31 October entry, "From the gallery of an ancient synagogue we enjoyed a view of the Temple area, the Mount of Olives, and the whole storied landscape in the morning sunshine." Does he have a word to say about the majesty of the Dome of the Rock and al-Aqsa mosque? He does not. On the way to Motsa and back, does he notice the oceans of terraced olive groves to the north and south? Not at all.[9]

Herzl's successor, Chaim Weizmann, was similarly afflicted when it came to Palestine's indigenous inhabitants. Here he is speaking at a Zionist meeting in Paris in April 1914:

> In its initial stage, Zionism was conceived by its pioneers as a movement wholly depending on mechanical factors: there is a country which happens to be called Palestine, a country without a people, and, on the other hand, there exists the Jewish people, and it has no country. What else is necessary, then, than to fit the gem into the ring, to unite this people with this country? The owners of the country must, therefore, be persuaded and convinced that this marriage is advantageous, not only for the people and for the country, but also for themselves. On this basis grew Zionism.[10]

By 'owners of the country,' of course, Weizmann did not mean the people who actually *lived* there, but whichever imperial power

9. Walid Khalidi, *The Jewish-Ottoman Land Company: Herzl's Blueprint for the Colonization of Palestine*, Journal of Palestine Studies, Winter 1993, pp 40-41

10. Chaim Weizmann, *Zionism Needs a Living Content (1924)*, quoted in *The Zionist Idea: A Historical Analysis & Reader*, Arthur Hertzberg, The Jewish Publication Society, Philadelphia, 1997, p 575

happened to rule over the country at the time. In April 1914, it was Ottoman Turkey. The only 'people' who figure in his conception are 'the Jewish people.' The non-Jews who actually inhabit the country are nowhere to be seen. As the following anecdote reveals, when asked directly about Palestine's majority Arab population, Weizmann literally showed his hand:

> Soon after Sir Herbert Samuel's arrival [July 1920], some of us were summoned to Government House to meet Dr. Weizmann, and to hear him expound his theory of Zionism. His pronouncement was as clear as daylight. In fervid sentences he told us of the hopes that Jews had held for 2000 years, and how these hopes were at last to be fulfilled. At first under British protection, later perhaps as an autonomous state... Palestine was to be handed over to the Jews. At the end we were invited to ask questions. One of us asked him what he intended to do about the Arabs. "Those who wish to remain here can of course do so," was Dr. Weizmann's reply; "but for those who do not so wish, there is Egypt, there is Syria, and" (pointing with a significant gesture to beyond the horizon of the Moab hills visible from the window) "there is the great desert from whence they originally came."[11]

This gesture of Weizmann's could be considered the first iteration of the contemporary claim by hardline Zionists that the Palestinians already have a state of their own – Jordan.

From Flirtation to Affair
'The thesis became an idea present in the air, and soon was a possible line of conduct'

As with the Arab nationalists, Turkey's entry into the war provided the Zionists with the opportunity they needed to advance their cause. While the Arabs were fighting and dying on the battlefield for theirs, the Zionists were schmoozing with British politicians in the corridors of power. Led by Chaim Weizmann, a chemist, and Nahum Sokolow, a journalist (both Russian Jewish émigrés), the Zionists succeeded in winning over to their cause such key political figures

---

11. Humphrey Bowman, *Middle East Window*, Longmans, Green & Co., London, 1942, p 284. Bowman was Mandate Palestine's director of education.

as Herbert Samuel (a British Jew and Liberal MP), Arthur James Balfour (a Conservative MP and former prime minister), David Lloyd George (the Liberal MP who would succeed Asquith as prime minister in December 1916), and Sir Mark Sykes, the diplomat.

Tibawi points out that Weizmann and Sokolow made 'two fantastic claims: that they represented the Zionist movement all over the world and that they acted on behalf of world Jewry,' adding that 'It is very strange indeed that neither of these wild claims was seriously challenged by the British Foreign Office. Without such a challenge the two men were emboldened to claim that they could sway Jewish public opinion in Russia and America from indifference or hostility to Britain and her allies to whole-hearted support.'[12]

Jeffries describes how the Zionist idea went viral in British political circles:

> M. Sokolov and others were busy in the fostering ante-chambers of the English political world. They made converts, and the converts made their converts, and Zionism by degrees became a topic amidst the persons and the groups that count in that world, and in its social centre. The thesis which Asquith had found extravagant as a novel of Disraeli's became through repetition not so extravagant to other statesmen, and then became an idea present in the air, and soon was a possible line of conduct.[13]

Inevitably, however, a line was crossed:

> [Weizmann and Sokolov] knew nothing about the Arab alliance which had ushered in the year [1916]. Besides, what were Arabs in their schemes at any time? However, for the statesmen who had dealings with the Zionist pleaders the new-made alliance should have marked a great difference. To date they had been able to toy with the Zionist project with some show of legitimacy, but now to consider a Zionist State, which was what they were asked to consider, whether it were created immediately or by degrees, upon territory where we were engaged to support Arab independence, ceased to be legitimate. In diplomatic language what they began to do was undesirable; in plain language it was dishonest."[14]

---

12. Tibawi, p 202
13. PTR, pp 98-99
14. PTR, p 99

Britain's rulers had begun the process of weaving the mother-of-all tangled webs:

> The situation in February, so far as it can be disentangled, was that we had a genuine treaty with the Arabs, an "arrangement" pending with the French, an "affair" developing with the Zionists. Some people knew of some of these and a few may have known of all of them, though nobody with much clarity. The French "arrangement" was being kept secret from the Arabs and the Zionists, the Arab treaty was being kept secret from the Zionists, and the French only had general notions of it...[15]

According to Jeffries, 'The first *official* step along the path which led to the dishonouring of Great Britain's obligations [to the Arabs],' came in the form of a Foreign Office memorandum, presented to the Russian foreign minister by Britain's ambassador in Petrograd, Sir George Buchanan, in March 1916. It reads in part,

> A telegram has been received from [foreign secretary] Sir Edward Grey stating that the attention of His Majesty's Government had recently been drawn to the question of Jewish colonization in Palestine.
>
> Although, as is known, many Jews are indifferent to the idea of Zionism, a numerous and most influential section of them in all countries would highly appreciate the proposal of an agreement concerning Palestine, which would fully satisfy Jewish aspirations.
>
> If the point of view set forth above is correct, it will be clear that by means of utilizing the Zionist idea, important political results might be achieved. One of these would be the conversion to the side of the Allies of Jewish elements in the East, in the U.S.A., and other places, whose present attitude towards the cause of the Allies is, to a considerable extent, hostile [...]
>
> The only object of His Majesty's Government is to devise some agreement which will be sufficiently attractive to the majority of Jews to facilitate the conclusion of a transaction securing Jewish support. Having this consideration in view, it appears to His Majesty's Government that if the scheme provided for enabling the Jews, when their colonies in Palestine are sufficiently strong to be able to compete with the Arab population, to take in hand the administration of the internal affairs of this region (excluding

---

15. PTR, pp 100-01

Jerusalem and the Holy Places), then the agreement would be much more attractive for the majority of Jews. His Majesty's Government would not wish to express a preference for this or another solution of the question. However, it is informed that an international protectorate would meet with opposition on behalf of influential Jewish circles.

Communicating all this telegraphically, Sir Edward Grey instructs Sir George Buchanan to solicit from the Russian Government a serious consideration of this question and to favour him at the earliest possible date with the communication of the Russian point of view.[16]

Jeffries' reaction to such a document (as with others of its kind, such as the Balfour Declaration) is visceral: 'What a document! It is scarcely credible that within ten weeks of pledging Arab independence... to the Shereef of Mecca, the Foreign Minister was thus preparing to hand over the administration of Palestine to the Zionists.' He remarks pointedly that this was to be done without thought of its Arab people except to how soon they could be outnumbered, or could be reduced to parity - 'The Arabs' natural right to their country, and the bond into which we had just entered to give them their independence if they fought beside us, alike were disregarded.'

In conclusion, he writes,

That is enough concerning this deplorable document, the first of a series in which British policy and the aims of political Zionism were welded together. The alliance is reflected in the evidently composite text, passing as the voice of the Foreign Secretary alone.

There is but a single plea of any kind to be made on behalf of the memorandum. In one place it has a frankness of its own. At least the reasons for favouring political Zionism are stated without hypocrisy.

Of course, this message was not intended to reach the general public, and so hypocrisy could no doubt be left out. The Government refers in it to nothing but the main chance, and proposes acquiescence in the Zionist schemes as a halfpenny-for-you-penny-for-me politico-commercial transaction. Such bargains, it is true, are the common stuff of alliances. The alliance with the Arabs was a give-and-take affair also. But since nearly all those

---

16. PTR, pp 101-02

who have imposed the support of the arbitrary type of Zionism upon Great Britain have presented it regularly to the nation as radiant with a halo of selfless intentions, it is very satisfactory to have the reality disclosed in such business-like terms as "utilizing" the Zionist idea and "achieving important political results."

The way in which these results were to be realized is very interesting. Russia was an unfortunate ally at the time, in the sense that her maltreatment of her Jewish subjects had set the minds of Jews against her all over the world. Various violences done to them during the early War years, undisclosed in Great Britain, but published in the United States, had deepened the antagonism of the Jews in that country. This made them lukewarm to the cause of Russia's companions-in-arms. Indeed, as the Petrograd memorandum acknowledges, their attitude towards the cause of the Allies to a considerable extent was hostile. An espousal of political Zionism by the British Government might remedy this Jewish hostility. The Zionist leaders in England then, and later, guaranteed that it would. They gave a special guarantee for the United States.[17]

In his autobiography, Weizmann trumpeted the Memorandum as the culmination of a Zionist triumphal march across Europe:

> Zionism was rapidly passing from the preliminary stage of propaganda and theoretical discussion to that of practical realities. Our contacts had become firm enough, public opinion was sufficiently developed for the transition. We had travelled a long way from the tentative 'feelers,' the scattered individual sympathies, of 1914. The picture of the forces for and against us had clarified. We knew who was with us and who against us in the Jewish world. We had discovered, in the English political world, a heavy preponderance of opinion in our favour. As early as March 1916, the subject was being mooted in the European chancelleries. Sir Edward Buchanan, the British Ambassador to Russia, was instructed by Sir Edward Grey to sound out the Russian Government on 'the question of Jewish colonization in Palestine'.[18]

Weizmann's final sentence should not be taken at face value. Jeffries suspected that Grey had been the victim of departmental

---

17. PTR, p 110
18. Chaim Weizmann, *Trial & Error: The Autobiography of Chaim Weizmann*, Hamish Hamilton, London, 1949, p 234

secrecy, a suspicion confirmed by American historian Jonathan Schneer, who attributes authorship of the Memorandum to Hugh O'Beirne, a Foreign Office official, and the Marquess of Crewe, Asquith's secretary of state for India. According to Schneer, Crewe, a relative of the Rothschilds by marriage, had been 'substituting [at the time] as foreign secretary for Sir Edward Grey, who was ill.' Significantly, Schneer also reveals that O'Beirne and Crewe had drafted and sent the Memorandum in the full knowledge that, if word of it were ever to reach the Arabs, there could well be a backlash:

> That the Arabs' reaction would be negative if they learned about such plans, nobody doubted. "It must be admitted," O'Beirne noted, "that if the Arabs knew we were contemplating an extensive Jewish colonization scheme in Palestine (with the possible prospect of eventual Jewish self-government), this might have a very chilling effect on the Arab leaders." [...] In other words, at this very preliminary stage of their courtship of "world Jewry," British officials who had previously been wooing Arabs now understood that they faced a fork in the road. "It is evident," wrote the percipient O'Beirne, "that Jewish colonization of Palestine must conflict to some extent with Arab interests. All we can do, if and when the time comes to discuss details, is to try to devise a settlement which will involve as little hardship as possible to the Arab population. We shall then, of course, have to consult experts."[19]

The Invention of a National Problem
'Political Zionism was not something engrained in the soil of the Near East, nor had it any place amidst the problems which the Ottoman Empire handed on to its successors'

The third and last of Britain's wartime undertakings concerning the Arab East was, as we know, the Balfour Declaration of 2 November, 1917, the culmination of Zionist efforts to obtain a statement of

---

19. Jonathan Schneer, *The Balfour Declaration: The Origins of the Arab-Israeli Conflict*, Random House, New York, p 160. Tibawi's reference to Grey's policies being undermined by his Foreign Office subordinates should be recalled here.

British support for their settlement project in Palestine. These began with the formulation of a Zionist program in October 1916. As Jeffries explains,

> [I]n October 1916 the Zionist Organization felt justified in putting forward a formal statement of its views as to the future government of Palestine in the event of its coming under the control of England and of France [...] The document was rather a long one... One clause demanded that a Jewish Chartered Company should be established of which the purpose should be the resettlement of Palestine by Jewish settlers... [I]t was to have power "to exercise the right of pre-emption of Crown and other lands and to acquire for its own use all or any concessions which may... be granted by the suzerain Government." [...]
>
> The most significant clause of all, though, was that in which the Arabs came in for mention... in a Zionist document of that date. But in what manner? "The present population, being too small, too poor, and too little trained to make rapid progress, requires the introduction of a new and progressive element in the population, desirous of devoting all its energies and capital to the work of colonization on modern lines."
>
> The Arabs, the "present population" of the above paragraph, at the time numbered some 675,000, and Palestine is of merely county dimensions. These however were not facts to detain the Zionist Organization. It dismissed the Arabs without further consideration, after what seemed without doubt the conclusive remark that their population was "small and poor." To be small and poor is the supreme crime in a category of thought which, curiously, is itself small and poor.
>
> Therefore these Arabs, exiguous in their hundreds of thousands, required "the introduction of a new and progressive element." Sentences of such surpassing effrontery as this one are rare, and it would be hard to find anything matching in insolence the whole clause. What right had the Zionist Organization to talk of what the Arabs needed? None whatsoever.
>
> Still, whether the clause or the whole programme of which it was a part were insolent or not, the programme of the Chartered Company was accepted as a foundation-stone by the British Government. "The Government," says the Zionist Report, "seems to have regarded the Zionist claims embodied in the programme as forming a basis for discussion." Negotiations thenceforth went on steadily. Talks with individual statesmen "gave place to discussions of a more formal character. Zionism won recognition as one of the complex problems connected

with the Middle East on the one hand and the question of small nationalities on the other." (Zionist Official Report.)

There it is. A better example could not be supplied of the sophistries by which the hapless Arabs were to be supplanted. Zionism, political Zionism, not alone was confirmed in the status it had acquired out of the skies, but now was advanced a stage beyond. Political Zionism became one of the "complex problems connected with the Middle East." All in a flash it was enrolled amidst the problems which by and by the Allies must face.

The role thus assumed by political Zionism was one unwarranted by any law, any deed, any political conditions which were then in existence, or previously had been for over a thousand years. Zionism as a political entity had owned no situation outside the brains of its own recent devisers. Political Zionism was not something engrained in the soil of the Near East, nor had it any place amidst the problems which the Ottoman Empire handed on so profusely to its successors.

The Ottoman Empire had been approached and had refused to introduce this amidst its many complicated factors. It would not have a Jewish enclave. No statesmen in the world had toiled for years over Zionism, no statesmen in the world had inherited dossiers in hundreds filled with the negotiations of his predecessors-in-office concerning it. It simply was not a problem at all. There was a Jewish problem in Eastern Europe; there was none in Palestine. It was intended now to introduce the problem where it had never existed, but that was to create a problem – something vastly different. In fact, to say that political Zionism was a complex problem connected with the Middle East was a thumping lie. Its true situation in the realm of politics was that of a theory just beginning to be exploited in London and Paris and New York.

The complexity attributed to it was wholly unreal. What was called complexity only meant the difficulty of finding a formula opaque enough to disguise the immediate or future annexation of Palestine.

But sophistry did not confine itself to slipping political Zionism in this way in among the problems of the Middle East. With the same stroke Zionism also won "recognition as a problem connected with the question of small nationalities." Indeed it did. The operative word... is "connected." By more adroitness that which had been nothing, but had been transmogrified into a problem, was now again transmogrified from a problem into a small nation, by coupling it to various lesser lands.

The scheme for this can be visualized. In 1916 the small nations were already forming up to put their pleas to the (it was hoped) conquering Allies. Together they made a political caravan, a train if you like. When the moment came they would all set off together, the train would depart for the terminus where the victorious Peace was being prepared. The political Zionists were ready for this. Rapidly and unostentatiously a van labelled "Zionist Problem" would be connected to the last carriage. The train would puff away. Somewhere *en route* the label would disappear, and a van inscribed "Jewish National Home" would draw eventually alongside the arrival platform, behind Czechoslovakia, Lithuania, Latvia and all the others. The whole scheme is very simple. But the chance of watching the manoeuvre is not often given.[20]

So much for 1916. More Zionist victories would follow in 1917. As the Arabs were taking the Hejaz port of Wejh from the Turks in March of that year, with 'nearly twenty killed,'[21] the Zionists were advancing from their redoubt in the Foreign Office to lay siege to the War Cabinet, and, having got wind of the Sykes-Picot Agreement and its proposal to internationalise Palestine, they launched a pre-emptive strike on Paris. Jeffries writes that,

> It was proof of the growing power of the Zionist leaders... that they should have tried to secure the annulling of the Sykes-Picot pact. What is more they succeeded in doing so, or securing what was tantamount to the annulment of the portions which affected them. Not only did the French Government admit the recognition of Zionism, though it had no place in the Sykes-Picot provisions, but the international zone was deleted from the text. Nothing was stated or disclosed officially, but internationalization vanished, *spurlos versenkt*. When the revised Sykes-Picot documents became the basis of the abortive Treaty of Sevres in 1920, the clause providing for internationalization was gone. With that clause disappeared too the conscientious stipulation that the prospective ruling body of Palestine must consult Arab representatives before disposing of the future of that country and its Arab populace.[22]

The next major Zionist advance came when the United States entered the war on the Allied side in April 1917, in the form of a

---

20. PTR, pp 127-130

21. T.E. Lawrence, *Seven Pillars of Wisdom*, Jonathan Cape, London, 1926/1950, p 168

22. PTR, pp 141-142

British statement of war-aims in the Near East, designed specifically to win the support of American Jews:

> It is proposed that the following be adopted as the heads of a scheme for a Jewish re-settlement of Palestine in accordance with Jewish National aspirations: 1) *Basis of Settlement*: Recognition of Palestine as the Jewish National Home. 2) *Status of Jewish Population in Palestine generally*: The Jewish population present and future throughout Palestine is to enjoy and possess full national, political and civic rights. 3) *Immigration into Palestine*: The Suzerain Government shall grant full and free rights of immigration into Palestine to Jews of all countries. 4) *The Establishment of a Chartered Company*: The Suzerain Government shall grant a Charter to a Jewish Company for the colonization and development of Palestine, the Company to have power to acquire and take over any concessions for works of a public character... and the rights of pre-emption of Crown lands... not held in private or religious ownership... 5) *Communal Autonomy*: Full autonomy is to be enjoyed by Jewish communities throughout Palestine in all matters bearing upon their religious or communal welfare and their education.

Jeffries asks rhetorically,

> What was this "British" statement of war-aims in the Near East? Again nothing other than a Zionist document taken over and re-edited. It is the programme of the previous October, complete with references to the "suzerain," and with several other of the original phrases reappearing. When first issued, as the October Programme, it had been termed a "basis for discussion" between the Zionists and Whitehall. The basis had crept up by now and had become the main structure of the Government's statement of policy; a magic formation.[23]

'Magic formation'? Jeffries explains,

> First of all political Zionism floats in the minds of some adepts. A few books giving its theories, in the Russian or German tongues chiefly, come to England. A handful of the adepts also transport themselves to England, and translate, in both senses of that word, their doctrines to this country. In the mind of a Cabinet Minister of their race [Sir Herbert Samuel] the culture finds an appropriate medium for growth, and expands, till he eases what

---

23. PTR, pp 142-43

has been thronging his brain into a memorandum on paper. This passes to his colleagues and working through them develops, with additions from the original adepts, into a further memorandum, the Petrograd document, which half inquires about this Zionism, half supputes the advantages of patronizing it, if a satisfactory form for it can be found.

In order to supply this form, the doctrine is tabulated thereon by its original propagators, in a manner which they dub official, but, since they have no status, is official for them alone. This is presented to British ministers, to the Ambassador in Paris. Shortly afterwards it is recognized, or rather is accepted as an official presentation by the Government. Upon which those who presented it by an inevitable process themselves turn into official persons.

The next step is for the now official Zionist leaders to submit a document, the latest embodiment of all that has gone before, the October Programme, and this the Government says it will take into consideration, thereby half sharing it. Soon, and finally, comes the Government's own announcement of war-aims, which proves to be, in all that matters, identical with this October document. So what began as a remote idea in the heads of a few strangers, in the far parts of Europe, has now become the mind and the policy of the British Empire. And though this development has been crammed into three years, the violence of the process has escaped observation, and has appeared to be in the order of nature.

In reality the growth of political Zionism had not been natural at all. It corresponded to nothing so much as the mango-tree trick, now in this political version of it practised upon the greatest scale and with the nimblest sleight-of-hand in the history of conjuring statesmanship.[24]

Not all, however, were fooled. Britain's largely anti-Zionist Jewish establishment was becoming concerned at the rising

---

24. PTR, p 143. By way of explanation: 'An amazing trick of generating a mango tree from a seed within a few minutes. The seed is placed in an empty pot under a tripod formed by three sticks. The tripod is then covered with a sheet after which the pot containing the seed is taken out and filled with soil. Water is poured into it and the pot is again placed under the covered sticks. Onlookers are asked to look under the cloth from time to time. After a while, the performer opens the cloth and takes out a mango plant. Then the plant seems to grow bigger under the cloth and ripe mangoes start falling and rolling out from under it. Finally, the magician removes the cloth to reveal a mango-tree laden with fruit.' (www.mazmaindia.com)

influence of Zionism in government circles. Jeffries cites a 24 May *Times* letter from David Alexander, the president of the Conjoint Committee of the Board of Deputies of British Jews, and Claude Montefiore, the president of the Anglo-Jewish Association:

> They began by declaring their sympathy with Zionism, if it were carried out in a non-political manner... They went on to say that the "establishment of a Jewish nationality in Palestine, founded on the theory of Jewish homelessness, must have the effect throughout the world of stamping the Jews as strangers in their native lands and of undermining their hard-won positions as citizens and nationals of those lands."
>
> They pointed out that the theories of political Zionism undermined the religious basis of Jewry. The only alternative to a religious basis would be "a secular Jewish nationality, recruited on some loose and obscure principle of race and of ethnographic peculiarity. But this would not be Jewish in any spiritual sense, and its establishment in Palestine would be a denial of all the ideals and hopes by which the survival of Jewish life in that country commends itself to the Jewish conscience and to Jewish sympathy. On these grounds the Conjoint Committee of the Board of Deputies and the Anglo-Jewish Association deprecates most earnestly the national proposals of the [political] Zionists." The second part in the Zionist programme which has aroused the misgivings of the Conjoint Committee is the proposal to invest the Jewish settlers [in Palestine] with certain special rights in excess of those enjoyed by the rest of the population, these rights to be embodied in a Charter and to be administered by a Jewish Chartered Company. In all the countries in which Jews live the principle of equal rights for all religious denominations is vital to them. Were they to set an example in Palestine of disregarding this principle they would convict themselves of having appealed to it for purely selfish motives. In the countries in which they are still struggling for equal rights they would find themselves hopelessly compromised.
>
> The letter of protest ended with these words: "The [political Zionist] proposal is the more inadmissible because the Jews are... a minority of the population of Palestine, and it might involve them in the bitterest feuds with their neighbours of other races and religions, which would severely retard their progress and find deplorable echoes throughout the Orient".[25]

---

25. PTR, pp 147-148

Later developments in Europe would bear out the fears of Alexander and Montefiore. Their fear that the 'establishment of a Jewish nationality in Palestine' would lead to Jews being seen 'as strangers in their native lands,' for example, was borne out by events in 1932 Vienna: 'Crowds of Nazis attacked Jews in the principal streets, on the tram-cars and in the cafes to-day, on the occasion of the opening meetings of the Vienna City Council and the Vienna State Parliament. The cry "Jews, go to Palestine!" was raised repeatedly by the Nazis...'[26]. Their fear that Jews would become involved 'in the bitterest feuds with their [Palestinian] neighbours of other races and religions,' of course, needs no elaboration.

What, then, enabled Britain's Zionists to prevail over this anti-Zionist opposition? For Jeffries, the answer lay as much in the peculiar mindset of Britain's political elite as it did in the Zionists' powers of persuasion:

> [T]he issues raised by these [anti-Zionist] pronouncements, both in America and in Europe, were met by their being ignored. In England, Mr. Lloyd George, Lord Balfour, Lord Milner and presently General Smuts, imbued with an indescribable mixture of false idealism, of ingenuity and ingenuousness, of biblical dilettantism and Hebrew pedantry, of expediency and of gratefulness and of bargaining statesmanship, were bent upon the political Zionist plan.[27]

Drafting the Balfour Declaration
Drafts went back and forth to the Foreign Office. They also went back and forth over the ocean'

The drafting process that resulted in the issue of the Balfour Declaration of 2 December, 1917 began in earnest, in June 1917, with a visit to Lord Balfour by Weizmann, Lord Rothschild (to whom the Declaration would later be addressed) and Sir Ronald Graham, the Assistant Under Secretary of the Foreign Office.

---

26. *'Jews go to Palestine!' Nazis shout attacking Jews in Vienna streets*, jta.org, 25/5/32
27. PTR, p 154

Weizmann's own account of the meeting is, alas, all too brief:

> [A] few days later [after 13 June] I went, with Sir Ronald and Lord Rothschild, to see Mr. Balfour... and put it to the Foreign Secretary that the time had come for the British Government to give us a definite declaration of support and encouragement. Mr. Balfour promised to do so, and asked me to submit to him a declaration which would be satisfactory to us, and which he would try and put before the War Cabinet.[28]

Thankfully, Jeffries does it justice:

> The arrival of the two Zionist delegates at the Foreign Office with their plea for a declaration of British support was no surprise of course to the Secretary of State. All the negotiations since February had tended to the sole end that Britain should adopt the Zionist cause publicly, and various formulas, such as that of the previous October, had been elaborated with this in view. The delegates' visit to Lord Balfour and their request for a pronouncement therefore were so much stage-play. It was not that the time had come for him, in the Army phrase, to be issued with a declaration. Balfour knew his role in a performance so much after his own mind: he took his cue, and asked the visitors for "a draft that he would put before the War-Cabinet for sanction."
>
> His Majesty's Government, be it noted, was to define its policy in the forthcoming document. The Foreign Secretary's way of setting about this was to ask Dr. Weizmann, and his honorary companion, to furnish him with a draft of this policy of His Majesty's Government. As soon as he got it, Lord Balfour would put Dr. Weizmann's policy of His Majesty's Government before His Majesty's Government for approval. The walls of the Foreign Office without doubt have enclosed many a singular scene, but they might well have inclined together to hide from view the spectacle of a Secretary of State asking a visitor from Russia to give him a draft of his own Cabinet's measures. The situation was what is called Gilbertian, or would have been so but for the great issues of national honesty involved.[29]

Balfour had, in fact, just returned from five weeks in the United States where he had met with Weizmann's American counterpart, Louis D. Brandeis, a US Supreme Court Justice and confidant

---

28. Chaim Weizmann, *Trial & Error: The Autobiography of Chaim Weizmann*, Hamish Hamilton, London, 1949, pp 255-256

29. PTR, p 156

of President Woodrow Wilson. What is more, he had reportedly proclaimed while there, 'I am a Zionist.'

According to Brandeis' biographer, Balfour 'sought out Brandeis almost immediately upon his arrival in Washington, and the two men took an immediate liking to each other.'[30] He continues,

> At a White House reception on 23 April, and in several interviews, they explored the problems of a declaration, the need for an American endorsement of it, and the intricacies of Anglo-French rivalry. When Balfour suggested that perhaps the United States would assume a protectorate over the Holy Land, Brandeis quickly told him that it was out of the question. The justice knew that the Wilson administration had no interest in expansion on the other side of the globe; American Zionists wanted British control. Balfour had been hoping to hear this, since a British protectorate over Palestine would make England the dominant colonial power in the region, and he urged the justice to secure American approval of a declaration.[31]

The drafting of the Declaration was, in fact, very much an Anglo-Zionist-American affair, as Jeffries indicates:

> Balfour returned home with a thoroughly cultivated Mission, gave his formal interview to Dr. Weizmann and Lord Rothschild, and the drafting of the Declaration began on both sides of the Atlantic. In England "many different versions of the suggested formula were drafted by various members of the (Zionist) Political Committee." (*Zionist Official Report*) Drafts went back and forth to the Foreign Office. They also went back and forth over the ocean. "A considerable number of drafts were made in London and transmitted to the United States, through War Office channels, for the use of the American Zionist Political Committee." (de Haas.) President Wilson himself lent a hand to the drafting, or at least bent a supervising eye upon the text of the suggestions from England. "The field of international discussion was accordingly widened, and all the Drafts of the proposed Declaration were submitted for approval to the White House." (Wise & de Haas.)[32]

---

30. Melvin I. Urofsky, *Louis D. Brandeis: A Life*, Pantheon, New York, 2009, p 517

31. Urofsky, p 517

32. PTR, p 163

Two developments of particular interest at this time are missing from Jeffries' account of the matter. We learn from Tibawi that 'the publicity given to [Zionist] ambitions provoked a public protest [on 9 June] by the Muslim community in London [and] at the same time Balfour called for a statement, probably prompted by the Palestine question, of the British obligations to the Arabs and the allies regarding Turkish territory.'[33]

The Muslim protest, in fact, resulted in the production of a 23-page pamphlet titled *Muslim Interests in Palestine*. Tibawi relates that this was handed to the Foreign Office, where it 'finally reached Balfour who may or may not have read it for it bears only his initials.'[34]

The statement of Britain's 'obligations to the Arabs and the allies' was drawn up by the Foreign Office official Harold Nicolson. Tibawi speculates that,

> Nicolson must have sensed the unexpressed aim of the memorandum he was asked to prepare to be a search for an escape from the obligation to the Arabs regarding Palestine. Hence his great reticence. He was right in the midst of the Zionist pressure at the Foreign Office... He started with the obligations to Russia, France and Italy (and added, though he was not asked to do so, under Britain 'Mesopotamia, independence of Egypt from Turkey; ?Palestine.') The question mark before Palestine shows that he knew the wishes of the Prime Minister but found no contractual warrant for them. He said nothing about the international regime...
>
> The Arabs were considered last. Britain was under an obligation by virtue of McMahon's letter of 14 December, 1915 not to conclude any peace treaty that does not include in its terms 'the freedom of the Arab peoples from German and Turkish domination'. Otherwise the British obligations to the Arabs through the Sharif were 'far more complex' than to the allies, and 'the position was rendered more delicate by the fact that our prestige in Arabia and the Middle East will stand or fall by the extent to which we are enabled to act up to our promises'. He did not detail these but quoted the exact paragraph from the first letter from the Sharif defining the boundaries of the Arab countries

---

33. Tibawi, p 213
34. Tibawi, p 214

for which he sought British recognition of independence. Then he quoted, also textually, the areas in Syria excluded in favour of France. Nicolson judged that the Sharif 'signified his somewhat grudging acquiescence in French claims in Syria.' He said nothing about Iraq or Palestine, the main object of the enquiry. But he adroitly shifted the responsibility on to Sykes with the flattering remark that he 'alone will be able to state with authority how far any evasion or modification of our engagements to the Sharif are likely to be resented by Arab opinion.'

The question mark against Palestine in Nicolson's memorandum is full of meaning. The intention was either to evade or modify British engagements to the Arabs, and Palestine was the area to which the one or the other was to be applied. It is in the highest degree unfortunate that the matter was not more deeply investigated.[35]

The earliest draft declaration of British support for Zionism documented by Jeffries appeared in July 1917. It reads as follows:

His Majesty's Government, after considering the aims of the Zionist Organization, accepts the principle of recognizing Palestine as the National Home of the Jewish people and the right of the Jewish people to build up its National life in Palestine under a protection to be established at the conclusion of Peace following upon the successful issue of the War. His Majesty's Government regards as essential for the realization of this principle the grant of internal autonomy to the Jewish nationality in Palestine, freedom of immigration for Jews, and the establishment of a Jewish National Colonizing Corporation for the re-settlement and economic development of the country. The conditions and forms of the internal autonomy and a charter for the Jewish National Colonising Corporation should, in the view of His Majesty's Government, be elaborated in detail and determined with the representatives of the Zionist Organization.[36]

Of particular interest here is the fact that there is no reference in the text to the Zionist project as *a refuge for persecuted Jews*, only to the alleged right of that Zionist ideological construct, 'the Jewish people,' to 'build up its national life in Palestine.' In fact, at a later (4 October) meeting of the war cabinet, Balfour also had

---

35. Tibawi, p 215-216
36. PTR, pp 163-164

nothing whatever to say of Jewish suffering, and spoke only of Jewish nationalism:

> What was at the back of the Zionist movement was the intense national consciousness held by certain members of the Jewish race. They regarded themselves as one of the great historic races of the world, whose original home was Palestine, and these Jews had a passionate longing to regain once more their ancient national home.[37]

It should be noted too that there is no mention whatever in the draft of the country's existing non-Jewish population. It is as if, as Jeffries points out, Palestine 'were empty.' This first, unamended, Zionist draft of the Balfour Declaration clearly spells out the settler-colonial agenda behind the much amended final version, the first being for private consumption, the second for public.

Too frank to survive in its original form, the first draft demanded drastic revision. Characteristically, while Jeffries attributes this to the need to placate anti-Zionist Jewish opposition to the Zionist scheme, Leonard Stein (in his 1961 study *The Balfour Declaration*) disingenuously claims that it resulted merely from objections to its length and detail by Sykes and Graham.

Be that as it may, the second Zionist draft of 18 July reads as follows:

> 1. His Majesty's Government accepts the principle that Palestine should be reconstituted as the National Home of the Jewish people.
>
> 2. His Majesty's Government will use its best endeavours to secure the achievement of this object and will discuss the necessary methods and means with the Zionist Organization.[38]

Mark the word 'reconstituted.' An ancient regime that had existed, in Jeffries' words, 'for a [mere] gnat's span' was to be revived, some '18 centuries after the last shadow of the Israelite flicker of power faded,' as the national home of the aforementioned Zionist 'Jewish people' construct.

---

37. Doreen Ingrams, *Palestine Papers 1917-1922: Seeds of Conflict*, John Murray, London, 1972, p 11

38. PTR, p 164

Although this new formulation met with Balfour's approval in August, Lord Milner, a member of the War Cabinet, watered it down still further, removing the word 'reconstituted' and making other changes. Milner's draft reads,

> His Majesty's Government accepts the principle that every opportunity should be afforded for the establishment of a National Home for the Jewish people in Palestine and will use its best endeavours to secure the achievement of this object, and will be ready to consider any suggestions on the subject which the Zionist Organisation may desire to lay before them.[39]

As always in these matters, Jeffries' eye is firmly on the ball:

> In the new draft Palestine was no longer mentioned as the National Home of the Jewish people: instead the Government signified its desire to establish "a National Home for the Jewish people" *in* Palestine. A vast deal of printers' ink and a vast deal of speakers' breath has been wasted upon the exact significance of this change of formula. All that it signified in fact was a lack of courage on the part of the Governmental persons involved. Confronted with Jewish opposition, they took fright at announcing that they would patronize the turning of Palestine *en bloc* and at once into a Jewish National Home. They decided to announce their patronage only of a first instalment of this process. They suffered no change of heart: they did not reconsider their position in the light of the McMahon-Hussein Treaty: they made no effort to consult any Arab representatives or to preconize as essential and to promise such a consultation as soon as it should be possible. They went on with their illegitimate deal, but they phrased it differently and began to develop it more warily [...]
> "National" was a key-word. For Jews to have not a social or religious home, but a "National Home," meant that the germ of the future Jewish State in Palestine was implanted in the formula. Also the attribution of a national quality to the so-called "Home" extricated the Jews who formed it from allegiance to any State founded upon the popular suffrage of all denizens of Syria or of any section of Syria.[40]

---

39. Curiously, Ingrams (p 9), Stein (*The Balfour Declaration*, p 521) & Tibawi (p 221) omit the word 'national.' Jeffries notes that 'this key-word was kept in succeeding drafts by the Government.' (PTR, p 166) Schneer (*The Balfour Declaration* p 336) concurs with Jeffries.

40. PTR, pp 165-166

Milner's draft was duly approved by Balfour and referred to the War Cabinet meeting of 3 September, where it ran into stiff anti-Zionist opposition in the form of Edwin Montagu, the Secretary of State for India, the Cabinet's only Jew, and a confirmed anti-Zionist.

Since neither Lloyd George nor Balfour attended the meeting of 3 September, it seems that Montagu pretty much had the floor on this matter. Drawing on arguments from a provocatively titled memorandum he had prepared and circulated in August (*The Anti-Semitism of the Present Government*), he sought to 'place on record [his] view that the policy of His Majesty's Government is anti-Semitic in result and will prove a rallying ground for Anti-Semites in every country in the world.'

Montagu's scathing polemic is worth quoting at length, not only for its prophetic foreshadowing of current Zionist attitudes towards the Palestinians, but for its remarkable prediction of Israel's key apartheid Law of Return (1950):

> Zionism has always seemed to me to be a mischievous political creed, untenable by any patriotic citizen of the United Kingdom. If a Jewish Englishman sets his eyes on the Mount of Olives and longs for the day when he will shake British soil from his shoes and go back to agricultural pursuits in Palestine, he has always seemed to me to have acknowledged aims inconsistent with British citizenship and to have admitted that he is unfit for a share in public life in Great Britain, or to be treated as an Englishman. I have always understood that those who indulged in this creed were largely animated by the restrictions upon and refusal of liberty to Jews in Russia. But at the very time when these Jews have been acknowledged as Jewish Russians and given all liberties, it seems to be inconceivable that Zionism should be officially recognised by the British Government, and that Mr Balfour should be authorized to say that Palestine was to be reconstituted as the "national home of the Jewish people." I do not know what this involves, but I assume that it means that Mahommedans and Christians are to make way for the Jews and that the Jews should be put in all positions of preference and should be peculiarly associated with Palestine in the same way that England is with the English or France with the French, that Turks and other Mahommedans in Palestine will be regarded as foreigners, just in the same way as Jews will hereafter be treated as foreigners in every country but Palestine. Perhaps also citizenship must be granted only as a result of a religious test.

Montagu went on to argue that there was no 'Jewish nation'; to predict that 'when the Jews are told that Palestine is their national home, every country will immediately desire to get rid of its Jewish citizens, and you will find a population in Palestine driving out its present inhabitants, taking all the best in the country...'; to deride Balfour and Rothschild as false messiahs; to advocate the 'disenfranchisement' of British Zionists and even the 'proscrib[ing] of the Zionist Organisation as illegal and against the national interest'; to assert that Palestine was just as associated with Muslims and Christians as it was with Jews; to predict that Palestine would become 'the world's Ghetto'; and, finally, to urge that the government 'go no further' than 'be prepared to do everything in their power to obtain for Jews in Palestine complete liberty of settlement and life on an equality with the inhabitants of that country who profess other religious beliefs.'[41]

It was the principled opposition of Montagu and Lord Curzon ('the most travelled man who ever sat in a British cabinet,' according to his biographer, David Gilmour), which was to prove the most significant impediment to the smooth passage of a British declaration in support of the Zionist cause.

As it happened, the War Cabinet voted a) to defer the draft declaration, and b) to ascertain whether US President Wilson favoured a 'declaration of sympathy with the Zionist movement.' According to Leonard Stein, 'This idea seems to have emerged as an afterthought from the discussion on September 3rd, when the War Cabinet was shaken by Montagu's protest against a pro-Zionist declaration, but not to the point of being prepared to dispose of the matter then and there.'[42] According to the minutes, 'The Acting Secretary of State for Foreign Affairs [Lord Robert Cecil] pointed out that this was a question on which the Foreign Office has been very strongly pressed for a long time past. There was a very strong and enthusiastic organisation, more particularly in the United States, who were zealous in this matter, and his belief was that it

---

41. www.jewishvirtuallibrary.org
42. Leonard Stein, *The Balfour Declaration*, Vallentine Mitchell & Co. Ltd, London, 1961, p 503

would be of most substantial assistance to the Allies to have the earnestness and enthusiasm of these people enlisted on our side.'[43]

On 11 September, Colonel Edward House, Wilson's adviser, telegraphed the Foreign Office that 'the time was not opportune for any definite statement further, perhaps, than one of sympathy, provided it can be made without conveying any real commitment.'[44] Alarmed at this development, Weizmann prevailed upon Brandeis to intervene with House. Brandeis telegraphed Weizmann on 24 September as follows: 'From talks I have had with President and from expressions of opinion given to closest advisers I feel that I can answer that he is in entire sympathy with declaration quoted in yours of 19th [September] as approved by Foreign Office and Prime Minister. I of course heartily agree.'[45]

One is left wondering whether Brandeis was being entirely honest here. Stein has this to say on the matter:

> If on September 11th Wilson was satisfied that the time was not opportune for a pro-Zionist declaration unless it could be made without 'conveying any real commitment,' how did it come to pass that, less than two weeks later, Brandeis was able to report that the President 'was in entire sympathy with' the Rothschild formula? The obvious explanation is that... Brandeis had used his personal influence with the President to undo the harm that had been done. He had either persuaded Wilson that there was nothing in the Rothschild formula which could be interpreted as 'conveying any real commitment' or he had induced the President to change his mind about the kind of declaration he could approve. It looks, however, as though this may not be quite the whole story. In assuring Weizmann... that the President was in entire sympathy with 'the declaration quoted in yours of 19th,' Brandeis referred to 'talks I have had with the President.' Was he referring to recent talks or only to conversations he had had with the President in the past? If he had Wilson's direct authority for his message to Weizmann, why should he have troubled to refer also to 'expressions of opinion given to [the President's] close advisers'? These 'close advisers' would certainly include Colonel House... It seems probable... that, having been convinced by

---

43. Ingrams, p 10
44. Stein, p 505
45. Stein, p 507

Brandeis that a declaration on the lines of the Rothschild formula ought to command American support, House had advised the President in the same sense and got him to agree. This would fit in with what is known of the background to Wilson's favourable reply when he was again consulted by the British government early in October. There is... good reason to believe that it was on House's advice that he approved the proposed declaration.[46]

Jeffries very much regretted that while working on his book he had not been able to travel to the United States 'to inquire into what happened in the political ante-rooms of the United States before the proclamation of the Balfour Declaration.' In the absence of first-hand information, he could only conclude that Wilson had 'erred... through ignorance of the far-off country whose fate he attempted to settle.'[47]

The American historian Lawrence Davidson offers the following summation of the matter:

> It was [his] very full agenda that helps explain Wilson's delayed response to the British request for preapproval of the Balfour Declaration. Working through Wilson's adviser and confidant, Edward House, the British sought the president's agreement to the wording of the document that would be the Balfour Declaration. In a memo of September 7, 1917, House asked Wilson, "Have you made up your mind regarding what answer you will give [Sir] Cecil [Arthur Spring-Rice, British ambassador in Washington] concerning the Zionist Movement? It seems to me that there are many dangers lurking in it." The Zionists added their own pressure for a positive response to the British draft, again through House, until he complained to Wilson in a note of October 3, 1917, that "the Jews from every tribe have descended in force, and they are determined to break in with a jimmy if they are not let in." Finally, on October 13, 1917, the president literally rediscovered the issue amidst all the other problems he daily confronted. On that day he memoed House, "I find in my pocket the memorandum you gave me about the Zionist movement. I am afraid I did not say to you that I concurred in the formula suggested from the other side. I do, and would be obliged if you would let them know it." So Wilson, rather offhandedly, gave his blessings to the Balfour Declaration.

---

46. Stein, pp 507-508
47. PTR, p 157

It is to be noted that Wilson seems to have given his approval for the Balfour Declaration without serious consultation with the State Department. This is a pattern that would persist over time and create repeated confusion over U.S. foreign policy for Palestine. Thus years later, when the State Department was reviewing all its documents referring to the Balfour Declaration, it could conclude that "there is no confirmatory evidence of [President Wilson's support for the declaration] in the records of the Department... On the contrary it would appear... that this Government was not kept officially informed of negotiations leading up to the Balfour Declaration." From the beginning the State Department stood apart from, and often uninformed about, presidential thinking on the subjects of Zionism and Palestine.[48]

Unfortunately, Wilson's precise role in the matter remains, at this juncture, something of a mystery.

In late September, with Montagu's opposition very much in mind, Weizmann prevailed upon Lloyd George to place the question of Palestine on the agenda of the 4 October meeting of the War Cabinet and followed this with a memorandum to the Foreign Office, pressing for a favourable decision by the War Cabinet to 'counteract the demoralising influence which the enemy press is endeavouring to exercise by holding out vague promises to the Jews.'[49]

This was essentially a scare tactic ('the German scare' as Tibawi calls it). Predictably, it was trotted out at the 4 October meeting by Balfour, who warned that 'the German government were making great efforts to capture the sympathy of the Zionist Movement.'[50]

Stein comments that 'Misleading as they can now be seen to have been, the reports current at the time as to the German Government's intentions were taken seriously by the Foreign Office and to the long-term case for a pro-Zionist policy added a cogent argument for a speedy decision in its favour.' Stein refers only to 'misleading... reports current at the time.'[51]

---

48. Lawrence Davidson, *America's Palestine: Popular & Official Perceptions from Balfour to Israeli Statehood*, University Press of Florida, Gainesville, 2001, pp 16-17

49. Stein, p 514

50. Stein, p 516

51. Stein, p 516-517

Tibawi goes further, suggesting that these reports were, in fact, Zionist concoctions:

> Simultaneous with Weizmann's move, Rothschild addressed a private letter to Balfour, and the *Jewish Chronicle* published an item of news the previous day making the same point, namely that German newspapers were advocating Jewish settlement in Palestine under German protection. It was therefore imperative to forestall Germany, as if German foreign policy was made by newspapers. There is no record in the file that Balfour did reply to Rothschild's note. Nor is there any evidence from any British embassy or consulate anywhere in the allied or neutral countries to support the Zionist claims. And yet these were now implicitly believed by those in charge of the Zionist question at the Foreign Office, notably by Graham.[52]

Montagu's contribution to the meeting of 4 October was again substantial. In Tibawi's paraphrase,

> He objected to any declaration that included the expression 'national home' for the Jewish people, for that would prejudice the position of all Englishmen of the Jewish faith including himself. How could he deal with India on behalf of a British government that proposed to proclaim to the whole world that his national home was 'in Turkish territory.' The majority of Jewish supporters of Zionism in England were either foreign or foreign-born. The voting at the Conjoint Committee [composed of what Weizmann dismissed as assimilationist Jews] was not decisive nor was it on the issue of Zionism. No accurate plebiscite of the supporters of the opposing sides was made. He concluded by saying that President Wilson was opposed to the proposed declaration.[53]

Curzon raised the question of questions. Tibawi again:

> His main point had already been raised by Montagu who feared that the Muslim and Christian inhabitants of Palestine would be doomed to give way to the Jews. But Curzon put the problem in the form of a specific question: 'How was it proposed to get rid of the existing majority of Mussulman inhabitants and to introduce the Jews in their place?' There is no record in the minutes that this question received any answer.[54]

---

52. Tibawi, p 224
53. Tibawi, p 226
54. Tibawi, p 226

The interventions of Montagu and Curzon resulted in yet another decision to seek President Wilson's approval, as well as those of Zionist leaders and representative Anglo-Jewish anti-Zionists.

Tibawi notes the meeting's predictable failure to solicit the Arab view:

> What was not ascertained, and ought to have been ascertained through British diplomatic channels, were the views of Jews and Zionists outside Britain in whose favour the declaration was to be made. Another omission was the neglect to consult the Muslim community in London [...] But the greatest omission was the complete disregard of the Arab case. The Sharif of Mecca also had certain rights regarding Palestine under the Sykes-Picot agreement, even if his rights under the McMahon pledge were to be 'evaded'. Furthermore he was Britain's ally whose prestige and some of his forces were employed in furthering the conquest of Palestine. Since its Arab inhabitants were inaccessible under Turkish military rule, the Sharif ought to have been consulted on their behalf through the usual British channels. He might not have averted the injustice to the Palestinian Arabs, but at least the insulting reference to them, constituting as they did over ninety per cent of the population, as 'non-Jewish communities', might have been amended to specify two, instead of one, national homes in the country.[55]

Montagu and Curzon's concerns led to a significant rewriting of Milner's draft. It now read,

> His Majesty's Government views with favour the establishment in Palestine of a national home for the Jewish race and will use its best endeavours to facilitate the achievement of this object, it being clearly understood that nothing shall be done which may prejudice the civil and religious rights of existing non-Jewish communities in Palestine, or the rights and political status enjoyed in any other country by such Jews who are fully contented with their existing nationality.[56]

Balfour telegraphed the new draft to House on 6 October (with the addition, at its end, of the words '... *and citizenship*'). The following response was received on 16 October:

---

55. Tibawi, pp 226-227

56. Stein, p 521. Stein attributes the new draft to Leopold Amery, Assistant Secretary to the War Cabinet.

> Colonel House put formula before President, who approves of it but asks that no mention of his approval shall be made when His Majesty's Government makes formula public, as he has arranged that American Jews shall then ask him for his approval, which he will give publicly here.[57]

Further alterations, at Brandeis' behest, were made at this point. The draft now read,

> His Majesty's Government views with favour the establishment in Palestine of a national home for the Jewish people and will use its best endeavours to facilitate the achievement of this object, it being clearly understood that nothing shall be done which may prejudice the religious and civil rights of existing non-Jewish communities in Palestine, or the rights and civil political status enjoyed by Jews in any other country.[58]

Jeffries credits the opposition of Britain's anti-Zionist Jews with this significant watering down of the Milner draft:

> Edwin Montagu, Sir Philip Magnus and their associates in British Jewry by the stand they made enjoy the everlasting credit of having prevented either of these Balfour Declarations, of July or September, from being issued. It is a rider of importance upon the character of political Zionism that it was Jews who prevented it from carrying out the arbitrary seizure of Palestine which it intended. The Arabs therefore owe a great debt to these upright Jews.
>
> What stands out most, though, is that but for their action the British Government too would have handed over Palestine to the Zionist Organization. In both formulas the Government passed the Arabs by completely, as though they did not exist. Here therefore is an absolute answer to the countless subsequent protestations during twenty years that the British Government never, never intended to put Palestine into Zionist hands. These protestations are falsehoods. Mr. Lloyd George, Lord Balfour and their confederates in the matter did so intend. Here is the documentary proof of it.[59]

That Weizmann saw these 'upright Jews' very much as a thorn in his side emerges clearly from the following passage in his autobiography:

---

57. Stein, p 530
58. Stein, p 531
59. PTR, pp 164-165

> It was an extraordinary struggle that developed within English
> Jewry in the half-year which preceded the issue of the Balfour
> Declaration... Here was a people which had been divorced from
> its original homeland for some eighteen centuries, putting in a
> claim for restitution. The world was willing to listen, the case
> was being sympathetically received, and one of the great Powers
> was prepared to lead in the act of restitution... And a well-to-
> do, contented and self-satisfied minority... rose in rebellion
> against the proposal, and exerted itself with the utmost fury
> to prevent the act of restitution from being consummated.
> Itself in no need – or believing itself to be in no need – of
> the righting of the ancient historic wrong, this small minority
> struggled bitterly to deprive the vast majority of the benefits
> of a unique act of the world conscience; and it succeeded, if
> not in baulking the act of justice, at least in vitiating some of
> its application.[60]

Montagu, unfortunately, had to leave for India on 14 October,
but not before leaving behind a second memorandum (*Zionism*, 9
October), in which, among other things, he accused Weizmann of
being 'a religious fanatic.'

With respect to the 4 October Cabinet decision to solicit the
views of prominent Zionist and anti-Zionist Jews, five Zionists
and three anti-Zionists lodged submissions. It is noteworthy that
four of the five Zionists chose to comment on the new guarantee
in the draft declaration that 'nothing shall be done which may
prejudice the civil and religious rights of existing non-Jewish
communities in Palestine.' Their comments on this subject speak
volumes about their perceptions of Palestine's Arab majority, and
none, significantly, expressed any reservations when it came to
according the Arabs only 'civil and religious rights.'

Britain's Chief Rabbi, Dr J. H. Hertz, declared,

> I welcome the reference to the civil and religious rights of
> the existing, non-Jewish communities in Palestine. It is but a
> translation of the basic principle of the Mosaic legislation:
> 'And if a stranger sojourn with thee in your land, ye shall not
> vex (oppress) him. But the stranger that dwelleth with you

---

60. Weizmann, p 252. The pejorative term 'self-hating Jew' had yet to appear as an
   ideological weapon with which to silence Jewish opposition to Zionism.

shall be unto you as one born among you, and thou shalt love him as thyself [for ye were strangers in the land of Egypt...].' (Lev. xix.33, 34)...[61]

Tibawi was moved to remark on Hertz's theological arrogance as follows:

'The bracketed explanation of vex is in Hertz's text. His reference to the Bible is indeed revealing. What a prospect for the Arab majority to be regarded as strangers and their land to be somebody else's.'[62]

Lord Rothschild took umbrage at the reference to 'non-Jewish communities' - 'Personally, I think that the proviso is rather a slur on Zionism, as it presupposes the possibility of a danger to non-Zionists, which I deny...'[63]

Sir Stuart Samuel, Chairman of the Jewish Board of Deputies, offered the following suggestion: 'Non-Jewish opinion would, I think, be conciliated if a statement were made simultaneously that the Holy Places in Jerusalem and vicinity would be internationalized, or at any rate not be placed under entirely Jewish control.'[64]

Finally, Sokolow boldly asserted that 'The safeguards mentioned in the draft are not open to any objections, since they are and always have been regarded by Zionists as a matter of course.'[65]

This of course, was untrue. They had only been mentioned to mollify Curzon.

In addition to Montagu's second memorandum of 9 October, Curzon had also circulated a memorandum among his War Cabinet colleagues. Titled *The Future of Palestine* (26 October), it reiterated and expanded upon the question he had posed at the 4 October meeting. Most significantly, it referred not to 'existing non-Jewish communities,' but to 'Syrian Arabs':

---

61. Ingrams, p 13
62. Tibawi, p 230
63. Ingrams, p 13
64. Ingrams, p 14
65. Ingrams, p 15

'What is to become of the people of this country?', Curzon queried, 'assuming the Turks to be expelled, and the inhabitants not to have been exterminated by the war? There are over half a million of these, Syrian Arabs – a mixed community with Arab, Hebrew, Canaanite, Greek, Egyptian, and possibly Crusaders' blood. They and their forefathers have occupied the country for the best part of 1,500 years. They own the soil, which belongs either to individual landowners or to village communities. They profess the Mohammadan faith. They will not be content either to be expropriated for Jewish immigrants, or to act merely as hewers of wood and drawers of water to the latter. Further, there are... 100,000 Christians, who will not wish to be disturbed...'[66]

The 31 October meeting of the War Cabinet, which finally decided the matter, was dominated by the pro-Zionists. Tibawi's account of the proceedings, given his Palestinian birth, is understandably bitter:

'When the morning was come, all the chief priests and elders of the people took counsel against Jesus...' The modern parallel of the tragic scene was enacted on Wednesday 31 October 1917. All the *dramatis personae* were there. Lloyd George was in the chair and all the members of the cabinet (Curzon, Milner, Bonar Law, Smuts, Carson and Barnes) were present. The last three were newcomers... Balfour spoke first. He gathered that 'everyone' was agreed (did he intend this as a slight for Curzon?) that a declaration in favour of 'the Jewish nationalists' was desirable. He repeated the Zionist assertions that 'the vast majority of the Jews in Russia, America and all over the world 'appeared' favourable to Zionism. If the government made such a declaration 'we should be able to carry on extremely useful propaganda in Russia and America'. (That clearly means that he had not yet received 'the thirty pieces of silver'!) He took the term national home to mean 'some form of British, American or other protectorate, under which full facilities would be given to the Jews to work out their own salvation' by building up a centre of national culture and a focus of national life. It did not necessarily involve the early establishment of an independent Jewish state, which he said 'was a matter for gradual development in accordance with the ordinary law of political development'. This is an even more ominous suggestion than that of Chief Rabbi Hertz. The Arab majority, to which Balfour made

66. Robert John & Sami Hadawi, *The Palestine Diary*, The Palestine Research Centre, Beirut, 1970, p 89

no reference at all, was in the *extraordinary* circumstances to become a minority in its own native land so that a Jewish state becomes possible sometime in the future.

Curzon spoke next. He was still concerned about the holy places and still not reconciled to the language of Milner's draft. He agreed that some expression of sympathy with Zionist aspirations would be an 'adjunct' to propaganda, but any such expression should be couched in guarded language. There is no record that anyone else opened his mouth. The subject was the last item on an agenda with eleven other items including such important matters as the Western front, the invasion of Italy, air raids and food supplies... After the reference to Curzon's statements the austere minutes abruptly state that the cabinet authorised Balfour to issue the following declaration, reproducing the Milner text with only the Zionist amendments taken into consideration but none of the others.

There is no evidence in the minutes to indicate that, with the exception of Curzon, the ministers who approved the declaration were aware of its manifest injustice to the Arabs: that it named only one national entity, the absentee Jewish people, half of whom were enemy subjects or under enemy control, and relegated the indigenous majority to the insulting grade of non-Jewish communities; that civil rights were no substitute for political and national rights, and that the authors of the documents arrogated to themselves the function of taking away the rights of the majority and giving them to a minority. Never has greater folly been committed without even the justification of British national interests.[67]

The Balfour Declaration, in its final form, came in the form of a letter from Balfour to Rothschild. This 'product of polyandry,' as Jeffries called it, reads as follows:

Foreign Office,
November 2nd, 1917.

I have much pleasure in conveying to you, on behalf of His Majesty's Government, the following declaration of sympathy with Jewish Zionist aspirations, which has been submitted to, and approved by, the Cabinet.

His Majesty's Government view with favour the establishment in Palestine of a national home for the Jewish people, and will

---

67. Tibawi, pp 232-233

use their best endeavours to facilitate the achievement of this object, it being clearly understood that nothing shall be done which may prejudice the civil and religious rights of existing non-Jewish communities in Palestine or the rights and political status enjoyed by Jews in any other country.

I should be grateful if you would bring this declaration to the knowledge of the Zionist Federation.

Yours sincerely,
Arthur James Balfour.

'Nothing more cynically humorous than the final couple of lines of this letter,' writes Jeffries, 'has ever been penned.'[68]

To sum up:

The Balfour Declaration was a jointly drafted, Anglo-Zionist statement, issued by a group of senior British politicians, principally, Lloyd George and Arthur Balfour, who had been raised on Old Testament mythology. Misled by the essentially anti-Semitic myth of Jewish power, propagated by a pair of Russian Zionist emigrés, Weizmann and Sokolow, they gave government support to the fantastic claim, espoused by the Zionists, a militant minority of the world's Jews, that world Jewry constituted a people/nation, possessing not merely an historical connection with Palestine, but a right to sovereignty over it. In the process, they ignored the compelling objections of the only British Jew among them, Edwin Montagu, and the only one of their number who had actually set foot in Palestine, George Curzon. Worse, they violated a prior pledge to their Arab ally, the Sharif of Mecca, that Palestine would be an integral part of an independent Arab state, and ignored entirely the wishes and interests of Palestine's majority Arab population.

It is difficult to conceive of a more bizarre and immoral foreign policy decision than this.

---

68. PTR, pp 170-171.

5

The Balfour Declaration
Under the Microscope

Dissecting the Balfour Declaration
'The most discreditable document to which a British Government has set its hand within memory'

While Weizmann, predictably, hailed the Balfour Declaration as 'the Magna Carta of the Jewish people,' Jeffries condemned it as 'the most discreditable document to which a British Government has set its hand within memory.' As one would expect from the author of such a categorical condemnation, he has given the Declaration the most thorough forensic going over of any scholar to date – to the point where further commentary on the matter could well be considered superfluous.

Given its supreme importance in the history of the Zionist settler-colonial project in Palestine ('obtaining the consent of governments... to reach the goals of Zionism,' it will be recalled, was a key goal of the Basel Program of 1897), Jeffries' unsurpassed analysis of the Balfour Declaration - Chapter 11 of *Palestine: The Reality*, is reproduced here in major part:

> There is a great deal which has to be said now concerning the Declaration which, like water seeking its source, came to the Zionist leaders on that 2nd of November in 1917. But the first thing of all to be said of the Balfour Declaration is that it was

Arthur Balfour

a pronouncement which was weighed to the last pennyweight before it was issued. There are but sixty-seven words in it, and each of these, save perhaps the Government's title and a few innocent conjunctions, was considered at length before it was passed into the text.

This too memorable document is not so much a sentence of English as a verbal mosaic. Drafts for it travelled back and forth, within England or over the Ocean, to be scrutinised by some two score draftsmen, half co-operating, half competing with one another, who erased this phrase or adopted that after much thought. At long last, out of their store of rejections and of their acceptances the final miscellany was chosen, ratified and fixed. There never has been a proclamation longer prepared, more carefully produced, more consciously worded [...]

So there is one point upon which there is no doubt. Whatever is to be found in the Balfour Declaration was put into it deliberately. There are no accidents in that text. If there is any vagueness in it this is an intentional vagueness. If it is vague, the admiral is vague who orders his destroyers to emit a smoke-screen.

It is most important to have this established before more is said, for the reason that for some time past the controversy concerning Palestine, in so far as the Declaration is concerned, has been given a false turn. A secondary apologia has been evolved, which by-passes the *bona fides* of Lord Balfour's pronouncement to concentrate upon its terminology. It is described as "uncertainly phrased," or as "containing implications not foreseen when it was written," or as "not so definite as was thought"; or contrariwise it is said that "too much has been read into it."

Behind this apologia often enough there may have lain a good intention. The Balfour Declaration, alas! has been made by a series of our Governments the pedestal of British policy in Palestine. Because of this a number of persons have reasoned that the Declaration must be accepted as it stands, 'with all its imperfections.' Scrutiny of it might reveal that it was written in bad faith. But to expose bad faith in the Declaration would be the same as exposing it in the conduct of the country itself, since one Government of Great Britain published it and subsequent Governments have confirmed it. The people who have shrunk from scrutinizing it may not have put their thoughts to themselves as starkly as that, but it was thus they did think in their hearts' recesses. Therefore, as they conceived, the only course which lay open to them, if the country's honour was to be saved, was to assume that the Declaration had been loosely composed, and to lead the controversy on to that ground. They made great show of riddling out what it meant, with a little deprecatory criticism thrown in.

In this way they could escape perhaps having to acknowledge that this nationally issued and nationally endorsed document was nothing but a calmly planned piece of deception. That is why for years past we have heard statesmen, publicists and politicians, and members of the public too, assert that the authors of the Declaration either did not mean what they appear to say in it, or did not succeed in saying in it what they meant. Other apologists have given their own interested versions of its meaning. In this order were the explanations of Mr. Winston Churchill, as intricate and as lasting as worm-casts in the sand.

Behind excuses and shifts of the kind there may lie, in this way, something of good intention. But it is an intention deplorably translated into practice, and I am not going to follow the example thus set. Since the Balfour Declaration was without excuse, I see no reason to excuse it. There is no pleasure in taking such a course (as I have said before now): there is no relish in exposing one's country or in exposing at least the men who spoke in her name. But the world of 1939 has no room for displays of patriotic cowardice. Nor is there any sort of advantage in them. We want an England which can confess her sins, and thereafter take her place at the head of the nations in the strength of her cleared conscience.

With this borne in mind, let us return to the Declaration. It reached the general public on the 9th of November, when Lord Balfour's letter was reproduced in the newspapers. It was given forth, of course, under the guise of an entirely British communication embodying an entirely British conception. Everyone concerned was made the victim of this false pretence. The British people were given to believe that it was an unadulterated product of their own Government. To the mass of Jews it was presented as a guarantee sprung of nothing but the conscience of the Cabinet – and thereby it served to allure them towards political Zionism. As for the Arabs, when it was proclaimed eventually upon their soil (which was not till much later), to them too a text in which Zionists of all nationalities had collaborated was announced as the voice of Britain. They were told that it was a pledge made to the Zionists: they were not told that the Zionists had written most of it. They were asked to respect it on the ground that it was given to the world by the British Government out of its native magnanimity, after the said Government had extended its profound, solitary and single-minded consideration to the "problem of Palestine."

Let me be quite clear about this. The onus of deception does not lie upon the Government of 1917 because before issuing its Declaration *it consulted* the Zionists. As far as the mere form of the proposed announcement went (leaving aside other considerations), the Zionists could have been asked quite reasonably to submit their ideas on the species of "support and encouragement" for which they hoped. The Government could have examined whatever the Zionists submitted, and have consulted further with them, till both had agreed upon a final text. Had this text been published for what it was, an agreement between the two parties which the British Government was willing to sponsor, then the form of the Declaration would have been blameless. The form would have been honest, even if the policy was indefensible.

When however the bipartite Declaration – and to call it bipartite is to swell the Governmental share in its drafting – was given out as the composition of His Majesty's Government alone, a plain deception was committed. In subsequent years too these synthetic *ipsissima verba* have been paraded with unyielding obstinacy to the Arabs as a sacred obligation of Great Britain to the Jews, even after it had been disclosed that all the time various Zionists had themselves framed the obligation to themselves. This makes later Governments partakers in the deception of the 1917 Cabinet, a deception only mitigated by culpable ignorance in the case of certain members of these Governments.

The Zionists themselves are in a better position in the matter than their British collaborators are. To do them justice, it was they who made known the real conditions under which the Declaration was composed. They did so after an interval which I cannot give exactly, since I have not read all Zionist publications and writings that ever were. But the Zionist Organization certainly had divulged its share in the Declaration within four years of its publication, and for all I know this may have been divulged earlier. I shall not say that the motives of the Zionist Organization were of the first rank. Everything seemed to be going swimmingly for their cause then and some members or other of the Organization staff could not resist gathering kudos in the eyes of the mass of Zionist supporters by disclosing the important part which their body behind the scenes had taken in the Declaration. Still, their statement was a frank one.

And now to analyse the text of the Declaration. "*His Majesty's Government view with favour the establishment in Palestine of a national home for the Jewish people...*" This first clause is often printed with the words "national home" with capital initials. But in the original copy, as reproduced in *The Times*, Lord Balfour used the discreeter apparel of what printers call "lower-case" letters for his protégé. Neither he nor his colleagues can claim the invention of this title, which had been imagined by Leon Pinsker in Odessa thirty-five years before. Pinsker himself did not intend it to apply to Palestine... But Balfour and his colleagues adopted the title from the Zionist programmes and drafts, and made use of its ambiguity. For most people in 1917 "National Home," with or without capitals, was a new phrase. Naturally no one could give it a meaning, for it had no established meaning, and was put into practice in Palestine without one.

But in a formal document announcing the support of the British Government for this institution, it was indicated by all rules of statesmanship that ere committing itself to such support, the Government should define for the nation exactly what it was supporting. Not to do so was to pledge (without touching on the right to give a pledge) the aid of Great Britain for no one could say what. The same culpable lack of definition was to be found in the preamble, wherein the Declaration was described as "a declaration of sympathy with Jewish Zionist aspirations," but no clue was supplied to these desires. What were Jewish Zionist aspirations? They were not identified. How could a British Government guarantee its sympathy to an enigma?

The truth of course is that these unfathomable phrases were employed just because they were unfathomable and could be interpreted to pleasure. They had the air of promising Government support of what the Zionists wanted in Palestine, a Jewish State, to be reached through a fictitious condominium of Jew and Arab. This was the meaning which the Zionists who helped to draw up the Declaration accepted in the end, and this was the meaning which Zionists and Jews in general were given to understand the Declaration would hold. They were disappointed no doubt that they did not receive full ruling rights immediately. But they were confident that they could engender conditions in Palestine involving a more rapid finish for the transition period than might be expected. The Government on its part did mean to give as much of the Zionists' sense to the Declaration as was safe, from the very start. As the margin of safety grew, as its own hold on the land became stronger, as a menial prosperity enticed the mass of Arabs, and the opposition of the remainder had been measured and met, then the Government would increase its support of the Zionist establishment in widening degrees, till the Jewish State at last arose.

On the other hand, the government kept a way of retreat open in case some formidable opposition, in Britain or outside, might make headway against official alliance with political Zionism. In that event, the Declaration was phrased so that it could be explained away as nothing but an expression of unengaged, friendly interest in the Zionist movement. If it came to that, what *did* "view with favour" amount to as a gage of support? Pretty little. It could be taken to signify no more than that the Government would cast a benign eye upon the "national home," pleased if the Zionist plans worked out, regretful but quite unimplicated if they failed.

To sum up: the paths of the Government and of Zionism had crossed; the Government had liked the wanderer's look; the pair had dallied, and then they had agreed to walk on together. So far so good. But if trouble arose on the way before home was reached, well, the path which the Government had crossed the Government, in a manner of speaking, could cross again. The final drafting of the Declaration was a great play of wits, in fact. The opposition to the previous drafts had brought it home to the Government that it must be more careful. So in the final draft, while still conceding everything to the Zionists in its own intent, the Government achieved a wording which would allow it an exit, if needs were, from any definite obligation of any kind. In this the Governmental drafters outwitted the Zionist drafters, who thought that they had the Government securely tied up. The Government was anxious for these ties, which it had invited, but it preferred now to draft so that even they could be slipped in the last resort. All first-class chicanery, but how far fitting in a Declaration by Great Britain is another matter.

In the succeeding clause the same dubious skilfulness prevails as in the first. The Government "*will use their best endeavours to facilitate the achievement of this object.*" What is to be understood of this facilitation? To "facilitate" may signify to lend a hand in the way, passively. The sentence in fact is composed upon the same lines as its predecessor, that is, it covers the private intention of giving active help, provides a public screen of passive interest, and in the last resort contains a way out. As in the preceding sentence the situation of the Zionist drafters was that they considered that the nucleus of their special intentions was contained in the words used.

However, it is not until we reach the third and final clause of the Balfour Declaration that its character is quite revealed. "*… it being clearly understood that nothing shall be done which may prejudice the civil and religious rights of existing non-Jewish communities in Palestine or the rights and political status enjoyed by Jews in any other country.*"

The first part of this clause is the supposed "safeguard" of the Arabs of Palestine, which protects them from Zionist encroachment. As far as protection goes, I am reminded of the experience of a relative. When about to land from a ship in a lonely corner of some docks in a distant country, he was warned to take very little money with him and, above all, "to be aware of the police." A similar warning applies to this "protective" clause.

At first sight it does not seem so craftily phrased as the earlier clauses. The will-to-deceive in it is so patent; the description of the Arabs as the "non-Jewish communities in Palestine" is so obviously slippery. At the time the Declaration was issued the population of Palestine was in the neighbourhood of 670,000. Of these the Jews numbered some 60,000. These are broad figures, but reasonable: there is no accurate census to quote [...]

Therefore we have Palestine with 91% of its people Arab and 9% Jew at the time of the Declaration. It was an Arab population with a dash of Jew. Half of the Jews were recent arrivals.

Before this unpalatable reality, what did the framers of the Balfour Declaration do? By an altogether abject subterfuge, under colour of protecting Arab interests, they set out to conceal the fact that the Arabs to all intents constituted the population of the country. It called them the "non-Jewish communities in Palestine"! It called the multitude the non-few; it called the 670,000 the non-60,000; out of a hundred it called the 91 the non-9. You might just as well call the British people "the non-Continental communities in Great Britain." It would be as suitable to define the mass of working men as "the non-idling communities in the world," or the healthy as "the non-bedridden elements amongst sleepers," or the sane as "the non-lunatic section of thinkers" – or the grass of the countryside as "the non-dandelion portion of the pastures."

But of course there is more than mere preposterous nomenclature in the use of the phrase "non-Jewish communities in Palestine" to describe the Arabs. It is fraudulent. It was done in order to conceal the true ratio between Arabs and Jews, and thereby to make easier the supersession of the former. [...]

Just now it was stated that at first sight this phrase seemed not so crafty, because it was too manifestly deceitful. But on second examination it is perceived to be adroit in its mean way. It plays upon general ignorance. What in 1917 did the war-worn British public, what did the deluded Jews of Russia, what did any general body of people outside the Near East know about the composition of the population of Palestine? Nothing.

It was upon this, then, that the drafters of the Declaration played. They concealed the Arabs' very name and called them "existing communities in Palestine"... The qualification "existing" provides the finishing touch. The impression given is that these Arabs have just managed to survive, that an explorer has returned and reported to Lord Balfour that he has discovered non-Jews existing in the hills. Consequently the average citizen, when he read the Declaration, concluded, if he gave the matter any further thought at all, that proper steps would be taken under its terms to safeguard the occasional remnants of other races than the Jews who might be found in the Holy Land. This was what it intended he should conclude. As for any odd individuals who in the thick of war might have sufficient interest to question the phraseology employed, for them what may have been thought a neat reply had been prepared. "Community is the correct word to use since the population of Palestine is divided into the Moslem, Christian and Jewish communities." The Druses and Samaritans might have been added for effect: otherwise there is no more to say about this equivocation. It is enough to write it down to expose it. Words are wasted on it.

But the Declaration was not issued merely to falsify the status of the Arabs. It was also to offer them a spurious guarantee, in the phrase *"it being clearly understood that nothing shall be done which shall prejudice the civil and religious rights"* of the aforesaid so-called "communities." That their religious rights should not be prejudiced, indeed, was satisfactory, though there was not very much in that. Happily, it could be taken for granted. Wherever Britain rules religious rights are preserved.

The crux arrives with "civil rights." What are "civil rights"? All turns on this point. If civil rights remain undefined it is only a mockery to guarantee them. To guarantee anything, and at the same time not to let anyone know what it is, that is *Alice in Wonderland* legislation. "I guarantee your civil rights," said the White Queen to Alice in Palestine-land. "Oh, thank you!" said Alice, "what are they, please?" "I'm sure I can't tell you, my dear," said the White Queen, "but I'll guarantee very hard."

If only the Declaration had been as innocent as the text of *Alice in Wonderland*. Its nonsense is deceptive nonsense, written with vicious intention. The Arabs were guaranteed civil rights, again because to the unalert ear it sounded as though they were being assured a man's normal rights, the freedom to choose the government of his country which every decent man should enjoy, the common political rights of a democratic regime.

But in fact the Arabs were not assured these at all. The effect, and the aim, of the clause actually was to withdraw from the Arabs (fighting or suffering for us at the time under promise of independence) those very rights of independence for which they had contracted; to say nothing of their natural title to them. By sleight of tongue civil rights were substituted for political rights. If civil rights meant anything, which was uncertain and would take long legal proof (which was never offered) they meant most likely civic or borough rights, or such rights as a foreign householder can exercise in a country of which he is not a citizen. But this was untested theory. As practice went, "civil rights" was an expression which was left without out any interpretation, and so had no existence as a surety or guarantee at all. [...]

There can be no doubt that the authors of this particular "guarantee" were the Zionists themselves, and that the phrase was introduced from America. [NB: I omit here Jeffries' tracking down of the wording of the 'guarantee' to a US Jewish manifesto of October 1916 calling for civil, religious and political rights for Jews.]

Observe, though, what a difference occurred in the new use of the formula. In the United States the Zionist drafters had employed the formula to define their own rights. In the Balfour Declaration they had to employ it to define, for safeguarding purposes, their own rights, but also, so to speak, to undefine the Arabs' rights. They conceded therefore to the Arabs the notorious "civil rights": for themselves they dropped this word "civil" altogether. They had seen from the beginning that it had no value, since in the manifesto they had taken care to demand religious and political rights *in addition* to civil rights. In the Balfour Declaration they took the same care.

But they improved the phraseology in the "Balfour Declaration." Not only was "civil" jettisoned, but with great agility the cardinal word "political" was shuffled from "rights" on to "status." To have granted in the same clause only civil rights to the Arabs but to the Jews political rights would have been too glaring a contrast. It might have drawn attention even from the indifferent eyes of 1917. Therefore, for the Jews their "rights" were left apparently unclarified but really expanded in principle through the removal of the constricting adjective, while "political status" was brought in as something of another order peculiar to the Jews, and to do the work of a definite guarantee.

Let me halt for a space to explain why it was essential to have such a guarantee. Without it when Palestine became a Jewish State all Jews might be conceived as belonging to it. This might occur even during the preliminary stage, during the illusory period when Jew and Arab running in harness were building up a new Palestine together (or whatever mixed metaphor best describes this atrocious mixed metaphor of policy). Antisemitism spreads easily, and an agitation might arise in any country to dispatch Jewish citizens to Palestine, or if not to expel them, to catalogue them as aliens, citizens of Palestine, and to deprive them of the vote.

The insertion of the guarantee is further proof, besides, of the character of the regime intended under the Declaration in the Holy Land. If the "National Home" was to be something innocuous, a mere "national home from home" with a modicum of establishment receiving a stream of visitors, an institution without any political status, then there was no need to guarantee hosts or guests against losing their overseas or overland political status in their place of origin. If "National Home" meant a State or quasi-State, there was every need for the guarantee.

The "guarantee" clause of the Declaration, then, with its deceptive text by which the Arabs were to be deprived of their citizenship, sprang undoubtedly from Zionist brains, though it was adopted of course by Balfour and the others and issued by him as though the British cabinet had thought it out. Considering the joint authorship of the Declaration, this perhaps might have been expected. Its British drafters were mostly guided by expediency: the Zionist drafters were doctrinaires. The British thought it necessary to shut their eyes to Arab rights; the Zionists were convinced or convinced themselves that the Arabs had no rights as men, save those the Turks might have conceded them.[1]

It should be noted that Weizmann himself was quite scornful of the value of mere 'civil and religious rights' – when applied to Jews. In the context of his jousting with Britain's anti-Zionist Jews, he recalled, in his autobiography, 'all the old arguments that I had learned to expect since the time of my encounter with Western assimilation in the person of Dr. Barness of Pfungstadt.' He listed these as follows: 'The Jews were a religious community, and nothing more. The Jews could not claim a National Home. The utmost that could be demanded for the Jews of Palestine was enjoyment of religious and civil liberty, 'reasonable' facilities for immigration and colonization, and 'such municipal privileges in towns and colonies as may be shown to be necessary,' and so on, and so on.'[2] 'Religious

---

1. PTR, pp 172-181
2. Chaim Weizmann, *Trial & Error: The Autobiography of Chaim Weizmann*, Hamish Hamilton, London, 1949, p 254

and civil liberty,' however, was apparently good enough for the Arabs of Palestine. Weizmann also complained, again in his autobiography, (while comparing the second July draft with the watered-down October draft, which he described as a 'painful recession from what the Government itself was prepared to offer'), that 'the [latter] introduces the subject of the 'civic and religious rights of the existing non-Jewish communities' in such a fashion as to impute possible oppressive intentions to the Jews, and can be interpreted to mean such limitations on our work as completely to cripple it.'[3]

Following his analysis of the Declaration's 'sham character and deceptive phraseology,' Jeffries turns to the fundamental question of whether or not Britain had any right to issue the document. His answer is unequivocal:

> The Government had no business to issue a declaration enacting, let alone crystallizing the situation of the Zionists in Palestine. The preceding Cabinet had covenanted to recognize the independence of this Arab land "in every sense of the word independence." This agreement was still standing: the Arabs were carrying out their side of it by waging war upon the Turks. Therefore the Government had no right to father and to patronize officially the special action in Palestine of a third party, which did not intend to ask any permission for this special action from the Arabs, and so contravened their independence. That is the position in short. The Balfour Declaration, barred by the treaty with King Hussein, and issued without any previous consultation or consent of the Arabs, was illicit.[4]

Tibawi addresses the same question:

> But had the British government any right to issue the declaration? On 31 October when the cabinet decided to do so the British army, before Allenby's offensive on that same date, was in occupation of a very small strip at the southern extremity of Palestine. [...] Since the voice of the moral philosopher was seldom heard in the corridors of power throughout history, let morality and philosophy be silent, but let two legal considerations be emphasised: (1) Because the whole territory of Palestine was under Turkish sovereignty, the British government was, even as an occupying

---

3. Weizmann, p 260
4. PTR, p 186

power, debarred by *The Laws and Usages of War* from taking any measures, political, legal or administrative, to change the character of the country before the conclusion of a peace treaty with the legal sovereign. (2) Because the British cabinet had no jurisdiction over the territory of Palestine, one of its members warned that the territory had a vast majority of Arabs, both Christian and Muslim, the issue of the Balfour declaration amounted to an ultimate British intention to deprive this majority of its natural right to self-determination. The injustice of the sentence was heightened by the fact that it was passed in absentia.[5]

Finally, before moving on to other matters connected with the decision to issue Balfour Declaration, one particular passage in *Palestine: The Reality* affords us an insight into the kinds of attitudes towards the Declaration that Jeffries encountered in the interwar years, not with Zionists as such, but with those Britons who simply wished to avoid facing the moral implications of their country's pact with the Zionist movement:

> Another sort of excuse [for our course of action in Palestine] is so common that it must be mentioned also. As an excuse it is worth just as much as the gold in a farthing. Nothing *ought* to be more astonishing than the facility with which such a silly thing is repeated. But it has gained currency because it suits so well the too common laziness of mind which does not wish to make the least effort of inquiry into the rights or the wrongs of any question. The exercise of the brain is escaped by saying of any such question that it is all wrongs, that the situation of everyone concerned in it is deplorable, and that it is a waste of time to search for shades of culpability amidst them. "Drop grudges and start afresh" or "keep out of it," says the excuse-broker, and gets off to his golf.
>
> In the case of Palestine, the excuse is that we have made promises all round, to Arabs and to Jews, in public and in private. The only commonsense, straightforward course therefore is to cancel "the lot of them" and to make a new beginning. So runs a plea which is as ignoble in attitude as it is indefensible in argument. If there were any basis to it, what a prospect it would open.
>
> Anyone who had repented of a contract which he had made could slip out of it always, by making another and later contract or contracts which were incompatible with the previous one.

---

5. A.L. Tibawi, *Anglo-Arab Relations & The Question of Palestine 1914-1921*, Luzac & Company Ltd, London, 1977, p 235

If the person to whom he was contracted ventured to hold him to their bargain he could go to court, display his documents, and plead "All these engagements of mine are in contradiction one with another." The judge, finding that they were, would announce, "So they are. The court annuls them all therefore." What morality and what nonsense!

No, when an individual invokes a plurality of contracts, or a nation boasts a superfluity of treaties or of official declarations, there is but one means of deciding which of them holds good. Which was the first of them? If that was duly transacted, it is by that the citizen or the cabinet must adhere.

The Balfour Declaration was issued over two years after the pact with King Hussein had been made. It is incompatible with this previous pledge and therefore it is null and void. It has no more status than have the vows made to a woman before the altar by a man who has a discarded wife still living. The best description in fact of the Balfour Declaration is that it is a bigamous declaration.

The worst of bigamy is the suffering it inflicts upon two persons, the true wife and the false "wife." In the present example of this crime, many thousands of Jews – I do not say their leaders – have been decoyed to Palestine by the junior marriage-lines to which Balfour set his name. Between these immigrants and their leaders the responsibility is their own affair. As far as we are concerned, who have inherited the responsibilities conferred on Britain by the 1917 Cabinet, we owe to these poor people a considerable reparation, which we shall have some difficulty in paying. But we do not owe it to them to install them in the situation of the lawful spouse, or side by side with her in *her* home.[6]

The bigamy analogy, as it happens, was also deployed in the Arabic-language newspaper, *Falastin* (Palestine) in the form of a cartoon, *The Man with Two Wives*, dating from the 30s (possibly 1933). A troubled John Bull (the English version of Uncle Sam) seeks advice from the Archbishop. The caption runs as follows:

John Bull: My Lord, I married first an Arab woman and then a Jewess and for the last 16 years I have had no peace at home...

The Archbishop: How did you manage to have two wives, are you not a Christian?

---

6. PTR, pp 187-188

John Bull: It was the pressure of the Great War, my Lord.

The Archbishop: Well, my son, if you are sincerely looking for peace you must divorce your second wife, because your marriage to her is illegal...[7]

The Question of Motives
'He had a theory to demonstrate, which was that the world had not paid the Jews sufficiently for their contributions to civilization'

What was it that possessed David Lloyd George and Arthur James Balfour, the principal progenitors of the Declaration on the British side, to issue 'the most discreditable document to which a British Government has set its hand within memory'? Certainly, Jeffries asserts, 'the celebrated "historic rights," by which the Zionists claimed entry [to Palestine], counted for little or nothing, despite all the orating about them, in the concession of the National Home. The Government did not issue the Declaration because the whole Cabinet was penetrated with a romantic determination that the Jewish race should enjoy its own again.'[8] What then was it that counted? What, in short, were the *motives* of the prime minister and his foreign secretary?

Indelibly associated with the Declaration, let us begin with Lord Balfour. Jeffries asserts that,

> He had a theory to demonstrate, which was that the world had not paid the Jews sufficiently for their contributions to civilization. The world was backward in its payments, and it was a piece of intellectual book-keeping for Balfour to balance the payments. This supplied him with a sort of *do quia dedisti* motive; a reasonable gratitude. But his strongest impulse was the putting into practice of his own theory. It was such a moral theory to him that he did not care how immorally it was put into practice.
>
> So it was that Balfour, despite everything that happened following upon his Declaration, after all the outcries and the riots, after all the protests and the testimony of misdoing showered

---

7. Fred Pragnell, *Palestine Chronicle 1880 – 1950*, Pragnell Books, Kingston Upon Thames, 2005
8. PTR, p 188

forth by the Arabs, still went on professing in his chair of Zionism with the placidity of unconcern. His theory satisfied himself: interruptions were tiresome, but could be lived down. [...]

Balfour's own first and last journey to Syria, where he nearly fell, in the northern zone, into the power of an infuriated Arab mob, raised no doubts in him. Ere then, in the southern zone, like another Catherine surrounded by bevies of Potemkins, he had been led, with his armed escorts hidden from view, through the permanent set of the Zionist colonies, and had been heralded by the cheers of their permanent chorus. The set delighted him: it was the Palestine he wanted to see, something remote from the realities of the situation.

This attitude of his has induced some to call him a dilettante in politics. He was and he was not. He pursued politics with iron determination, and yet it was out of politics, despite his tennis and his golf, that he won his supreme entertainment. In all his statesmanship there was a strain of recreation and he would not be baulked of it. He was like a man who *will* have his exercise, and goes trudging over other people's gardens and wheatfields in the honest cause of health. The Arab acres of Palestine lay on the route of Balfour's mental exercise, and he led his Zionist companions into them, exclaiming on the emptiness of the site and its suitability for occupation as he trampled the corn and strode past the vociferating owners.

To accomplish and to vindicate his theories, then, Lord Balfour signed the Declaration. He was not ignorant of course of the material advantages which might come of it, but these hardly provided him with a motive. There is a piece of advice which says not to marry for money but to go where there is money. It was on these lines, as far as the nuptial settlement went, that Balfour married Britain to Zionism, very much *en secondes noces*. He would very probably have been even more satisfied if his rarefied idea of getting the United States to take over the lady had been accomplished. The United States as an Oriental ruler under an untried scheme was so irresistibly unlikely and therefore so fascinating.[9]

Jeffries' portrait of Balfour trampling the 'Arab acres of Palestine' suggests a kind of Strangelovian figure. Yet it is entirely consistent with what those who knew or observed him have reported.

Lord Curzon, who succeeded Balfour as foreign secretary, wrote of him that,

---

9. PTR, pp 188-189

The truth is that Balfour, with all his scintillating intellectual exterior, had no depth of feeling, no profound convictions, and strange to say (in spite of his fascination of manner), no real affection. We all know this. When the emergencies came, he would drop or desert or sacrifice any one of us without a pang, as he did me in India, as he did George Wyndham over Ireland. Were any of us to die suddenly, he would dine out that night with undisturbed complacency, and in the intervals of conversation on bridge would be heard to murmur 'Poor old George.'[10]

Stephen Bonsal, an aide to Colonel House, head of the US delegation to the Paris Peace Conference of 1919, recorded the proceedings of a meeting of the Council of Ten on 11 February, chaired by Balfour, as follows:

I was very much on hand when the morning of the ninth dawned on which the pro-Arab and the pro-Sykes-Picot forces were to meet each other face to face before the Council of Ten... I went to the field of battle with Lawrence and there I joined Faisal and Nouri who were flanked by handsome young aides arrayed in robes and tunics of many colors, all of them with flashing, hungry eyes like the hawks of the desert. I could not refrain from saying, "Sir Mark must be a brave man to face that phalanx," and Lawrence answered quietly, "He is a brave man and, worse luck, a stubborn one."

There was a great shuffling of papers and then Balfour mumbled to the serviceable Hankey, "I think we'll put Sykes on now. What?"

"Have just had a message: Sykes has a bad cold. Can't talk."

"Dear, dear. How provoking. I had so hoped we would get on with this business today. Tell him it will go over until the eleventh but he must not fail us then. I suppose we shall have to take up the next item on the agenda. What's that? Oh, yes, those islands in the Baltic. I never can remember their names."

The Arab contingent filed out. They were inclined to think that Sykes was playing possum, but not so Lawrence. "If Sykes admits he's sick I fear he's ill," he said.

On the eleventh we all assembled again. Balfour was as usual quite a little late in arriving; blushing like a bride and with profuse apologies he said to his colleagues of the Ten: "Now we'll

---

10. Leonard Mosley, *Curzon: The End of an Epoch*, Longmans, London, 1960, pp 165-166

get on with it. I'll put Sykes on the stand immediately. Hankey, where is Sykes?"

"His servant has just brought me sad news," said Hankey in a low voice. "Sykes is dead. He died this morning at daybreak – septic pneumonia following on flu."

"Dear, dear," muttered Balfour. "It seems as though we shall never get on with this problem. And now, Hankey, what is the next item on the agenda? And do please see to it that I get the proper papers and that the important paragraphs are flagged. I so hate wading through interminable documents..."[11]

Arnold Toynbee, the noted British historian, who had worked in the Intelligence Department of the Foreign Office in 1918, commented succinctly on the then foreign secretary, 'I will say straight out: Balfour was a wicked man.'[12]

If one were to conduct a search among the statements and speeches of Balfour for one that would best illustrate the validity of Toynbee's judgment, it would surely be the following memorandum, addressed to Curzon on 11 August, 1919, on the subject of the United States' King-Crane Commission. Few foreign policy statements in history could possibly be as cold-blooded as this:

> Let us assume that two of the 'independent nations' for which mandatories have to be provided are Syria and Palestine. Take Syria first. Do we mean, in the case of Syria, to consult principally the wishes of the inhabitants? We mean nothing of the kind... Are we going 'chiefly to consider the wishes of the inhabitants' in deciding which of these [mandatories] is to be selected? We are going to do nothing of the kind... So that whatever the inhabitants may wish, it is France they will certainly have. They may freely choose; but it is Hobson's choice after all.
>
> The contradiction between the letters of the Covenant [of the League of Nations] and the policy of the Allies is even more flagrant in the case of the 'independent nation' of Palestine than in that of the 'independent nation' of Syria. For in Palestine we do not propose even to go through the form of consulting the wishes of the present inhabitants of the country, though the American Commission has been going through the form of asking what they are.

11. Stephen Bonsal, *Suitors & Suppliants: The Little Nations at Versailles*, Prentice-Hall Inc., New York, 1947, p 42

12. *Arnold Toynbee on The Arab-Israeli Conflict*, Journal of Palestine Studies, Spring, 1973, p 3

The Four Great Powers are committed to Zionism. And Zionism, be it right or wrong, good or bad, is rooted in age-long traditions, in present needs, in future hopes, of far profounder import than the desires and prejudices of the 700,000 Arabs who now inhabit that ancient land.

In my opinion that is right. What I have never been able to understand is how it can be harmonised with the [Anglo-French] declaration [of November 1918], the Covenant, or the instructions to the Commission of Enquiry.

I do not think that Zionism will hurt the Arabs, but they will never say they want it. Whatever be the future of Palestine it is not now an 'independent nation', nor is it yet on the way to become one. Whatever deference should be paid to the views of those living there, the Powers in their selection of a mandatory do not propose, as I understand the matter, to consult them. In short, so far as Palestine is concerned, the Powers have made no statement of fact which is not admittedly wrong, and no declaration of policy which, at least in the letter, they have not always intended to violate.

If Zionism is to influence the Jewish problem throughout the world Palestine must be made available for the largest number of Jewish immigrants...

A Foreign Office official, George Kidston, minuted on Balfour's memorandum as follows:

Mr Balfour's suggestions are admirable as indicating a broad line of policy, but I doubt if he realizes the difficulties of the details... Palestine is to go to the Zionists irrespective of the wishes of the great bulk of the population, because it is historically right and politically expedient that it should do so. The idea that the carrying out of either of these programmes will entail bloodshed and military repression never seems to have occurred to him.[13]

---

13. The first paragraph of Balfour's memorandum is taken from Walid Khalidi, *From Haven to Conquest: Readings in Zionism & the Palestine Problem Until 1948*, Institute for Palestine Studies, Washington, 2005, p xxxii. For the rest see Doreen Ingrams, *Palestine Papers 1917-1922: Seeds of Conflict*, John Murray, London, 1972, p 74. Walid Khalidi's introduction to Balfour's memorandum reads as follows: 'Neither of the two Western powers had any illusions about what they were doing by endorsing Zionism. However glib his public utterances concerning the safeguarding of Palestinian Arab political rights, Balfour knew better. He made some particularly revealing comments in his secret memorandum to the British cabinet on the paragraph in the Covenant of the League of Nations which enshrined the Wilsonian principle of self-determination... The paragraph in question reads: "The wishes of these communities... must be a principal consideration in the selection of a mandatory".'

Such was Balfour. Let us now turn to Lloyd George.

The character of Lloyd George doesn't emerge as vividly from the pages of *Palestine: The Reality* as that of Balfour. Nonetheless, it is clear that he inhabited much the same Judeo-centric mental terrain as Balfour, as the following passage by one of his biographers, Peter Rowland, indicates:

> Lloyd George's one consolation [following British military reverses on the Western Front] was the capture of Jerusalem, which surrendered to Allenby on December 11th [1917]... This was a conquest he had set his heart on. "I am looking forward," he had written to [his son] William on March 30th, "to my Government achieving something which generations of the chivalry of Europe failed to attain," and Churchill told Wilson on May 30th that the premier wanted it "because the Welsh people would like it." Its capture would, obviously, be a resounding blow to Turkish prestige, but the idea of doing something for the Jews was something which also appealed to him. Asquith had noted with some amusement, as long ago as March 1915, that Lloyd George was the only member of the Cabinet who supported Herbert Samuel's proposal for acquiring Palestine, "into which the scattered Jews would in time swarm back from all quarters of the globe, and in due course obtain Home Rule."[14]

Just how important a place the Jews of the Bible occupied in Lloyd George's thinking may be gleaned from the following extract, taken from Laurence Housman's satirical portrait of him, *Trimblerigg*:

> If he seemed to be always carrying the New Testament in his coat-tail pocket and making it his foundation for occasions of sitting down and doing nothing, while, up and doing, it was the law of Moses with which he stuffed his breast: and if, when he wanted to thump the big drum (as he so often did), he thumped the Old Testament, he was only doing with more momentary conviction and verve and personal magnetism what the larger tribalism of his day had been doing all along...[15]

---

14. Peter Rowland, *David Lloyd George: A Biography*, Macmillan Publishing Co., New York, 1975, p 424

15. Laurence Housman, *Trimblerigg: A Book of Revelation*, Jonathan Cape, London, 1924, p 11

Certainly, if most of us today have forgotten Lloyd George's role as co-father of the Balfour Declaration, the Zionists of his day knew exactly who their patrons and benefactors were. Having already named one of their colonies after Balfour (Balfouria) in 1922, they accorded Lloyd George the same honour by naming another Ramat David in 1926.

Jeffries refers to Lloyd George's motives as follows:

> He did not say much about them at the time of the Declaration, but he has explained them on various occasions since. Three years ago, in the House of Commons, he gave his view of "Jewish historic rights" in Palestine. A general debate on Palestine was going on, and it was in the course of an indication of the special points to which he would speak that he threw out a reference to the "historic rights." It was just in his style to pass casually, as he did, over what was a primary question, but the little he said upon it was categoric enough. "I am not now putting the case," he said, "that the Arabs are only a modern introduction into Palestine and that the ancient inhabitants were the Jews. There is nothing in that case, because, after all, the Jews turned out the Hittites and the Ammonites." This was a quarter of the truth, which left out the factor of the brief duration and of the minor extent of Jewish occupancy, and left out the Arab inheritance from the "Ammonites and Hittites." But even so it is quite enough.
>
> The Zionists claimed the right of establishment in Palestine on the grounds of historic right, on the grounds that they *were* the ancient inhabitants. "There is nothing in that case," said the ex-Prime Minister, yet it was on that very case, which was the only ostensible case, that he encouraged and supported their entry in 1917. What is to be said of such action? Really there is no canon, no axiom of justice, no propriety which has not been violated in the endeavour to install the Jewish National Home in Palestine.
>
> However, if this one was not, what *was* Mr. Lloyd George's real motive, as head of the Government, in issuing the Declaration and in supporting the case in which he saw nothing? He himself has named for us two motives which do not agree altogether, but have something in common. The one is personal: he supported Zionism as a reward for Dr. Weizmann's help in manufacturing chemicals during the war. The other is impersonal: he wanted to win over the Jews in general to the Allied cause.[16]

16. PTR, pp 189-190

Jeffries concludes that 'The Balfour Declaration, as far as it concerned the Prime Minister, was a salary he paid the Zionists for their services, no more, and if the metaphor be taken to the end, I fear it must be said that it was paid out of Arab trust-funds.'[17]

The 'chemicals,' or rather chemical, Jeffries refers to is acetone, a solvent used in the production of cordite, a propellant used in ammunition. Weizmann had discovered a more efficient method of synthesising it. In so far as acetone figured in Lloyd George's support for the Balfour Declaration, Jeffries' indignant reaction, as follows, is more than justified:

> No British commander obtained more than an Earldom from the Great War... Yet for Dr. Weizmann history is turned inside out, geography is suppressed, a people is disenfranchised and an empire is forsworn. All in return for a formula for making propellant-paste, which was valuable for a while and after a while was superseded.
>
> The thing is outrageous. The whole sum of war-profiteering is a mite in comparison with this. Even if the Palestine prize were not given for acetone, but for the enlistment of Jewish support in the United States and other countries (Mr. Lloyd George's alternative essential motive) what then? It would still be outrageous, it would still be the most gigantic and most intolerable "deal" of the War.[18]

In his investigation of the former prime minister's motives for assenting to the issue of the Declaration, Jeffries drew mainly on Lloyd George's speeches. Unfortunately, the latter's *Memoirs of the Peace Conference* (1939), which dwells on these motives at some length, came too late for Jeffries to draw on. It contains much, however, that would have fired him up. Those passages which relate to Palestine and the Balfour Declaration were obviously written against the background of Palestine's Arab Revolt of 1936–39, and

---

17. PTR, p 193

18. PTR, p 196. Weizmann remarked in his autobiography that: 'I almost wish it had been as simple as that, and that I had never known the heartbreak, the drudgery which preceded the Declaration. But history does not deal in Aladdin's lamps.' (Chaim Weizmann, *Trial & Error: The Autobiography of Chaim Weizmann*, Hamish Hamilton, London, 1949, pp 192-193

suggest nothing so much as a politician struggling to justify his worst ever political decision. They are also replete, you will note, with Old Testament references:

- At the beginning of the war, Palestine was not in the picture... The destiny of Palestine was left to the haggling of experts in the various Foreign Offices of the Allies. In 1915 and 1916, Britain massed huge armies to check the menace of the Turk on the Suez Canal. At first they crawled drearily and without purpose across the desert towards the land of the Philistines. But in 1917, the attention of her warriors was drawn to the mountains of Judea beyond. The zeal of the Crusaders was resumed in their soul. The redemption of Palestine from the withering aggression of the Turk became like a pillar of flame to lead them on. The Sykes-Picot Agreement perished in its fire. It was not worth fighting for Canaan in order to condemn it to the fate of Agag and hew it in pieces before the Lord. Palestine, if recaptured, must be one and indivisible to renew its greatness as a living entity.[19]

- The next factor which produced a momentous change was the decision to come to terms with Jewry, which was clamouring for an opportunity to make Canaan once more the homeland of their race... No one imagined that the 14,000,000 of Jews scattered over the globe could find room and a living in Palestine. Nevertheless this race of wanderers sought a national hearth and a refuge for the hunted children of Israel in the country which the splendour of their spiritual genius has made forever glorious.[20]

- The fact that Britain at last opened her eyes to the opportunity afforded to the Allies to rally this powerful people to their side was attributable to the initiative, the assiduity and the fervour of one of the great Hebrews of all time: Dr. Chaim Weizmann... Dr. Weizmann enlisted my adhesion to his ideals at a time when, at my request, he was successfully applying his scientific skill and imagination to save Britain from a real disaster over the failure of wood alcohol for the manufacture of cordite. In addition to the gratitude I felt for him for this service, he appealed to my deep reverence for the great men of

19. David Lloyd George, *Memoirs of the Peace Conference*, Yale University Press, New Haven, 1939, pp 721-722
20. Lloyd George, p 722

his race who were the authors of the sublime literature upon
which I was brought up. I introduced him to Mr. Balfour, who
was won over completely by his charm, his persuasiveness and
his intellectual power.[21]

On the subject of the crucial War Cabinet decision of 31 October,
1917, Lloyd George had this to say:

> That policy [of support for the Zionist movement] was after
> prolonged enquiry and reflexion decided by the Cabinet on
> merits, and I have no doubt in my mind that some such provision
> would by common consent of all the Allied Powers have been
> inserted in the Peace Treaty even had there been no previous
> pledge or promise. But the actual time of the declaration was
> determined by considerations of war policy. It was part of our
> propagandist strategy for mobilizing every opinion and force
> throughout the world which would weaken the enemy and
> improve the Allied chances.[22]

Like some demented anti-Semite, Lloyd George saw evidence of
Jewish power and influence everywhere:

> [T]he Germans were the first to realise the war value of the Jews of
> the dispersal. In Poland, it was they who helped the German army
> to conquer the Czarist oppressor who had so cruelly persecuted

---

21. Lloyd George, p 722. Nor was the phenomenon of seeing European Zionist
leaders as biblical Israelites confined to Lloyd George: 'Many years later
[Churchill's son, Randolph] recalled a visit by Weizmann to Churchill's home
at Chartwell at the time of the 1929 White Paper discussions, when Randolph
was eighteen. His father, he said, had been fascinated by Weizmann's talk
and appearance; "Just like an Old Testament prophet," he told his son when
Weizmann had left.' (Quoted in Martin Gilbert, *Churchill & The Jews*, Simon
& Schuster, London, 2007, p 95). Weizmann too was given to similar flights
of fancy. For example: 'After a heavy day, having seen 15 or 20 *Va'adim*
[committees], I leave my Bureau and go out under the Palestinian sky; I hear
the voices of the people rising from the grave, voices of prophets, seers, wise
men. They seem to say to me: Be patient; salvation will come. It is bound to
come.' (Chaim Weizmann, *Speech to Conference of Jews in Liberated Area of
Palestine*, Jaffa, 17/6/18, in *The Letters and Papers of Chaim Weizmann*, Series
B. Papers Vol. 1 August 1898-July 1931, Israel Universities Press, Jerusalem,
1983, p 191). 'Am I too bold if today, in this place among the hills of Ephraim
and Judah, I state my conviction that the seers of Israel have not utterly
perished, that under the aegis of this university there will be a renaissance of
the divine power of prophetic wisdom that once was ours?' (Weizmann, *Speech
at Foundation-stone laying of Hebrew University*, Mt Scopus, 24/7/18, p 193)

22. Lloyd George, p 723

their race. They had their influence in other lands – notably in America, where some of their most powerful leaders exerted a retarding influence on President Wilson's impulses in the direction of the Allies. The German General Staff in 1916 urged the Turks to concede the demands of the Zionists in respect of Palestine...[23]

The Zionist offer to harness this power for the Allies was, it seems, simply too good to refuse:

> The Zionist leaders gave us a definite promise that, if the Allies committed themselves to giving facilities for the establishment of a National Home for the Jews in Palestine, they would do their best to rally to the Allied cause Jewish sentiment and support throughout the world. They kept their word in the letter and in the spirit, and the only question that remains now is whether we mean to honour ours.[24]

In one extraordinary passage, Lloyd George even has the Balfour Declaration inspiring Bolshevik resistance to the Germans and providing Hitler with a rationale to persecute German Jews in the 30s as payback for alleged Russian and American Jewish support for the Allies following its publication in November 1917:

> Immediately the declaration was agreed to, millions of leaflets were circulated in every town and area throughout the world where there were known to be Jewish communities. They were dropped from the air in German and Austrian towns, and they were scattered throughout Russia and Poland. I could point out substantial and in one case decisive advantages derived from this propaganda amongst the Jews. In Russia the Bolsheviks baffled all the efforts of the Germans to benefit by the harvests of the Ukraine and the Don, and hundreds of thousands of German and Austrian troops had to be maintained to the end of the War on Russian soil, whilst the Germans were short of men to replace casualties on the Western front. I do not suggest that this was due entirely, or even mainly, to Jewish activities. But we have good reason to believe that Jewish propaganda in Russia had a great deal to do with the difficulties created for the Germans in Southern Russia after the peace of Brest-Litovsk. The Germans themselves know that to be the case, and the Jews in Germany

---

23. Lloyd George, p 722
24. Lloyd George, p 737

are suffering to-day for the fidelity with which their brethren in Russia and in America discharged their obligations under the Zionist pledge to the Allies.[25]

In respect of the above, lest Lloyd George's professed concern for the suffering of German Jews under the Nazis be taken too seriously, the following passage from his biographer should place the matter in context:

> Lloyd George had an undisguised sympathy for the German leader which was gradually transformed, as the months went by, into an intense admiration. 'Hitler,' he continually remarked in private, 'is a great man.' The Führer was, after all, carrying out in Germany all the policies which he, Lloyd George, had wanted to implement in Britain: unemployment was being cured by the construction of splendid new motorways and magnificent new buildings, the people were being settled on the land in their thousands, engineering industries were humming with activity and the telephone service was, presumably, being improved beyond recognition. It was tough luck, admittedly, if one happened to be a Jew, a staunch pillar of the local church, a trade union leader or a Communist, but every revolutionary movement was bound to have its over-zealous devotees and the Western Powers were really to blame, in any case, for any atrocities that might be committed. For Britain's own potential Führer, Sir Oswald Mosley, who had lost his seat at the general election, Lloyd George continued to have a soft spot. He wrote an article for the *Sunday Pictorial* of June 24th 1934 in which he referred to a recent Blackshirt meeting at Olympia in admiring tones.[26]

Finally, note this desperate clutching at straws:

> There is no better proof of the value of the Balfour Declaration as a military move than the fact that Germany entered into negotiations with Turkey in an endeavour to provide an alternative scheme which would appeal to Zionists. A German-Jewish Society, the V.J.O.D. [*Vereinigung Judischer Organisation en Deutschlands zur Wahrung der Rechte des Osten* – Alliance of the Jewish Organizations of Germany for the Safeguarding of the

---

25. Lloyd George, p 737

26. Peter Rowland, *David Lloyd George: A Biography*, Macmillan Publishing Co., New York, 1976, pp 705-06

Rights of the Orient], was formed, and in January, 1918, Talaat, the Grand Vizier, at the instigation of the Germans, gave vague promises of legislation by means of which "all justifiable wishes of the Jews in Palestine would be able to find their fulfilment."[27]

Value for Money?
'The declaration was extracted under false pretences'

So what, if anything, did the British get in return for the Balfour Declaration? According to Jeffries, precious little:

> [P]ossibly the truest comment on the reward paid to the Zionists is to examine what in sober reality *was* gained for the Allies by the "National Home" transaction. So much is assumed upon this point, and so little is established. Certainly one of the anticipated recompenses never came to hand. "The Foreign Office," writes Lord Balfour's biographer [Blanche Dugdale] when dealing with the October-November period, "was now in fact anxious to reap all the immediate advantages there might be in the Declaration." She goes on, "It was expected apparently to have some direct results on the Russian revolution, then passing out of its Menshevik phase. Lenin and Trotsky took power in the same week of November 1917 that Jewish nationality won its recognition." There is much unrealized satire in this last sentence. However, the direct results which were expected will have been that Russia would go on fighting. This Russia did – at Archangel.
>
> But it would be unfair to suppose that Zionism was to make its real return for the Balfour Declaration in Russia. This was only dangled as an attractive possibility. The real return was to be in the United States, where Zionist adherents and the Zionist machine were (as we have seen more than once) to tip the trembling scale and bring the great Federation into the War.
>
> It is sustained that they did so, but I have never read any satisfactory proof of it. I agree that it would be a difficult thing to prove, for there was no day or short critical period when you could say at the end of it that the United States changed over from opposing participation to favouring participation. If there had been such a critical incident, there would have been some chance

---

27. Lloyd George, p 738

of showing who or what supplied the decisive twist. But there was no such occasion, though certain events provided factors to participation. Therefore there is this difficulty of proof.

At the same time, it is clear that the obstacles in the way of proving the case do not permit it to be assumed. If the Zionists cannot easily show how they brought America in, they are equally unentitled to say without producing evidence that they did bring America in, and to profit by this unverified assertion.

Such evidence as there is on the whole tells altogether against their being the deciding factor. No doubt they were one factor amongst a quantity. They won a number of their own people over from indifference or semi-support of the other side, but they have made claims as though they were *the* factor which brought in the United States. It is an interesting point that in the volume of Mr. Lloyd George's memoirs[28] which treats of the American entry into the War he makes no mention of Zionism as a contributory cause. We have the sinking of the *Lusitania* and of various United States merchant-vessels, the Zimmerman dispatch to Mexico, and other such events. We have an expose of President Wilson's developing opinions, and so on. But of Zionist help, nothing. It seems to me that if it had been so valuable as all that, had been as valuable as Mr. Lloyd George is by way of sustaining in other passages of his memoirs... then it should not have slipped his memory completely at the moment of cardinal computation.

The run of the evidence in fact does not square with Zionist help having been the determining factor. The leaders such as Brandeis and de Haas had enough to do, it is quite evident, in gathering supporters for the Zionist cause itself and in trying to counteract the anti-Allied sentiment amidst these supporters, particularly amidst all the seniors who had been in Russia or remembered Russia [...] It might perhaps be asserted that the Balfour concession, as it were, was given in exchange for Zionist influence amidst just a few men in the United States, the great Jewish bankers and financiers and other magnates. But that assertion cannot be borne out either. Mrs. Dugdale herself records that Balfour when in the United States found "the Jewish magnates hostile to the national [that is, Zionist] movement." Two months after the Declaration was issued our Ambassador at Washington "reported on Brandeis's authority that the Zionists were violently opposed by the great

---

28. This is a reference to Lloyd George's multi-volume *War Memoirs*, published between 1933 and 1936.

Capitalists." More evidence could be cited, but this is evidence enough. Any great Jewish financial interests in the United States which came to our support did not do so because of the pleadings of any Zionist.[29]

Jeffries' claim that American Zionist leaders had their hands full 'in gathering supporters for the Zionist cause itself and in trying to counteract the anti-allied sentiment amidst these supporters' accords with the evidence. Some Zionists had, in fact, been bastions of America's anti-war movement. However, when push came to shove, they deserted its ranks and toed the Zionist line, as the following passage from a study of American Jewish women's activism indicates:

> The American Jewish community was divided in its response to the war... Some Jewish women found that maintaining their commitments to both peace and other causes, such as Zionism, was virtually impossible in a world at war. Henrietta Szold and Jessie Sampter, two of the most prominent Zionist women in America, joined a pacifist group called the People's Council for Peace & Democracy but were pressured into resigning by other members of the American Zionist leadership, including Louis Brandeis, who regretted the war but saw in it an opportunity to transform the map of the Middle East.[30]

There is perhaps no more dramatic example of the phenomenon of American Zionists switching from an anti- to a pro-war position than the case of Brandeis' deputy, the progressive Reform rabbi, Stephen Wise. The author of the following telling passage, Oswald Garrison Villard, was the wartime editor of the *New York Evening Post*:

---

29. PTR, pp 196-198. Jeffries' reference to Archangel, of course, was not to the Bolsheviks continuing the fight against the Germans (Russia's participation in the war ended in March 1918 with the Treaty of Brest Litovsk), but to the fighting which broke out in October 1918 between the Red Army and Allied forces in North Russia. Tibawi, moreover, wonders pertinently why the Foreign Office expected any 'advantages' after being informed by its ambassador in Petrograd, Sir George Buchanan, on 27 April, that 'He doubted "very much" whether the proposed declaration would help and gave the reason: "There is no great enthusiasm for Zionism among the Jews in Russia, more especially since the overthrow of the old regime".' (p 206)

30. Melissa R. Klapper, *Ballots, Babies & Banners of Peace: American Jewish Women's Activism, 1890-1940*, New York University Press, New York, 2013, p 113

Only a relative few of the peace-loving hauled down the flag when war came [April, 1917]. A session of the American Union against Militarism produced a most dramatic scene. In the midst of a discussion of what our policy should be, Rabbi Stephen S. Wise said that he felt the time had come for a re-orientation of the pacifist point of view and that he wished to read us extracts from a sermon he intended to deliver the next Sunday. It bowled us over for it was a complete yielding on every point, an acceptance of the war as high-minded and all for the best – a complete reversal of everything he had stood for. He asked us to state our frank opinion one after the other and he got what he asked for... Never have I heard such plain, straightforward language; never have I seen a man so flayed to his face. When my turn came I reminded him that in several public sermons he had penned the finest tributes to my grandfather's non-resistant doctrines yet published, that he had declared his allegiance to them, and I said that if he read that sermon I should never wish to speak to him again.

During this ordeal by fire the perspiration ran in streams down the rabbi's face. When it was over he remarked that it was evident that he could not deliver that sermon and that he would not do so. A few weeks later the sermon was delivered, with modifications, and thereafter the rabbi became one of the war's great supporters.[31]

Nor did the Balfour Declaration cause German Jews to rally to the Allied cause. According to Jeffries, 'In Germany none of the great Jewish supporters of the imperial regime ceased their part in the struggle for German success. And when the imperial regime collapsed, the scissions in the will-to-win of the German people did not come from Zionist streams percolating through the national system. It was not by Zionist aid that the Allies conquered Germany, but by their arms.'[32]

We conclude with Tibawi's cold-water conclusions, both on the subject of British motives, and on the alleged benefits of the Declaration to Britain's war effort:

---

31. Oswald Garrison Villard, *Fighting Years: An Autobiography*, Harcourt, Brace & Company, New York, 1939, pp 323-324

32. PTR, p 203

The myths that invested the issue of the declaration with haloes of 'idealism' may all now be laid to rest. There was no idealism at all. Nor was the declaration inspired by British imperial or strategic interests, still less by humanitarian consideration of providing a haven for persecuted Jews. Least of all was it a *douceur* for the scientific work of one Jew... There is nothing in the minutes of the four cabinet meetings nor in the statements made at the relevant meetings by Cecil [Balfour's deputy] or Balfour to justify any of these myths. Its only justification, repeatedly made at the cabinet meetings and in the Foreign Office minutes and memoranda, was its as yet not proven service as an adjunct to propaganda. It was supposed to forestall a German declaration, and was imagined to influence the Jews in Russia and America in favour of the war effort.[33]

You will note, in particular, Tibawi's second sentence: 'Nor was the declaration inspired by British imperial or strategic interests.'

Tibawi dismisses out of hand the idea of an impending German declaration of support for Zionism:

The German scare was used by Balfour at the cabinet meeting on 4 October and in the telegram to Wilson two days later. On both occasions Balfour asserted that the German government was making great efforts to win the support of the Zionist movement. The Foreign Office went further in warning of an impending German declaration that would forestall the British. The first assertion was based only on newspaper reports that came through Zionist, not British diplomatic, channels. And no evidence at all was produced in support of the second assertion. Both have since proved to be entirely without foundation. The German government, far from making overtures to the Zionists, repeatedly rejected the representations made to it by the German members of the Zionist Executive in Berlin. At no time did the German government even consider the issue of a declaration. All of this has been conclusively established, on the basis of the Zionist records relating to the time, by none other than the historian of the Balfour Declaration, himself a Jew and a Zionist who under Weizmann became secretary of the World Zionist Organisation.[34]

---

33. Tibawi, pp 233-234
34. Tibawi, p 234. See Stein p 533f.

He also dismisses the idea that it was the Zionists who brought the United States into the war:

> In America the Jews, and still less the Zionists, played no part in her entry into the war. After her entry the main British and allied interests were the two vital matters of financial credits and the production of war materials. The credits were directly from the American government to the allied governments. Hence the Jewish financiers, who at any rate fought shy of Zionism, had no influence on the transactions. The Jews, and still less the Zionists, were powerless to hinder or expedite the production of munitions of war. They lacked the managerial and labour force to do that.[35]

Tibawi's conclusion is sobering:

> An historian who considers these facts against the Zionist claims in 1917 cannot escape the conclusion that they were a colossal bluff to which Balfour and the Foreign Office conditioned themselves to succumb, with the result that the declaration was extracted under false pretences. Its immediate effect was to impose the Zionist creed upon unwilling Jews in Britain and to some extent also abroad, and ultimately to give Weizmann a free warrant to assume the leadership of the Zionist movement. Britain's reward was very small indeed: largely inspired, and couched in similar terms, messages of gratitude.[36]

Finally, support for Tibawi's thesis that the Balfour Declaration was the result of a 'colossal bluff' may be found in Weizmann's own words. Speaking at a banquet in Czernowitz, Romania, in 1927, the Zionist leader declared that,

> We Jews got the Balfour Declaration quite unexpectedly; or, in other words, we are the greatest war profiteers. We never dreamed of the Balfour Declaration; to be quite frank, it came to us overnight... The Balfour Declaration of 1917 was built on air, and a foundation had to be laid for it through years of exacting work; every day and every hour of these last ten years, when opening the newspapers, I thought: Whence will the next blow come? I trembled lest the British Government would call me and ask, "Tell us, what is this Zionist Organisation? Where are they,

---

35. Tibawi, p 235
36. Tibawi, p 235

your Zionists?" For these people think in terms different from ours. The Jews, they knew, were against us; we stood alone on a little island, a tiny group of Jews with a foreign past.[37]

The Question of Responsibilities
'The largest share of responsibilities must be borne by the 1917 Government'

Jeffries' verdict on those responsible for the Balfour Declaration has all the finality of the fabled Judgment of History:

> The largest share of [responsibilities] must be borne by the 1917 Government. The Zionists have a big burden to carry, but their action would have come to nothing without first the acquiescence, and later the collusion, the backing and finally the incitement of Whitehall.
>
> They were inspired too by an ideal, even though it was ill-interpreted and should have been carried out in a purer way. Unfortunately their leaders rejected the pilgrimage to Zion in favour of the appropriation of Palestine. But the presence of an ideal, however subverted, does attenuate in a minor degree their fault, and there is not much counterpart to be found for it in the bargaining motives of our own Government.
>
> No doubt the Government was in some straits because of the perils of the war at the time. In the then Prime Minister's own words, "It was important for us to seek every legitimate help we could get." The help though had to be legitimate. It could not be that form of help which is helping oneself to another's property. The Government was, indeed, fighting to save England, and that would seem to supply it with a motive equal, or superior to the Zionists'. But it was precisely to save England that the members of the Government were waging the War. It was to preserve the England that had come down to them, not to substitute for it an England of easier conscience and then to claim this as a survival.
>
> There was the question too of position and of setting an example. It was for the British realm to set the example, not to conform to the standards of the Zionists. Methods understandable from a self-appointed fresh-made caucus such as the Zionist

---

37. Chaim Weizmann, *Reminiscences*, quoted in *The Zionist Idea: A Historical Analysis & Reader*, Arthur Hertzberg, The Jewish Publication Society, Philadelphia, 1997, p 581

Organization were beyond belief when proposed by the heirs of a hundred Parliaments.

The responsibility for not taking this view must lie therefore upon the Cabinet of 1917, and principally upon Lord Balfour, who insisted on working out, in a sphere which the War placed at his mercy, an academic thesis of his own, in a particular way. When that way was barred to him by facts, he scorned them and scorned that elementary justice which was altogether too much in the foreground for his style of seeing things. He persisted wilfully in his course, and as we have seen, it was he who broke every opposition.

"From the first," his biographer assures us, "he threw his whole weight on the side of the Zionists, and without it they might not have prevailed." "The Balfour Declaration," say the officials of the Zionist Organization in their report upon it, "is justly so-called, not only because it fell to Sir Arthur Balfour as Foreign Secretary to write the historic letter, but also because he, more than any other single statesman, is responsible for the policy embodied in the Declaration."

As happens now and then in the course of public events, words which were written to be a eulogy have stayed to be an impeachment.

With this the immediate examination of the Balfour Declaration may end. These were its principal characteristics:

1) Its publication broke our pledged word to the Arab race.

2) Its object was to establish the Jews in a privileged position in Palestine without the assent of the population, as a prelude to the absorption of the latter, under plea of their co-operation, in a future Jewish state.[38]

3) It was written in great part by those who were supposed only to have received it, and was deliberately worded so that the truth might be hidden by it, its guarantees to the Arabs be useless and its promises intangible.

4) It was ostensibly a recognition of Zionist aspirations to return to Palestine under the sanction of historic rights, but in reality, it was the published clause of a private bargain by which war-spoils were to be given in payment for war-help.

There is relief in quitting this subject. The Balfour Declaration will recur in the remaining chapters, but at least in combination with

---

38. With the benefit of hindsight, Jeffries might have amended the final clause of point two to read: '... as a prelude to the expulsion and exile of the latter from their homeland in order to ensure a Jewish majority in a future Jewish state.'

other proclamations or papers or speeches and in conjunction with other events. So it will be less prominent.

But it is a pity that that it cannot be lost from sight, and a greater pity that it has not yet been removed from our public records. Unlawful in issue, arbitrary in purpose, and deceitful in wording the Balfour Declaration is the most discreditable document to which a British Government has set its hand within memory.[39]

---

39. PTR, pp 199-201

Winston Churchill

6

Challenging the
Balfour Declaration

Lord Northcliffe in Palestine
(February 1922)
'The Dyaks of Borneo are better behaved'

As a journalist for Lord Northcliffe's *Daily Mail*, Jeffries enjoyed the support of its owner, who harboured serious reservations about the wisdom of Britain's support for a Jewish national home in Palestine. Northcliffe, in fact, was so concerned that he decided to include Palestine in the final leg of a world tour to assess the situation for himself.

The following extract from his diary encapsulates his feelings at the time:

> We stopped at two "Colonies," where young Lithuanian and Galician Jews were very slackly at work on road-making. Fine young fellows, many. We entered the eating tent and huts of some of them. They are rude people. If you make them stand up, which they don't otherwise, they go on eating in your face, with their hats on the backs of their heads, and put their hands in their pockets. The Dyaks of Borneo are better behaved. If they do that to us, whose coming they have awaited for hours, what do they do to the natives? I spoke my mind to their leader, much to the pleasure of British officers with me. People daren't tell the Jews the truth here. They've had some from me. I didn't come uninvited.[1]

---

1. Lord Northcliffe, *My Journey Round the World*, John Lane, London, 1923, pp 276-77

Google the names Northcliffe and Jeffries and the following invariably appears: 'In 1922 Lord Northcliffe visited Palestine, accompanied by a journalist, Mr. J.M.N. Jeffries (whose subsequent book, *Palestine: The Reality*, remains the classic work of reference for that period).'[2] They were penned in the early 50s by the journalist Douglas Reed, who promoted the belief that Northcliffe, who died on 22 August, 1922, was poisoned in order to prevent his editorial attacks on the Balfour Declaration from spreading to *The Times*, of which he was a part owner.

As his diary reveals, Northcliffe was accompanied, not by Jeffries, who was in Ireland at the time, but by Philip Graves, a correspondent for *The Times*, whom he described as 'my secretary and correspondent *pro tem.*' Graves was the half-brother of the poet Robert Graves and author of a 1923 book, *Palestine, the Land of Three Faiths*.[3]

Jeffries' own account of the press baron's visit may be found in *Palestine: The Reality*:

> Lord Northcliffe... brought to Palestine what the Colonial Secretary [Winston Churchill] so conspicuously had failed to bring, an objective mind. He learned the facts on the spot and formed from them his judgment of the situation...
>
> He was accessible. The news spread that here was a great Englishman who listened, and during his stay two hundred visitors waited upon him. Petitions were drawn up and presented to him not only by the Arabs but also by the maltreated Jewish bodies, those Zionists who had committed the ultimate mistake of demonstrating by their presence that "rights" and exemption from "sufferance" were superfluous for Jews who came in faith to Palestine.[4] The Rutenberg monopoly was made clear to him, and the fiction that Palestine was a Jewish country faded as he used his ever-open eyes.
>
> His general judgment went straight to the truth. "This country," he said in the words used to open this book, "runs

---

2. Douglas Reed, *The Controversy of Zion*, Dolphin Press, Durbin, 1978, p 295
3. Lord Northcliffe, p 273
4. By 'Zionists' Jeffries means here Jews living in, or visiting, Palestine solely for reasons of faith, as distinct from political Zionists. The reference to 'rights' and 'sufferance' comes from Churchill's White Paper of June 1922: 'It is essential that [the Jewish community] should know that it is in Palestine as of right and not on sufferance.'

the risk of becoming a second Ireland." The prophecy was only too accurate. Balfour, not satisfied with his achievement of one embittered Ireland, had arranged for us a second one.[5]

The great consequence of Lord Northcliffe's visit was that the Arabs henceforth obtained in his newspapers some space for the presentation of their wrongs. His last illness came, alas! on his return home, and in August he was dead, England losing more than has ever yet been realized, a purely candid mind. But his impetus in the Palestine affair stayed, and was given a fresh impulse by his brother and successor, Lord Rothermere. I was dispatched there in the autumn of 1922 by Mr. Thomas Marlowe, the editor of the *Daily Mail*, with general instructions to go fully into the question.[6]

The following account of Northcliffe's visit by his biographers corroborates that of Jeffries':

[Northcliffe] concluded his diary notes of his visit of less than a week with the declaration: 'There will be trouble in Palestine.' He had seen for himself that the British troops 'hate their work of repression,' and he believed that unless more regard was shown for Moslem and Christian rights the country would become 'a second Ireland.' He told the High Commissioner, Sir Herbert Samuel, in a letter (February 11): 'As a supporter of sane Zionism, I am frankly unhappy at many things that it is impossible to ignore. Time may obliterate many, but tact on the part of the overseas zealots and newcomers would do more. If Zionism be not ruined by its fanatics it can, in my very humble opinion, be eventually achieved peacefully and to the good of the world.' But he thought the 'National Home' ideal a British mistake because it ignored Moslem sentiment and interests. He told Lovat Fraser: 'We mustn't suppose that because a man wears a turban or a tarboosh that he is a fool or slow or unable to combine.' One of the lessons of his journey, he said, was the discovery that 'these people are not so much unlike ourselves as we thought they were.'[7]

---

5. Balfour was Chief Secretary for Ireland from 1887–1891. He opposed Irish Home Rule and was nicknamed 'Bloody Balfour' by Irish nationalists.

6. PTR, p 497

7. Reginald Pound & Geoffrey Harmsworth, *Northcliffe*, Cassell, London, 1959, pp 826-827

Jeffries in Palestine
(October–December 1922)
'It was as though I were a Royal Commission of one'

'Before the year closed I had to investigate the whole Palestine question,' Jeffries wrote in *Front Everywhere*:

> I was satisfied to have to do this, for it was real work on an important issue. It took some months of enquiry; Sir Herbert Samuel gave me every facility. He was High Commissioner then, and opposed as I am to Zionism as interpreted in Palestine I retain genuine respect for him. My pages of notes ran to over a thousand by the time I had finished; it was as though I were a Royal Commission of one. This was the most difficult and onerous piece of work I ever had, and of all I have done that by which I stand most firmly. When I returned to England I wrote a long series of articles, and the facts in them were not controverted. Incidentally I gave the text of part of a Treaty which the Government had (and still has) not published. According to the book the publication of a secret treaty is the classic feat of journalism and should bring renown, but in practice it does not make any difference at all.
>
> The general conclusion of my inquest on the "Palestine Question" was that the name prejudged the issue. The Colonial Office talked so loudly about the "Question" that it concealed cleverly that there was no Question till we had made one. As for the Jews, their attitude is understandable. If I were a Jew, I believe I should imagine I had rights in Palestine, and be a Zionist. The more guilty parties are not the Jews, but our politicians who know the Jews have no such rights but for their own purpose encourage them to think they have. The furthest limits of fraudulence have been reached by these same politicians' offer to the Arabs of half the seats in a Parliament which is to represent their native country![8]

There is an understandable note of bitterness in Jeffries' observation that, 'according to the book the publication of a secret treaty is the classic feat of journalism and should bring renown, but in practice it does not make any difference at all.' At the time, he had

---

8. FE, pp 280-281. As has been indicated, Jeffries' 'long series of articles' and 'the text of part of a Treaty which the Government had (and still has) not published,' have been edited by William M. Mathew and republished as *The Palestine Deception 1915-1923: The McMahon-Hussein Correspondence, the Balfour Declaration & the Jewish National Home* (2014).

dared to hope that the publication of the McMahon Treaty would effect a real change in the government's pro-Zionist Palestine policy. Sadly, it was not to be. Nevertheless, Jeffries' first-hand reports in the *Daily Mail* on the situation in Palestine in 1922 would help to fuel a major assault on the government's Palestine policy in the House of Lords in 1923. As he put it in *Palestine: The Reality*,

> [W]hile I was in the Near East, where I spent several months in my investigation, I procured my copy of the McMahon papers, and besides drawing attention when I returned to the absence of any Mandate I published the salient portions of these in the *Daily Mail* during the months of January and February 1923. So far the only knowledge of the McMahon texts had come from the single-line excerpt made by the Arab Delegates the previous year and from Mr. Churchill's brief quotation in reply, if indeed this can be described as a quotation from the text.
>
> Their fuller publication caused some stir, and led to the House of Lords' debate on the 27th of March, which must be recalled, as it was the only occasion upon which one of the Houses of Parliament passed a direct vote upon the legitimacy of the Mandate as framed and exercised by Great Britain. Lord Islington moved, in fact, that "The Mandate for Palestine in its present form is inacceptable to this House because it directly violates the pledges made by His Majesty's Government to the people of Palestine in the declaration of October 1915 [in the McMahon] papers and again in the Declaration of 1918 and is, as at present framed, opposed to the sentiments and to the wishes of the great majority of the people of Palestine: that therefore its acceptance by the League of Nations should be postponed until such modifications have been effected therein as will comply with the pledges given by His Majesty's Government."
>
> By this time there was a change of government. Mr. Lloyd George had gone in the previous autumn. The Bonar Law Ministry had succeeded, and there was a new Colonial Minister, the Duke of Devonshire, who in the business of Palestine lived in a state of being prompted continually by permanent officials. The defence of the Government in the Lords rested really with the new-made Earl of Balfour.
>
> The debate, admirably introduced by Lord Islington, furnished the already quoted and several times mentioned speech of Lord Grey. Balfour came into the House late, with clear expectations of conquest. It was his first speech, I think, in the Lords, and probably his worst. "I ask my noble friend [he said] who takes up

the cause of the Arabs, and who seems to think that their material well-being is going to be diminished [*this had in nowise been his noble friend's thesis*] how he thinks that the existing population of Palestine is going to be effective unless and until you get capitalists to invest their money in developing the resources of this small country."

He made a too usual display of affected ignorance, expressing surprise that the question at issue, if it meant so much to his opponents, "had never been raised in the House," whereas, as Lord Sydenham answered, it had been raised many times.

He trifled with the amusing texture of truth, turning it in his fingers as it were and playing with it and saying, "I cannot imagine any political interests exercised under greater safeguards than the political interests of the Arab population of Palestine." This from the man who had abolished the Arabs' political rights! He ended on his favourite note, "This is a great adventure. Are we never to have adventures?"

As for the McMahon pledges, he slid past them. Lord Grey, who had been responsible for their being given, made his pathetic statement of unacquaintance with their details. The most striking speech came from Lord Buckmaster, who had been Lord Chancellor. Referring to the McMahon-Hussein papers he said, "If these documents are accurate – and I am bound to say that on the face of it they appear to me to be perfectly sound – they show unmistakably that there has not been, as the noble viscount, Lord Grey, suggested, something in the nature of casual inconsistency between different announcements at different times, but that a deliberate pledge has been given on the one hand and has been abandoned upon the other."

From a man who had been the first lawyer in the realm, this was crushing testimony. On a rather full division the ministerial case was defeated by fifty-two votes to twenty-nine, and Lord Islington's motion that the Government had violated its pledges was passed. That day was about the high-water mark of the poor Arab cause... But the Government resisted by paying no attention to anything and by doing nothing.[9]

It should be pointed out here that Jeffries has inadvertently conflated two House of Lords debates on Palestine, namely that of 21 June, 1922 and that of 27 March, 1923. An examination of Hansard, for example, reveals that,

---

9. PTR, pp 497-499

- The government's Palestine policy was rebuffed by the Lords on 21 June, 1922 by 60 to 29 votes, not, as Jeffries has it, by 52 to 29.

- Since the debate of 27 March, 1923 arose not from a formal motion, but from a question by Lord Islington, no vote occurred.

- Islington's motion, quoted by Jeffries, pertains instead to the 1922 debate.

- Balfour took part in the 1922 debate, not that of 1923. The key government spokesman in the latter was the Colonial Secretary, the Duke of Devonshire.

- Lords Grey and Buckmaster took part in the 1923 debate, not that of 1922.

Be that as it may, there were, in fact, four debates in all at this time on government policy in Palestine, spanning June 1922 - March 1923:

21 June, 1922 (Lords)
4 July, 1922 (Commons)
1 March, 1923 (Lords)
27 March, 1923 (Lords)

Jeffries' reports, particularly his translation from the Arabic of the Hussein-McMahon Correspondence, supplied the ammunition for those in 1923. As William M. Mathew notes,

> The fact that Jeffries presented such a translation at a juncture when the Mandate for Palestine was still some months short of its full legal implementation, when opposition to the Balfour policy was mounting in the British press and parliament, and when the Zionists themselves were vigorously establishing facts-on-the-ground to the acute dismay of the indigenous Arab population – and to much of the pre-existing Jewish community as well – came as an obvious shock to the troubled colonial authorities. So intense was their discomfort, indeed, that public denial was extended to *self* denial. Remarkably,

when the Colonial Office had the Jeffries articles cut out from the *Daily Mail* for its official record, it completely excluded the fifth of these – 'Broken Faith with the Arabs. McMahon Letters Disclosure' – and much of the sixth – 'Inventing a Province. Vilayet of Churchill. Pledge in White Paper Basket' (referencing the *British White Paper of* [June]1922, which reaffirmed the undertakings of the Balfour Declaration). Copies of the pieces in a popular newspaper were available to a wide public; officials themselves, however, seemed adamant that they should have no place in any government documents.[10]

Since these four debates represent the only serious parliamentary challenge to the government's draft Mandate for Palestine (which incorporated the Balfour Declaration), and since other sources which reference them have relied solely on Jeffries' conflated account,[11] it is important to examine each of them as recorded in Hansard. In doing so, we can see more clearly the part played by Jeffries' journalism in informing and strengthening the case of the anti-Mandate forces in the Lords' debate of March 1923.

As Mathew indicates, the timing of these four debates was dictated by the fact that those who initiated them had a window of opportunity in which to challenge Britain's Palestine policy. In the case of the 1922 debates, Britain's draft Mandate for Palestine had not yet been confirmed by the League of Nations Council. This would not take place until 24 July, 1922. And, with regard to those of 1923, the draft Mandate still had to await the signing and ratification of a peace treaty with Turkey, which did not take place until 24 July, 1923, and 28 September, 1923, respectively.

---

10. William M. Mathew, *The Palestine Deception 1915-1923: The McMahon-Hussein Correspondence, the Balfour Declaration, and the Jewish National Home*, Institute for Palestine Studies, 2014, pp 8-9

11. Izzat Tannous' *The Palestinians* (pp 68-69) and Robert John & Sami Hadawi's *Palestine Diary*, pp 190-192. The latter, for example, misconstrue Lord Islington's June 1922 speech as a reaction to Jeffries' *Daily Mail* reports of 1923: 'In his speech Islington quoted extracts from the 'Correspondence' which had appeared in the *Daily Mail*...' p 190

The Palestine Debates of 1922
'Are we never to have adventures?'

1. Palestine Mandate, House of Lords, 21/6/22

Lord Islington (Liberal), speaking as one 'familiar with the conditions in Palestine, and the traditions of the people in that country,' moved 'That the Mandate... in its present form is inacceptable to this House because it directly violates the pledges made by His Majesty's Government to the people of Palestine in the [McMahon] Declaration of October 1915, and again in the [Anglo-French] Declaration of November 1918, and is, as at present framed, opposed to the sentiments and wishes of the great majority of the people of Palestine; that, therefore, its acceptance by the Council of the League of Nations should be postponed until such modifications have been therein effected as will comply with pledges given by His Majesty's Government.'[12]

'There have been several occasions when the subject of the Mandates has been raised in this House,' he noted, 'but I think this is the first occasion when a Motion has been made, and a debate will take place... proposing a modification of the policy in regard to the most vital aspects of this Mandate.'

Islington went on to argue that certain pro-Zionist Articles of the Mandate conflicted with Article 22 of the Covenant of the League of Nations, which stipulated that 'the well-being and development of [ex-enemy] peoples form a sacred trust of civilisation,' and that 'the wishes of [their] communities must be a principal consideration in the selection of the Mandatory.'

While the British people accepted the 'principle of the Mandate,' he maintained, 'the moment it was decided to... introduce into it the principle of the Zionist Home, the whole of that great ideal of leading the people on in their own way and by their own means to self-government in their own country was at once and forever abandoned. The Zionist Home must, and does, mean

---

12. Lord Islington had been under-secretary of state for the colonies from 1914-15, and under-secretary of state for India from 1915–18. According to his *Times* obituary, he was a politician and colonial administrator, 'notable for his devotion to the cause of Palestine Arabs.'

the predominance of political power on the part of the Jewish community in a country where the population is preponderantly non-Jewish. And that is what the Palestine Mandate... sets forth permanently to establish. If ratified, it imposes on this country the responsibility of trusteeship for a Zionist political predominance where 90% of the population are non-Zionist and non-Jewish. In saying this I want to make it clear that I speak in no sense in hostility to the Jewish race.... In fact, very many orthodox Jews, not only in Palestine but all over the world, view with the deepest misapprehension, not to say dislike, this principle of a Zionist Home in Palestine. The scheme of a Zionist Home must, and does, entail direct Jewish bias as against the people of the country, who are mainly Arabs and Mahomedans. And it not merely introduces this influence by utilising the Jewish forces within the territory of Palestine, but it brings about this influence by importing into the country extraneous and alien Jews from other parts of the world, in order to make that predominance effective.'

The second prong of Islington's attack on government policy concerned Britain's failure to honour its pledges to the Arabs: 'The Proclamation made on the instructions of His Majesty's Government in 1915 by Sir Henry McMahon... to the Sherif, stated that 'Great Britain is prepared to recognise and support the independence of the Arabs within the territories included in the limits and boundaries proposed by the Sherif.' It is contended that those limits include Palestine. It is true that there is a verbal quibble as to whether Palestine is included or not, but I shall not enter into that.'

With regard to the above, you will recall Jeffries' words: 'So far the only knowledge of the McMahon texts had come from the single-line excerpt made by the Arab Delegates the previous year and from Mr. Churchill's brief quotation in reply, if indeed this can be described as a quotation from the text.' The Arab delegates referred to were a group of Palestinian notables who had come to Britain to state their case. While there (from August 1921 to May 1922), the Palestine Arab Delegation, as they were known, published a pamphlet in November 1921, *The Holy Land: The Moslem-Christian Case against Zionist Aggression*, in which, under the heading *Pledges to Arabs*, the following account of the Hussein-McMahon Correspondence appeared:

> In a letter addressed on July 14th, 1915, to Sir Henry McMahon, King Hussein, who had decided to take up arms on the side of the Allies, asked, first, "that England should acknowledge the independence of the Arab countries bounded on the north by Mersina and Adana up to the 37th degree of latitude, on the east by the frontiers of Persia up to the Persian Gulf, on the south by the Indian Ocean with the exception of Aden, and on the West by the Red Sea and the Mediterranean up to Mersina," Palestine thus coming within these boundaries. Replying to the above on October 24th, 1915, Sir Henry McMahon wrote: "I am empowered in the name of the Government of Great Britain to give the following assurances:- Great Britain is prepared to recognise and support the independence of the Arabs within the territories included in the limits and boundaries proposed by the Sherif. Regarding the Vilayets of Baghdad and Basra, the Arabs will recognise that the established position and interests of Great Britain necessitate special measures of administration and control in order to secure these territories from foreign aggression."

That, it appears, was the only account of the Correspondence available to Islington and his colleagues when they raised the issue of the McMahon pledge in 1922. Jeffries' more substantial translation would, of course, not become available to them until January 1923.

Islington's reference to an Anglo-French Declaration of November 1918 was to a document issued by General Allenby assuring the Arabs, including those in Palestine, that Britain's aim in the Near East 'was the complete and final liberation of all peoples formerly oppressed by the Turks and the establishment of national Governments and administrations in those countries deriving authority from the initiative and free will of those peoples themselves,' and that 'Great Britain agrees to encourage and assist the formation of native Governments and their recognition when formed.'

Islington maintained that 'the Proclamations of 1915 and 1918 constitute a definite undertaking to the Arab community by Great Britain, whilst Zionism, as embodied in the Balfour Declaration, as implied in the Palestine Mandate, and as given effect in the administrative system now prevailing, cannot constitute other than a direct repudiation of these solemn and authoritative undertakings.'

Most significantly, in light of assertions to the contrary by the Colonial Secretary, Winston Churchill, in the Commons debate to follow, Islington reminded the Lords that 'Parliament is not committed to Zionism' and 'has never given its decision in regard to it.'

Finally, he declared that 'this Zionist scheme really runs counter to the whole human psychology of the age. There has never been a time in our history, I believe, when nationality, as such, has been a stronger force. By nationality, I mean the jealous adherence on the part of a people to its own rights and its own privileges... This scheme of importing an alien race into the midst of a native local race is flying in the very face of the whole of the tendencies of the age. It is an unnatural, partial and altruistic experiment, and that kind of experiment is a very grave mistake to-day, wherever it is tried, and particularly in the East...'

Lord Balfour (Conservative) asserted (in what was, in fact, his maiden speech in the Lords) variously that the mandatory system 'always contemplated the Mandate for Palestine on the general lines of the Declaration of November 1917'; that 'it is known to the Council of the League of Nations that we are carrying out that policy'; that 'Jewish domination over the Arabs... is no necessary consequence'; that 'I cannot imagine any political interests exercised under greater safeguards than the political interests of the Arab population of Palestine'; and that, 'as soon as all this Mandate question is finally settled... [the Arabs] will... come forward and freely help in the development of a Jewish Home.'

These delusional assertions were followed by a statement which encapsulates, in no uncertain terms, the thinking which motivated him to issue the Declaration which bears his name:

> My noble friend told us in his speech, and I believe him absolutely, that he has no prejudice against the Jews. I think I may say that I have no prejudice in their favour. But their position and their history, their connection with world religion and with world politics, is absolutely unique. There is no parallel to it... in any other branch of human history. Here you have a

small race originally inhabiting a small country... at no time in its history wielding anything that can be described as material power, sometimes crushed in between great Oriental monarchies, its inhabitants deported, then scattered, then driven out of the country altogether into every part of the world, and yet maintaining a continuity of religious and racial tradition of which we have no parallel elsewhere.

That, itself, is sufficiently remarkable, but consider... how they have been treated during long centuries... consider how they have been subjected to tyranny and persecution; consider whether the whole culture of Europe... has not from time to time proved itself guilty of great crimes against this race. I quite understand that some members of the race may have given, doubtless did give, occasion for much ill-will and I do not know how it could be otherwise, treated as they were; but, if you are going to lay stress on that, do not forget what part they have played in the intellectual, the artistic, the philosophic and scientific development of the world.

(One peer was prompted to quip at this point, 'The noble Earl, Lord Balfour, said that he had no prejudice in their favour. Following upon that, he delivered a eulogy of that nation which I hope he will not think it impertinent if I say was almost as good as Disraeli at his very best in his two chapters on the Jews in his *Life of Lord George Bentinck*. In listening to the noble Earl I almost wished that I was a Jew myself because they came in for some very handsome treatment at his hands.')

Balfour pleaded,

[D]o not your Lordships think that if Christendom, not oblivious of all the wrong it has done, can give a chance, without injury to others, to this race of showing whether it can organise a culture in a Home where it will be secured from oppression, that it is not well to say, if we can do it, that we will do it? And, if we can do it, should we not be doing something material to wash out an ancient stain upon our own civilisation...?

He concluded his case for the 'great ideal' of the Jewish national home with the following astonishing words:

It may fail. I do not deny that this is an adventure. Are we never to have adventures? Are we never to try new experiments? I hope your Lordships will never sink to that unimaginative depth, and that experiment and adventure will be justified if there is any case or cause for their justification. Surely, it is in order that we may send a message to every land where the Jewish race has been scattered, a message that will tell them that Christendom is not oblivious of their faith, is not unmindful of the service they have rendered to the great religions of the world, and, most of all, to the religion that the majority of your Lordships' House profess, and that we desire to the best of our ability to give them that opportunity of developing, in peace and quietness under British rule, those great gifts which hitherto they have been compelled from the very nature of the case only to bring to fruition in countries which know not their language and belong not to their race. That is the ideal which I desire to see accomplished, that is the aim at the root of the policy I am trying to defend; and, though it be defensible indeed on every ground, that is the ground which chiefly moves me.

It is worth noting that nowhere in his defence of Britain's Jewish national home policy does Balfour cite the 'extremely useful propaganda [among Jews] in Russia and America,' which he claimed, at the War Cabinet meeting of 31 October, 1917, would flow from 'a declaration of support' for Zionism, and which was the only reason for doing so advanced by him at the time.[13]

Four Lords rose to speak in support of Islington's motion.

Lord Sydenham (Unionist) raised the matter of another buried document – the report of the 1919 American King-Crane Commission, 'which went all over Palestine, and made a very important Report to the Government of the United States, which we have never been able to see...'

The report of the King-Crane Commission had recorded the overwhelming opposition of the Palestinian Arab population to the idea of a Jewish national home in Palestine. What is of particular interest here is Sydenham's reference to the government's refusal to table the Commission's report.[14]

Two further points made by Sydenham deserve inclusion.

---

13. Doreen Ingrams, *Palestine Papers 1917-1922: Seeds of Conflict*, John Murray, London, 1972, p 16

14. The King-Crane Report remained a 'secret' in the files of the US State Department until Ray Stannard Baker published excerpts from it in his book on President Wilson late in 1922.

The first relates to the establishment of a precedent, namely the entertaining of prehistoric claims as a basis for twentieth century foreign policy decisions:

> If we are going to admit claims based on conquest thousands of years ago, the whole world will have to be turned upside down.

The second could be considered the definitive response to Balfour's question, 'Are we never to have adventures?':

> It is really a painful and humiliating fact that the Palestinians under Turkish rule were more contented, more lightly taxed, and had far more share in their Government, than they have under the British flag at the present moment. Nowhere in history could you find a parallel to that case. In no place where we have gone has freedom become less. What we have done is, by concessions, not to the Jewish people but to a Zionist extreme section, to start a running sore in the East, and no one can tell how far that sore will extend.

Lord Buckmaster (Liberal), a former Lord Chancellor, stressed the fact that a pledge was a pledge:

> I have to say that while accepting all the splendid idealism of the noble Earl and being most anxious to accompany him in all his new idealistic adventures, I find myself quite unable to vote against this Motion, unless I am sure that the Mandate, as it stands to-day, does not violate the pledges that we gave to the native races.

Lord Lamington (Conservative), who had earlier in the Lords (20 April, 1921) pointed out the conflict between the draft Mandate and Article 22 of the League Covenant, also took umbrage at the government's suppression of the King-Crane Commission's report:

> I was in Damascus at the time Mr. Crane came out with a Commission to try to find out what the people of Syria really wanted... I have before now asked for the publication of their Report, but His Majesty's Government, with their usual clever evasiveness, said they could not obtain it. I have no doubt they could have obtained it time after time, and I fancy, if that Report had been put before the public, it would have been found that there were three main deductions arrived at by that Commission.

> One was that Syria was wholly indivisible... The second is that on no account should the French obtain any Mandate over Syria... The third was that the Zionist organisation should have no control whatsoever in Palestine.

Lamington also had a confession to make:

> The noble Earl said that when the Declaration was made all the Allies at that time were in favour of it. I was myself. As I have stated before in this House, I went to address an overflow meeting held to celebrate the fact that this Declaration had been made. But I have learned wisdom since then. I have been out to that country, and found that if you try to establish this Zionist settlement in Palestine you are bound to have trouble.

In its account of this important debate, 'the high-water mark of the poor Arab cause,' as Jeffries put it, *The New York Times* merely reported that 'The Earl of Balfour made his first speech in the House of Lords this evening in circumstances of uncommon interest with an unfortunate result. The die-hards did not treat him kindly and the Government was defeated 60 to 29.' The paper went on to assert that 'Lord Sydenham proved himself an advocate of Turkish rule,' and that the vote was 'a blow for the League of Nations.'[15]

2. Colonial Office, House of Commons, 4/7/22

In an attempt to replicate the Lords' pro-Arab vote of June 1922 in the Commons, Sir William Joynson-Hicks, the Conservative MP for Twickenham,[16] supported by Sir John Butcher, the Conservative MP for York, took advantage of a debate on Colonial Office funding to move 'That, in the opinion of this House, the Mandate for Palestine, the acceptance of which must involve this country in financial and other responsibilities, should be submitted for the approval of Parliament; and further, that the contracts entered into by the High Commissioner for Palestine with Mr Pinhas Rutenberg should at once be referred to a Select Committee for consideration and report.' The Rutenberg contracts referred to the government's

---

15. *New York Times, Palestine Mandate defeated in Lords*, 22 June, 1922
16. Joynson-Hicks would go on to become Home Secretary from 1924-1929.

granting of a monopoly to the Zionists over the production and distribution of electrical power in Palestine.)

Joynson-Hicks began by declaring, 'I can hardly conceive it possible, that in a democratic country such as this, ruled by a democratic Parliament, the Government should undertake the very grave responsibility of taking over the government and management of Palestine, or any other country, under a mandate which is in fact a title deed and a Constitution combined, originated and prepared by the League of Nations, without submitting that mandate to this House.'

He then raised the matter of the Hussein-McMahon Correspondence:

> It is quite clear that we wanted the help of the Arabs during the War. A certain correspondence took place between the High Commissioner in Cairo, Sir Henry McMahon, and the Sherif of Mecca, King Hussein. I have that correspondence here – a translation of it. It is in very flowery language... but it is quite clear from the very outset that, before accepting the suggestion of the High Commissioner, King Hussein said, "I want to know exactly what the territories are in which you are going to acknowledge the Arab rights." Sir Henry McMahon replied, "Do not let us deal with boundaries now: these territories are in the hands of the enemy. Let us drive the enemy out first..." "Not a bit," said King Hussein, who was a wise old king. "Let us first get these boundaries defined, and I will tell you what boundaries I want." In his correspondence he sets out these boundaries, and on 24th October, 1915, Sir Henry McMahon replied: "Subject to the above modifications, Great Britain is prepared to recognise and support the independence of the Arabs within the territories included in the limits and boundaries proposed by the Sharif of Mecca. When the situation admits, Great Britain will give to the Arabs her advice, and will assist them to establish what may appear to be a most stable form of government in the various territories." In August Sir Henry wrote to the Sherif: "We rejoice with your Highness that your people are of one opinion that Arab interests are English interests and English interests are Arab interests." In consequence of that, which I suggest is a treaty made between the High Commissioner and King Hussein, the Arabs took action.

Joynson-Hicks' account of the McMahon pledge, like Islington's, appears to have derived from the Palestine Arab Delegation.

Like Islington, he, too, referred to the Anglo-French Declaration with which, as he put it, General Allenby had 'placarded the whole of Palestine.'

Joynson-Hicks, like Lord Lamington, also felt the need to explain his earlier support for the Balfour Declaration. 'I was not then,' he said, 'cognisant of the pledges which had been given to the Arabs.' He was minded to do this because, before he had even risen to speak in the debate, the Conservative MP (and Weizmann ally), William Ormsby-Gore (soon to be Under Secretary of State for the Colonies) had raised the matter during an earlier debate that very day. His attack on Joynson-Hicks is worth recording here as it provides a fascinating insight into Zionist tactics immediately following the issue of the Balfour Declaration in November 1917:

> I understand that [the Member for Twickenham] is going to lead the attack not only on the Rutenberg scheme, but on the British Mandate in Palestine and the Zionist movement generally. If I may be allowed to say so, I think it comes singularly ill from him. On 4th November, 1917, at the time of the Balfour Declaration, which is the foundation of British policy in Palestine, the hon. Member... wrote to the Zionist organisation, in response to a request for his views on the Declaration, as follows: "I consider that one of the greatest outcomes of this terrible War will be the rescue of Palestine from Turkish misgovernment, and I will do all in my power to forward the views of the Zionists in order to enable the Jews once more to take possession of their own land." [...] Personally, I hope that when the Debate comes on, the Government will be in no way deterred by the criticism, either in this House or in another place, from carrying out what was not merely the pledge given by the Lord President of the Council – now the acting Foreign Secretary [Balfour] – in 1917, but was also an allied pledge, given at the time by the French Government, the Italian Government, and the Japanese Government, adhered to by the United States Government, reaffirmed only recently by the Foreign Affairs Committee of the Senate of the United States, reaffirmed in the Peace Treaty, included in the Draft Treaty of Sevres, decided at San Remo, and submitted in the Draft Mandate.

Ormsby-Gore portrays the Balfour Declaration here as a joint Anglo-French-Italian-Japanese affair. In his 1923 booklet, *The Palestine Deception* (see Chapter 7), however, Jeffries reveals that

'After the Declaration was issued the other allied Governments were approached by the Zionist leaders to confirm it. The French communique they obtained was adequate but cold. But the Marchese Imperiale, then Italian Ambassador in London, in giving the Italian reply, used the Balfour formula more or less, with a sardonic addition. He said that the Government of the King of Italy "will use their best endeavours to facilitate," etc., "it being understood that this shall not prejudice the civil *and political* rights of existing non-Jewish communities." The italics are mine. The credit is Italy's.' (p 30)

Ormsby-Gore went on to ask of Joynson-Hick's coming 'attack,'

> What is there against [the Declaration]? Certain excerpts are dragged up out of certain confidential letters written to King Hussein before King Hussein came into the War. If those are to be quoted as the reason why the Balfour Declaration should now be torn up, why is not the whole correspondence quoted, and why is it not made clear, as was made clear in the subsequent letters, that Palestine was excluded from the undertakings that were made to King Hussein? A further declaration that was made, at about the time of the Armistice, specifically mentioned Syria and Mesopotamia, and specifically did not mention Palestine. The campaign which has been engineered against the Balfour Declaration and against the policy of His Majesty's Government in Palestine, where it is not anti-Semitic, is anti-British.

As an intelligence officer attached to Sir Henry McMahon in 1916, his reference to the Hussein-McMahon Correspondence is disingenuous to say the least.

Ormsby-Gore's words 'in response to a request for his views on the Declaration' indicate that, no sooner had the Zionists secured the Declaration, than they began soliciting endorsements of it from British MPs. The latter could not have known at the time, however, that such endorsements would be used against them in the event that they later, in Lamington's words, 'learned wisdom' and felt the need to backtrack. As we will soon see, this is exactly what happened when it came to the pro-Zionist Colonial Secretary Winston Churchill's turn to enter the debate against Joynson-Hicks and Butcher.

To return to Joynson-Hicks' speech, the member for Twickenham told the Commons that a 'national home for the Jewish people' in Palestine meant simply Zionist political control of the country. In evidence, he quoted Weizmann's own words that it meant, ultimately, that Palestine would become 'as Jewish as America is American and England is English,' and went on to describe how 'Zionist political control has been gradually created in the administration of Palestine':

> I said just now that Palestine had been Zionised. I am not saying a word against the Government officials, but we have the High Commissioner himself [Sir Herbert Samuel], we have the High Commissioner's son, who is, I think, one of the Assistant Governors of Jerusalem, the Legal Secretary is a Zionist, the Director of Commerce and Industry is a Zionist, the Director of Central Stores is a Zionist, the Director of Labour is a Zionist, the Assistant Director of Public Security, the Assistant Director of Railways and Traffic Manager, the Assistant Director of Emigration at Jaffa, the Director of Emigration at Haifa, the District Engineer at Haifa, the District Engineer at Jaffa, the Director of Companies Registration, the Senior Quarantine Officer at Jaffa, the Assistant Public Custodian at Haifa, are all of them Jews and Zionists. I do not make the slightest charge against them, but when you have got a population, as you have in Palestine, very jealous and very much on edge, who are quite prepared to have English officials, observing that the whole administration of the country is gradually being put into the hands of men whom, rightly or wrongly, they hold to have different views as to the development of Palestine, is it not natural that there should be unrest in the country and that they should feel that we have not perhaps played the game fairly by them?

Coming to the subject of the Rutenberg contracts, which he wanted referred to a select committee for review, Joynson-Hicks declared that these were 'the most astonishing concessions I have ever seen or read of in my life.' He accused the government of 'blocking all applications for concessions... except from the Zionists,' whether Arab, British or Dominion, and submitted that 'this House is the only place to which the inhabitants of Palestine can appeal... They say, "We have confidence in Great Britain. We are diametrically opposed to the Zionist domination of Palestine.

We represent 90% of the people of Palestine. We do not want the country to be converted into a Zionist dominion, and its development to be handed over to Mr. Rutenberg who is to have a monopoly for the electrical and commercial development of Palestine. We ask that a committee may be appointed to inquire into the whole matter."'

Sir John Butcher, speaking in support of Joynson-Hicks, asked, with respect to the Rutenberg Concessions, 'What right has His Majesty's Government to tie up the development of Palestine for 70 years or for an indefinite time longer? This is all the more remarkable because the Treaty of Sevres [with Turkey] is not yet ratified. The mandate is not granted. We are there simply… as a conquering nation. It is the elements of jurisprudence that when one country is in possession of another country by the right of conquest, until some new government is established, you can only act according to the previous laws of the country. You cannot introduce new laws into the country. Still less can you grant at the expense of the inhabitants of the country large concessions, binding the present and the future for some purpose of your own.'

While other MPs spoke against Joynson-Hicks' motion, it was the forceful intervention of Colonial Secretary Churchill that appears to have saved the government's bacon. To be sure, his speech was all bluff and bluster, but sufficient, it seems, to have persuaded the Commons not to replicate the pro-Arab vote of the House of Lords barely a fortnight before.

Seeking to counter Joynson-Hicks' assertion that the Palestine Mandate had not been submitted to Parliament, Churchill asserted that,

> The House, as a whole, has definitely committed itself on more than one occasion to the general proposition that we should use our best endeavours to make good our pledges and facilitate the achievement of a National Home for the Jewish people in Palestine. There never has been any serious challenge to that policy in Parliament.

When one alert MP, Rupert Gwynne (Conservative), interjected that the House 'had not yet had the opportunity of discussing it,' Churchill insisted that,

The House again and again on most formal occasions has approved of the great series of negotiations in which these were included, and which is associated with the name of Versailles. There is no doubt whatever that the fulfilment of the Balfour Declaration was an integral part of the whole mandatory system, as inaugurated by agreement between the victorious Powers and by the Treaty of Versailles. These are decisions in which I have taken only a very subordinate part, and which the House at every stage has approved. And speaking as Colonial Secretary, charged with the execution of a particular policy, a policy adopted and confirmed by this country before the whole world, I am bound by the pledges and promises which have been given in the name of Great Britain in the past, and by the decisions which Parliament has taken from time to time. I know it is dangerous to go back upon the declarations which people have made in the past – at any rate, to go back for a very long period. For about 15 years.

The Balfour Declaration, in fact, was not yet five years old at the time. As to whether it had been approved by parliament, the former British foreign secretary, Viscount Grey, would later put Churchill's lie to rest by remarking in the House of Lords debate of 27 March, 1923 that 'Palestine is but one example... since the Armistice into which commitments had been entered into, or Mandates applied for, without... Parliament having an opportunity of expressing an opinion.'

Like his underling, Ormsby-Gore, Churchill read out Joynson-Hicks' words of support for the Balfour Declaration in 1917, using the opportunity to mock both him and Lord Sydenham:

There is an extraordinary similarity between the declaration of my hon. Friend in 1917 and the declaration of Lord Sydenham at that date. The terms are almost identical... It is very remarkable. Two great minds have moved together. Together they made this immense promise to the Zionists, together they pledged their faith, together they revised their judgment, and together they have made themselves the leaders of the opposition to this Government carrying out their policy... You have no right to say this kind of thing as individuals; you have no right to support public declarations made in the name of your country in the crisis and the heat of the War, and then afterwards, when all is cold and prosaic, to turn round and attack the Minister or the Department

which is faithfully and laboriously endeavouring to translate
these perfervid enthusiasms into the sober, concrete facts of day-
to-day administration.

For Churchill, apparently, there was no such thing as 'the cold
light of day.'

The highlight of his speech in defence of the Rutenberg Concessions
is surely its prologue, with its gross misreading of Palestine's rural
landscape and its gratuitous scorn for its Arab population.

After first claiming that the Balfour Declaration contained 'an
equally important promise' to the Arab inhabitants in Palestine 'that
their civil and religious rights would be effectively safeguarded and
that they should not be turned out to make room for newcomers,' he
claimed that the Zionists would 'create new sources of wealth' such
as 'a greatly extended and revived agriculture.' He then launched
into the following variation on the familiar Zionist propaganda
trope of making the desert bloom:

> As I explained to the House when I addressed hon. Members a
> year and a half ago, anyone who has visited Palestine recently
> must have seen how parts of the desert have been converted
> into gardens, and how material improvement has been effected
> in every respect by the Arab population dwelling around. On
> the sides of the hills there are enormous systems of terraces,
> and they are now the abode of an active cultivating population:
> whereas before, under centuries of Turkish and Arab rule, they
> had relapsed into a wilderness...

What in fact Churchill is slyly intimating here is that these
'enormous systems of terraces,' a traditional feature of Palestinian
Arab agriculture,[17] were in fact either the handiwork of recent
Zionist settlers or were inspired by them. One wonders just how
many MPs were taken in by this verbal sleight of hand.

---

17. 'The terrace is a thing of great utility to the hill farmer of Palestine. To
the traveller it is a thing of beauty as it climbs the hills with its artistically
irregular breaks in what would be otherwise a rather monotonous slope.
But with terraces and some water the earth is caught and filled with many
possibilities of fruit and vegetables. A hill well terraced and well watered looks
like a hanging garden. Much of the farming in Judea is on the sides of hills.'
(Elihu Grant, *The Peasantry of Palestine: Life, Manners & Customs of the
Village*, J.B. Lippincott Company, Philadelphia, 1921, p 49)

He continued,

> Apart from this agricultural work – this reclamation work – there are services which science, assisted by outside capital, can render, and of all the enterprises of importance which have the effect of greatly enriching the land none was greater than the scientific storage and regulation of the waters of the Jordan for the provision of cheap power and light needed for the industry of Palestine, as well as water for the irrigation of new lands now desolate… [I]t was only by the irrigation which created and fertilised the land, and by electric power which would supply the means of employing the Arab population, that you could take any steps towards the honest fulfilment of the pledges to which this country and this House… is irrevocably committed.
>
> What better steps could we take in order to fulfil our pledge to help them to establish their national home, without breaking our pledge to the Arabs that they would not be disturbed, than to interest Zionists in the creation of this new Palestinian world which, without injustice to a single individual, without taking away one scrap of what was there before, would endow the whole country with the assurance of a greater prosperity and the means of a higher economic and social life? Was not this a good gift which the Zionists could bring with them, the consequences of which, spreading as years went by in general easement and amelioration – was not this a good gift which would impress more than anything else on the Arab population that the Zionists were their friends and helpers, not their expellers and expropriators, and that the earth was a generous mother, that Palestine had before it a bright future, and that there was enough for all? Were we wrong in carrying out the policy of the nation and of Parliament in fixing upon this development of the waterways and the water power of Palestine as the main and principal means by which we could fulfil our undertaking? I am told that the Arabs would have done it themselves. Who is going to believe that? Left to themselves, the Arabs of Palestine would not in a thousand years have taken effective steps towards the irrigation and electrification of Palestine. They would have been quite content to dwell – a handful of philosophic people – in the wasted sun-scorched plains, letting the waters of the Jordan continue to flow unbridled and unharnessed into the Dead Sea.

Churchill concluded his lengthy defence of the Concessions with an appeal to the Commons to offset the earlier vote in the Lords by giving the government a vote of confidence, 'because we cannot carry out our pledges to the Zionists, with which the House is fully familiar, unless we are permitted to use Jews, and use Jews freely, within what limits are proper, to develop new sources of wealth in Palestine. I am bound also to ask the Committee to attach significance to this vote because of the adverse vote recorded in another place a few days ago. I think that it was a very unfortunate vote. As far as this House and the country are concerned, it does not make much difference [but] this vote may have a serious result in Palestine. It might lead to violent disturbances... a vote like this, unless dealt with by the House of Commons, might lead to distress and bloodshed.'

In the event, Joynson-Hick's motion was voted down, 292 to 35.

It should never be forgotten that by behaving as if the Balfour Declaration were holy writ, and blindly defending it at every turn, both in and out of the Commons – despite the obvious injustice to the Arabs of Palestine which it entailed – Churchill has ensured his place as number three in the unholy trinity, along with Lloyd George and Lord Balfour, responsible for a century's worth of 'distress and bloodshed' in Palestine.

Needless to say, Weizmann was quite alarmed by these two debates. As he explained in his autobiography,

> From Paris we returned to London, to find debates on Palestine pending in both Houses of Parliament. Lord Sydenham, Lord Islington and Lord Raglan led the attack in the Lords, and in spite of a rather lively debate, their motion for the repeal of the Balfour Declaration won by a substantial majority. In the Commons, with such champions as Mr. Churchill and Major Ormsby-Gore, we had better luck, and a similar motion was heavily defeated. Still, I was greatly distressed by the outcome of the debate in the House of Lords. I went to see Mr. Balfour... and expressed my perturbation. He advised me not to take it too seriously, saying: 'What does it matter if a few foolish lords passed such a motion?'[18]

---

18. Chaim Weizmann, *Trial & Error: The Autobiography of Chaim Weizmann*, Hamish Hamilton, London, 1949, p 360

The Palestine Debates of 1923
'The pledge to Palestine to be an independent country is as clear as daylight'

By 1923, the Coalition government of Lloyd George and Balfour, which had suppressed the McMahon pledge, issued the Balfour Declaration, and laid the foundation for a Jewish state in Palestine under the cover of a League of Nations Mandate, had given way to the Conservative government of Andrew Bonar Law. Despite the change, however, the new government showed little interest in changing course on Palestine. Since a peace treaty with Turkey had still to be concluded, the Declaration's opponents in the Lords seized the opportunity to renew their attack on Britain's Palestine policy. This time around, however, they were armed with the data provide by Jefferies. Jeffries' January–February 1923 series on Palestine in the *Daily Mail*, particularly his translation of, and commentary on, the Hussein-McMahon Correspondence, can be seen in the March 1923 debates on Palestine in the House of Lords.

1. Pledges to the Arab Peoples, House of Lords, 1/3/23

Lord Sydenham (Conservative) sought 'To draw attention to the pledges given to the Arab peoples, and to ask His Majesty's Government whether they will lay on the Table the correspondence in 1915 between Sir Henry McMahon and the Sherif of Mecca, now King Hussein, on which their predecessors based the claim that Palestine is geographically excluded from those pledges.'

He reminded the House that 'His Majesty's Late Government [i.e., the government of Lloyd George & Balfour] always refused to publish this important correspondence because on it depends the whole of our pledges to the Arab peoples which were made in the year 1915. Ever since then,' he went on, 'the Arabs have consistently maintained that we have not fulfilled our solemn pledges made to them at that time. Surely it is only right and just that we should know exactly how our national obligations stand in this respect. As so often happens in cases of this kind, a version of this correspondence, containing the crucial parts relating to the pledges, has been made public. I am informed that this version is correct, and I hope that His Majesty's Government will say whether the portions which I quote are correct or not.' Sydenham then proceeded to quote Jeffries' translation before stating that, 'If the extracts which I have quoted can be relied upon as authentic, then it is perfectly clear that Palestine is included among those countries which are to be independent...'

Citing the Churchill White Paper of 3 June, 1922, Sydenham drew attention to the Colonial Secretary's bizarre interpretation of the McMahon pledge therein:

> The excluded territory is defined... as the portions of Syria lying to the West of Damascus, Homs, Hama and Aleppo. Palestine is, of course, a country in which France has no special interest whatever. Damascus is well north of Palestine, and the other towns mentioned lie almost on a bee line further north of Damascus. Mr Churchill, therefore, had to invent a theory of the existence of a vilayet [province] of Damascus which contained in its ambit the province of Trans-Jordania. Unfortunately, there was no vilayet of Damascus, and Trans-Jordania had never had any administrative connection with Damascus. I understand, therefore, that this distinct "terminological inexactitude" has now been officially abandoned, though I am afraid it served its purpose for a time. Your Lordships will, I think, see that the pledge to Palestine to be an independent country... is really as clear as daylight.

Sydenham also cited the Anglo-French Proclamation of November 1918, and quoted Lloyd George as saying, in September 1919, that "The Arab forces have redeemed the pledges given to Great Britain, and we should redeem our pledges." 'In spite of that,' he continued, 'I contend that these pledges were violated by His Majesty's Government. Nearly two years after this formal bargain was sealed and signed there was what I am afraid I must call a disastrous declaration which was made... in a private letter to Lord Rothschild. That declaration created astonishment and consternation in Palestine and throughout the whole Arab world...'

'By violating our solemn pledges,' he reminded his fellow Lords, 'we have brought upon us a host of unnecessary troubles and we have been involved in quite unnecessary expenditure. That, it seems to me, is the just nemesis of our wrong doing in the Near East...'

Then he reiterated a point he'd made in the debate of June 1922: 'In Palestine, I am ashamed to say, most of the Arabs would now prefer the return of Turkish rule to living under the Zionist administration under which they now find themselves.'

Sydenham concluded his speech with these words:

> I hope that the Government will say whether the version of this important and crucial correspondence, of which I have given specimens, is correct or not. If it is correct, then are we not bound in honour to fulfil the pledges which I hope I have succeeded in proving do actually exist? If it is not correct, then I really think that we should have the true version of this correspondence so that we may see exactly how we now stand and be able to judge of the facts for ourselves.

Churchill's successor as Colonial Secretary, the Duke of Devonshire, began his response by declaring that he 'was not in a position to satisfy the demands of his noble friends' because 'the correspondence is long and it is inconclusive' and its publication 'would be detrimental to the national interest.'

On Palestine, Devonshire invoked the official line laid down in his predecessor's White Paper. 'This promise was given subject to a reservation... which excluded from its scope... the portions of Syria lying to the west of the district of Damascus. This reservation has always been regarded by His Majesty's Government as covering the vilayet of Beirut and the independent Sanjak of Jerusalem. The whole of Palestine west of the Jordan was thus excluded from Sir Henry McMahon's pledge.' He further maintained that 'undoubtedly there never was any intention, when the pledge was given, to recognise the independence of the Arabs so as to include Palestine.'

In response to a final request from Sydenham to release at least 'those parts in which our promise is stated by the Arabs to reside,' Devonshire agreed merely to 'consider the point.'

2. Palestine Constitution, House of Lords, 27/3/23

Mere weeks later, Lord Islington sought 'To ask His Majesty's Government whether in the election for the Legislative Council just concluded in Palestine it is not a fact that the whole Arab electorate refrained from voting in protest against the new Constitution: whether, in view of this protest... His Majesty's Government will not now consider the desirability of modifying the Constitution so as to bring it into closer accord with the sentiments of the native population and the Arab community throughout the East: and to move for Papers.'

The proposal to establish a Legislative Council had been announced in the Churchill White Paper. The body was to consist of 12 elected and 10 official members, with the High Commissioner as its president. Islington saw it as a measure 'calculated to prevent the Palestinian sentiment being fully represented in the future,' and called it 'a parody of a Constitution.'

He pointedly asked,

> Is it not a positive irony that Great Britain, of all the countries in the world, under a succession of Governments, should be a party to enforcing this unnatural form of government upon a native people? Is there any other corner of the world where such a system could be contemplated, still less put into operation? I ask the question with all deliberateness: Why should Palestine be selected as the playground of this eccentric constitutional experiment? We have been told... that Jewish traditions for centuries past were connected with the territory of Palestine. But are there no Christian traditions, and those of the most sacred character, to be taken into account? Are there no Arab traditions, which, through the ages, cover a far greater period of time than the traditions of the Jewish race?

Islington raised the issue of those MPs and Lords who had had second thoughts about the wisdom of Britain's support for Zionism, after initially endorsing the Balfour Declaration in response to a request by the Zionist Organisation:

> When first this policy of a Zionist home was proposed there is no doubt that it appealed to many people in this country. They accepted it in good faith and intention, and were attracted by its conception. It was adopted very precipitately, and it was adopted, I venture to say, with a very imperfect knowledge of the local conditions and sentiments of the country. Many who held the view four years ago, on closer acquaintance with this problem and after the experience of the past four years, have completely

changed their opinion. Among those who have done so are many members of the Jewish persuasion. I wonder whether the noble earl, Lord Balfour – whom I do not see in his place – as the author and parent of this movement, would have directed his energy and exercised his powerful influence in its adoption could he have foreseen its effect? I very much doubt it. It must be admitted by all fair-minded people to-day that this adventure has proved to be a hopeless failure. It has failed politically. It has failed financially. And the longer it continues the greater will be the failure.

As would Lord Lamington later in the debate, Islington drew on Jeffries' expose of the illegality, under international law, of Palestine's civil administration:

> Speaking as a layman, I believe that the whole of this Palestine scheme is steeped in irregularity if not in illegality... There is to-day a Constitution in the country, which was established presumably under the authority of a Treaty and a Mandate. The Treaty has never been signed and the Mandate has never been ratified.

In light of this, he raised the matter of a substantial loan, made 'through the Crown Agents,' which required 'heavy taxation of the native population – a small and poor population' to pay interest on it, and wanted to know under what authority that money had been advanced.

Inevitably, Islington raised the matter of the McMahon pledge, asserting that 'the present Constitution is a definite violation of the pledge;' that the delineation of Arab territorial boundaries to accommodate French interests – 'territory which lay to the west of a line from the city of Damascus, through Homs, Hama, up to Aleppo and away up to Mersina' – was 'quite clear;' and that, therefore, 'all the rest of the Arab territory would come under the undertaking.'

He remarked on how Churchill, 'with considerable ingenuousness, of which when in a difficult situation, he is an undoubted master, [had] produced an entirely new description of that line... His interpretation was that it was not the city of Damascus that was referred to but the vilayet of Damascus [which] he implied... included Palestine, and that, therefore, Palestine was in the excluded territory, despite there being no such thing as the vilayet of Damascus.'

He raised, yet again, as he had done in June 1922, the matter of the Anglo-French Proclamation of November 1918, and asked how its posting throughout Palestine could possibly be reconciled with Churchill's interpretation of the McMahon pledge and his successor Lord Devonshire's support for that interpretation. 'No one,' he insisted, 'who has studied... the whole correspondence... believes for one moment that it was ever suggested that Palestine should be excluded. There is not an Arab throughout the East who believes in it, and nobody outside the Colonial Office who has studied it believes in it in this country.'

Following a lengthy statement on the need for an Arab federation, including Palestine, Islington moved '1) for papers showing the Budget accounts in Palestine during the past year both in regard to taxation and loans; and 2) for a full report of the recent elections in Palestine, explaining the methods employed and giving the numbers of both those who voted and those who did not vote.'

He was seconded by Lord Sydenham, who reminded his colleagues that he had called on the Colonial Secretary in the previous debate to publish the Hussein-McMahon Correspondence, and indicated that he 'still cherish[ed] a faint hope that the noble Duke will be able to publish the whole of that correspondence, or at any rate those parts of it which are relevant to my contention.'

Sydenham also raised the matter of Britain's right to hold elections in Palestine, or in any way alter the *status quo ante bellum*, without a peace treaty with Turkey. He touched too on the matter of Zionist immigrants, both those 'dumped on the shores of the Holy Land,' and those 'constantly passing over the northern frontier.' 'All this,' he declared, 'is directly contrary to the wishes of the vast majority of the people of Palestine, including, I am certain, a great many of the old Palestinian Jews. The people of Palestine would stop it at once were it not for the British Forces, maintained in Palestine at the expense of the British taxpayer.'

Viscount Grey, who had been foreign secretary from 1905 to 1916, and was at the time leader of the Liberal Party in the Lords, was clearly discomfited by what he had heard. He did his best to excuse the behaviour of the Lloyd George government, which had succeeded his in December 1916:

I do not propose to go into the question whether the engagements are inconsistent with one another, but I think it exceedingly probable that there are inconsistencies. In time of war you have to consider the direct and immediate consequences of what you do, and the pressure of the emergency is so great that no Government has much time in which to consider what the indirect and ulterior consequences may be.

However, he admitted to finding the post-war consequences of those engagements, 'exceedingly embarrassing.' As he implicitly acknowledged, this was because of Jeffries' published investigation:

A considerable number of these engagements... which have not been officially made public by the Government, have become public through other sources... I seriously suggest to the Government that the best way of clearing our honour in this matter is officially to publish the whole of the engagements relating to the matter, which we entered into during the war. If they are found to be not inconsistent with one another our honour is cleared. If they turn out to be inconsistent, I think it will be very much better that the amount, character and extent of the inconsistencies should be known, and that we should state frankly that, in the urgency of the war, engagements were entered into which were not entirely consistent with each other.

Grey then embarked on the following pointed critique of the Balfour Declaration:

Without comparing one engagement [the McMahon pledge] with another, I think that we are placed in considerable difficulty by the Balfour Declaration itself... It promised a Zionist home without prejudice to the civil and religious rights of the population of Palestine. A Zionist home, my Lords, undoubtedly means or implies a Zionist Government over the district in which the home is placed, and if 93% of the population are Arabs, I do not see how you can establish other than an Arab Government, without prejudice to their civil rights. That one sentence alone of the Balfour Declaration seems to me to involve, without over-stating the case, very great difficulty of fulfilment... I do not speak with any want of sympathy about a Zionist home. We have all, or most of us, been brought up to be very familiar with Jewish history from about the year 1,400 B.C. to the early years of the Roman Empire, and I admit that I was one of those who, when the Declaration was made, did not feel any antipathy to the idea of a Zionist home, but, on the contrary, so far as the principle of a Zionist home was concerned, I regarded it with a certain degree of sentiment and sympathy. It is not from any prejudice with regard to that matter that I speak, but I do see that the situation is an exceedingly difficult one, when it is compared with the pledges which undoubtedly were given to the Arabs.

He suggested, sensibly, that,

> It would be very desirable, from the point of view of honour, that all these various pledges should be set out side by side, and then, I think, the most honourable thing would be to look at them fairly, see what inconsistencies there are between them, and, having regard to the nature of each pledge and the date at which it was given, with all the facts before us, consider what is the fair thing to be done.

But Grey did not stop there. He not only called for a complete review of Britain's commitments in Palestine, but warned against what is called today 'mission creep':

> [F]rom the point of view of [the national] interest, I think that we should get rid of these commitments in the Near East. I know that the present Government inherited these commitments as a Government, and that although some individual members were parties to them, the Government as a whole are not responsible for them. That gives them an opportunity of reviewing these commitments with an open and impartial mind. All new commitments since the war which may involve this country in the use of force are things which need very careful consideration, and which ought to be avoided if possible, but the most undesirable commitment of all is the commitment which is likely to involve the use of force not against an external enemy, but against the very people in the territory in whose interests the commitment purports to have been undertaken. It is in Palestine that I am afraid we are drifting into that very sort of commitment.

Finally, he urged that 'commitments of this kind, including application to the League of Nations for Mandates, should not be entered into without... giving Parliament an opportunity of discussing them.'

Grey's political stature was such that prominent Zionists such as Sir Herbert Samuel, Britain's High Commissioner in Palestine, were filled with alarm. 'In March 1923,' Samuel recounted in his *Memoirs*, 'I was concerned to find that, in a debate on Palestine in the House of Lords, Lord Grey of Fallodon had used words which seemed to imply that he thought there was substance in [the argument that Palestine was part of the territory referred to in the pledge.]'[19]

Colonial Secretary Devonshire, clearly under pressure, claimed that 'the assent of King Hussein' would be needed 'before the Despatches are published,' but that, in any event, because it involved 'many other matters,' it would not be 'in the public interest' to do so. He promised, however, to give the matter (as well as that of the election results and the Crown loan) his 'most serious consideration.'

Devonshire also appealed to Islington and his colleagues to refrain from using language 'which may embitter a very difficult position locally.' He regretted that 'so large a number of Palestinians rejected this first instalment' of what he termed 'self-government,' and felt that they were not 'wisely inspired.' Instead of 'adopting this negative attitude... they would have been better advised,' he said, 'to co-operate with the High Commissioner and the British Government in... laying the foundations of that which it was hoped would eventually lead to a complete form of self-government.'

He concluded by saying that he would 'endeavour to see whether the information [requested] can be given for the benefit of the House and of the country.'

Needless to say, despite his undertaking, the Hussein-McMahon Correspondence remained officially under wraps until 1939.

Finally, in a reference to Jeffries' translation, Lord Buckmaster (Liberal) suggested that the publication of the Correspondence should present no 'serious' difficulty because 'what purports to be a complete copy of these Despatches has already been published in the Press, and I have yet to learn that the Government has repudiated those communications as inaccurate.'

Buckmaster continued, in no-nonsense fashion,

---

19. Viscount Samuel, *Memoirs*, The Cresset Press, London, 1945, p 172

We ought, surely, to know that, because it is impossible that documents of such importance should be publicly broadcast without the Government accepting or rejecting the accuracy of their contents. If those documents are accurate – and I am bound to say that, upon the face of them, they appear to me to be perfectly sound – they show unmistakably that there has not been, as the noble Viscount, Lord Grey, suggested, something in the nature of casual inconsistency between different announcements at different times, but that a deliberate pledge has been given on the one hand, which has been abandoned on the other. No amount of examination and no amount of comparison will ever enable the two things to be reconciled, because these documents show that, after an elaborate correspondence in which King Hussein particularly asked to have his position made plain and definite so that there should be no possibility of any lurking doubt as to where he stood as from that moment, he was assured that within a line that ran north from Damascus through named places should be the area that should be excluded from their independence, and that the rest should be theirs. After that it certainly does seem to me a little strange that in 1918 steps should be taken to secure the dominion of another people who were never mentioned at the time, and that the noble Duke should ask the inhabitants of Palestine to accept a Constitution so set up in order that they might work it as a step towards the independence which they had been deliberately and solemnly promised eight years before. I am bound to say that I am not in the least surprised that these people have rejected it.

In conclusion, the concerns of these British politicians with regard to Palestine, whether Conservative (such as Lamington, Sydenham and Joynson-Hicks) or Liberal (such as Islington and Buckmaster), may be summarised as follows:

a) That, in proceeding with the implementation of the policy of the Jewish National Home in Palestine, the government was reneging on a prior pledge to the Arabs, a pledge, moreover, the details of which the government was refusing to disclose. Once cognizant of the existence of the McMahon pledge, the Anglo-French Declaration, and the Report of the US King-Crane Commission, these politicians experienced a 'this changes everything' moment, which, in some cases, prompted a retreat from a prior position of unthinking support for the Jewish national home policy.

b) That the government, in this matter, was attempting to bypass parliamentary debate of the policy's merits or otherwise.

c) That important principles of international law were at stake, namely, the principle that, where occupied enemy territory is concerned, the status quo must prevail pending the signing and ratification of a peace treaty with the territory's former owner.

d) That the Mandate, which incorporated the Balfour Declaration, was little more than a vehicle for the transformation, against the wishes of its Arab majority, of an Arab land into a European, Jewish colony. Early signs of same were the stacking of the Palestine administration with British Zionist officials, most notably the appointment of a British Zionist politician, Sir Herbert Samuel, as Palestine's first High Commissioner; the attempt to set up unrepresentative political institutions weighted in favour of the largely immigrant Jewish minority; the mass immigration of European Jews; and the granting of monopoly concessions to Zionists.

e) That, to paraphrase the words of Viscount Grey, Britain risked drifting into a military confrontation with Palestine's majority Arab population, a fear borne out by the need to put down an escalating series of Arab intifadas (1920, 1921 & 1929), culminating in the bloody Palestinian Revolt of 1936-1939.

Coming from different political traditions and perspectives, the men who initiated and contributed to these debates should be given credit for having spoken out in the spirit of the Conservative statesman, William Gladstone, who famously described Britain's intention to initiate the first Opium War with China (1939–1842) thus: 'I am not competent to judge how long this war may last, but this I can say, that a war more unjust in its origin, a war more calculated in its progress to cover this country with permanent disgrace, I do not know, and I have not read of.'

As for the British Labour Party, which had a representative (George Barnes) in the War Cabinet of 1917, it is worth remembering that the leaders of the British working class at the time had no issue with the thrust and tenor of the Balfour Declaration. Jeffries, for example, cites a resolution from 'the Parliamentary Labour Party, the Executive Committee of the Labour Party and the Parliamentary Committee of the Trades Union Congress,' urging the government to support Britain's assumption of a Mandate for Palestine. It reminded the Lloyd George government of the terms of the Balfour Declaration, and urged 'upon His Majesty's Government the necessity of redeeming this pledge by the acceptance of a Mandate under the League of Nations for the administration of Palestine with a view to *its being reconstituted the National Home of the Jewish people.*' This, it claimed, was 'both in the interests of Palestine itself as well as being in the interests of the Jewish People.'

As Jeffries remarks, 'the Labour Party, or its leaders... intended that the Zionists in 1920 were "to get Palestine," though their language was more circumspect... Their petition asked that entire Palestine, no mere portion of it, should be reconstituted as the Jewish National Home.' He added, 'This is not the moment to compute the guilt, or innocence in every sense of that word, of the Labour movement in this affair. Enough to disclose that it took its part in the disenfranchisement of the Arab people and that it entreated the Prime Minister to accept (sweet word!) the Mandate.'[20]

---

20. PTR, pp 341-342

7

'A Series of Savage Articles'

We have seen how Jeffries' 'series of savage articles,' as Weizmann called them, impacted on the Palestine debates in the House of Lords in 1923. We turn now to the considerable discomfort they caused Weizmann and his comrades at the time, and examine how the Zionists sought to counter their impact.

Chaim Weizmann and Philip Graves
'I think Graves will be very useful'

The first indication of concern on Weizmann's part can be found in a letter he sent to James Malcolm on 5 February, 1923:

> When Mr. Jeffries was in Palestine I could not see him because he went up north about the day of my arrival, but my friends saw him and gave him all information, documents, etc. You see what use he made of it. I don't think he is altogether a free agent and he is probably acting under orders. Under the circumstances I don't think it would be wise for me to see him as I am afraid I could do very little good.[1]

---

1. *The Letters & Papers of Chaim Weizmann January 22-July 23*, Transaction Books, Jerusalem, 1977, p 239

By contrast, Jeffries' assessment of Weizmann, which appeared in the *Daily Mail* of 11 January, 1923, was, if anything, too charitable:

> Dr. Weizmann... bears the reputation in Palestine of being a moderate man. How far he was later concerned in personal efforts to oust British Chief Administrators it is not possible to say. But the greater evils of political Zionism were perpetrated in Palestine while he was not there: he was always travelling. In any case, his influence was on the wane when I left that country: we shall have to deal with strange faces and other minds. But he may be given some benefit of doubt over the Balfour Declaration; he may not have known the British Government were breaking their word to present him with it. When it was later to be made clear that it was a bogus present he should have returned it, most surely.[2]

Weizmann again referred to Jeffries in a 7 February, 1923, letter to F.H. Kisch:

> The one paper which is still trying to run us to death is the *Daily Mail* in which Jeffries continues to bombard us with articles, but one hears on all sides that this stunt has fallen flat. By the way, I have heard that Jeffries is an ardent Catholic. The *Daily Mail* is also isolated in its Turkish policy and in its Ruhr policy. The *Times* is quite friendly. Philip Graves is writing a book, which will practically be an answer to the *Daily Mail*. Sokolow, Stein and I have had various conversations with him and I think he will be very useful.[3]

In fact, Jeffries was *still* under Weizmann's skin some three decades later, prompting the then first President of Israel to pen the following words in his autobiography:

> [T]hough *The Times* remained dignified – if mistrustful – on the subject of Palestine, the other Northcliffe papers – the *Daily Mail*, the *Evening News*, and so on – launched out into a virulent campaign against us. In particular a certain Mr. J.M.N. Jeffries succeeded, in a series of savage articles, in presenting a wholly distorted picture of Jewish life in Palestine. His conclusion was

---

2. J.M.N. Jeffries, *The Palestine Deception 1915-1923: The McMahon-Hussein Correspondence, the Balfour Declaration & the Jewish National Home*, ed. William M. Mathew, Institute for Palestine Studies, 2014, p 50 (Hereinafter: Mathew)
3. *The Letters & Papers of Chaim Weizmann*, p 242

that the only thing to do was to annul the Balfour Declaration and scrap the whole British Palestine policy... [However], through all this maze we still managed somehow to progress, if with maddening slowness, towards the ratification of the Mandate.[4]

As it happens, Graves did indeed prove useful to the Zionists, publishing in 1923 the book, *Palestine, the Land of Three Faiths*, which Weizmann had envisaged, in his letter to Kisch, as 'an answer to the *Daily Mail.*'

In the preface to his book, Graves positions himself above the settler-colonial fray. On the one hand, he professes to 'not believe in political Zionism,' which he describes as 'an attempt to promote the artificial Judaization of the country by the importation of large numbers of Jews in the hope that this will lead to Jewish political dominance,' while, on the other, claiming that he is 'equally sceptical of the ability of the Palestinian Arabs, unaided by Jewish brains and capital and by British administrators, to make anything of the country, except in a distant future for which the modern world will not wait.'

In reality, Graves served Weizmann (whose fear at this time, as we have seen, was that the British would 'annul the Balfour Declaration and scrap the whole British Palestine policy') by attacking those such as Jeffries, Islington and the rest who were hoping for just such an outcome:

> Nor do I see what advantage can accrue to the British Empire from obedience to the commands of our Press Stentors, who cannot yet realize that our abandonment of Palestine would involve, not merely the abandonment of the Holy Land first to anarchy and then to the first foreign Power which desired to put an end to that anarchy, but the loss of the bridgehead of the Suez Canal and of one of our principal stations on our Imperial Air Line to the East.[5]

Jeffries had in fact made *The Times* correspondent's acquaintance in Egypt, in 1914, and (always the iron fist in the velvet glove)

---

4. Chaim Weizmann, *Trial & Error: The Autobiography of Chaim Weizmann*, Hamish Hamilton, London, pp 351-352

5. Philip Graves, *Palestine, the Land of Three Faiths*, Jonathan Cape, London, 1923, p 3

had written of Graves' *Palestine, the Land of Three Faiths* that 'His book upon Palestine... deserves reading. I disagree altogether with its conclusions, but if it strands the reader in the wrong terminus at midnight he will, none the less, have travelled first class throughout.'[6]

Philip Graves and J.M.N. Jeffries
'Stranding the reader in the wrong terminus at midnight'

Graves' book and Jeffries' *Daily Mail* reports constitute the first two substantive works in English on Britain's self-created Palestine problem. Since *Palestine, the Land of Three Faiths*, at least in part, was written as 'an answer to the *Daily Mail*' (in Weizmann's words), we will focus at this point on Graves' bones of contention with Jeffries, drawing on the latter's 'savage' journalism where required.

Chief among these of course, was the Balfour Declaration. Graves' treatment of it is superficial to say the least:

> At the end of 1916 it came to the knowledge of the British Government that Germany contemplated making certain offers to the Zionist Jews in order to win their moral support. It was also alleged that Talaat Pasha, the Grand Vizier of Turkey, had approached prominent German and neutral Zionists... and had made offers to them with the same object. Learning of this attempt to secure moral support and perhaps financial assistance from neutral Zionists, the British Government began to study the Zionist problem. There had always been considerable sympathy with Zionist aspirations in Bible-reading England, and the problem of the Eastern Jews had been studied... by British observers.[7]

He notes that, 'In October, 1916, the leading Zionists in England made certain proposals to the British Government... regarded as forming a basis for discussion'; mentions a February 1917 meeting with Sykes; notes that 'Meanwhile the Russian Revolution took place and the Foreign Office appears to have laid a memorandum

---

6. FE, p 222
7. Graves, pp 41-42

before the War Cabinet in which it pointed out that British support
of Zionism might have a good effect in Russia'; and asserts that,
because 'Jews were playing a prominent part in the Russian
Revolution,' Zionism became 'an important political issue' for
Britain's war cabinet, which realised that 'something must be done
to bring Jewish opinion in Russia to the side of the Allies and to
influence American Jewish sentiment.'[8]

Then comes his first direct reference to Jeffries:

> On July 18, 1917, a draft text of what was afterwards known as
> the Balfour Declaration was submitted by Lord Rothschild to Mr.
> Balfour. But both the British Government and a number of non-
> Zionist British Jews raised objections to the wording of the draft.
> Mr. J.M. Jeffries, in one of a series of anti-Zionist articles recently
> published in *The Daily Mail* (January 9, 1923), suggests that
> the word "National" in the "key-phrase," viz. "National Home
> of the Jewish People," was retained in the Balfour Declaration
> against the wishes of these non-Zionist Jews and in deference to
> the insistence of the Zionists.[9]

In rebuttal, Graves quotes the Jewish writer and philosopher,
Dr. Asher Ginzberg's (Achad Ha-Am) assertion that the Zionists
'attached far more importance to the article 'a' preceding the
adjective "National" than to the adjective itself.'[10]

His one and only criticism of the Declaration comes next:

> Vague, perhaps purposely vague, as is the phraseology of the
> Declaration – *cf*. The reference to the "civil" rights of the non-
> Jews of Palestine wherein the adjective "civil" has no clear
> meaning – it aroused the enthusiasm of large numbers of Jews.[11]

Needless to say, Graves' perfunctory account of the history
of the Declaration, and his single reference to its phraseology,
hardly bear comparison with Jeffries's bold critique, as set forth
in his *Daily Mail* reports of 1923. Two extracts suffice to show
the difference.

---

8. Graves, pp 43-44
9. Graves, p 44
10. Graves, p 45
11. Graves, p 46

The first is taken from his article of 8 January, under the headline, "*National Home for the Jews.*" *Insincerity & Illusion. An Exhaustive Expose*:

> When, in the course of the war, our late Cabinet had to decide what should be the fate of the Holy Land, and especially what part Great Britain was to play there, surely only one course was open to them. That was to be just and straightforward; to determine that at least on that sacred soil each word they uttered should bear nothing but its plain meaning, and each act be done for no other reason than the reason openly they gave.
>
> What they did was the exact opposite. They forced political Zionism on Palestine's unwilling people, while pretending to leave their rights unimpaired. They let it be understood they were moved with deep sympathy with Zionism, whereas the sympathy with Zionism of most of them was mediocre, and in the case of one or two more akin to curiosity upon the results of a quaint experiment. Their real motives were, firstly, to obtain the world-wide support of Zionism's supposed hidden powers; secondly, to establish in a strategic corner of the Near East a body of people in close coalition with Britain. To have, as a mirthless Zionist propagandist put it once, "a little loyal Jewish Ulster amid the enveloping hosts of Arabism."
>
> While, as an essay in plain speaking, our then Government produced as their gospel in Palestine the Balfour Declaration, a triumph of drafting of the plausible sort, in which deception is replaced by definition. A document which is not, as the general public believes, Lord Balfour's solitary emotional act, but the work of many minds, frequently modified and rearranged as its British part-authors shrank from the frankness of the various texts which its Zionist part-authors provided.[12]

The second comes from his article of 10 January, under the headline, *The Balfour Declaration. Unmeaning Promises*:

> 1) What exactly is a "National Home"? Nobody knows. The expression was used because it was ambiguous. To the Syrians it is explained as a home. To the Jews it is explained as containing the germ of Nationality, of a Jewish State.
>
> Fifteen months after the British Government had declared that it viewed this ambiguity with favour, Mr. Lansing, the

---

12. Matthew, p 25-26

American Foreign Secretary, was obliged to ask at a meeting of the Peace Conference in Paris what "National Home" meant. Dr. Weizmann replied that it meant there should be established such conditions ultimately in Palestine that "Palestine shall be just as Jewish as America is American and England is English." Mr. (as he then was) Balfour is described as having been "very pleased" with this reply. It is difficult to see why, since Dr. Weizmann had removed with his frankness a good deal of ambiguity.

2) "Nothing shall be done," says the vigilant Declaration, "which may prejudice the civil and religious rights of existing non-Jewish communities in Palestine." No phrase could sound better, but what exactly *are* "civil rights"? Again nobody knows. That is why the Declaration is so anxious to guarantee them. Observe that the phrase "political rights" is not used. Political rights would have been something definite. The political rights of a people are its ownership of its country. The right to have, as the Syrian-Arabs demand, "a National Government created, which shall be responsible to a Parliament elected by the people of Palestine – Moslems, Christians, and Jews."

"But to grant this demand," acknowledges the foremost defender of Zionism, Mr. Israel Cohen, "would be to enable the preponderating Arab majority – Moslems and Christians – to make short work of the projected Jewish National Home." For that reason there is no mention in the Balfour Declaration of "political rights" for the preponderating majority. There is no intention of guaranteeing political rights ending in a National Government. But in order to have the air of doing so, the vague expression "civil rights" is inserted. I asked one of the highest personages in the present Government of Palestine what was meant by "civil" rights, and he said, "Well, they are difficult to define." Precisely [...]

3) The people of Palestine are referred to as the "non-Jewish communities in Palestine." There are about 80,000 Jews and 670,000 non-Jews in Palestine. The wording would give anybody the impression that the "non-Jewish communities" were some specialised sort of bodies and not the mass of the population. Is this intended? Does Lord Balfour call the British people the "non-foreign community in England"?

4) Nothing, according to the Declaration, is to prejudice the "political status enjoyed by Jews in any other country." What

does this mean? It means that Jews, besides being put on the road to establishing a Jewish State in Palestine, are also guaranteed against not belonging to it if they don't wish. Political Zionism may look forward, therefore, to having their cake and eating it.

The truth peeps out very clearly from this part of the Declaration. If there existed no intention in the minds of its framers of founding a Jewish State, why were they moved to protect their co-religionists from the necessity of belonging to it? If the National Home was to be only a home, the political status of Jews elsewhere could no more be altered by it than is the status of Englishmen because thousands of them have homes in France and Italy. But if a State was erected in Palestine? Ah, then!... Gentlemen framers of the Balfour Declaration, what say you?[13]

Graves cites three other areas of disagreement with Jeffries:

[I]t is maintained in anti-Zionist quarters that the Balfour Declaration was concealed from the population of Palestine until 1920, and conflicted with the proclamation issued with the approval of the British and French Governments in Syria and Palestine in November, 1918, and still more with the terms of the undertaking into which we entered with the Grand Sherif of Mecca in 1915.[14]

Regarding the first, Graves writes that 'The statement that the Declaration was concealed from the inhabitants of Palestine has been recently published in England.'[15] For this he cites Jeffries in a footnote: 'The Daily Mail, January 10, 1923.' If we look up Jeffries' article for this date, we find the following:

"There can be no doubt," maintains the Zionist report, "but that General Allenby knew by the time that such a Declaration had been issued. But the military authorities obviously thought that any official mention of this fact in the newly conquered territory might mar the jubilation of certain sections of the population. Naturally anxious to avoid any friction which might hinder the freedom of further military operations, they preferred to abstain

---

13. Mathew, pp 43-45
14. Graves, p 47
15. Graves, p 47

from any mention of the fact that the British Government had promised to support Zionist aspirations."[16]

That is correct. Jeffries cites a 'Zionist report,' which says that Allenby 'preferred to abstain from any mention' of the Declaration following its issue, which is to say, he *concealed* it.

Jeffries continues,

> Now what does this mean, put into plain English? It means that the British Government has issued a Declaration so high-handed, unwarranted, and dangerous that it was an impediment to the progress of the British Army. It had to be suppressed. It does not matter essentially by whose orders it was suppressed. If it was suppressed by the orders of the Army, has any British Government before been censored by its own forces in the field, as if its pronouncements had been written by the enemy? If the Declaration was suppressed by order or agreement of the Government itself, how in the name of anything that is honest could the Government pretend that the issue of it was a just and straightforward act towards Palestine? It is a strange Magna Carta which cannot be published in Runnymede.
>
> The point needs no pressing. The very fact that the Balfour Declaration was not proclaimed in Palestine till 1920 is sufficient proof of its character.[17]

Now here is Graves' attempt to rebut the obvious:

> The German Wireless had already spread it abroad in the interval between its publication and the capture of Jerusalem on December 8, 1917, and after December 8 British newspapers were available.... It was not made public in the form of an official proclamation, since such publication was deemed unnecessary and also somewhat presumptuous. When the result of the war was in grave doubt, it was not a fitting moment to make any official proclamation of our intentions as regards hostile territory. The bear was not dead but very aggressive; why advertise our designs upon his skin before we had killed him?[18]

---

16. Mathew, p 41
17. Mathew, p 41
18. Graves, p 48

As for the man behind the Declaration, Weizmann, Graves is suitably impressed, discerning in him 'great driving power and the gift of personal magnetism joined to impressive mental ability, which is necessary to any Jew who aspires to leadership among a critical, intellectual people.'[19]

Graves' second assertion is that the Balfour Declaration did not 'conflict' with the Anglo-French Declaration of November 1918. Jeffries is again the subject of a footnote, which cites the *Daily Mail* of 11 January, 1923. If we turn to Jeffries' article of that date (*Misleading the Arabs. Contradictory Pledges. The New Babel*), we read as follows:

> It was November 1918, and everywhere there were lesser peoples under enemy rule the Allies were assuring them of their support in a formal fashion. The Arabs could not be left out. The Army authorities were determined they should not be left out, and so, with their interest in North Syria, were the French. What the attitude of our Government was it is impossible for any man to understand. As far as I can see, they had a lapse into integrity. But was it voluntary? In any case the following joint Anglo-French proclamation was published throughout Syria with full formality. Read it now, you who have read the Declaration of all the Balfours, and again when you have a little time to spare for wonder:
>
> "The end that France and Great Britain have in pursuing in the East the war unloosed by German ambition is the complete and definite freeing of the peoples so long oppressed by the Turks, and the *establishment of National Governments and Administrations deriving their authority from the initiative and free choice of the indigenous populations.*
>
> "In order to give effect to these intentions, France and Great Britain have agreed to encourage and assist the establishment of indigenous Governments and Administrations in Syria and Mesopotamia, now freed by the Allies, and in the territories whose liberation they seek, and to recognise them as soon as they are effectively established.
>
> "Far from wishing to impose any particular institutions on the populations of these regions, their only care is to assure by their support and efficacious assistance the normal working of the Governments *which they shall have freely given themselves.* To assure impartial and equal justice for all, to facilitate the

---

19. Graves, p 42

economic development of the country by promoting and encouraging local initiative, to foster the spread of education, to put an end to the divisions too long exploited by Turkish policy – such is the role which the two Allied Governments claim in the liberated territories."

The British Government did not push its claim, did it? What is to be said of a Government which spoke in such solemn tones, engaging the credit of every British subject, and yet had issued the Balfour Declaration and was treating even then with political Zionists "as of right" in Whitehall? If the government had been an individual, a judge of the High Court would have sent the papers to the Public Prosecutor.[20]

Graves tries to get around the inconvenient truth of the Anglo-French Declaration by claiming, speciously, that it 'was not addressed to the Palestinians but to the peoples of Syria and Iraq (Mesopotamia) and other peoples the Allies hoped to free from the Turks.'[21]

The problem for Graves here, however, as Jeffries reminds us in his article of 8 January, 1923 (presumably read by Graves), is that Palestine is merely the southern part of Greater Syria:

Palestine is nothing but the southern part of Syria. Our grandfathers, better read and informed in many ways than we are, were familiar with the name "Syria" as a country, and in their days many engravings and books of travel dealt with that country. The name had, of course, been handed down to them. Palestine had been recognised for generations as part of Syria, just as Sussex is part of England. The exigencies of the present half-mandatory system in the Near East have now, as it were, prised Palestine out of Syria and, for the sake of politico-Zionism in great part, driven us into creating the half-nationality of the Palestinian.[22]

Graves continues, unconvincingly, 'It seems to have been published in Palestine as a matter of routine by the Military Authorities who were responsible for the whole huge area of General Sir E.H. Allenby's command...'[23]

---

20. Mathew, pp 52-53
21. Graves, p 49
22. Mathew, p 27
23. Graves, p 49

We come now to Graves' third assertion, namely, that the Balfour Declaration does not conflict with the McMahon pledge.

He begins by stating that the Anglo-French Declaration 'cannot override the Balfour declaration, which was published a year earlier,' adding that 'The Palestinian Arabs, who assert that our "agreement" with the Grand Sherif in 1915 cancels the later Balfour Declaration, cannot argue that the Proclamation of November, 1918, cancels the Balfour Declaration *because* it is later than it!'

He goes on,

> But far more serious is the charge made by the Palestinian Arab Delegation and other opponents of Zionism and subsequently taken up by the sensational Press of this country, that the Balfour Declaration conflicts with the terms of our "agreement" with the Grand Sherif of Mecca... concluded in 1915 by Sir Henry McMahon... On the strength of this charge the Balfour Declaration has even been described as 'illicit.' ['By Mr. J.M. Jeffries, *Daily Mail*, 11 January, 1923.'] What are the facts? In the first place there was no "agreement" with Hussein of Mecca in the sense of a Treaty... Sir Henry McMahon gave certain undertakings to the Grand Sherif in return for assurances of eventual military support on the Sherif's part.[24]

So, for Graves, the pledge is not a pledge, it is merely an 'undertaking.' Yet, as Jeffries reveals in his article of 12 January (*Broken Faith with the Arabs. The McMahon Letters Disclosures.*) even Balfour knew a pledge when he saw one:

> Such is the McMahon correspondence. The pledges in it were formally confirmed in 1918, when the Turks tried to get the Arabs to enter into a separate treaty with them on the understanding that Turkey would recognise the independence of the Arab countries. King Hussein cabled the news of this offer to the British Government. Our Foreign Minister, then Mr. Balfour, replied through the British representative at Jeddah, thanking King Hussein for the loyal information, and declaring: "His Britannic Majesty's Government, in agreement with the Allied Powers, confirms its previous pledges respecting the recognition of the independence of the Arab countries".[25]

---

24. Graves, pp 49-50
25. Mathew, p 60

In relation to McMahon's deal-clinching letter of 24 October, 1915, Graves even quibbles (in a footnote) about Jeffries' translation: '*The Daily Mail*'s correspondent translates the Arab word *mawathik* as "Covenant." This goes beyond the ordinary meaning (cf. *The Daily Mail*, January 12, 1923).'[26]

Graves is simply wrong here. The word can be translated variously as covenant, agreement, contract, treaty, pact, alliance or charter.[27]

Graves also mounts a defence of Churchill's 3 June, 1922 White Paper and its thesis that Palestine was excluded from the area of Arab independence:

> The Secretary of State added that he was ready to bring evidence to show that Sir Henry McMahon was convinced that the Grand Sherif of Mecca was not under the impression that Palestine was included in the "independent" Arab area. But all his denials have not prevented the Arab Delegation from inditing a long reply full of verbal and geographical quibbles to his enclosure, in which its members refuse to accept his interpretation. Nor have they prevented the industrious Mr. Jeffries from writing nearly two columns in *The Daily Mail*, based on the rather singular premise, Syria=Palestine, to prove that Mr. Churchill threw his pledge and "the word and honour of England" into "the waste-paper basket."[28]

In his article of 13 January, 1923 (*Inventing a Province. Vilayet of Churchill. Pledge in Waste-Paper Basket*), presumably read by Graves, Jeffries refers to the Palestinian Arab Delegation, which had come to London to press for 'the revocation of the Balfour Declaration,' and points out that its case was based on the 1915 McMahon pledge, the 1918 Anglo-French Proclamation, Balfour's 1918 reaffirmation of the McMahon pledge, and the Arabs' natural rights of possession. Jeffries writes,

> The [Arab] claim is luminous in its simplicity. In the Shereef's letter he proposes among the boundaries of the Arab kingdom… the Mediterranean on the west. *Within these limits lies Palestine.*

---

26. Graves, p 51

27. See Hans Wehr, *A Dictionary of Modern Written Arabic* (Arabic-English) Edited by J Milton, Cowan, Otto Harrassawitz, Wiesbaden, 1979, p 1229

28. Graves, pp 52-53. See also PTR, p 477

Sir Henry McMahon in his letter says, "*We accept these boundaries with modifications.*" Could anything be clearer? Unless Palestine falls within the sphere of the modifications, all is up with the Declaration of all the Balfours and the legitimacy from any point of view of the "National Home"... Now the modifications with equal clarity specify that "portions of Syria lying to the west of the districts of Damascus, Homs, Hama, and Aleppo cannot be said to be purely Arab and therefore should be excluded" from the Arab boundaries.

He continues, in the manner of a geography master addressing a particularly thick student by the name of Winston Churchill:

Get an atlas of your own out, if you like, to find what are these portions of Syria. It is as easy as possible. Find Damascus first: it is the key place. There it is in the centre of Syria; roughly speaking, the French mandatory area is north, the British south. The French overlaps a little. Where is the next place, now, Homs? North. Where is Hama? North again. Where is Aleppo? Northernmost of all. The four towns form a line, as it were, on the desert's edge. What are the excluded portions lying west of them? Approximately it is the country facing Cyprus, comprising the towns of Sidon, Beyrout, Tripoli, Latakia, Antioch as we go up towards Alexandretta, Mersina, and the rest of the excluded land.

Where does Palestine lie? Where are Haifa, Nablus, Jaffa, Jerusalem, the cities and towns of Palestine? South, south, far to the south. The decisive line that went westward from Damascus struck the coast between Tyre and Sidon... Below it, safe from exclusion, are the cities of Palestine, 60, 80, 120 miles below. Besides, does not Sir Henry McMahon only speak of reconsideration where "the interests of France are interwoven"? And the Shereef Hussein in his final letter, has he anything more to ask for but "*the northern parts* and their coasts... now left to France"? And "France" stops some 15 miles below Tyre. All that is south goes, by the word of Sir Henry McMahon, which is the word of Great Britain, to form an independent kingdom for the Arabs. And yet our Cabinet could impose a "Jewish National Home" within these boundaries to the conservation of which it was pledged!

Did that Cabinet put forward no defence of its action? Better by far for that Cabinet if it had never done so. But through the mouth of Winston Churchill it did. Listen to him: "This promise to recognise the independence of the Arabs was given subject to a reservation made in the same letter, which excluded from its scope the country lying to the west of the vilayet (province) of Damascus."

The then Colonial Secretary added that since this vilayet included the whole of Transjordania, therefore the portions to the west of it, the excluded portions, covered Palestine as it now is. That is to say, he paid no attention to the names of Homs, Hama, and Aleppo, in the McMahon text, the line of towns going north from Damascus, but produced as from a conjuror's tall hat a line going *south* from Damascus which satisfied his requirements.

Now, if this Churchillian line were genuine the whole of Syria would have been excluded, since Homs, Hama, and Aleppo would have excluded the northern part. It stands to reason that if the British high contracting parties had meant to exclude all Syria they would have specified "Syria." The phraseology imputed by Mr. Churchill to himself and his colleagues is preposterous...

But there is worse than this to come – far worse. In order to give a show of fact to his plea, Mr. Churchill spoke of "the vilayet of Damascus." The vilayets or provinces of Syria were those of Aleppo, Beyrout, and Suriya (our word Syria is a corruption of this). Deir-ez-Zor, the Lebanon, and Jerusalem were self-sufficing sanjaks or counties outside the vilayets... These were the only divisions of the country. *There is no vilayet of Damascus; it does not exist!* Naturally, it is not to be found in the McMahon text; if you read you will see the word used is "district" (*moukataa* in the Arabic). As in English, it is a word of loose general meaning, with the sense of the immediate surroundings of a city. Whereas, by speaking of a supposed vilayet or province, Mr. Churchill could make it stretch far south, and exclude any desired stretches of territory that got in its way. The Palestine delegates icily pointed out to him the inexistence of the "vilayet of Damascus."

A pretty position for a British Minister. He had invented a province and invented a territory. It was in vain. He was proved wrong. The pledge stood. Now comes what I regret to have to recall. It may well have been that when Mr. Churchill made his reply he had depended upon geographical information drawn from an official of his Ministry who had made a mistake. Ministers and officials are human and make such mistakes. *But,* when the errors are discovered, what do they do? We have been prone to think that they honourably repair them and revoke any action founded upon the error. Did Mr. Churchill set about redeeming the British pledge? Listen to his astonishing reply to the Syrian Delegation.

"The comments you were good enough to offer [J.M.N.J.: i.e., 'There is no vilayet of Damascus'] ... were carefully considered by the Secretary of State, who, after consulting the authorities concerned with the early correspondence between Sir Henry McMahon and the King of the Hedjaz" [J.M.N.J.: i.e., after consulting Sir Henry McMahon] "decided to make a modification in the draft on a point of fact." The Syrians were proved right, so Mr. Churchill altered a word or so in his draft reply to them. No more.

Please understand what this means. The Secretary of State took up his reply to the Syrian Arabs, crossed out his own vilayet, "the vilayet of Churchill," put in "District of Damascus," left out "Homs, Hama, and Aleppo," added "this district has always been regarded as covering the vilayet of Beyrout and the independent sanjak of Jerusalem." Where was the recognition of the proved pledge? There was none. Where was the pledge? It had gone into the waste-paper basket. It had been suppressed. Unable to disprove it, the British Minister says, "it has always been regarded" as what it is not, and for him that closes the affair.

And the word of England, built up so painfully and lengthily by generations of Civil Servants and soldiers and merchants who have always in all parts of the globe kept their word? In the waste-paper basket, too.[29]

Graves makes one final attempt to cast doubt on the relevance and importance of the McMahon Treaty by paraphrasing a 12 March, 1922, letter of McMahon's in which he (McMahon) 'places on record the fact that in his letter of October 24, 1915, it was his intention to exclude Palestine from an independent Arabia. His reasons for restricting himself to specific mention of the towns of Damascus, Homs, Hama, and Aleppo in that connection in his letter were that these were places to which the Arabs attached vital importance and that there was no place he could think of at the time of sufficient importance for purposes of definition farther south of the above. It was as fully his intention to exclude Palestine as it was to exclude the more northern coastal areas of Syria. He did not make use of the Jordan to define the limits of the southern area, because he did not know whether at

---

29. Mathew, pp 61-65

some later stage of the negotiations with the Grand Sherif a more suitable frontier might be found east of that river. He concludes by stating that he does not remember having ever heard anything from King Hussein that gave the impression that the latter did not understand Palestine to be excluded from an independent Arabia. This is surely conclusive.'[30]

'It cannot be denied,' continues Graves, 'that the provisions of the McMahon undertaking conflicted with those of the Sykes-Picot agreement... But as far as Palestine is concerned, there can be no question that the country was excluded from the McMahon undertaking, and that, whatever criticisms may be levelled against the Balfour Declaration, it does not conflict with that undertaking in any respect because Palestine does not come within that undertaking's scope.'[31]

With regard to McMahon's gloss on his October 1915 letter to Hussein, it is worth recalling what Jefferies had to say in response to another letter of McMahon's (to *The Times* in 1937) along the same lines:

> This is well stated. The writer confines himself rigidly to certifying what he is in a position to certify, that is, the nature of his own intentions. He does not say that the pledge of independence for Palestine was not given to the Arabs; all he says is that he did not mean to give it. Very rightly, too, in the same measure in which he is categoric about himself he refuses to be categoric about King Hussein. He can speak for himself, but concerning Hussein, whom he was not meeting, though he was exchanging documents with him, he was dependent upon the reports of other parties. So he is careful not to put any rumours into Hussein's mouth nor to father upon him unprovable attitudes.[32]

He also makes the obvious point that,

> What any signatory of a treaty thinks or intends or imagines at the time it is signed is not of the slightest consequence. It is what the signatory signs that matters, and that alone... If engagements are to be abrogated by retrospective inattention or forgetfulness

30. Graves, pp 53-54
31. Graves, p 54
32. PTR, p 481

or failure to express oneself, then there is no longer any safety in texts, there is no longer any reason for texts at all, nor for faith amidst peoples. [33]

One is driven to the conclusion that, whatever insights *Palestine, the Land of Three Faiths* may contain about the state of affairs in Palestine in 1922, it is primarily a vehicle for Zionist propaganda, which is to say that it will leave the reader 'stranded in the wrong terminus at midnight.' Typically, while it is readily obtainable online, an original copy of *Palestine: The Reality* is nowhere to be found.

The Anti-Zionist Press
'Nothing but embarrassment, war and ruinous expenditure await us in Western Asia'

On 9 February, 1923, the editor of the *Daily Mail*, Walter George Fish, followed up Jeffries' series of reports with the following call for the government to pull out of Palestine and Mesopotamia, under the title *Evacuate the Near East! The Palestine Deception*:

---

33. PTR, p 483. Tibawi catches McMahon out with reference to a much earlier communication of his: '[McMahon] tried to explain his sins of commission and omission in a despatch scarcely two days after sending the letter to the Sharif. He said the aim was to write something at once acceptable to the Arabs and keeping 'as free a hand as possible' for the British Government in the future. Thus, and here comes a very serious misrepresentation, he claims that he made Britain recognise 'the principle of Arab independence in purely Arab territory.' But the word 'principle' does not occur in the letter at all. He then says that he was definite 'in excluding Mersina, Alexandretta and those districts on the northern coast of Syria, which cannot be said to be Arab, and where I understand that French interests have been recognised.' This is a most revealing passage. It refers to Mersina and Alexandretta without attaching any administrative description to either, accurate or inaccurate. It locates those portions of Syria lying to the west of Damascus-Aleppo excluded in favour of France as 'on the northern coast of Syria'. It refers to them, moreover, in the general geographical sense as districts. It is therefore certain that 'districts' in the passage above means *sanjaqs* in the *vilayets* of Aleppo and Beirut. Thus unwittingly McMahon himself provides the conclusive proof that Palestine was not among the excluded areas. That he asserted years later in a letter to *The Times* that he intended in what he wrote to the Sharif to exclude Palestine is of no consequence, since it is flatly contradicted by what he actually wrote to Grey only two days later specifying what exactly was excluded. Palestine was far away from it.' (*Anglo-Arab Relations & The Question of Palestine 1914-1921*, pp 89-90)

We published yesterday the last of the series of articles in which our Special Correspondent, Mr. J.M.N. Jeffries, has reported the results of his prolonged and systematic inquiries in Palestine into the financial position there and the attitude of the people to the Zionist regime.

Mr Jeffries was admirably equipped for such an investigation. During the war he served as War Correspondent in the Near East, and after the war he paid various visits to Palestine, so that he knows that country, as it was before the Zionist regime, and its problems. An experienced and careful inquirer, he spent many weeks in the mandated area last year ascertaining the facts. These he has now given to the public through our columns; and they throw a flood of new light on the Palestine situation and lead to certain inevitable conclusions, following as they do on the similar reports made for *The Daily Mail* by our Special Correspondent Sir Percival Phillips, last year on the position in Mesopotamia.

The first conclusion is that *British Policy in this business of the Near East and Middle East mandates is entirely wrong.* Mr. Bonar Law admitted on November 7 last year that he wished "we had never gone to Mesopotamia," and he said some days earlier that he was being "bombarded" with requests from the British public to "go out of Mesopotamia and Palestine." In fact, the evacuation of these regions would be hailed with intense relief by the whole country as an escape from constant risk of complications and war and from an expenditure which the nation can no longer afford.

Behind all our difficulties with Turkey are the questions of Mosul, Mesopotamia, and Palestine. We might have claimed these countries on the ground of conquest, but we did not. We claim them because the League of Nations has handed them over to us. But the League has no right to do this. Its action was entirely illegal, as it had not consulted the Turks. Moreover, the alleged mandate which it issued to us to establish a National Home for Jews in Palestine struck at the first principle which the League professes to uphold – namely, self-determination.

Mr. Jeffries has shown, however, that *the mandate does not really exist, and that our presence in Palestine is based on an elaborate system of deception* and political fraud, for which the unfortunate British public have to pay the bills.

Two arguments have been advanced for our continued presence in Palestine, and both have been effectively answered by Mr. Jeffries. The first is that we must remain there because of our pledges. As a matter of fact, Mr. Jeffries has proved that a whole series of contradictory promises has been given to the population of Palestine. The first pledge was that of 1915, when the Arabs were guaranteed independence and the possession of Palestine. The Balfour Declaration was not made till November 2, 1917, and was in flagrant contradiction with this older promise, as it asserted the British Government's sympathy with the Jewish "National Home." The third pledge was that of November 18, for "the establishment of national Governments and Administrations, deriving their authority from the initiative and free choice of the indigenous population," and was again contradictory of the Balfour Declaration.

So far as our pledges go, we ought to evacuate Palestine at once and not remain there. We ought, that is to say, to fulfil our first and earliest promise to the Arabs, who are seven-eighths of the population of Palestine, and give them independence, instead of trying to force on them with our aircraft and bayonets the rule of a mere fraction of Zionists.

The second argument is that we owe it as a duty to humanity to remain, and that in any case we are bound by the mandate (which, as had already been seen, does not exist). The best answer to this argument is to point out that the *United States was importuned to accept the mandate for Armenia. It refused to do so* as the American people would not take the risk of constant complications and heavy expenditure in Asia.

But there is a broader and stronger reason for evacuation. The British Empire has waxed great by "governing men as they wished to be governed." It is not doing this to-day in Palestine or Mesopotamia. In Palestine it is trying to foist on the Arabs the Zionist regime. In Mesopotamia and Kurdistan it is forcing on the population the alien regime of King Feisal. If we persist in this policy, then it may be predicted with certainty that nothing but embarrassment, war, and ruinous expenditure await us in Western Asia.[34]

Just how prescient that final prediction was becomes apparent when read in the light of the following passage, taken from the Colonial and Foreign Office document announcing the termination of Britain's Mandate for Palestine on 15 May, 1948:

---

34. J.M.N. Jeffries, *The Palestine Deception 1915-1923: The McMahon-Hussein Correspondence, the Balfour Declaration, and the Jewish National Home,* Edited by William M. Mathew, The Institute for Palestine Studies, 2014, pp 149-151

His Majesty's Government had now striven for 27 years without success to reconcile Jews and Arabs and to prepare the people of Palestine for self-government. The policy adopted by the United Nations had aroused the determined resistance of the Arabs, while the states supporting this policy were themselves not prepared to enforce it. 84,000 troops, who received no cooperation from the Jewish community, had proved insufficient to maintain law and order in the face of a campaign of terrorism waged by highly organized Jewish forces equipped with all the weapons of the modern infantryman. Since the war, 338 British subjects had been killed in Palestine, while the military forces there had cost the British taxpayer £100 million.[35]

Jeffries' articles on Palestine for the *Daily Mail* were published (with certain omissions and rearrangements) by the *Daily Mail* later in 1923 as a 72-page booklet, *The Palestine Deception: 'Daily Mail' Inquiry on the Spot*. A powerful and pungent polemic, it can only be found today in the odd state or academic library.

Other sections of the press at this time were unhappy with Britain's growing commitments in the Middle East. Lord Beaverbrook, owner of the *Daily Express* and the *Sunday Express*, visited Palestine in March 1923. The following report of his visit, in the *Daily Express* of 11 March, 1923, suggests, if anything, an even more implacable opponent of Zionism than Northcliffe:

At the request of the Grand Mufti, Lord Beaverbrook met in Jerusalem a representative gathering of Moslem and Christian Arab leaders from various parts of Palestine. After hearing a statement of the Arab case, Lord Beaverbrook replied:

'I was glad to hear the warm reception you gave to the name of the late Lord Northcliffe. I had for him a deep affection and a great admiration. When he saw the right course he always took it boldly. You will, perhaps, be surprised to know that he looked with friendly eyes on the Balfour Declaration when it was first made. But he quickly saw that the policy was mistaken. He became in his lifetime the principal champion and the greatest fighter for the cause of government by the people.

'For myself, I am a convinced opponent and enemy of Zionism. I believe Lord Balfour made a mistake. In order to prove that this is not an anti-Semitic movement, I may tell you I was first asked to oppose Zionism by a committee of British Jews.

---

35. Palestine: Termination of the Mandate, p 10

'Today in our opposition to Zionism we are unjustly branded as anti-Semitic. Our opposition is not inspired by any hostility to the Jews. It is due to the sheer injustice and utter folly of the Zionist policy in operation in Palestine. I have only spent three days here. In that time I have seen little. What little I have seen has strengthened and confirmed me in my hostility to the system of Zionism.

'You may trust in the righteousness of the British people, which has not often failed in the past. They will in good time respond to the explanations of the position that are being laid before them by newspapers so different in character as the *Morning Post* and the *Daily Mail*. The *Express* newspapers are glad to cooperate with these newspapers in a common hostility to Zionism. Mr. James Douglas, the Editor of the *Sunday Express*, is at this meeting today in order to get a closer and better understanding of the injustice which is being perpetrated upon you. The *Daily Express* and the *Sunday Express* will continue the struggle. We have only to persevere in order to conquer and to triumph over Zionism.'[36]

It is inconceivable that Beaverbrook's anti-Zionism was not informed and bolstered by Jeffries' eye-opening journalism in the *Daily Mail*.

Another source of media opposition to Britain's policies in the Middle East at this time came from the influential conservative weekly, *The Spectator*, owned and edited by John St Loe Strachey. The following editorial emerged only a little over two weeks *after* Jeffries' investigation in the *Daily Mail*:

Although we feel happy indeed in the possession of the present Government when we compare their directness, simplicity and absence of prevarication with the tortuousness and the shallow but glittering promises of their predecessors, we can see that the danger of the present Government is going to be the disinclination to assert a very definite and prompt policy upon critical subjects... A matter in which the qualities we have described seem to us to be urgently required is the problem of Mesopotamia. Although the case of Palestine is different from that of Mesopotamia we cannot help coupling the names of the two countries. We sincerely advise the Government to give up both. It is true that on paper the accounts of the new State in Palestine show no loss and that the British troops which are at present maintained in Palestine

36. Mathew, pp 154-155

would in any case have to be maintained somewhere. We are looking, however, at the future rather than at the present. So far as we can understand, the authorities in Palestine do not feel able to develop the country on the revenue which is at present available, and where more money is to come from is a problem as yet unsolved. But quite apart from the money question... we frankly dread what might happen in Palestine. The Jews who have found there a national home are in a tiny minority, and the feeling against them of the overwhelming majority of the Arabs becomes more bitter instead of more conciliatory. It is quite possible that there might be an explosion. If there were riots, if there were a constant state of disturbance, if there were a massacre, Great Britain would be held responsible. It would then be extremely difficult for us to wash our hands of the whole business without seeming either callous or dishonourable. We strongly urge the Government, therefore, to make up their minds to get out, not only of Mesopotamia, but of Palestine, while there is time to do so quietly and creditably.[37]

The 'tortuous' government with its 'shallow but glittering promises' referred to by the editorialist was, of course, that of David Lloyd George and Lord Balfour.

Christopher Sykes and J.M.N. Jeffries
'A brilliant correspondent'

Jeffries' role in the campaign to reverse (or at least, modify) Britain's Palestine policy at this time has also been acknowledged by Christopher Sykes, the writer, historian, and son of Sir Mark Sykes:

> The Times and the Daily Mail, both under Northcliffe's direction, undertook systematic anti-Zionist propaganda. The most important move in this newspaper campaign was made by Mr. J.M.N. Jeffries, a brilliant correspondent who was sent out to Palestine in the Autumn of 1922 in order to gather material for a series of articles in the *Daily Mail*. He served Northcliffe extremely well. He obtained a copy of the Arabic text of the McMahon correspondence. His articles appeared in the *Daily Mail* during January and February of 1923 and in them he made

---

37. John St Loe Strachey, *The need to withdraw from Mesopotamia and Palestine*, 24/2/23

public a retranslation of the full text of these letters which the Government had been at such pains to keep hidden.

Publication came too late for Northcliffe's purpose. If the letters had been made accessible to politicians and the public in the early part of 1922 they would quite certainly have altered the outcome of the Churchill White Paper [of June 1922], probably in an anti-Zionist sense though not necessarily so: by making it impossible for the Middle East Department to indulge in their vilayet-fantasies, they might have forced the pro-Zionist argument on to good ground. But whatever might have been the effect of publication then, it was another matter with the long and tedious negotiations at last terminated, the White Paper accepted, and public interest elsewhere. (The French had entered the Ruhr.)[38]

What follows, however, is puzzling:

The effect was also weakened by the manner in which the letters were presented. Jeffries's articles, for all their brilliance, were too long, too elaborate and too intemperate, drawing no distinction between the Jewish moderates and extremists, trying to make a bogey-man out of Mr. Norman Bentwich (a hopeless task), and launching into absurd accusations that Winston Churchill had embezzled public money at the Cairo Conference [of March 1921].

Sykes' criticisms of Jeffries are, of course, unjustified. To begin with, Jeffries did not find it necessary to draw fine distinctions between Zionist moderates and extremists, because, as he would later point out in *Palestine: The Reality*: 'Zionism from the start... stood for sovereignty. The pretences of partnership and of blended authority in Palestine – themselves indefensible – with which... it had been thought to delude the Arabs, never were the aim of the movement. This always was what Herzl said it was – sovereignty. The other formula was only put forward while it was believed that the Arabs might be deceived by a system under which they would only lose their authority by degrees.'[39]

---

38. Christopher Sykes, *Cross Roads to Israel*, Collins, London, 1965, pp 93-94 To clarify: Jeffries had made public, in his own words, only 'the relevant portions' of the correspondence.

39. PTR, p 39

As for the charge of demonising Bentwich, Mandate Palestine's first (and Zionist) attorney-general, Jeffries had done no more than report the 'complaints of Syrians and Europeans against the legal administration, and the complaints of the Jews themselves, for among the Jews in Jerusalem there is as bitter antagonism to political Zionism as anywhere in the world.'[40] And of the man responsible for that state of affairs, Bentwich, he had written merely, 'There is no Zionist on earth more ardent than he...'[41]

Moreover, if one turns to the dust jacket of Sykes' book, from which his criticisms of Jeffries are taken, one may read the following encomium from none other than 'Professor Norman Bentwich': 'Crossroads to Israel' is the most informing and most exciting book on the history of modern Zionism and Palestine, under the British Mandate.'

As for Sykes' allegation that Jeffries' had accused Churchill of 'embezzling public money,' quite how he managed to derive such a charge from the following passage in the relevant Jeffries' article is anyone's guess:

> The less said the better about this episode of the notorious £700 a week trip. The Companion of Honour came; reaffirmed the Declaration of All the Balfours, which was the least he could do with several of the original Balfours in his entourage; bullied a Syrian delegation which asked him to be sincere and abrogate it; was the cause of a riot in Haifa with two casualties; saw a Zionist orange-grove; took this as a proof that only Zionists could make anything of the country; and went back to Cairo. All that has to be said of this is that at £100 a day the cost of word-breaking had been raised upon the luckless British people. The then Premier even broke more economically at San Remo.[42]

'Nevertheless,' concluded Sykes, 'the publication of the letters was the cause of grave Jewish anxiety, and it heartened the anti-Zionists in the House of Lords to return to the attack.'

---

40. Mathew, p 94
41. Mathew, p 93
42. Mathew, p 88

William M. Mathew, in the introduction to *The Palestine Deception 1915-1923*, offers this measured assessment of Jeffries' role and achievement at the time:

> The timing of Jeffries' articles... was opportune and almost certainly intended as a determining contribution to debate in London... Absolutely critical to Jeffries' influence was his offering, for the first time, of extended translations from the Arabic of the [Hussein-McMahon Correspondence]... Successive British governments, conscious of the contradiction, for Palestine at least, between this pledge and the subsequent commitment to a Jewish national home, refused to publish these documents until 1939. As the parliamentary debates make clear, it was the accusation of official double-dealing that constituted the principal significance of Jeffries' work.[43]

Aftermath
'The future of Palestine cannot possibly be left to be determined by the temporary impressions and feelings of the Arab majority in the country of the present day'

Finally, to round off the story of Lord Islington's interventions to pre-empt what he termed Palestine's 'Zionist system of Government,' it should be pointed out that, three months after the 27 March, 1923 debate, on 27 June, he again called on the government to 'reconsider their present policy,' warning that 'There is only one way of maintaining a system which is disliked... by the people of a country, and that is by force.'[44]

On this occasion, he found himself up against Viscount Milner (Conservative), one of the architects of the Balfour Declaration, and Churchill's predecessor as Colonial Secretary. Milner breezily

---

43. Mathew, pp 3-4

44. During a 3/12/30 debate on Zionist land purchases, Islington remarked that 'we have already had 3 explosions – one in 1920, one in 1921, and a more serious one in 1929, and, unless effective measures are taken, I have not the slightest doubt that we shall hear of another one before very long.' He died on 6 December, 1936, but lived long enough to see the beginnings of the biggest Palestinian 'explosion' of them all, the revolt of 1936–39.

assured the House that 'we have only to go on steadily with the policy of the Balfour Declaration as we have ourselves interpreted it in order to see great material progress in Palestine and a gradual subsidence of the present agitation... which I believe to be largely due to artificial stimulus and... excited from without.'[45]

Milner's main plea, however, was that Palestine was not just another Arab country:

> If the Arabs go the length of claiming Palestine as one of their countries in the same sense as Mesopotamia or Arabia proper is an Arab country, then I think they are flying in the face of facts, of all history, of all tradition, and of associations of the most important character – I had almost said the most sacred character. Palestine can never be regarded as a country on the same footing as the other Arab countries. You cannot ignore all history and tradition in the matter. You cannot ignore the fact that this is the cradle of two of the great religions of the world. It is a sacred land to the Arabs, but it is also a sacred land to the Jew and the Christian, and the future of Palestine cannot possibly be left to be determined by the temporary impressions and feelings of the Arab majority in the country of the present day.

This outrageous statement echoed Balfour's equally outrageous statement, already cited, namely that 'Zionism, be it right or wrong, good or bad, is rooted in age-long tradition, in present needs, in future hopes, of far profounder import than the desires and prejudices of the 700,000 Arabs who now inhabit that ancient land.'

The Colonial Secretary, the Duke of Devonshire, who had, in the earlier 27 March debate, promised to give the matter of the release of the Hussein-McMahon Correspondence his 'most serious consideration,' resorted this time around to a flat assertion that it was 'contrary to the public interest.'

---

45. Palestine, 27/6/23, Hansard

8

Pre-Reality Writings

Foreign Correspondent (1923–33)

The remaining ten years of Jeffries' career as a foreign correspondent for the *Daily Mail* – 1923–33 – receive only the most cursory coverage in the final chapter of *Front Everywhere*. (Since the latter was published in 1935, it is possible that a fuller account of these years fell victim to the more urgent call of *Palestine: The Reality*, on which he would also have been working at the time.) Be that as it may, the salient details are as follows.

- In 1923, he was in Switzerland, writing about winter sports, and then in England, covering the general election of 6 December, which led to the formation of Britain's first Labour government.

- In 1924, following a stint in the south of France, he was back in London, 'in Piccadilly, in the Strand, in Cheapside and in Oxford Street, in Knightsbridge and in all the thoroughfares where everything is centred but life.'[1]

- In 1925, Jeffries covered the joint French-Spanish military campaign against Abd-el-Krim al-Khattabi's Rif Revolt in Morocco:

---

1. FE, p 284

Outposts; camp-fires; Foreign Legionaries loping into hill-posts; forts falling under my eyes; Senegalese suddenly emerging from trenches, like jets of earth; ambushes crossed; rivers dried or swollen; slithering on camels in the rains; a cause imperilled; messages leading to Cabinet Councils in Paris; messages in cypher improvised from Roget's *Thesaurus* – that was a great year.[2]

'How is it,' he asked, in an essay, *Dangers & Doubts in Morocco*, published in *The English Review* of January 1926, 'that the second soldier of France [Marshal Petain] and the virtual ruler of Spain [General Primo de Rivera], with great guns and tanks, battleships and squadrons of aircraft and many men, are found leagued together against a mere mountain chieftain?'

In his essay, Jeffries described the diminished state of post-war France:

Bled ashen white by the Great War and the terrible epidemics which followed it... France has now literally not enough of her sons left to carry on the full work of the nation [and so] has turned to her great Colonial Empire, and has filled the thinning cadres of her army with her black or dark-skinned subjects. From Algeria, Senegal, Indo-China, Madagascar, and Tunis she draws conscripts; from Morocco she draws volunteer levies.

And he saw in this diminution the perverse rationale for this obscure colonial war:

France's empire, like any other, wholly depends upon the maintenance of prestige. Let that army fail to defeat Abd-el-Krim, and not only would it cease to be the international asset it has been, but also its own discipline... could not but be corroded by her native troops' loss of confidence in a ruling race which had failed to worst a man of African blood.

- In 1926, Jeffries reported on the work of the League of Nations in Geneva.

- He found 1927 'a mixed sort of year, wherein Spain and Southsea, George Bernard Shaw and King Zogu were blended in a diet tending to indigestion. But King Zogu's Albania provided engrossing material for me. Nearly everyone still

---

2. FE, p 284

wore national costume there; the people were so simple that when one of the few cars in the country splashed them with mud they thought it a great joke and roared with laughter, just as men laughed at mishaps in the Middle Ages in England.'[3]

- In 1928, Jeffries spent time on a variety of British warships, and, in 1929, in places as far apart as Middlesex and Grenada. Of the latter, he recalls whimsically that 'in planters' dining-verandas lizards clung to mid-wall in rapt poses of attention, struck to a standstill by my conversation.'[4]

- The period from 1930-31 saw him variously in Italy, the Isle of Man, Wales, Blackpool, the Argentine and Brazil.

- From 1932-33 he was in Ireland and the United Kingdom.

In addition to his regular reporting, Jeffries occasionally wrote highly evocative travel sketches. An example of these is *Stone Upon Stone*, published in *The English Review* of February, 1928. In the following extract from that piece, Jeffries wonderfully describes Montenegro's barren karst country between the old royal capital of Cetinje and the Adriatic Sea:

> From point of vantage to point of vantage, spiral by spiral, we went on till we reached a great divide. There all thought of the backward view was lost at sight of that which stretched away, not into the depths alone, but to the limit of prospect. For from that divide I gazed out for uncounted miles upon nothing but mountains and valleys of stone. By these the stone basin of Cetinje was but a pebble. No grass, no bushes, no tree nor plant nor house, nor sight of man or animal broke the measureless expanse, naught in any way retrieved the doomsday look of that desert heaved into the sky. Here and there in it, said my driver, there were some huts, and goats wandered about in the lure of provender. But as I stood and watched, nothing of that was to be seen. Grey and empty to the horizon, dry stone upon dead, it showed like a vision of the world's finish, of the shocking end of a materialist world. Broad day shone down, for the sun rode in a cloudless sky, but it was no more than an aloof display in the heavens, for there was no green, no soil, no

---

3. FE, p 285
4. FE, p 287

tint upon the land to receive its rays and to cast them back in the glow and the rebound of hope which enlighten the human scene. As I looked, I seemed to be rapt to some far and fatal hour, to some terrible eve closing in round the unbeliever. Out of the earth itself the sap was sucked and the marrow was drawn, and upon it silence had fallen. Men, too, were failing with their failed world: hearing and touch and sight were numbed to the last hold on life, and the whole universe was waning into nothingness. So felt I as I stared at that magnificent and monstrous sight; and then I turned from it and jumped into my car, and sped away towards Cattaro and the moving sea and time with a morrow. [5]

Jeffries retired at some point in 1933. By our reckoning (which is to say that of his *Times* obituary), he would have been 53 years old. Between the year of his retirement and 1939, he produced, in addition to *Palestine: The Reality* (1939), *Front Everywhere: The Reminiscences of the Famous Special Correspondent* (1935), the memoir we have drawn on, and *London & Better* (1936), a book of travel sketches of the United Kingdom and its capital. A short critique of the League of Nations, *Sanctions without Sanction*, also appeared, in 1936.

We turn now to a brief overview of the aforementioned works.

Front Everywhere (1935)
'A fascinating book by a knight errant of our own times'

The primary source for Jeffries' life thus far, *Front Everywhere*, was published by Hutchinson. Judging by the reviews I have been able to find, the book was warmly received by the press, a tribute to Jeffries' standing and reputation among his fellow journalists.

The journalist and historian Sir Philip Gibbs described it as '[a] fascinating book by a knight errant of our own times who went on his way to adventure, in peace and war, with a fountain pen, a gallant spirit, a quick eye, a poet's heart, and a whimsicality of humour which never failed him. 'Jeffries of the Mail' is already a legendary hero of Fleet Street, and in this book he writes of his own chronicles and gestes. They are vastly interesting.'

---

5. *Stone Upon Stone*, p 217

Gibbs had been in the same group of war correspondents sent to France soon after the outbreak of the war in 1914 as Jeffries. As Jeffries put it in *Front Everywhere*, 'An unaccredited, earnest group of outlaws crossed with me upon the boat to Boulogne. Amongst them was Philip Gibbs, then correspondent of the *Telegraph*. I was very proud of sharing difficulties with a man of such reputation. The future narrator of the British Army's valour and compassionate extoller of its sacrifices was in no better case than I was.'[6]

Jeffries' old friend, Compton MacKenzie, writing in the *Daily Mail*, called *Front Everywhere* an 'absolutely absorbing book... Mr Jeffries' account of the first days of the war in Belgium is of considerable importance besides being as exciting a tale of adventure as anybody could wish to read... there are too many plums in this magnificent cake to be picking out any more of them... one of the most vivid books about the war that has been written.'[7]

H.V. Morton of the *Daily Herald*, a pioneer in the field of travel writing, declared it to be 'The most readable book published on the war by any newspaper correspondent... enthralling because it is a splendid adventure story, and because it is illuminated from first to last by the charm of its author's personality... I heartily recommend *Front Everywhere* to all who like a book without one dull page in it.'[8]

An anonymous reviewer, writing for *The Times* of 24 May, 1935, had nothing but praise for the book:

> Mr. Jeffries, of Anglo-Irish-American stock, had scarcely found his feet in the reporters' room of the *Daily Mail* (Lord Northcliffe used to call it "the dog fight," and Mr Jeffries would not sharply disagree) when he was sent to Belgium. The War had broken out. Seven years of life abroad and a good knowledge of French were by no means the only equipment of this very young man for the work of war correspondent. Any brother of the journalistic craft who has had the good fortune to travel with Mr. Jeffries on a mission will be aware that he combines scrupulous loyalty to his paper with very unscrupulous interpretation of its commands, minute care in providing against possible obstacles with the most high-handed ingenuity in overcoming them when they oppose

6. FE, p 130
7. Quoted on the book's dust jacket.
8. Quoted on the book's dust jacket.

him. In Belgium he had very soon shown his metal. Told to stay in Brussels, he hurried off to Liège, and there saw General Leman as nearly as possible captured in his own headquarters by a marauding band of Germans.

He went, with a correspondent of this journal [Gibbs], to the Western Front, in the days before war correspondents were welcome there, and was duly foiled. He saw the defence of Antwerp; and, as he tells in one of his most brilliant chapters, bicycled back against the exodus of refugees in order to see the actual fall of the city. He went to Egypt, and wrote an account of the Turko-German attack in February 1915, which he wisely here reprints in full. He went to Serbia and saw horrors which his photographs and his writing substantiate; he went thence to Corfu, and reveals another side of his nature in a beautiful passage about that most beautiful island. He can fill, in fact, nearly a paragraph with the list of his "national shifts" during the war; and his last chapter makes it clear that he has not been idle or stay-at-home since.

Mr. Jeffries' book is more than a lively narrative of adventurous days. In its generous temper, its brilliant but always kindly sketches of his fellow correspondents (not least of two whose memories are affectionately honoured in the office of this journal, Harry Perry Robinson and Gerald Campbell), its level-headed shrewdness and, best of all, the revelation that it unconsciously gives of the attitude of the best sort of journalist to his employers and to his work, it stands out from the common run of reminiscences.[9]

Britain's Catholic press was especially fulsome in its praise for *Front Everywhere*.

The following review, by R.J.J.W., appeared in *The Catholic Herald* of 8 June, 1935:

J.M.N. Jeffries was a name long familiar and now sadly missed from the columns of daily newspapers. He was, and still is, a journalist with a personality. He writes with distinction, every paragraph is a signature in itself, and his sub-editorial interposition stood out in his copy like an electric grid pylon in the English scenery.

Naturally, there has been no such interference with his published reminiscences, *Front Everywhere*, a book which will be welcomed and seized upon with avidity by all of those thousands of loyal readers who can afford it. Its price [18/-] is the one drawback to one of the best war books that has reached us yet...

Front Everywhere is as exceptional as its writer. The fulsome praise the book deserves would be hackneyed. Everybody knows

---

9. *Two journalists*

the straightforward simplicity that has always been the hallmark of J.M.N. Jeffries' writing, his pen snapshots, his little kindly quirks, his unconscious trick of holding your interest by seeming to write up to you, the personality outstandingly self-effacing. [...]

Jeffries is at his best writing of his colleagues, and how those colleagues love the things he says! This notice has been held back purposely so that its writer might have the opportunity to pick up the impressions made by this book upon the minds of those who are doing the work of its author. It is spoken of with something more than any praise. It has been greeted with an affectionate appreciation by the men who know and whose appreciation will be most welcome to its author.

J.M.N. Jeffries wrote on nearly every front. He was scissored by nearly every censor with less knowledge, discrimination or reason even than was shown later by sub-editors, "the tailors of the Press... if they often slash broadcloth with wanton scissors there are times when they remove grease-spots from it in a twinkling and there are times when they mend invisibly the holes and the tears in shoddy... they join up the paragraphs which they have amputated with a dollop of a peculiar liquid-prose of their own, akin to such products as the liquid leather used to mend shoes... Many of the greatest talents of the press have sprung from amongst them... it is from amidst the sub-editors that the editors and the assistant-editors of papers generally are chosen."

Jeffries, so much of whose best stuff was in the nature of asides, suffered at least as much as anybody from those enemies who lie in ambush waiting for the lovely errant phrase that wanders from the point to make the story literature; and yet he can write like that about them and not have to stick his tongue in his cheek. That is Catholicity in journalism, and that is characteristic of his book, of his work and of the man himself. *Front Everywhere* finishes with the war, but it must not be allowed to finish with J.M.N. Jeffries. It must be the first of a series from a typical journalist and model for all Catholic pressmen.

Buy *Front Everywhere* if you can afford it; if you cannot, then get it from your library or, better still, write to Messrs Hutchinson and ask about that three-and-sixpenny edition.[10]

The Catholic weekly, *The Tablet*, carried the following appreciation, by W.B.N.C., in its issue of 15 June, 1935:

To readers of the *Daily Mail* the name of Mr. Jeffries must be very familiar, but few can realize the extraordinary nature of the

---

10. *War book of distinction*

career of this old Stonyhurst boy, who "butted in" to Carmelite House, and within a year sent the first telegram from the Belgian Front which got through to England. The *Daily Mail*, in the days of the first Harmsworth [Northcliffe], specialized in bright young men, as everybody knows, but it can be seldom that Mr. Marlowe "spotted a winner" as quickly as when he singled out Mr. Jeffries for what was then an adventure into the unknown.

A review cannot deal adequately with the mass of matter brought together in this volume, the fruit of the author's first leisure time since he entered the uninspiring portals of Carmelite House and kicked his heels in the reporters' room there in 1913, for it is a summary of the world's history of bloodshed for the intervening years. Many people labour under the idea that the reporter's job is to distort facts and to make "a story" which, in nursery parlance, is mainly "a story"; but Mr. Jeffries bares his breast and confesses to one story only, and a half story, in all his journalistic career. This engaging frankness, and the documentation of all the more important episodes, adds to the value of this great book as one of the byways of History; and, as we all know, it is the byway that gives verisimilitude to the dry-as-dust official historian's work [...]

How like to ancient history the events in Belgium in 1914 now seem! The hopelessly unequal struggle of a handful of ill-equipped men against the great and efficient army of the invaders; the sudden shock of it all – Antwerp, and the gallant but ineffectual attempts to stem the tide. It is hardly possible to realize that a generation has all but come to its majority since those dreadful days, which to some of us seem as but yesterday in their surprise, confusion and horror.

But, as we have indicated, the reader must go to Mr. Jeffries' own narrative for details. We must not omit his tribute to the "Venerible" in Rome, where, at the end of his school days, he spent a year before deciding that "I had mistaken my bent, and whatever my walk in life was to be it was not to be with a crozier. I was rather ashamed of myself; the English College had given me all it knew during that year, and I had given it nothing."

Interspersed throughout the narrative are thumbnail sketches of the great men of the war epoch, both on the field and at home, and many an anecdote lightens the gloom of the war pages. In this Mr. Jeffries catches the spirit of the trenches; for never surely, was there so much good fellowship and fun when we were all under the same condemnation, the same danger and the same miseries, in those ghastly ditches and frowsy dugouts...

Doubtless some of Mr. Jeffries' statements and judgments will be questioned from time to time, in the ordinary course of living history; but there can be no doubt as to his entire sincerity, his great powers of observation, and his remarkable memory, any more than there can be doubt as to his ability to "put his stuff over" in a pleasant, readable and humorous way. There is ample matter here for a long series of readings – now happily in peace – which will recall to many of us days which few of us would care to go through again, but which fewer still will regret having experienced. To Mr. Jeffries in his retirement (for how long, we wonder) our thanks are due and our good wishes are already paid.[11]

Sanctions without Sanction (1936)
'Weeping for the national rights of the Abyssinians and laughing at the national rights of the Arabs'

In 1936, Jeffries published a 14-page pamphlet called *Sanctions without Sanction*, a copy of which I have not been able to procure. Essentially a reflection on the hypocrisy of the League of Nations, a guide to its contents may be found in the following editorial letter by Jeffries, published in *The Catholic Herald* of 27 March, 1936:

> I am much obliged by your notice of my pamphlet *Sanctions without Sanction*. But will you allow me to make a poor return for your kindness by disagreeing with your own conclusions upon it?
>
> My argument is that the League of Nations, passing final judgment upon Italy, is in the situation of a supreme court. But this same court notoriously shrank from passing like judgment upon Japan in a kindred situation, and the moral authority of such a court vanishes when it fails to apply a uniform code impartially in all cases. Therefore the League's condemnation of Italy, given without proper credentials, was *ultra vires* and illicit.
>
> You reply that "a supreme court which has failed once or is even notoriously corrupt only yields its authority to a purer ordering of justice." Therefore, pending continuous justice, what I may call the League's justice-every-second-case-or-so keeps its authority.
>
> It all depends upon what you understand by authority. A corrupt court, it is true, can continue to sit for lack of any better tribunal, fulfilling a purpose which escapes me, but retaining, I concede, physical authority. Not retaining moral authority, though. I made the point in my pamphlet. The League still has the physical backing of the powers which compose it, and it has the practical

---

11. *A pressman's reminiscences*

authority to emit and to impose its verdict. But it no longer has the moral authority which alone can make that verdict just.

This is very important, because the League claims the adherence of the peoples upon moral grounds. It was created, of course, as part of the extremely physical Treaty of Versailles, but it makes its appeal, as our tired ears know well, to the conscience of the world.

Nor can I see that we are obliged to accept the standard of the League because none better is available at present. In the conspicuous absence of saints we ordinary frail mortals are all that is available on the whole to make up the Church, yet she does not take her standard from us.

A League which had a code and kept to it would have claims on the allegiance of all of us. But a League which defaults and pretends it has been inflexible, a League which condemns Italy for not keeping the provisions of a covenant which it has evaded itself, which weeps for the national rights of the Abyssinians and laughs at the national rights of the Arabs – no, sir, as the French say... *tres peu pour moi*.[12]

---

12. Jeffries refers here to Japan's conquest of Manchuria (1932-33), and Italy's of Abyssinia (1935-36). He is highly critical of the League of Nations in *Palestine: The Reality*, asserting that 'The sole effect of the League's connection with Palestine has been the discrediting of the League.' (p703) With respect to Italy and Abyssinia at this time, another English observer, Thomas Hodgkin, the left-leaning private secretary to Palestine's High Commissioner, General Sir Arthur Wauchope, wrote along similar lines: 'The contrast between England's attitude to Italy's treatment of Abyssinia and her own treatment of the Arabs of Palestine is one frequently pointed out by Arabs, with much justice. At a time when right-minded people in England are expressing their disgust at the successful conclusion of Mussolini's imperialist adventure in Abyssinia, and their contempt for the hypocrisy of Italy's gesture in "liberating the Abyssinian slaves" they might spare some of these feelings for the events of their own democratic empire. Palestine, like Abyssinia, was conquered in the course of an imperialist war. The act of aggression by which Palestine was brought within the British Empire, like the act of aggression by which Abyssinia was brought within the Italian Empire, was represented as an act of liberation, and for some time the Arabs of Palestine were compelled to observe the day on which Allenby marched into Jerusalem and their country was formally occupied by the British as 'Liberation Day.' The British and Zionists claim that they have brought 'prosperity' to Palestine: the Italians are going to bring 'prosperity' to Abyssinia. You cannot have it both ways. Either it is just that Italy should annex Abyssinia by force in order that that country should serve the interests of Italian capital and Italian imperial strategy, and incidentally enjoy better roads and railways and a more efficient system of posts and telegraphs. Or it is unjust that England should have annexed Palestine by force, and should now be holding the Arabs down by force, to serve the interests of British and Zionist capital and British imperial strategy, and incidentally enjoy better roads and railways and a more efficient system of posts and telegraphs. You cannot eat your neighbour's cake and then look shocked when another fellow eats his neighbour's sugar biscuit.' Thomas Hodgkin, *Letters from Palestine: 1932-36*, Edited by E.C. Hodgkin, Quartet Books, London, 1986, pp 200-201

London & Better (1936)
'An involuntary tribute to the city of London'

Hutchinson followed its publication of *Front Everywhere* with *London & Better* in 1936. This was a collection of verbal sketches, anecdotes and erudite, witty reflections on London and other sites around the United Kingdom, which Jeffries had written for the *Daily Mail*.

'Perhaps I should explain the title of this book,' Jeffries wrote in its Introduction. 'It is an involuntary tribute to the city of London. No tribute could be more involuntary than this is, for of all places which I know London is the place which I most detest. Why I detest it so I shall not delay to expound at the moment, beyond affirming that for five months of the year London blunts all human faculties and that then in its bleary atmosphere even the youngest perforce see the world with the vision of the aged.'[13]

Since our primary focus here is *Palestine: The Reality*, *London & Better* need not detain us further – save for the one sketch that conveys a hint of sunnier, Middle Eastern, climes - *Incident Off the Ministry of Health*. Here it is in full:

> This last week-end there was an incident off the Ministry of Health. Whether it was upon the Friday or the Saturday I am not at all sure, for, to tell the truth, it took place below the Ministry of Health rather than off it. It took place in the subway which leads to the Ministry from the bridge. When a subterranean location such as that is given to an incident upon one of these January days of London, who shall distinguish Friday from Saturday in the gloom?
>
> It was, indeed, a terrible SatiFriday afternoon. The pavements ran with rain and the wind howled round the inhuman piles of Government buildings. Into the cold sky the pinnacles of Westminster rose like academic prayers. Newsboys, hidden in doorways from the driving torrents, protruded sodden bills which told of "Floods Rising." Passers, struggling in the wind with cheap umbrellas, splashed by mud on their mud-coloured clothes, wet, hurried and crossed, jostled each other for omnibuses or scuffled into the subway under Whitehall to the corner of Bridge Street.

---

13. J.M.N. Jeffries, *London & Better*, p 15 (Hereinafter: L&B)

And there, on the fourth or fifth step down to the subway, occurred the incident. I almost stepped on a branch of mimosa, dropped by a forgetful purchaser. Its delicate articulations were hidden in the grime, its small puffs of sunshine were here and there trodden into the dirt and grit of the reeking stair. But it was not altogether trodden down; it still retained something of its true self; in a cluster of its buds still shone a thin, filigree flame of the south.

I had a notion to pick it up, for so to speak many a mimosa tree has been kind to me in foreign parts, and I felt the stirrings of gratitude. But we are a poor lot, most of us, as the poets so correctly say. I should have dirtied my gloves if I had picked it up, and besides I was on my way to a Government Office and already had half-prepared my Government Office mood. You cannot file mimosa. So I passed it by.

Poor branch of mimosa, no doubt it was crushed to death. It died in the dark beneath a blind heel, by the foot of one of those either lunatics or prisoners who inhabit London in the winter, and its scent went out.

Yes, that was a sad, a nasty incident in Whitehall. Where were the police? Having an At home in Scotland Yard, when they might have saved the mimosa from decease, and have saved me, as possibly you think, from writing this present falsely sentimental passage. But if you had met me in the flesh upon the steps of the Westminster subway, had marked how forlorn I was between dirty pavements, dirty rain and dirty sky, and I had whined to you: "Buy a bit o' sentiment, mister. It's 'and-worked," do you really believe that you would have spurned me?[14]

14. L&B, pp 84-85

9

Zionising Palestine
(1919–23)

The root causes of the Palestine problem, as Jeffries points out in *Palestine: The Reality*, 'have been kept concealed or as far out of sight as possible,' and are 'all to be sought within the period from the War to 1923.'[1] The year 1923, of course, saw the British Mandate for Palestine finally in place, or in Jeffries' words, 'the long-planned Zionising regime... finally in command, and the course of the country... fixed.'[2]

Thus far we have focused on the tangled skein of British wartime pledges, culminating in the issue of the Balfour Declaration, and examined at length the heroic efforts of Jeffries and others concerned with such matters to prevent the government from taking Britain down the path of 'embarrassment, war and ruinous expenditure... in Western Asia,' as the editor of the *Daily Mail* put it, or, as Churchill put it, when the British administration in Palestine came under sustained attack by Zionist Irgun and Stern Gang terrorists in the 1940s, 'a hell-disaster.'[3]

In this chapter, we will shift focus to examine how Britain went about installing the 'Zionising regime' of 1923, which paved

---

1. PTR, p 574
2. PTR, p 409
3. Norman Rose, *Churchill & Zionism*, in *Churchill*, edited by Robert Blake & Wm. Roger Louis, Oxford University Press, New York, 1993, p 165

David Lloyd George

the way for the later Zionist regime of 1948. The key events and developments in this process, with commentary by Jeffries and others, are outlined in the remainder of this chapter.

The Paris Peace Conference (1919)
'Was it worse to be slain and tyrannized over by French soldiers, or to be made comfortable but disinherited by the more subtle British?'

The year 1919 was dominated by the proceedings of Paris Peace Conference, which saw a struggle develop over the text of the Covenant of the League of Nations (founded in January 1920) between Wilsonian idealism (as embodied in the US president's celebrated Fourteen Points) and Big Power realism/ rapacity, a matter to which we shall shortly turn.

The Peace Conference is perhaps best known for the Treaty of Versailles, graphically described by John Maynard Keynes as a 'Carthaginian peace,' imposed by the Allied Powers on their defeated German enemy. But what of the Arab *allies* of these Powers? How did they fare at the Conference? Given that the Arab Nationalist forces had fought the Turks all the way from Mecca to Damascus on the strength of a British promise to recognise Arab independence in the Middle East, one might have expected them, all things being equal, to have done very well out of the post-war peace settlement.

Not so. Their very first experiment in independence, Faisal's Damascus-based Kingdom of Syria, was ruthlessly crushed by the French in July 1920, and Palestine (that is, *southern* Syria) was severed from its northern half by the British, and opened up to Zionist settlers bent on establishing a Jewish state regardless of the rights or wishes of the indigenous Palestinian Arab population. If, indeed, a 'Carthaginian peace' was imposed on the German *enemy* of Britain and France, what was imposed on their Arab allies could only be described as 'a-worse-than-Carthaginian-peace.' The following sketch by Jeffries in *Front Everywhere*, quoted earlier in Chapter 2, encapsulates this bizarre outcome:

> A curious memory of those days is a violent quarrel between two Syrians in a hotel in Beyrout. One came from the British and one from the French mandatory area, and they quarrelled about the conditions of their areas. Each insisted that his own was in the more deplorable state under foreign government. Was it worse to be slain and tyrannized over by French soldiers, or to be made comfortable but disinherited by the more subtle British? The two were yelling and trying to settle the point by fisticuffs when I departed.[4]

So how did it come about that the Arabs ended up faring worse at the Peace Conference than the Germans? Their only hope, in the face of Anglo-French designs on Greater Syria, lay with the newly formed League of Nations. But would it be robust enough to protect their interests from the rapacity of the victorious European powers, or little more than a rubber stamp in their hands? As a small people, exhausted by war and famine, and without influence either in London or Paris, the Arabs' prospects for meaningful input, let alone influence on the course of events at the Peace Conference, were bleak. As Jeffries puts it: 'The Arabs... dependent in the main on such copies of the Arabic papers of Cairo and of the European papers as reached their shores irregularly and long after events, were at the most extraordinary disadvantage. How could they fight their cause in Paris? How could they mobilize national opinion at proper moments and make Paris aware at once, in any important juncture, they were the most vitally affected body of all, and that account must be taken in full of what they thought and desired, and were determined upon? They could not do this: they had no chance. They were placed or fell into the role of a far-off, unconcerned, uninterested body... How could they manifest with effectual speed against what was being done to them, and the Conference, with Zionists fleeting through its corridors, took no measures to have them informed.'[5]

'Zionists fleeting through its corridors'? As Jeffries explains,

> At this extremely personal, almost private Peace Conference, the great thing was to be admitted to the privacy of the principals. The Zionists had all the necessary admissions, as inner Peace

---

4. FE, p 280
5. PTR, p 280

Conference history attests. In another world from the public conferrings, far from tournaments, in movements easeful and triumphant as high summer's, like bees visiting and fecundating flowers, Messrs. Weizmann and Sokolov and Wise flew from the President to House and from House to Balfour and Balfour to Lansing and from Lansing to Tardieu, and from Tardieu to Lloyd George through long honey-making days... Yet the Zionist group was the sole group in Paris which almost could have dispensed with these intimate visits. In one sense the Zionists scarcely needed to have anyone working for them in Paris at all, since it was superfluous to court principals, half of whom (and the dominant half of whom) were themselves vowed already to the Zionist dogma. Of the various Zionist delegations in Paris the chief was the official delegation of the British Government. Lloyd George and Balfour! Acetone and accessory! The next in importance was the official delegation of the United States of America. When Feisal presented the Arab case to the Council of Six he did so before men who had helped to create the Zionist case.[6]

Be that as it may,

[His] gist... was that the Allies were asked to recognize that the Arabs generally formed a unit in blood, in history, in faith and in speech. There was no question of trying to place them all under a single Arab Government, but they would form a natural confederacy, of which each section, the Hedjaz, Nejd, Syria, Irak and so forth would govern itself according to its own traditions and desires. But the whole should be placed under the supervision of a single Mandatory European Power which would superintend the construction of roads, telegraphs and such matters... [H]e also asked for the postponement of any decision on Palestine. No doubt he thought that this was the best he could do for Palestine to prevent the immediate development of the non-Arab projects, and... to get British help in saving Damascus. But his endeavours in this direction, and anything that he said indeed, were destined to be fruitless, for the Zionists already had arranged with the Conference leaders for their form of Mandate in Palestine, and by the 30th of January the division of Syria between Britain and France tacitly was agreed upon.[7]

---

6. PTR, pp 258-259. Rabbi Stephen Wise, Zionist Organization of America; Robert Lansing, US Secretary General; Andre Tardieu, Commissioner General for French-American Affairs and aide to Prime Minister Georges Clemenceau
7. PTR, pp 259-260

General Smuts
Drafting the Balfour Declaration and the League Covenant

Since the British ruled Palestine under what is known as a 'mandate,' it is important to know something of the word's provenance. The term originated with South Africa's General Jan Christian Smuts in deference to Wilson's opposition to the Allies' annexationist inclinations: 'Wilson dealt firmly with others who wished to annex conquered territory,' wrote Smuts' son and biographer. 'The best they got was a Mandate. Such were his scruples that he even turned down all the mandates offered to America.'[8]

Smuts, as it happens, was the key figure in the drafting of Article 22 of the Covenant of the League of Nations, 'the constitution of the Mandatory system' as Jeffries calls it. Its opening clauses read as follows:

> 1) To those colonies and territories which as a consequence of the late War have ceased to be under the sovereignty of the States which formerly governed them and which are inhabited by peoples not yet able to stand by themselves under the strenuous conditions of the modern world, there should be applied the principle that the well-being and the development of such peoples form a sacred trust of civilization and that securities for the performance of this trust should be embodied in this Covenant.

> 2) The best method of giving practical effect to this principle is that the tutelage of such peoples should be entrusted to advanced nations who by reason of their resources, their experience or their geographical position can best undertake this responsibility, and who are willing to accept it, and that this tutelage should be exercised by them as Mandatories on behalf of the League.

Smuts, however, was both an unabashed colonialist and a member of the British War Cabinet, with Leonard Stein describing him as 'among the architects of the [Balfour] Declaration,' although 'not quite of the same order as Balfour, Milner or Lloyd George.'[9]

---

8. Jan Christian Smuts, *Jan Christian Smuts by His Son*, Cassell & Co. Ltd, London, 1952, p 220
9. Leonard Stein, *The Balfour Declaration*, Vallentine-Mitchell, London, 1961, p 482

When it came to the former Ottoman territories of Greater Syria and Mesopotamia, the challenge for Smuts was to find a way around Point 12 of Wilson's 'Fourteen Points,' which stipulated that the non-Turkish 'nationalities which are now under Turkish rule should be assured an undoubted security of life and an absolutely unmolested opportunity of autonomous development.' This fine sentiment, however, was watered down by Smuts, eventually emerging as clause four of Article 22 thus:

> Certain communities formerly belonging to the Turkish Empire have reached a stage of development where their existence as independent nations can be provisionally recognized subject to the rendering of administrative advice and assistance by a Mandatory until such time as they are able to stand alone. The wishes of these communities must be a principal consideration in the selection of the Mandatory.

Jeffries describes how Wilson's drafts on the subject were progressively whittled down by Smuts, with the result that the Mandatory power, rather than the League, ended up having the upper hand over its Mandated territory. The Mandatory power was required merely to furnish the League with an annual report on its handling of the territory.

As Jeffries puts it, 'in the Smuts Resolution, all safeguards had been witched away. No longer merely manning the League, but superseding the League, stood the P.A.P., the Principal Allied Powers. No longer could the League appoint or dismiss a Mandatory. No longer could the League fix the terms of a Mandate. By the Resolution the role of the League was reduced to what it has been ever since in Palestine, that of a gas-inspector who is not allowed upon the premises, but receives the record of such ohms or therms as the Mandatory chooses to send him from such meters as the Mandatory chooses to install.'[10]

---

10. PTR, p 518

Drafting the Palestine Mandate
'Drawn up by someone reeling under the fumes of Zionism'

It was bad enough that Article 22 effectively ceded all authority over Palestine to the world's leading colonial Power. Worse, however, was that that Power was so deeply in thrall to Zionism that it unashamedly incorporated the Balfour Declaration into the text of its Mandate for Palestine. So how did this manoeuvre come about? Jeffries remarks that,

> Any person coming fresh to the subject – which is to say pretty well evertybody – will see on reading the text of it... that therein is not the slightest clue to where the Mandate was composed nor to how it was composed nor to when it was composed nor to the identity of those who composed it... This mystery goes hand in hand, or glove in glove, with the most reverential attitude towards the Mandate on the part of those who have occasion to speak of it. In an unmindful House of Commons and upon innocent public platforms such respect is paid to it that one might imagine that it had been revealed from some holy source."[11]

But with Jeffries on the case, no mystery was safe:

> The construction of the Mandate began before the Peace Conference had been held or the War had come to a close. The ultimate sources of it mainly are to be found, not in the archives of Geneva, nor in those of Whitehall itself but in the various Zionist documents which led up to the Balfour Declaration [...] For the Mandate followed the precedent of the Balfour Declaration. It was drafted in quiet between the Government and the Zionists, mostly by the Zionists, and then was issued under the cover of the League of Nations [on 29 September, 1923], as though it were the result of the collected debates of the world's lawgivers.[12]

Of the document's 28 articles, Jeffries traces nine back to their Zionist originals:

> These [nine Zionist Articles] and the equally Zionist Preamble controlled everything in Palestine. The Preamble contained the

---

11. PTR, p 521
12. PTR, pp 522-523

authorization and the title-deeds of the Mandatory. The nine Zionist Articles governed immigration, the establishment of the National Home, the installation of the Jewish Agency as a public body, local government, the land system, the laws of citizenship, the use of natural resources, the programme of education and the official mediums of speech. The political structure, the development, the whole of Palestine's national life was under [the Zionists'] sway.[13]

Weizmann, in fact, acknowledged the Zionist provenance of the Mandate in his autobiography:

> Curzon had by now taken over from Balfour at the Foreign Office, and was in charge of the actual drafting of the Mandate. On our side we had the valuable assistance of Ben V. Cohen, who stayed on with us in London after most of his fellow Brandeisists had resigned from the Executive and withdrawn from the work. Ben Cohen was one of the ablest draftsmen in America, and he and Curzon's secretary – young Eric Forbes-Adam, highly intelligent, efficient and most sympathetic – fought the battle of the Mandate for many months. Draft after draft was proposed, discussed and rejected, and I sometimes wondered if we should ever reach a final text. The most serious difficulty arose in connection with a paragraph in the Preamble – the phrase which now reads: 'Recognizing the historical connection of the Jews with Palestine.' Zionists wanted to have it read: 'Recognizing the historic rights of the Jews to Palestine.' But Curzon would have none of it, remarking dryly: 'If you word it like that, I can see Weizmann coming to me every other day and saying he has a *right* to do this, that or the other in Palestine! I won't have it!' As a compromise, Balfour suggested 'historical connection,' and 'historical connection' it was.[14]

According to Tibawi, 'the draft prepared in Paris by the Zionists and accepted by Forbes-Adam and Robert Vansittart came under consideration at the Foreign Office, together with the draft mandate for Iraq. The great contrast between the two was obvious, and the Zionist character of the Palestine mandate, with its omissions and stresses were at once evident to Curzon.' He continues,

---

13. PTR, p 558
14. Chaim Weizmann, *Trial & Error: The Autobiography of Chaim Weizmann*, Hamish Hamilton, London, 1949, pp 347-348

It is thus evident that Forbes-Adam and Vansittart who worked with the Zionists in Paris with Balfour's approval intentionally neglected to refer the matter to the Eastern Committee under Curzon or to the Foreign Office for almost a year. Now Curzon saw through the intrigue and wrote indignantly: 'I have never been consulted as to this mandate at an earlier stage, nor do I know from what negotiations it springs or on what understanding it is based. On another file I have noted a single compromising sentence. But here I may say that... I think the entire conception is wrong. Here is a country with 580,000 Arabs and 30,000, or is it 60,000 Jews (by no means all Zionists). Acting upon (? against) the noble principle of self-determination and ending with a splendid appeal to the League of Nations, we then proceed to draw up a document which reeks of Judaism in every paragraph and is an avowed constitution of a Jewish state – and the poor Arabs are only allowed to look through the keyhole as a non-Jewish community. It is quite clear that this mandate has been drawn up by someone reeling under the fumes of Zionism. If we are all to succumb to that intoxicant, this draft is alright. Perhaps there is no alternative. But I confess I should like to see something widely different.'[15]

A 'widely different draft,' however, never saw the light of day, with Tibawi attributing this to Curzon's 'ineffectualness and [tendency to] surrender even to subordinates.'[16]

Jeffries delivers an appropriately guilty verdict:

Such being the origin of the Mandate it is not strange that it was a document that broke every law and principle which it was supposed to safeguard. But though the Zionists had drafted it a hundred times over, it is not upon them that the supreme censure for this must fall. They were drugged by a delusion, and they were pretty frank about what they were doing. It is the Government of the day, the Government of Mr. Lloyd George which, to say nothing of its betrayal of national pledges, must bear once more the responsibility for deliberate violation in Palestine, through the imposition of such a Mandate, of the Covenant of the League which elsewhere it professed so glibly.

The Government's true duties under the Covenant, despite the game played with the text of the Mandate Article, were unmistakable. As Mandatory it was under bond to establish

15. A.L.Tibawi, *Anglo-Arab Relations & The Question of Palestine 1914-1921*, Luzac & Company Ltd, London, 1977, pp 427-428

16. Tibawi, p 432

Palestine as an independent nation, not ultimately nor in the long run nor some time, but provisionally at once. The Covenant was explicit upon this. "Certain communities," it said, "formerly belonging to the Turkish Empire have reached a stage of development where their existence as independent nations can be provisionally recognized subject to the rendering of administrative advice and assistance by a Mandatory, until such time as they are able to stand alone." The tense of the word "reached" is to be noted. Not "will reach" nor "may reach," but "have reached." Palestine *had* reached the required stage of development – the Covenant acknowledged it.

The Covenant was explicit too about the role of the Mandatory. The latter was to give nothing but administrative advice and assistance "until such time as they [the said communities or independent nations] are able to stand alone." But the Mandatory could not give administrative advice and assistance unless there were administrations, formed by the nations indicated, to which the two gifts could be proffered. Advice and assistance cannot be given to an Administration which is not there. Under this obligation alone, therefore, the creation in Palestine of a national government was predicated and presumed by the Covenant. The obligation, however, was resolutely evaded by the Lloyd George Government [...]

The action of the League Council in condoning this infringement of the Covenant by the Mandatory altered nothing. The Council's action was of no consequence, in the sense that it had no legitimizing value. The Council was not above the League. It was only (after a fashion) the custodian of its statutes. If it permitted the statutes of which it had the custody to be broken, all the Council did was to commit moral suicide. That was bad for the Council, but did not affect the Covenant. When the guardians of the law assist in its violation, it is not the law which is abrogated, but the number of the culprits and the extent of the guilt which are increased.[17]

Let us be quite clear. Far from the Mandatory regime 'rendering administrative advice and assistance until such times as [the Palestinians] are able to stand alone,' as per the words of Article 22, the Mandatory deliberately denied the Palestinians representative democracy for the duration of the Mandate's 25-years, *solely for the benefit of Palestine's Jewish minority.* Nor should it be forgotten

---

17. PTR, pp 559-561

that this extraordinary example of democracy denied was not only acknowledged but welcomed by Weizmann. Complaining in his autobiography that the Mandate did not go far enough (that is, 'place the country under such political, economic and administrative conditions as may facilitate the development of the Jewish National Home'), he was content with the fact that 'at least Palestine has not so far been put under a legislative council with an Arab majority.'[18]

The San Remo Conference (April 1920)
'When the Balfour Declaration was slipped into the Mandate'

The formal 'awarding' of the Middle Eastern mandates to Britain (Palestine and Mesopotamia) and France (Lebanon and Syria) took place at the San Remo Conference of 19–26 April, 1920, held in the palatial Villa Devachan in San Remo, Italy. Just how this transaction took place, however, remains yet another mystery in the Mandate story – one, however, which provided Jeffries with the opportunity to indulge his flair for comedy:

> [T]he sole official information given to the world upon what had happened at the morning session of the 25th, as far as the Near Eastern countries were concerned, was that "the question of the Mandates for Palestine, Syria and Mesopotamia was discussed." Discussed, indeed! During that session... the "examination of the Palestine question" which had begun upon the Saturday had been concluded, and Britain had been granted, or awarded, or indemnified with the nomination as Mandatory. And at this session... the Balfour Declaration had been inserted into the draft-Mandate which was being prepared as part of the coming Treaty [with Turkey].
>
> In fine, [this] was the fateful day... when the destinies of the most sacred land on earth were determined... A type of government, too, never before essayed in human society was inaugurated... and the countries which were to govern thus unprecedentedly were named. Yet no faintest suggestion of what had been done was vouchsafed by the Conference chiefs in their official report of their transactions [...]

18. Weizmann, p 348

Babies born that April morning have become young men and women, and yet we are about as ignorant as they were in their mothers' arms of what occurred at the Villa Devachan. This only we know, that the Balfour Declaration was slipped into the Mandate, and that it was Signori Nitti and Scialoja, M. Matsui, Lord Curzon, Messrs. Berthelot, Millerand and Lloyd George between them who somehow nominated as Mandatories the countries represented by MM. Berthelot and Millerand and by Lord Curzon and Mr. Lloyd George. It was a very intimate occasion, so intimate that four of those present suffered from ingrowing functions, nominated and being nominated at one and the same time. The sole clue to what a spectator might have witnessed of their proceedings from start to finish is to be found in the statement of a correspondent that "One cheerful feature about the Conference so far is the progress made in settling the Turkish Treaty. Discussions have run on the most cordial lines." Indeed they had done so.

This is the most living account of what happened which we possess. The League of Nations' own account of the birth of Mandates is highly significant because, in an Irish way, there is no account. "There is no record of the conversations by which Great Britain was selected as Mandatory for Palestine," confesses the League's official handbook.

Under such circumstances, it is impossible to prevent imagination from playing with the scene at the Villa Devachan. One pictures the bustling but superfluous helpfulness of the other delegates as Mr. Lloyd George efficiently levered the Balfour Declaration into the draft-Mandate. But the assumption of the draft-Mandate itself is not so easy to picture.

Did Signori Mitti, Scialoja, Millerand and Berthelot segregate themselves and then propose Great Britain as Mandatory for Palestine? Did Mr. Lloyd George simper and blush acceptance, or look sternly before him and say duty was duty? Did the French delegates then go to the chairs at the foot of the table? Did the British delegates take the vacated seats at its head, along with the Italians and the Japanese, meditate their choice with them for a pensive second, and then in chorus with them offer "Syria" to France? Whereon did the French delegates, with national immunity from humbug, nod and thank the British for carrying out the arrangement of the previous September?

Maybe it happened after this fashion: more probably it did not. Procedure demanded that all the Principal Allied Powers should nominate the Mandatory, so Mr. Lloyd George and poor Lord Curzon, completely out of his element, one imagines, will, in some way that we cannot guess and upon which unhappily silence has been maintained, have taken part in nominating themselves.

The official silence concerning the details of this odd performance has not prevented a hundred writers and orators in the service of the Zionist thesis from projecting ever since, through the best part of two decades, moving pictures of the moral glory which descended on the Villa Devachan that day. Mr Lloyd George has been presented, as upon the screen, in the role of the world's knight, bending a knee to receive Britain's obligations in Palestine. Like an accolade they were laid upon his shoulders by the incarnate kingly conscience of mankind.[19]

Jeffries makes two points with respect to this 'odd performance.' The first is that,

Britain and France had long fixed their respective Mandatory spheres between them, and the story of their being "chosen" now for these positions is only elaborate and disingenuous pretence. Mr Lansing, the American Secretary of State till that February, who knew all that was afoot, passed on these League and Mandate manoeuvres a judgment so apt that it must be quoted here. "If the advocates of the system," said he, "intended to avoid through its operation the appearance of taking enemy territory as the spoils of war, it was a subterfuge which deceived no one. It seemed obvious from the very first that the Powers, which under the old practice would have obtained sovereignty over certain conquered territories, would not be denied mandates over these territories".[20]

The second is that they were mandates in name only:

Great Britain was not awarded the Mandate for Palestine on the 25th of April, 1920. She could not be awarded what then was not in existence. The Mandates were sequels of the Peace Treaty, and the Peace Treaty with Turkey was not yet concluded. The flower could not appear in the air before its stem had risen from the soil. There were no Mandates in being as yet, and none could be created till the Peace Treaty had been concluded and ratified.

It was not therefore Mandates which were awarded to the two Powers at San Remo. It was nominations as prospective

---

19. PTR, pp 345-347. Francesco Nitti, Italian prime minister; Vittorio Scialoja, Italian foreign minister; Alexandre Millerand, French prime minister; Philippe Berthelot, French foreign minister; Keishiro Matsui, Japanese ambassador. (The US had observer status only.)

20. PTR, p 347

Mandatories which they received, a very different thing. The former would give them rights, the latter gave them no rights at all. But the Allied leaders were not anxious for the world to realise that their countries were only prospective Mandatories. They wanted to start straight off as (supposedly) invested Mandatories, having the full privileges of that status. They had their reasons for this desire, Mr. Lloyd George's being that he was anxious to bring the military administration of Palestine to an end, so as to set up a civil Government.

None the less the Allied Leaders, while they meant to act as though they possessed Mandates, shrank from putting evidence of their intentions upon paper. They were not quite so sure as they gave out that the Treaty with Turkey was going to be concluded at once. There was the possible prospect before them of a sort of no-man's-time, between nomination to the Mandate and the Mandate's entry into being.[21]

Despite this, the mere appearance of legality, sufficed for an 'elated' Weizmann, who announced in an interview that,

> Two decisions have been reached which are of the utmost importance. The first is the embodiment of the Balfour Declaration in the Treaty, thus giving it international sanction... The second decision is that the British Government, which is the Mandatory Power in Palestine... has agreed that a civil administration shall be set up immediately in Palestine to carry the Balfour Declaration into effect...[22]

This meant, writes Jeffries, that,

> The Balfour Declaration, so inserted, as an article of the Treaty would become binding upon Great Britain and upon her co-signatories of the Treaty, as an obligation... of the victors... This was the international sanction of which Dr. Weizmann spoke.[23]

Jeffries also reminds us that Britain and France's assumption of mandates at San Remo violated the stipulation, in Article 22 of the League Covenant, that the wishes of the communities concerned 'must be a principal consideration in the selection of

21. PTR, p 349
22. PTR, p 352
23. PTR, p 353

the Mandatory.' And further, that Dr Weizmann, 'who was not a native of Palestine,' was consulted 'at length.'

San Remo, avers Jeffries, was 'a treble betrayal':

> So here was a flagrant breach of the Covenant, a shocking act, because it showed such cynical appraisement of the new tables-of-the-law, which those who now broke them were even then proffering to the peoples of the world, to lead them out of the bondage of secret understandings and of false international promises. Theirs was a treble betrayal. By their act they betrayed the young League of Nations whose Covenant was to be inviolable. They betrayed the small peoples to whom they preached commandments which they themselves did not keep. They betrayed those of their own kin, the throng of men and women in the greater countries who were seeking to make of the Covenant the Constitution of a new and juster international polity.[24]

The Damascus Program (July 1919)
'A contrast to the rapine of political Zionism & the cabals of Whitehall'

On Faisal's return to Damascus from Europe in May 1919, a General Syrian Congress was convened, 'in lineal sequence from the early gatherings of Arab exiles in foreign countries and the meetings of the secret national societies under the Turks.' It constituted 'the first open convocation of Arab deputies upon Arab soil to the nucleus of an Arab parliament.'[25]

In July, the Congress issued a document known as 'The Damascus Program,' which called for 'complete political independence' for all parts of Syria, including Palestine; a 'democratic civil constitutional monarchy' under Faisal; no 'Mandatory Power'; no 'Jewish Commonwealth' in Palestine; no 'Zionist migration (for we do not acknowledge their title, but consider them a grave peril to our people from the national, economical, and political points of view)'; 'common rights [and] responsibilities' for 'our Jewish compatriots'; no 'separation' of Palestine or Lebanon from Syria; 'complete

---

24. PTR, p 355
25. PTR, pp 281-282

independence for emancipated Mesopotamia'; the 'complete annulment of secret treaties'; and the right to representation at the Paris Peace Conference.[26]

Jeffries sees in the Program a 'rejoinder' to Article 22 of the League Covenant, which patronisingly referred to ex-enemy territories 'inhabited by peoples not yet able to stand by themselves under the strenuous conditions of the modern world,' and hence in need of 'tutelage' by a mandatory 'on behalf of the League.'

He was moved to write of it that,

> When one reads it, and when one compares it with the programmes and the resolutions evolved by the Paris peacemakers, it is the words of the men "not able to stand by themselves" which shame the words of the men who so dubbed them. The feeling arises that these Arabs of Syria, in their pitiful disregarded charter, showed themselves more worthy of respect than the heads of great States advertising so widely, and so much in the way of business, the absolute purity of their principles. The Damascus Congressmen... showed wisdom; they asked for a State of a loose, decentralized character suited to the varying units of their race. They made due arrangements for safeguarding the rights of minorities. At a time when to their knowledge the Zionists were planning to supersede them in their native land they restrained themselves to a dignified protest against this, and thereafter guaranteed to their "Jewish compatriots" the enjoyment of common rights and the sharing of common responsibilities. What a contrast to the rapine of political Zionism and to the cabals of Whitehall.[27]

The King-Crane Commission (June/July 1919)
'The Zionists looked forward to a complete dispossession of the non-Jewish inhabitants'

In June 1919, President Wilson dispatched a fact-finding commission to the Middle East to determine the wishes of the people of Greater Syria (and Turkey). The King-Crane Commission, as it is known, received 1,863 petitions from all parts of the Greater Syria area.

---

26. PTR, pp 283-285
27. PTR, pp 297-298

Over 80 per cent demanded a United Syria, that is, a Syria that included Palestine. Of those petitions, 1,350 specifically rejected the Zionist program, particularly in Palestine, where 222 of the 260 petitions received declared against it.[28]

The commissioners recommended that there be a 'serious modification of the extreme Zionist programme for Palestine of unlimited immigration of Jews, looking finally to making Palestine distinctly a Jewish state,' and noted that a "national home" for the Jewish people is not equivalent to making Palestine into a Jewish State, nor can the erection of such a Jewish State be accomplished without the gravest trespass upon the "civil and religious rights of existing non-Jewish communities in Palestine." The fact came out repeatedly in the Commission's conference with Jewish representatives that the Zionists looked forward to a practically complete dispossession of the present non-Jewish inhabitants of Palestine, by various forms of purchase.'[29]

Jeffries writes of the Commission's report that,

> It is a full document and a frank one, amply argued. Its recommendations are well presented and were perfectly feasible. More than anything else, though, its main accomplishment was to expose unhesitatingly the aims of Zionism in Palestine – "practically complete dispossession of the non-Jewish inhabitants." To have this established at the outset by men of the independence and the ability of Messrs. Crane and King... was damning for the Zionist projects then. It is more damning if possible now for Mr. Lloyd George and the other Conference chiefs and cabinet ministers who were responsible for imposing these projects upon Palestine. The Americans informed them flatly that "nine-tenths of the population were most emphatically against the entire Zionist programme."
>
> If after reading the Report these statesmen entered upon a pro-Zionist policy in Palestine, they did so in full knowledge that they would be imposing it by force upon an unwilling and helpless people. If on the other hand they did not read the Report, because they did not want to have it in their hands, then their ignorance was culpable and their policy was no whit less guilty.[30]

---

28. PTR, pp 286-287
29. PTR, 292-293
30. PTR, pp 299-300

The Fall of the Kingdom of Syria (July 1920)

'Inside that revolving vicious circle it turned and turned and was abraded away'

Referred to by the Arabs as *'Am al-Nakba* (Year of Catastrophe), 1920 'saw the suffocation of what little Arab rule had been left in Syria and the end of military government in Palestine. It saw also the arrival of the first High Commissioner to establish there mandatory administration, under a Mandate, however, which was not yet in existence.'[31]

Under popular pressure 'to take a strong line with the Allies,' Faisal summoned the Syrian Congress in Damascus, resulting in a number of key resolutions. As Ali A. Allawi, Faisal's biographer, explains,

> The preamble to the resolutions summarised the position of the nationalists regarding the total independence of Syria within its natural frontiers, including Palestine, drawing on the right of the people to self-determination, the promises of the Allies and Wilson's Fourteen Points. The congress rejected the Zionist plan for a Jewish National Home in Palestine and called for administrative decentralisation and a special status for Lebanon. The resolutions then declared Syria to be a fully independent state within its natural boundaries and offered the crown of Syria to Faisal as its constitutional King.[32]

Faisal was duly crowned king of an independent Syria on 8 March, 1920. However, in Jeffries' telling,

> His Kingdom of Syria lasted only four months. In May his Government rejected the Mandate over north Syria which France had assumed in April, declaring that it was unacceptable to the mass of the Syrian population. Thenceforward relations with France worsened rapidly. A mixture of fighting and of tangled negotiations ended in mid-July with an ultimatum from General

---

31. PTR, pp 308-309
32. Ali A. Alawi, *Faisal I of Iraq*, Yale University Press, New Haven, 2014, pp 272-273

Gouraud, by which the Syrian Government was to accept the Mandate within four days, though Gouraud guaranteed that the Mandate would not take the form of annexation... Feisal tried to be conciliatory, and actually did accept the ultimatum. But his acceptance reached Gouraud too late. The French advanced. Final parleys were swept away by a tide of tribesmen and regulars who rushed out to give battle to the French. They were crushed, and on the 25th of July Damascus fell.

Feisal took refuge in Palestine, and after a period in Europe, about a year later he was installed as King of Irak, under a promise from Great Britain of temporary mandatory aid, of accruing national responsibility and presently, of independence. All of which has been carried out, so that in Irak at least our engagements have been honoured and the proprietary rights of the Arabs respected.

The kingdom of Syria, on the other hand, never had much of a chance. It could not attain recognition of its independence from the Allies till it accepted the Mandates, and it could not accept the Mandates without abandoning the independence of two-thirds of its citizens. It could not suppress disorder till it was given help, and it was refused help till it had suppressed disorder. Inside that revolving vicious circle it turned and turned and was abraded away.[33]

The Fall of the Military Administration (June 1920)
'Zionist influence in the high places of England'

Palestine's military government was also overthrown (in a manner of speaking) in 1920. The Zionist Organisation's arm in Palestine, the Zionist Commission, 'had arrogated to itself the privileges of a ruling hierarchy, and was endeavouring to act as a Government within the actual Government, and outside of it also, through its intimate relations with statesmen in England. The members of the military Government were driven into continual protests against it, protests which, alas, were disregarded studiously in London.'[34]

---

33. PTR, pp 328-329
34. PTR, p 309

Matters in dispute between the two parties included the Zionists' insistence on 'the installation of Hebrew as an official language, to a level with which Arabic, the common tongue of the country, was to be reduced,' and the administration's payment of subsidies to 'Zionist clerks and others who entered Government service' only to become 'a perpetual source of leakage of official information.' Most rankling, however, was 'the manner in which Zionist influence in the high places of England was brought to bear against officers who offended the Commission...'[35]

The first of what became a series of so-called Palestinian "disturbances" (1920, 1921, 1929, 1936–39) erupted in Jerusalem in April 1920, resulting in four Arab and five Jewish deaths, and 251 casualties. Its causes and circumstances became the subject of an official investigation by Major-General Sir Philip Palin,[36] who found as follows:

> 1) That the causes of the alienation and exasperation of the feelings of the population of Palestine are a) Disappointment at the non-fulfilment of promises made to them by British propaganda. b) Inability to reconcile the Allies' declared policy of self-determination with the Balfour Declaration, giving rise to a sense of betrayal and intense anxiety for their future. c) Misapprehension of the true meaning of the Balfour Declaration and forgetfulness of the guarantees determined therein, due to the loose rhetoric of politicians and the exaggerated statements and writings of interested persons, chiefly Zionists. d) Fear of Jewish competition and domination, justified by experience and the apparent control exercised by the Zionists over the Administration. e) Zionist indiscretion and aggression, since the Balfour Declaration, aggravating such fears. f) Anti-British and anti-Zionist propaganda working on the population already inflamed by the sources of irritation aforesaid...[37]

---

35. PTR, pp 312-313

36. Report of the Court of Inquiry Convened by Order of H.E, the High Commissioner & Commander-in-Chief, 12/4/20. For the full report see https://cs.anu.edu/people/Brendan.McKay/yabber. Astonishingly, even today the entire Palin Report is only available on academic Brendan McKay's "Middle East Yabber" website. McKay notes in his introduction to it that, 'Although this report had been cited by many historians, to our knowledge this is the first time the complete document has been published.'

37. Palin Report, Report D. Conclusions 69

Palin wrote of the Zionists that 'They are ready to use their powerful foreign and home influence to force the hand of this or any future Administration. If not carefully checked they may easily precipitate a catastrophe, the end of which it is difficult to forecast.'[38] (It should be noted that the Palin Report, like the Hussein-McMahon Correspondence, was suppressed by the British government.)

Jeffries' reading of this, the first of Palestine's many intifadas, speaks to its inevitability:

> I went back to Palestine after a month in Damascus and in other parts of the country. I found it, to say the least, in a more disturbed state than in March. The clash between Arabs and Jews had occurred in the interval. "*The* clash," not "*a* clash;" for there was no trace of accident about the affair. The policy of the Home Government had ensured it. When it took place there was naturally an uproar amidst Zionists throughout the world, and in the House of Commons a number of questions were asked. The Zionists said, and some members of Parliament too, that the authorities in Palestine were responsible for the rioting and bloodshed because they had not taken proper police or military precautions either before or during the crisis.
>
> This was not the true case. The authorities in Palestine could not prevent an explosion which the Government in London had foreordained from the time of the Balfour Declaration. The Arabs would not have been mortals if they had remained quiescent with the signs of Zionist power increasing daily and the whole future, as they saw now, dedicated to its development. The authorities might have delayed the rioting by displays of force here and there for a while, but they could not have displayed force always and everywhere. The national feeling which manifested itself in the riots was universal, and would have found another vent if the Jerusalem outbreak of early April had been stifled.[39]

Although 'the clash' had been predicted by Sir Louis Bols, Palestine's chief administrator from July 1919 to June 1920, his warnings fell on deaf ears. In fact, writes Jeffries,

> It is probable that he doomed himself and his Administration in mid-March, when he wrote home his comments upon a speech which had been made by Dr. Weizmann in London the month

---

38. Palin Report, Report C. Extent of Racial Feeling in Palestine 68
39. PTR, p 329

before... He felt it to be his duty to controvert several of Dr. Weizmann's assertions concerning Palestine, and to warn the future Mandatory Powers of the danger of accepting them as a true picture of the state of the country. "It must be understood," he wrote, "that 90% of the population of Palestine is deeply anti-Zionist. This opposition comprises all Moslems and Christians and not an inconsiderable proportion of Jews." [...] He continued... saying that if the policy outlined by Dr. Weizmann... were followed... that is, if exclusively Jewish labour were employed and Government lands were handed over to the Zionist Organization, then the situation would become untenable. In words which deserve to be recorded because of their foresight he declared, "I wish to state clearly that if such a policy is proposed it is certain that a revolution would ensue which would result in the Jews being driven out of the land unless they are covered by powerful military forces of the Mandatory Power."[40]

Bols, however, persisted with his protests to London over the conduct of the Zionist Commission, which he described as 'hostile, critical and abusive.' He declared in a memorandum that,

> This Administration has loyally carried out the wishes of His Majesty's Government, and has succeeded in doing so by strict adherence to the laws governing the conduct of the Military Occupant of Enemy Territory, but this has not satisfied the Zionists, who appear bent on committing the temporary Military Administration to a partialist policy before the issue of the Mandate. It is manifestly impossible to please partisans who officially claim nothing more than a "National Home," but in reality will be satisfied with nothing less than a Jewish State and all that it politically implies. I recommend therefore, in the interests of peace, of development, of the Zionists themselves, that the Zionist Commission in Palestine be abolished.[41]

That protest, however, appears merely to have hastened the abolition of the military administration itself, and, on 1 July, 1920, it was replaced by a civil administration under Palestine's first High Commissioner, Sir Herbert Samuel. As for the appointment's impact on the Arabs and the Zionists, Jeffries has this to say:

---

40. PTR, pp 333-334
41. PTR, p 359

Need it be said the appointment... was a blow to the Arabs. That a man of Jewish blood should be placed at the head of the Government surpassed their fears. The leading Zionists, too, made small secret of their predominant part in securing the nomination of the first High Commissioner. As time went on, they made no secret at all.[42]

Palestine's Civil Administration (July 1920/September 1923)
'It was called a Government but it was not a government'

The political complexion of its high commissioner was not the only problem with Palestine's new administration. Without an Anglo-Turkish peace treaty in place, it was illegal under international law, and would remain so until the ratification of the Treaty of Lausanne in August 1923. Jeffries states that,

> At the period which we have reached the Prime Minister and his friends started to act in Palestine as though under the impression that if they flouted all law there consistently enough, then they would establish a new order of conduct. From now on they pursued a regular course of illegality, through the deputy action of the Government which they had established in Palestine and, fundamentally, through the very establishment of this Government. For it is impossible to find that the supposititious Mandatory Administration for the three years between August 1920 and September 1923 had any Mandatory status or any legal status whatsoever. It was called a Government, but it had none of the title-deeds or rights of a Government. It was not a Government.
>
> Its deeds were all null and void, and presumably remain so to this day, in the absence of any remedial act. Among these was the quite arbitrary series of enactments by which Zionist immigration into Palestine was set on foot, as well as the enactment of the Constitution under which the country continues to be ruled.[43]

---

42. PTR, p 371

43. PTR, p 388. This issue had been raised by Jeffries in his 1923 reports in the *Daily Mail*.

This unprecedented situation elicited from Jeffries one of his most insightful reflections on the nature of the political class, and one which deserves to be accorded the status of an eternal verity:

> Mr. Edwin Montagu... told me that his colleagues of the 1917 Government mostly knew absolutely nothing about the Palestine Question as it presented itself then, and there is no reason to suppose, in their utter lack of access to unbiased information, that the bulk of Ministers of the later Governments knew anything more. Nor have Ministers of the various Cabinets between 1923 and this day, outside the responsible Ministry, the Colonial Office, and in a minor degree the Foreign Office, possessed any fuller knowledge or lesser ignorance than their predecessors. As time has passed, obviously they have grown to know less and less, indeed.
>
> It is but fair to emphasize this point, because public opinion never seems to allow for want of knowledge amidst statesmen and politicians in general. They are always thought to be so fully informed upon any given matter that, according as their actions disclose themselves later on, they are judged to have acted in respect of it either with entire honesty or entire dishonesty. This is far from being true: one of the first things a journalist learns from contact with major politics is that highly placed persons can be quite ignorant and can act in ignorance. It is fortunate in the present instance that this should be so. If it were not so we should have had a strange selection of rulers governing this country for the last fourteen or fifteen years.
>
> The Palestine Question has reached by now a stage in which those who have to take the greatest decisions concerning it may have the least information upon it. Ministers of to-day can only draw their information from the papers supplied to them by too interested Departments. Can anyone imagine that our present Prime Minister, Mr. Neville Chamberlain, has descended into the recesses of the matter? Or that he has ever had an opportunity of descending? Not for an instant is it to be believed that he has had such an opportunity. Till a short while ago, he has had to depend, for his information, upon a Colonial Office at the head of which was Mr. Ormsby-Gore. What did Mr. Baldwin know of the realities of Palestine? I have not the least hesitation in asserting that he knew nothing at all.[44]

44. PTR, pp 401-402

The fact of the military administration's indecently hasty termination, and the brazen illegality of its civil replacement, also moved Jeffries to broach the question of questions: was it really for no other reason than to facilitate 'the nine subterfuges of the Balfour Declaration' that British and Dominion troops fought and died in Greater Syria from 1917 to 1918?

> Granted that the Palestine Administration of 1920-3 was illegal, is it not begging reality to harp upon this? Palestine had been conquered by the British Army, the blood of British and Australian soldiers had been shed profusely to win it, it would not have been torn from Turkish rule without these many lives so bravely sacrificed. Is it not begging reality to accuse a British Government of being illegitimate where the return of peace, the prospect of plenty and the whole existence of civilized government had depended upon British arms?
>
> This argument has been put forward by some who have not thought much before they spoke, and by others who have masked a good deal of subtlety with a covering of bluff patriotism. The underlying assumption of it is that the soldiers who fell in Palestine fell fighting to provide there that form of government which Mr. Lloyd George installed. The 5th Norfolks, the 8th Hampshires bled so that the Sevres Treaty might not die: the men of the 53rd Division left six hundred casualties on the Samson Ridge so that the nine subterfuges of the Balfour Declaration might pass unchallenged: the Australian Light Horse charged crying, "Advance the National Home!"
>
> Was anything ever further from the truth? We know why our soldiers died – in loyalty to their country. Some of them too will have reflected as they marched to battle that they were going to redeem the land of their Saviour: all of them will have had some consciousness of this side of their emprise. If there was anything for which they did not die, it was that a British Government should use their bones as the foundation of a quibbling State unable to disclose its beginnings or avow its ends. It was for no such State in Palestine, nor for any political nostrum or thesis that they fought, and least of all in order that through their faithfulness their rulers should have ample opportunities for infidelity.
>
> They expected of course to inaugurate some kind of British rule, in their soldiers' way, as part of the campaign; but they looked no further. If they thought of the matter at all, they thought of a coming military Government by their chiefs. This was what they died to establish, if you will: and who disestablished it? Is

it maintained that the fallen men of the British Army in Palestine cried out from their graves that the survivors of the British Army must cease in 1920 to govern the land in which they lay, or else their own sacrifice was in vain?

If there is one plea in the world that will not do, it is this one that because of the Army's victory and for the sake of the dead lying on the battlefields, the tricks and the perfidies of statesmen must be condoned. More than in any other place it is intolerable in Palestine, where the Administration formed by the leaders and the comrades of the dead was ejected by these very statesmen. In 1920 there was no necessity for O.E.T. A [Occupied Enemy Territory Administration] to come to an end. It was the legitimate vehicle of rule under the conditions of armistice. All that could be said against it was that it was lasting a long while and that it cost money. But both of these things were disadvantages such as might be expected to spring from a great war: neither had the faintest pretension to rank as a lawful reason for ending the regime. Whatever the expense, too, of continuing O.E.T.A., a genuine effort could have reduced this, and indeed an administration on a restricted scale, physically and morally, would have been more apt for the country. Nothing, in fine, permitted the termination of the Military Government in order that the pseudo-Mandatory Administration might replace it.[45]

The second of Palestine's 'disturbances' broke out in May 1921. It was sparked by a clash between two Zionist organisations at a May Day march in Jaffa. 'To the Arabs,' remarks Jeffries, 'the Labour side of the demonstration was all gibberish: what they very naturally saw in it was a triumphal gathering and march of the flock of strangers who were settling like starlings upon their country.'[46]

A 'miniature rising' against the Zionist presence, both in Jaffa and in the countryside, ensued, resulting in the death and injury of 'close on 200 Jews... and some 120 Arabs.'

The inevitable inquiry into the matter, known as the Haycraft Commission, found that '... in our opinion the [Zionist] Commission's conception of its duties and functions has exercised an exacerbating rather than a conciliating influence on the Arab population of Palestine, and has thus been a contributory cause of the disturbances...'[47]

---

45. PTR, pp 402-404
46. PTR, p 419
47. PTR, p 422

As an example of the Zionist Commission's 'exacerbating influence' on the Arabs, the Haycraft Commission cited the views of its acting chairman, Dr Eder: 'In his opinion there can be only one National Home in Palestine, and that a Jewish one, and there can be no equality in the partnership between Jews and Arabs, but a Jewish predominance as soon as the numbers of that race are sufficiently increased.'[48]

The Report of the Haycraft Commission was the first available to the British public, that of the 1920 Palin Report, as we have seen, having been suppressed.

As one might expect, Weizmann was not at all happy with it, complaining in his autobiography that 'while condemning the brutality of the rioters, and denying most of the absurd allegations against the Jews in Palestine (e.g. that they were Bolshevists), [it] contrived to leave on the reader's mind the impression that the root of the difficulty was a British policy with which the Arabs were – perhaps justifiably – dissatisfied.'[49]

The Dreaded Effendis
'There is a magic for them in the word effendi'

In his discussion of this second intifada, Jeffries draws attention to 'a contention which has been put forward, over and over again, year after year, by the Zionists and the spokesmen of successive Home Governments.'[50] He explains that,

> This contention or allegation is that amidst the bulk of the Arab population there never has been any deep-seated or fundamental objection to the National Home and all it betokens, that most of the Arabs have been nothing but the tools of the leaders, of the Mufti of Jerusalem, of the Arab Higher Committee, of the sheikhs, of the whole crew of landlords, lawyers, usurers and such, who batten on the impoverished multitude. Under the Turks these sirrahs exploited the multitude to the top of their bent, and if they had a government of their own they would continue to

---

48. PTR, p 423
49. Weizmann, p 349
50. PTR, pp 423-424

do so. But the National Home bars the way to this government. Hence their campaign against the Home.

The Gentile protagonists of the Zionist cause are especially given to this argument, and seem to think that they have worded it to perfection when they say that the Arab agitation only aims at maintaining the subjection of the *fellaheen* [peasantry] to the *effendis*. There is a magic for them in the word effendi. They use it in a half-revolted, half-convinced matter, as though on the one hand they had but to mention it to win their case, and on the other hand as though it were a sort of verbal poison dangerous to retain upon the tongue. It figures and has figured in countless articles and speeches, in the sense of "capitalist" or "exploiter."

In fact effendi is a singularly modest agnomen, about equivalent in English to "educated esquire"... It is therefore as much nonsense to talk of effendis as though they were slave-driving capitalists as it would be to say that the poor are trodden down by esquires in England. Effendis are not a class at all, but comprise people of all views and all pecuniary conditions. A group of effendis in Britain would include, say, Maxton Effendi and Wedgwood Effendi, to say nothing of Sidebotham Effendi and Sacher Effendi, and most definitely would have included Snell Effendi ere he was advanced to the equivalent of Snell Pasha.[51]

He also quotes the following passage from the Haycraft report in rebuttal of the allegation:

A good deal has been alleged by Jewish witnesses about the instigation of the Arab mob to violence by their leaders. If this means no more than that while educated people talk and write the mob acts, then there is truth in the allegation. But if it means that had it not been for incitement by the notables, effendis and sheikhs there would have been no riots, the allegation cannot be substantiated... [T]he general belief that the aims of the Zionists and Jewish immigration are a danger to the national and material interests of the Arabs in Palestine is well-nigh universal among the Arabs, and it is not confined to any particular class.[52]

The idea that Palestinians are 'nothing but the tools of [their] leaders,' of course, is still a staple of Israeli propaganda today, with the word 'incitement' constantly heard on the tongues of Israeli politicians.'

---

51. PTR, p 424
52. PTR, p 425

10

Writing Reality

'An entire seclusion in the subject and the abandonment of every other interest'

What Jeffries referred to as 'the most difficult and onerous piece of work I ever had, and of all I have done that by which I stand most firmly,' his 1923 'inquest' on the Palestine problem, was obviously never far from his mind in the years which followed its publication. His rage against the injustice of Britain's Palestine policy, which he had worked so hard to expose in 1923, continued to simmer, prompting him, at some point, to conceive the idea of writing a definitive study of the origins of the Palestine problem.

The earliest indication that I have been able to find that he had begun work on *Palestine: The Reality* comes in a 1930 letter to Donald M. Brodie, a member of the 1919 King-Crane Mission. In it, Jeffries explained that he was 'in Paris looking up some essential references for my book in the National Library' and wanted to know if Brodie knew 'whether or not Lloyd George had seen the [King-Crane] report.'[1]

---

1. J.M.N. Jeffries, Letter to Donald Brodie, King-Crane Commission Digital Collection, Oberlin College Archives, collections.oberlin.edu

Six years later, we find him writing to George Antonius about Balfour's 1925 tour of Palestine and Syria, which sparked protests so fierce that Balfour was forced to beat a retreat from the region: 'I have heard that you were one of a group of two or three people with Balfour when he embarked at Beyrout after his experiences in Damascus and elsewhere. He is supposed to have said then, shaking his head, "Has all this happened because of me"? Was this so?'[2]

Antonius' response not only confirms the account of the visit that would later appear in Chapter 35 of *Palestine: The Reality*, but corroborates to a remarkable degree Jeffries' assessment of Balfour's character:

> About Balfour, I have a good deal of material and of personal information, for I was with him on that journey of his in Syria, from beginning to end; and his remarks about the origin and significance of the disturbances in Damascus were made to me. I am not using any of it, however, until the time comes when I decide to write the full story of that amazing journey. The remark which you attribute to him is, so far as I am aware, not literally true. But he did say something uncommonly like it, only worse, that is to say more revealing of abysmal ignorance about political forces in the Arab world. Between you and me, his remarks were to me a shocking revelation. Like yourself, I would treat him very severely. As you say, Palestine was to him a game, a sort of historico-intellectual exercise and diversion, into which he found himself drawn by the flattery of a plausible and astute Jew. Of the Arabs he was first not even conscious, except to the extent to which he may be said to be conscious of, say, the ground-lads who fielded the balls for him on the courts at Cannes. When the Arabs became vocal, he regarded them as a nuisance – hooligans who had never read Hume or Bergson and who must not be suffered to disturb the serene philosophy of his historical meditations or the delicate equilibrium of his fantastic experiment.[3]

In his introduction to *Palestine: The Reality*, Jeffries describes the process of writing the book as 'an entire seclusion in the subject and

---

2. Susan Silsby Boyle, *Betrayal of Palestine: The Story of George Antonius*, Westview Press, Boulder, 2001, p 129

3. Boyle, pp 130-131. Jeffries would go on in *Palestine: The Reality* to quote Balfour as follows: 'Is all this really because of my Declaration?' p 598. Unfortunately, Antonius' account of Balfour's visit is absent from *The Arab Awakening*, perhaps for diplomatic reasons.

the abandonment of every other interest.'[4] His 'seclusion,' however, was rudely interrupted by the turn of events in Palestine in 1936:

> From end to end the Holy Land has been running with blood. Evening after evening the voice of the wireless announcer has brought news of another combat, another ambush, another assassination perhaps, on the soil once pressed by the feet of Christ. Yet the more we are grieved by these events, the more it is incumbent upon us to examine into the causes which have produced them.[5]

For most westerners with a grasp of twentieth century history, the years 1936–39 conjure up only the Spanish Civil War. These four years, however, are of enormous significance in modern Palestinian history.

'In April 1936,' writes the American historian, Ted Swedenburg, 'Palestinian Arabs launched a general strike that lasted six months and turned into what became known as *al-thawra al-kubra* (the Great Revolt) of 1936–39, the most significant anticolonial insurgency in the Arab East during the interwar period. The strike began in the wake of a series of incidents initiated by the April 13 murder of two Jews by Arab insurgents. A wave of brutal reprisals and counter reprisals ensued, followed by the government's declaration of a state of emergency. "National committees" sprang up in all the Arab cities and towns and declared a general strike. Palestinian notables followed the wave of popular enthusiasm, and on April 25 the political parties met and established a coordinating body known as the Higher Arab Committee (HAC) headed by the Grand Mufti, Hajj Amin al-Husayni. The HAC, which represented a kind of alliance between traditional notables and emergent middle-class urban radicals, took over the leadership of the strike and articulated its demands: that Great Britain... put an end to Jewish immigration, ban land sales to the Jews, and grant the country its national independence.'[6]

---

4. PTR, p xvi

5. PTR, p xiii

6. Ted Swedenburg, *Memories of Revolt: The 1936-1939 Rebellion & the Palestinian National Past*, The University of Arkansas Press, Fayetteville, 2003, pp xix-xx

Dr Izzat Tannous

The HAC decided to send a delegation to London to put its case to the new Colonial Secretary, William Ormsby-Gore. Arriving in London in June 1936, it included a Palestinian Christian doctor, Izzat Tannous, who would later play a pivotal role in the publication of *Palestine: The Reality*. Happily, Tannous has left us an invaluable account of the delegation's activities in a 1988 memoir, *The Palestinians: Eyewitness History of Palestine Under British Mandate*, a source containing invaluable references to Jeffries. The first of these reads as follows:

> The first British friend we wanted to see was Lord Islington... The other[s] we were eager to meet were Colonel [S.F.] Newcombe who fought with Faisal in the Arabian campaign against the Turks; Mrs. Stuart Erskine, who wrote the book, *Palestine of the Arabs* [1935] in defense of the Arab cause; H.V. Morton, author of *In the Steps of the Master* and *In the Steps of St. Paul*... Miss Frances Newton, who lived among us in Haifa most of her life; Miss [Margaret] Farquharson, the Secretary of the National League of Women; J.M.N. Jeffries, an ex-correspondent of the *Daily Mail* for the Middle East, whose articles on the Palestine case were the example of honest reporting and who later wrote the most detailed book on the Palestine case: *Palestine: The Reality* (1939). Also Lord Lamington...[7]

The delegation was unfortunately unable to make any headway against the staunchly pro-Zionist Ormsby-Gore. 'It was futile to discuss any part of the Palestine Question with [him],' Tannous wrote, 'for he had a closed mind to everything that was Arab.'[8]

During the delegation's four-month stay in Britain, however, it accomplished several things. One of these was the production of an 11-page pamphlet, *The Palestine Case – Statement by the Palestine Arab Delegation* (1/7/36). This, wrote Tannous, 'was the first Arab document on the Palestine case published in the United Kingdom.' He added that 'This is a frank admission of our backwardness in the very important field of information and propaganda. I must

---

7. Izzat Tannous, *The Palestinians: Eyewitness History of Palestine Under British Mandate*, I.G.T. Company, New York, 1988, p 181
8. Tannous, p 183

admit again that it was wrong of the Arab people of Palestine to depend only on their indisputable natural rights to their country and on the Covenant of the League of Nations which decreed their self-determination. They also had too much faith in the promises of the British Government as found in the McMahon/Hussein Correspondence and in the Anglo-French Declaration of November 7, 1918... They had full trust in the Allies and in the United States of America whose word, because of Arab good heartedness and simplicity, was sacred.'[9]

On the subject of the pamphlet's content, he wrote,

> Our case is a straightforward case and we did not have to refer to a two-thousand-year-old connection to Palestine. We were in Palestine, and for thousands of years we had been deeply rooted in Palestine. We needed no promise from Balfour or from any other "tyrant." But, unfortunately, we were not a people who were left alone to enjoy peace. A great power had come to uproot us and to displace us; and in order to explain our problem, we included in our statement the following points: 1. Our natural rights. 2. Promise of independence in the McMahon/Hussein Correspondence. 3. Promise of independence in the Anglo-French Declaration of November 7, 1918. 4. Provision in the Covenant of the League of Nations stipulating the self-determination of people. 5. The illegality and the contradictions found in the Balfour Declaration. 6. The unjust government policy with regard to Jewish immigration and land sales as reported by the Shaw Commission, Sir John Hope-Simpson and Lewis French. 7. The landless Arabs. 8. Our demands. The publication of this pamphlet won for us a large number of British supporters who became very interested in our case.[10]

The delegation also oversaw the formation of a Pro-Arab Parliamentary Committee of approximately 60, mainly Conservative MPs, 'in order to counteract Zionist influence and coercion,' and established an Arab information office known as the Arab Centre under Tannous' direction.[11]

---

9. Tannous, p 183. Tannous has forgotten the 1921 Palestine Arab Delegation's publication, *The Holy Land: The Moslem-Christian Case against Zionist Aggression*. See Chapter 6.

10. Tannous, p 184

11. Tannous, pp 186-187

Following the ending of the Palestinian general strike in October 1936, Ormsby-Gore despatched a Royal Commission to Palestine under Lord Peel to look into the causes of unrest there. Unsurprisingly, these were found to have been 'the desire of the Arabs for national independence' and 'their antagonism to the establishment of the Jewish National Home in Palestine, quickened by their fear of Jewish domination.' Most controversially, the Peel Commission, as it is generally known, recommended that Palestine be partitioned between the two communities, a matter we shall return to later.

The Arab Centre
'The attachment of Jeffries to the Arab Centre was an asset to us all'

Tannous and his fellow delegates returned to Palestine in September 1936, leaving the operation of the Arab Centre in the hands of the delegation's British supporters. When he returned in January 1937, the work of the Centre began in earnest with the weekly production of an *Arab Centre Bulletin* for general distribution, and the holding of public meetings to present the Palestinian cause to a wider audience. Tannous described some of the Centre's visitors (following his return from a trip to New York on HAC business in August 1937) thus:

> I was very happy to find that the Arab Center... was doing well and its weekly *Bulletin* in great demand. Mrs. Stuart Erskine, who was the soul of the Center, was extremely happy to see me back, as she always felt sad at my leaving London for fear I might not return. However, I assured Mrs. Erskine, as I did on several occasions, that the Arab Center had become part of my life and it had taken the place of my clinic in Jerusalem.
>
> Musa al-Husseini, who was still studying at London University, was our most frequent visitor and was the person who took the deepest interest in the work of the Center. We used to call him the "Future Mufti" of Jerusalem. Of the Iraqi legation, Abdur-Rahman Bazzaz and Abdul Ghani Dally, were of great help. Other students who visited us less often were Nicola Ziadeh, now professor of Arab History at the American University of Beirut; Awni Daoudi, once the advisor of King Sinusi of Libya;

Issa Nakhleh, now in charge of the Palestine Arab Office in New York; Daoud Abu Ghazaleh and Farid Burtcosh. They all deserve worthy mention for their generous assistance to the Center. But they were not our only visitors. I can never forget the visits of Mr. Richmond, who, for a long time with architect George Shiber, were the responsible architects of the Dome of the Rock in Al-Haram Ash-Shareef in Jerusalem; Mr. [C.R.] Ashbee, an ex-civil servant in the Palestine Mandatory Government; the frequent visits of the members of the Pro-Arab Parliamentary Committee; Colonel Newcombe; Mr. and Mrs. H.V. Morton; Miss Newton who came almost every day and Mrs. Brooks who used to wear a badge indicating her love for the Arabs. It was also at that time that I came to know Ethel Mannin who has since written so many books on the Palestine Question and is still writing in support of the Arab cause. Both Ethel and her late husband, Mr. Fitzgerald, were pioneers in defending the Arab cause.[12]

It was Jeffries, however, whom Tannous singled out for special mention:

At this time, a special visitor came to the Arab Center. He was J.M.N. Jeffries, an ex-correspondent of the *Daily Mail* in the Near East during the First World War. He had written a book on Palestine and he wanted to be connected with the Center. I asked him to join and although he was not on the regular staff, he came to the Center every day and did a great deal of good work.

When acting as correspondent for the *Daily Mail* in the Near East, Jeffries sent to his paper several articles on Palestine which were of special interest. These articles stimulated Lord Northcliffe, proprietor of the *Daily Mail* and many other papers, to visit Palestine as soon as the war was over. During his stay in the Near East he listened to 200 visitors and received tens of petitions. He was among the first important Britishers who realized the dangers of the Balfour Declaration and said: "This country (Palestine) runs the risk of becoming a second Ireland." The prophecy was only too accurate. His conception of the Palestine problem allowed space in his papers to Arab complaints but, unfortunately, he died soon after his return from Palestine. However, his incentive was continued by his brother and successor, Lord Rothermere, who made it possible for Jeffries to return to Palestine in the autumn of 1922 to investigate fully into the Palestine Question. It was during that trip that Jeffries was able

12. Tannous, pp 214-215

to procure a copy of the McMahon/ Hussein Correspondence which was published, for the first time, in the *Daily Mail*.

The publication of the McMahon/ Hussein Correspondence in the London press caused great commotion in political circles. It was not easy to explain why so much had been published and said about the Balfour Declaration and nothing whatsoever had been published or said about its counterpart, the McMahon/ Hussein Correspondence. This disclosure, however, stimulated Lord Islington and others to debate the correspondence in March 1923 in the House of Lords. The noble Lord asked the Government to disclose the Correspondence which had been kept secret in the files of its Foreign Office since 1916. A vote was taken and the Government lost. The House voted 50 [sic] for the official disclosure of the Correspondence and 19 against it. But the Government did not until the year 1939 – sixteen years later.

The attachment of Jeffries to the Arab Center was a real asset to us all. He disclosed to us many of the secrets of the Palestine case which without him, would have remained secret. I have many interesting stories to tell about our colleague J.M.N. Jeffries which I will leave to the following chapters.[13]

---

13. Tannous, pp 218-219. It should be noted here that Tannous is relying on Jeffries' inadvertent conflation of the 1922 and 1923 Lords debates. See Chapter 6.

11

Crossing Swords

Norman Bentwich
'There is no Zionist on earth more ardent than he'

G iven his deep knowledge of the Palestine problem and his growing activism on behalf of the Palestinians through his work at the Arab Centre, it was inevitable that Jeffries would become involved in editorial sparring with Zionist advocates and propagandists. One important venue for this was the conservative weekly, *The Spectator*.

One such exchange, involving four correspondents in all, is of particular interest because two of the participants were prominent British Zionists, namely, Norman Bentwich and Blanche Dugdale, both of whom have figured earlier in this narrative, in Chapters 7 and 5 respectively.

Jeffries had referred to Bentwich, Palestine's attorney-general from 1920 to 1932, in his *Daily Mail* Palestine expose 13 years before, in the following terms:

> During the first ten days or so I spent in Jerusalem, to varying questions I put I would get every now and then the same sort of answer. "That was because of Bentwich," someone would say, or "Bentwich inserts this..." another would reply, or "Bentwich's idea has always been." The air is replete with the name of Bentwich; it is one of those names which gives vigour to

a conversation, because the moment it is uttered temperate talk flies out of the window. According to their political convictions, men in Palestine either bless or curse Mr. B... There is no Zionist on earth more ardent than he...[1]

Bentwich had written to *The Spectator* in response to a letter by Emile Ghory of the Palestinian delegation. This triggered a response from Jeffries, which in turn prompted a reply, not from Bentwich, but from Blanche Dugdale, Balfour's niece and biographer. This 'in turn' led to a lengthy exchange between Jeffries and Dugdale.

The eight-letter (Ghory/Bentwich/Jeffries/Dugdale) exchange (12 June, 1936 – 31 July, 1936) yields a fascinating insight into the thrust and parry of the debate between Zionist advocates and their pro-Palestinian opponents at this time. We begin with Emile Ghory's letter, written in his capacity as 'Secretary, Palestine Arab Party':

> The Press here, and its correspondents abroad, have certainly been generous in their news regarding the Palestinian situation. Unfortunately, however, they have presented only one side of the story, and ignored, deliberately or otherwise, many features and aspects pertaining to the Palestine disturbances. Below are only a few of the points which should be known by public opinion in this country.
>
> a) The Arabs and Moslems alone are supporting the general Arab strike. No foreign funds are given. The Arabs in Palestine are contributing very generously in money and food-stuffs. Jaffa alone has so far donated over P7,000. In Egypt, Syria, Iraq, and America – where there are many well-to-do Arab emigrants – funds are raised and sent to the Supreme Committee in Jerusalem. Moslem countries are now forming relief fund committees to support the Palestine Arabs.
>
> b) Incendiarism, arson, cutting of trees, and similar actions are not committed only by the Arabs, but also by the Jews. In fact the latter were the first to embark on the project of burning and demolishing property. On Monday, April 20th, the first incident took place, when Jews burned a two-storey

---

1. *Mr. Bentwich: The Key-Man of the Government*, 20/1/23, in J.M.N. Jeffries, *The Palestine Deception 1915-1923: The McMahon-Hussein Correspondence, the Balfour Declaration, and the Jewish National Home*, Edited by William M. Mathew, Journal of Palestine Studies, Washington, D.C., 2014, p 93. See Chapter 7.

Arab house at Jaffa. The statistics of the Jaffa municipality show that one hundred Arab houses were burned, and eleven demolished. Over 300 acres of crops belonging to the Arabs were burned in the Tulkarem district.

c) The Palestine troubles had their serious repercussions in both the Arab and Moslem worlds. Both worlds are becoming very restless. There were sympathy strikes and demonstrations in Syria, Iraq, and Egypt. In Transjordan the people (demonstrating) clashed with the police. Because the chieftains and tribesmen, arming to the teeth, announced their intention to come to the aid of their Palestinian brethren, the Mandatory Power despatched strong forces to guard the frontiers. All Arab and Moslem countries are now forming committees for the "Defence and Salvation" of the Holy Land.

d) The troubles have no flavour of religious (Islamic) strife. The Christian Arabs, numbering about 110,000, are taking actual part in the struggle against Zionism, side by side with their Moslem brethren. Incidents in the Holy cities of Nazareth, Cana of Galilee, Bethlehem, and Jerusalem, prove this fact.

On Ascension Day the Christian clergy, of all sects and churches, protested to the High Commissioner against the Mandatory's Zionist policy "which is threatening Christian sites." The Orthodox Patriarch of Damascus, Mgr. Alexandros Tahan, forwarded a letter to the Archbishop of Canterbury, drawing attention to the "apprehension of the Christians for the future safety of their Holy Places because of Jewish immigration," and appealing for a stoppage of that immigration.

e) The Arabs are complaining bitterly against the behaviour of the members of the Public Security forces. They see cases of beatings, destruction of property, insulting of women, invading homes, and similar actions. The following extracts are quoted in support of this assertion. (1) From a letter from a Jerusalem lady to a British lady: "… life is not worth living if we are going to keep on being treated so badly and brutally. The police and soldiers are behaving and treating us like no human being should be treated. They are very rude and unfair. Young boys and men are beaten, staffed, and searched at random. Even women are being insulted and beaten…" (2) From a telegram from the Arab National Committee at Nablus: "… Troops and police are destroying life and property… shooting of innocents with indiscrimination… officials of administration appointed judges are giving severe sentences while similar offences of Jews receive very slight punishment... the forces are violating the sanctity of the Koran by tearing it in the villages..."

I feel sure that such features of the situation in the Holy Land should be presented to the people side by side with the cases of "Arab snipers, marauders, rebels, bands," and similar names given to the young Arabs who are trying to defend their rights and liberate their country. (12/6/36)

Here now is Bentwich's response to Ghory:

The letter of Mr. Ghory... is neither designed nor calculated to make for better understanding in Palestine. And some of its statements are open to serious doubts. He says that Arabs and Moslems alone are supporting the general Arab strike, and no foreign funds are given. It is widely believed that the agents of one or more foreign Powers who are not sorry to foment trouble in the Middle East have contributed money to promote the strike. He states that arson, the cutting of trees, &c., are committed not only by the Arabs but also by the Jews. It is sufficient answer to that charge that the High Commissioner of Palestine has on several occasions borne witness to the restraint of the Jewish population in the face of most trying provocation. He says that the Arabs complain bitterly against the behaviour of members of the public security forces. "They see destruction of property, invading homes, and similar actions." The Palestine police, mainly British and Arab, are bearing a thankless task with a fortitude that compels general admiration. Daily British and Palestine Constables are wounded: almost daily innocent persons, Arabs as well as Jews, are murdered by bomb or revolver-shot or knife. In combating this terrorism the police and soldiers are forced to invade the home and damage property.

Recrimination, however, is useless and mischievous. The serious question is how to put an end to violence and restore peace. Palestine has been throughout history, and will remain, a bi-national country, one of the bridges between continents and civilisations where the East and the West meet. Arabs and Jews must live together, neither dominating the other nor being dominated. The Jews know that they cannot drive the Arabs of Palestine into other lands or the desert. The Arabs must realise that they cannot drive the Jews into the sea or stop their immigration. It is not economic interests which divide the peoples, but political passions. Jewish immigration has brought a general diffusion of well-being among all the dwellers of Palestine; and the immigration of the last years, which is the immediate cause of the outbreak, the thousands of Jews from Germany who are seeking a new home and a new life, are amongst the best elements which have come to Palestine. They are the fine flower of the German-Jewish youth, and they combine with their enthusiasm for a simple productive life the order and method which they learnt in Germany. The increased proportion of the Jewish population from one-tenth to nearly one-third, which has taken place in the last fifteen years, has not meant a diminution of the Arab population. On the contrary, the number of the Arabs rose between 1922 and 1931 by 200,000 through natural increase; and in the last years the numbers have risen not only in that way but by immigration of Arabs from the neighbouring territories, attracted by the prosperity of Palestine. The root of the trouble is that aggravated nationalism which today threatens the whole of civilisation. Politics dominates economics. The effort of all persons of good will must be to aid the fusion of the two peoples into one nation, sharing a common love for the fatherland, and working together in every aspect of public and economic life.

There are many examples of two nationalities originally hostile living side by side in a territory, and passing from feud and strife to the recognition of a common patriotism and to mutual helpfulness. That change has come about between peoples of different race in the Swiss Cantons, the English and French colonists in Canada, the British and Boer settlers in South Africa. The differences of language, culture and religion do not stand in the way once the will to understanding and co-operation is present.

Fifteen years ago Mr. Winston Churchill pointed out to an Arab Delegation in Palestine, which made the same demands as are being made by the Strike Committee today: "If, instead of sharing misery through quarrels, you will share blessings through co-operation, a bright and tranquil future lies before the country. The earth is a generous Mother. She will produce in plentiful abundance for all her children if they will cultivate her soil in justice and in peace." (19/6/36)

Bentwich's letter, it is worth noting, contains an early example of the Zionist propaganda trope about 'the Arabs wanting to drive the Jews into the sea': 'The Jews *know* that they cannot drive the Arabs of Palestine into other lands or the desert. The Arabs *must realise* that they cannot drive the Jews into the sea...' (italics mine) Ergo, the Jews are rational; the Arabs are not. Twelve years later, of course, the Jews would in fact be driving the Arabs of Palestine into both the sea *and* into 'other lands or the desert'. Had Bentwich been honest he would have written that 'The Jews know that they cannot *yet* drive the Arabs of Palestine into other lands...'

Jeffries responded to Bentwich as follows:

> For some seventeen years the Arabs of Palestine have been protesting to the British Government against the situation inflicted upon them. In answer they have received, officially or unofficially, either refusals to discuss the points they have raised or replies which – it is sad to have to say so – have wormed along from one subterfuge to another.
>
> Perpetually unheard, perpetually side-tracked, the Arabs have now broken into armed revolt in order to gain attention for their cause. It would have been better if they had not done this. None the less, the parallel for their rising is to be found in the uproars which in this country preceded the final Reform Bills, and in the violence which obtained women the vote after all logical pleas had failed them.[2]
>
> Everyone deplores the death of our soldiers in Palestine; everyone recognises that our authorities there must restore the public order of which they are the guardians. But the responsibility for the bloodshed in the Holy Land lies primarily where the responsibility for the bloodshed in England lay in 1839 – not on the rioters, but on the Cabinet Ministers who had refused consideration and had postponed reform.
>
> I am afraid that Mr. Bentwich's letter in your last issue is of no great service in this crisis. Indeed, it is harmful, for it is only too full of the phrases which for so long have been forcibly fed to the Arabs, which more than anything else have served to goad them into violence. Under each benevolent sentence some reversal of fact or some cold denial of their dues to the Arabs is barely concealed.
>
> "Arab and Jew," says Mr. Bentwich, "must live together, neither dominating the other nor being dominated." How equitable this sounds, yet in plain fact it means that the Arabs are not to have the ordinary majority rights of a population upon its native soil. "Palestine has been throughout history a bi-national country," says Mr. Bentwich, and thereby limits history to the last twenty years or so. In fact, between the Jews and Palestine there is a vacuum of centuries. Before the Mandate the Arabs were more

---

2. Reform Bills: a reference to the series of British electoral reforms which, by 1884, saw the vote extended to a majority of adult males.

firmly, longer, and more solely established in Palestine than are most of the races of Europe in their present habitat. During their long overlordship of Palestine precisely the one thing the Turks could not achieve was to make the country bi-national. Under its Turkish functionaries it remained integrally Arab. "It is not economic interests which divide the peoples (in Palestine)," continues Mr. Bentwich, "but political passions." The maintenance of the British Empire as British is a political necessity to which we all agree; but the maintenance on the same principle of an Arab land as Arab is a demand inspired apparently by political passion!

It is very adroit of Mr. Bentwich to try to substitute for the normal political birthright of peoples a new, uncodified, unlegalised economic birthright. But, however adroit, it is indefensible. In justice to him, though, it must be acknowledged that he is not alone in employing this stratagem, for the Colonial Office already has employed it. Amidst its dicta, in the Palestine Report of 1931, for example, is a statement that Jewish immigration should be "governed by the principle that it should not be so great in volume as to exceed whatever may be the economic capacity of the country at the time to absorb new arrivals."

Now, it is of the highest importance to grasp what this statement of British policy means. It means that political rights are abolished for the Arab. (In the "Balfour Declaration" significantly they are only promised "civil" rights, while the Jews are guaranteed in any part of the world against the loss of "political" rights because of the creation of the "National Home.")

The people of Palestine by this statement are shuffled secretly into a new category of human beings, as mechanical, economic units. Only economic reasons are allowed to stop the entrance into Palestine of an indefinite number of extraneous units. It is clear that as Zionist colonisation extends the economic capacity of the country increases, so that inevitably more and more units from outside have to be "absorbed." The original Arab units shrink from being nine-tenths of the population to being seven-tenths, and then a half, and presently a quarter.

Nothing comparable to this has been attempted elsewhere. If men are to be turned from men into economic units, if Great Britain wishes to apply this new theory of statesmanship, evidently she must begin by doing so on her own territory, after the British public has voted in favour of the project.

But she must not impose the new theory dictatorially on a small, weak population in the Near East by the strength of her aeroplanes and her bayonets and in despite of treaties. (26/6/36)

Blanche Dugdale
'Some of the "scorn" with which he views British policy has descended upon me'

At this point, Dugdale intervened. She was a woman devoted in equal measure to two things: keeping alive her uncle's flame – she had in fact written a two-volume biography of Balfour – and Chaim Weizmann, of whom she had written in her diary, 'When one is with Chaim one feels the infinite nobility of soul – the vast intellect – and knows that here is one of God's greatest instruments.'[3]

> It would be interesting if Mr. Jeffries would further elucidate his description of the Palestine Arabs as "perpetually unheard, perpetually side-tracked." Can he point to any occasion on which Arab representatives have been refused the ear of the High Commissioner in Palestine, or, for that matter, of the Colonial Secretary in London?
>
> I doubt whether Mr. Jeffries is doing the best service to the cause of peace when he encourages Palestinians to consider their racial problems in terms of "majority" or "minority" rights. But if he must do so, let him reflect which of the two races has most cause to fear being left, or placed, in the position of a minority.
>
> In the past eight weeks, damage has been done to Jewish property in fields, orchards and plantations, estimated at many tens of thousands of pounds. During this same period, not one Arab fruit-tree has been uprooted, nor one Arab crop burnt, by Jewish hands. Englishmen who have put their labour, their money or their love into the meadows or woodlands of their country can perhaps form some faint idea of the intense provocation, and the iron self-control which such a state of affairs must imply for the Jewish agricultural settlers.
>
> In the past twenty years, some 300,000 Jews (a number which, incidentally, does not exceed the increase in the Arab population itself during that period) have entered the land, trusting to the British assurance that they are there "as of right and not on sufferance."[4] Among their numbers are some 30,000 refugees from the Hitler Terror. Palestine, under the Mandate

---

3. Blanche Dugdale, *Baffy: The Diaries of Blanche Dugdale 1936-1947*, Edited by N.A. Rose, Vallentine, Mitchell, London, 1973, p 91

4. Right/sufferance: a reference to the Churchill White Paper of June 1922: 'In order that the [Jewish] community [in Palestine] should have the best prospect of free development... it is essential that it should know that it is in Palestine as of right and not on sufferance.'

administered by Great Britain, is so far the only country in the world in a position to afford some abiding shelter for the victims of the hideous revival of anti-semitism now defiling Germany. It is sad to find any Englishman who takes no pride or pleasure in that fact, but who seems to advocate yielding to the demands of the Arab extremists for the stoppage of immigration, which would, while the Arabs display their present spirit, in the end turn the Jewish National Home into a death-trap.

Lasting peace in Palestine will not come through the breaking of British promises to either section of the population, but its foundation might be laid through the speedy fulfilment of some of those promises which referred to large scale land development, in order to make room for a larger population. According to the experience and calculations of the best experts on Palestinian agriculture, a family scientifically cultivating irrigated land can live on five acres (as compared with a minimum of twenty-five acres of unirrigated land). There are still available at least three-quarters of a million acres of irrigable land which have not yet been developed.

The future of the great Arab nation is not bound up with that little notch in the vast territories inhabited by their race which Palestine represents.[5] What that future may be – politically or economically – no man can tell. But so far as it is possible to foresee the trend of events, it does appear likely that the Jewish National Home, established by virtue of historic right in the Land of Israel, will provide at any rate a partial solution for the Jewish problem, which is an international problem, and the direct concern of nearly every country in the world. (3/7/36)

The alert reader will of course note the echo in Dugdale's letter of later Israeli propaganda tropes. Before the Holocaust, the plight of Jews fleeing Nazi Germany could be invoked as a rationale for the Zionist project in Palestine. And before Hamas' rockets, 'raining down' on Sderot from Gaza, the burning of Jewish orchards could be hyped to arouse the sympathy of English farmers for their supposed counterparts in Palestine, 'Jewish agricultural settlers.'

Jeffries responded,

---

5. That little notch: a reference to Balfour's *Great Britain & Palestine* speech of 12 July, 1920: 'I hope that [the Arabs] will not grudge that small notch – for it is no more geographically, whatever it may be historically – that small notch in what are now Arab territories being given to the people who for all these hundreds of years have been separated from it...'

Mrs Dugdale, in your issue of last week, says that she doubts whether I am doing the best service to the cause of peace when I "encourage Palestinians to consider their racial problems in terms of 'majority' and 'minority' rights." The defenders of Zionism are very prone to mis-state their adversaries' case, and I fear that Mrs. Dugdale has done so in this matter. I cannot accept her definitions. Firstly, I do not encourage Palestinians. I encourage Arabs. The use of the word Palestinian is prejudicial because it assumes that there is a genuine nation established in the Holy Land, to be distinguished by this adjective from the Arab race which surrounds it. This is not so.[6]

Secondly, I am not encouraging the Arabs to consider, after any fashion whatsoever, a racial problem of theirs. Here again is a false assumption, but a much graver one. There is no racial problem in Palestine inherited by its inhabitants. We have created one by importing the Zionists. It is bad enough that we should be guilty of the wilful introduction of a problem into the Arabs' land, but that we should go on to describe it as 'their racial problem' passes all bounds.

Thirdly, it is very significant that Mrs. Dugdale, when dealing with Palestine, puts into inverted commas the words "majority" and "minority". I did not employ them and the text does not call for them. Mrs. Dugdale, however, inserts them because by those who support our present policy majority cannot be given its plain sense in Palestine. Yet, if one but looks into it, the long democratic struggle for free institutions comes to little else than the removal of inverted commas from the words "majority" and "minority" and the establishment of each as a practical body, the former enjoying its privileges, the latter its safeguards.

Today in Palestine, alone in the world, this is reversed. The minority has the privilege, the majority the safeguards. But now, indeed, is a reason for inverted commas; the "safeguards" of the majority in the Mandate are worded deliberately so that they cannot be accurately defined and enforced.

In the space of a letter I am not able to answer in full all the issues raised by Mrs. Dugdale. The Arabs have been able to give utterance to their grievances, but they never have been listened to. Their perfectly founded appeals against the legitimacy of the "Balfour Declaration" have been met by mere unproved denials from successive Colonial Secretaries. Mr. Winston Churchill, Mr. J.H. Thomas, Mr. Ormsby-Gore and others, after acting as the

---

6. In rejecting the word 'Palestinian' in favour of 'Arab', Jeffries is reflecting the original Arab national idea of a pan-Arab federation, of which Palestine was seen as an integral part.

witness for the Crown, have then returned to the bench and given judgements in their own favour. On the one occasion upon which it was possible to bring the acts of the Colonial Office before a neutral court of justice, in the matter of the Mavrommatis Concessions, the verdict was given by the Court of the Hague against the pretensions of the then Colonial Secretary [Churchill].[7]

Economic pleas are irrelevant. The death of British soldiers in Palestine is due to the insistence of Whitehall that the country is one where there are no political issues and that economic issues stand in their place.

Nor is there any Jewish right to Palestine. The historic claim mentioned by Mrs. Dugdale is not so much historic as prehistoric. If we are to engage in extravagant reconstitutions of the world of two thousand years ago, let us instal these enforced pageants amid our own people. I am sorry for the Jews driven from their homes by the tyranny of the Nazis, but we must not impose them on Palestine and try to cure tyranny with tyranny. Let us find room for them in our own Empire, not add to our reputation for hypocrisy by giving them a warm welcome to the shores of another people. (10/7/36)

Dugdale replied,

Mr. Jeffries objects to the use of the term "Palestinian" because he thinks that it "assumes that there is a genuine nation established in the Holy Land to be distinguished by this adjective (sic) from the Arab race which surrounds it." He is evidently not aware that

---

7. Mavrommatis Concessions: Euripides Mavrommatis was a Greek engineer who had obtained water and electricity supply concessions from the Ottomans. After the war, however, in Jeffries' words, 'the Mavrommatis Concessions... ran athwart the monopoly planned in complicity by the Zionists and the Colonial Office for the Rutenberg scheme.' (PTR, p 581) (It should be noted that when, on 4 July, 1922, Churchill told the House of Commons that 'At the time the Rutenberg concession was granted, no other application was before us,' he was misleading the House.) Mavrommatis, through the Greek government, took the matter to the Hague Court of International Justice. The Court found that the Rutenberg Concessions were 'not in conformity with the international obligations accepted by the Mandatory for Palestine.' Jeffries notes that this 'was the one occasion in which the Government of Mr. Lloyd George, the primarily responsible Government which had granted the Zionist monopoly, and the later Governments which had become accessory to this, were dragged by the hand of justice from the hiding-places where they lay screened by false Mandates, false vows, false Administrations and the debris of the Covenant of the League... Since then such a chance has never come again.' (PTR, p 595) Regarding Mavrommatis' concessions, delaying tactics by the Colonial Office led to him eventually settling for a payment of P60,000 in 1927.

the word "Palestinian" applies to all persons who were born in Palestine, or who, by fulfilling the necessary legal conditions, have become domiciled in the country, and are therefore entitled to receive a Palestinian Passport. The bulk of these people are Arabs and Jews, and it is in respect of them that I deplore Mr. Jeffries' allusions to majorities and minorities, because it is they who must find means of living in peace, side by side, and the gateway to peace is not through numerical calculations.

Mr. Jeffries excuses himself, on grounds of space, from any full reply to my last letter, but he selects from it one question – namely, on what occasions have the Arabs been "side-tracked" or "unheard"? In this context he quotes the decisions of the International Court of Justice at the Hague in the matter of the "Mavrommatis [sic] Concessions." This was a case involving a pure question of law, which turned on the question of whether, under the terms of the Treaty of Lausanne, certain Concessions granted to a Greek by the Sublime Porte before the War still remained valid. The Concessions were for supplying electricity to Jerusalem and to Jaffa. In the first case the verdict was in favour of M. Mavrommatis, in the other against him. But in neither case were Arab rights or interests in the slightest degree involved.

I cannot congratulate Mr. Jeffries on this choice of an illustration to support his theory that the British Government is deaf to Arab grievances. His general accusations against Mr. Winston Churchill, Mr. J.H. Thomas and Mr. Ormsby-Gore would require to be formulated before he could hope to make them impressive. (17/7/36)

Jeffries' penultimate letter delivered the mother of all *coups de grace*:

There is an Arab delegation from Palestine in London at the present movement. It is, I think, the fifth which has come to this country. Certainly it is one of a series of Arab delegations which have been spread over the years since the War and have remained in London, waiting on the Colonial Office, for periods varying from a complete twelvemonth.

The present delegation, though concentrating on the question of Jewish immigration, is making the same demands which its predecessors made. A couple of members, who belonged to previous delegations, are renewing the demands they made as much younger men. Last week a delegate said drily to me that he supposed their sons would come along in due course and repeat the pleas of their fathers to the same deaf walls. That is what I mean when I say that the Arabs have been unheard, a phrase by which Mrs Dugdale is rhetorically puzzled.

As for their being sidetracked, all that has been said or done, by the Arabs or on their behalf, in Palestine or out of it, during nearly two decades, has achieved what in reply? A succession of essays in verbiage from Whitehall. Public outcry and official enquiries have had the same answer. First one Colonial Secretary explains what the Balfour Declaration means, not to the Arabs, but to the Jews. Then another Colonial Secretary explains the explanation. This process has been continued till now the original Balfour Declaration is in a sort of mathematical situation, a surd surrounded by brackets upon brackets of explanation.

The final bracket very suitably was put in place by the hands of Mr. Ramsay MacDonald.[8] He excelled himself in a letter, a species of White Paper, addressed to Dr. Weizmann, who seems more and more to be winning the position of a sovereign State. That document, elicited by the most recent Commission of Enquiry into Palestine's affairs, touched upon all of these and deepened the obscurity surrounding each of them. Only one thing could be inferred with any likelihood, that the recommendations of the Commission would not be carried out. This proved to be true.

One of the persistent requests of the Arabs is that the recommendations of Commissions and of Reports appointed or instigated by British Governments should be carried out by those same Governments. It is a singular request for them to have to make. But, as Mrs. Dugdale would say no doubt, this request has never been sidetracked. The faithful observance, clause by clause, of the recommendations of the Shaw Commission, the Hope Simpson report, the French report, are equally familiar to her. I say nothing of old forgotten far-off things such as the Palin findings, given so widely to the world, and the rapid implementation of Lord Passfield's act of justice.

I write with scorn, but what other attitude is possible to anyone reviewing the behaviour of British rulers in the Holy Land? There are reasons excusing Mrs. Dugdale's advocacy, but into what pitiful artifices she is led. "The gateway to peace," she cries, "is not through numerical calculations." Does she believe that by calling the process which has placed the House of Commons at the head of the British people a "numerical calculation" she will hide its true nature? Is a man's vote a right in England and a wrong in Palestine? Is this country to profess

8. Ramsey MacDonald: Labour PM, 1924+1929-1931, National Government PM 1931-1935.

itself in Europe as the champion of democracy and in Asia as its enemy? Are we in England to set an example to despots of elective government, and out of England an example to elective governments of despotic control?

Pro-Zionists prate of the Mandate and of our "obligations" under it to the world. Is there a man in the world who believes in these "obligations," conferred by ourselves upon ourselves and for ourselves. As an honest and admirable writer has said, the San Remo Conference at which mandates were exchanged might have been termed by a cynic the "Inter-Allied Prize Distribution." The only obligation at San Remo to be heard of was in the spry tones of Mr. Lloyd George and the other national delegates, saying "Much obliged" as they passed the Mandates over the table one to another. "The utmost cordiality reigned," says a despatch of the period, describing the scene.

For reasons which escape me, we could not say then, nor have said since, that the retention of the adjacencies of the Suez Canal was necessary for the communications of our Empire. We could not straightforwardly proclaim there – as would have been quite proper – a Monroe doctrine of ours akin to the Americans' doctrine at Panama. Instead, under cover of a benevolent Mandate, we install the "National Home" violently, believing that its denizens will hold the fort for us. We refuse the population the freedom, under our guidance, which we had sworn to give them. We confer on Arabs *noms-de-plume* like "Palestinian" and proffer them safeguards which we are careful not to define. The tribes which cheered Allenby are fined by his successors, and ten battalions of British troops are in arms against a few devoted wretches where eighteen years ago a single infantryman could have garrisoned a town.

What is to be said of a policy which has brought us to this? (24/7/36)

Dugdale's was the final word:

I hate to confess myself beaten, but the effort to bring Mr. Jeffries' version of the history of British rule in Palestine into line with facts is becoming too great by comparison with the results obtained.

I do not understand what he means when he says that the British Government's successive White Papers have been "addressed not to the Arabs but to the Jews." These statements of policy are accessible to us all, and I would suggest that Mr. Jeffries should study the first of them, issued in 1922, and compare it with the text of the Mandate for Palestine and Transjordan. He will find that the White Paper restricts the area of the Jewish National Home to Palestine itself, whereas no such limitation is implicit in the Mandate. The reason for this very severe curtailment of Jewish settlement was that Transjordan lies within the boundaries of the territories where certain promises about Arab independence were made by the British Government to King Hussein. (See *Survey of International Affairs*, 1925, Vol.1, p. 361, published by the Royal Institute of International Affairs.) Mr. Jeffries dismisses all the White Papers as "essays in verbiage." It is a point on which he can claim to speak with authority, but it would be interesting to know whether this clause appears to him as redundant as the others. If it does not, then let him remember it next time he spills the vials of his wrath upon the British Government on the score of its alleged indifference to Arab rights.

Some of the "scorn" with which he views British policy has descended upon me, and the "pitiful artifices" with which I express my conviction that peace in Palestine does not depend on the relative numbers of its Arab and Jewish inhabitants. It depends upon the will to live together as neighbours, as both races must do, unless British promises to one or the other are to be disgracefully broken. Even today, Arabs and Jews are working harmoniously side by side in many of the enterprises which are bringing prosperity to the country, and have refused to allow their fellowship to be disturbed by political agitation. Surely it is by acknowledging, and encouraging, that spirit as far as we can that British people can best help to bring to an end the wreckage of hopes which is going on in Palestine at the present moment. (31/7/36)

The Jeffries-Dugdale exchange, it is worth pointing out, is the nearest thing we have to an editorial 'duel' between Jeffries and Balfour himself.

James A. Malcolm
'This hapless Prince seems to fill the role of a spar to which the defenders of political Zionism swim at intervals, when they can no longer maintain themselves even upon the dead sea of their "historic rights"'

Another letter of Jeffries' appeared in *The Times* of 14 July, 1936, this time on the subject of the Balfour Declaration:

I can bear out what Lord Islington, in your issue of the 7th, avers of the attitude of Mr. Edwin Montagu towards our policy in Palestine. Early in 1923, after returning from that country, I had a long conversation with Mr. Montagu at his house in London. He was uncompromising in his disapproval of the "Balfour Declaration" and of the whole system of forcible Zionist immigration under cover of the mandate. He told me that at the time the policy was first taken over by the Cabinet: this was done with altogether insufficient consideration. Mr. Lloyd George had insisted on the necessity for winning over Jewish-American influences in the United States to the side of the Allies (as indeed he has said himself lately) by a measure installing Zionism in Palestine. This measure was accepted hastily, every member of the Cabinet being intensely preoccupied with his own share of the general prosecution of the War. There was no proper consideration of previous countervailing pledges to the Arabs, no proper realization of the moral necessity of consulting the population of Palestine upon their fate, no proper understanding of the emptiness of the safeguards in the "Balfour Declaration" so far as that population was concerned.

Mr. Montagu was convinced that the aim of the Zionist body was to create a State under its control in Palestine under the envelope of the mandate. That explains his action in seeking to guarantee Jews elsewhere from the danger of losing their national citizenship in the countries of their birth, to which Mr. Franklin alluded yesterday.

Jeffries' letter drew the inevitable Zionist response from another of Weizmann's associates, James A. Malcolm, a Persian-born Briton of Armenian origin. (Malcolm would go on to boast, in a 1944 statement, how 'it fell to my lot to meet Dr. Weizmann and to initiate the negotiations which culminated in the publication of that historic charter of Jewish national resurgence.' In it, he claimed that it was he who had converted Sir Mark Sykes to Zionism and introduced him to Weizmann.)[9]

The late Mr. G. K. Chesterton wrote that the more unfounded a tradition was the more it persisted. A trite example of this is the supposed promise given to Palestine Arabs during the War, and this apparently is the theme of Mr. J. M. N. Jeffries's letter in your columns of July 14.

---

9. James A. Malcolm, *Origins of the Balfour Declaration: Dr Wiezmann's contribution*, 1944, mailstar.net/Malcolm

During the War the Palestine Arabs were active enemy belligerents, shut off from the world, and knew nothing whatever about any arrangement with Feisal in the Hedjaz. So if any promise was given to them it could only have been given presumptively through Feisal and that quite unbeknown to them.

Circumstances arose in the autumn of 1916 which necessitated a promise also being given to the Jews in the interests of the Allies, including such Arabs as cooperated with them. Although I have reason to believe that when the Balfour Declaration was made Feisal already had knowledge of its tenor, I do not think it matters when he was informed of it. The fact is that subsequently Feisal by his agreement with Dr. Weizmann and by joining the League of Nations, together with 52 nations, including two other Moslem States besides Irak, approved the Balfour Declaration and the Palestine Mandate.

While holding on to a promise if ever given and obtained for them by Feisal, the Arabs now repudiate his authority to speak on their behalf. In other words, they want to have it both ways.[10]

As to Mr. Jeffries's remarks about the late Mr. Edwin Montagu, I think everybody will agree that he was a Jew *sui generis* and there is no reason why his single if not singular opinion about Palestine as a Jewish national home should be accepted in preference to that of Jewry all the world over. In any case perhaps this year at least Mr. Jeffries will agree that one swallow cannot make a summer. (21/7/36)

Jeffries responded,

---

10. On Faisal, Malcolm writes as follows in his statement of 1944: 'At the request of Sir Mark Sykes I had an interview with General Haddad Pasha, the representative in London of the Sharif Hussein and his son Feisal. There were two other high Arab officers present. Although they had already some inkling from Sir Mark of the new developments in regard to Palestine, they were not at all pleased with the information I gave them that the Jews were to be promised Palestine in consideration of their help in gaining pro-Allied support in the United States. They did not want Jews to go to Palestine, which was an Arab land. But when I explained the importance of the matter and that the War Cabinet had resolved on it, they reluctantly agreed as they, too, realised the vital importance of American help. The fact that the much vaunted Arab revolt had been of such small dimensions was not without its effect on their decision. They undertook to raise no objections and said we could count on the Arab leaders agreeing to the settled British policy. During my interviews with T.E. Lawrence in London and in Paris during the War, and with Feyzal and Lawrence during the Peace Conference, I found Lawrence entirely favourable and Feyzal reconciled to the bargain being carried out. The agreement signed by him with Dr. Weizmann about April, 1918, bears this out.'

I have been moving about and by mischance did not see till to-day your issue of the 21st. In this Mr. Malcolm takes me to task for supporting, in a letter to your columns, the validity of the engagements to the Arabs which we contracted in the earlier part of the War. This is somewhat odd since I wrote nothing concerning this. My letter dealt only with Mr. Edwin Montagu. I testified to the strength of his feelings against political Zionism and recorded his complaint that the "National Home" policy had been foisted upon the Cabinet of which he was a member.

However, since Mr. Malcolm raises the question of my opinions, I may be permitted to state them perhaps. What Mr. Malcolm terms supposed promises were real engagements. They were not given to any section of the Arabs, but to the spokesman and head of their race at the time, the Shereef of Mecca.

These engagements were not dependent in any way upon the actions of the Emir Feisal. This hapless Prince seems to fill the role of a spar to which the defenders of political Zionism swim at intervals, when they can no longer maintain themselves even upon the dead sea of their "historic rights."

In this particular case Dr. Weizmann's agreement with Feisal, born after an unaccountably long parturition, does not seem to me of the slightest effect. It has a certain interest as recording the fleeting phases of mind of two distinguished men at a given moment, but as a treaty between the Arab State and any conceivable realm it does not begin to exist.

I am afraid Mr. Malcolm is making membership of the League of Nations altogether too attractive when he suggests that previous treaties can be abrogated for countries who join the League through any act of the League concerning their affairs. Treaties have to be abrogated formally by those who made them, as we have heard often enough of late. The Arabs so little agreed to the abrogation of the McMahon engagements that even when Lord Curzon himself in 1924 peremptorily summoned King Hussein to jettison them and accept the Balfour Declaration he refused. (28/7/36)

12

Partitioning Palestine

The Peel Report (1937)
'A new cause of the Palestine Question was created and a fresh acceleration to the initial velocity of revolt was applied'

7 July, 1937, marked a turning point in the Great Palestinian Revolt of 1936–39. It was on that day that the Peel Royal Commission published its report, recommending that Palestine be divided into Arab and Jewish states. In Jeffries' words, 'a new cause of the Palestine Question was created and a fresh acceleration to the initial velocity of revolt in that country was applied.'[11]

Jeffries responded ten days later with a trenchant critique, *Palestine, Arab or Jew: A Criticism of the Palestine Report*, published in the Catholic weekly, *The Tablet*. It is sobering to reflect, from the vantage point of the present, on the implications of his opening arguments, namely that (a) 'once a political issue grows complicated, however grave it may be, it never comes properly before the entire nation, because the abbreviated Press of today has no space for all its ramifications,' and (b) 'the guilty party may have twined a labyrinth of entangled deeds and words over the original case, and much time has to be given... for the painful unravelling

---

11. PTR, p 576

of this entanglement before the basic facts can be brought to light again.' If this were the case in 1937, how much more so is it today, 80 years later?

As in everything he wrote on the Palestine problem, whether it be an editorial letter or a 728-page book, Jeffries' essay on the Peel Report goes to the dark heart of the matter. Here it is in full:

> The Report of the Royal Commission upon Palestine, with its proposal to divide that country into two States, Jewish and Arab, has brought this great question again to the forefront. Discussion will now flow upon it again, or will flow as much as is possible, for the worst feature of the Palestine Question is precisely that it cannot be fully presented to the public. Once a political issue grows complicated, however grave it may be, it never comes properly before the entire nation, because the abbreviated Press of today has no space for all its ramifications.
>
> The Palestine Question is the first major example of this predicament. It cannot be treated in a column or in a couple of columns of a newspaper: certainly the Arab case cannot be presented within these limits, for much history has to be restated, a horde of documents have to be quoted, and many pronouncements of British statesmen and of Jewish leaders must be analysed at length. It is the common impression, I know, that in any dispute the innocent party has a short and immediately convincing case to give. But events do not always fall out like this. The guilty party may have twined a labyrinth of entangled deeds and words over the original case, and much time has to be given and much space has to be available for the painful unravelling of this entanglement before the basic facts can be brought to light again.
>
> The Report of the Royal Commissioners itself shows how this artificially produced intricacy of the Palestine affair operates against a proper understanding of it by the British nation. Indeed it operates too against the very solution of the Palestine affair which the Commissioners themselves, trying to conceal their despair, so bravely propose. On the twentieth page of their four-hundred-page Report, at the very start, therefore, they declare, "We have not considered that our terms of reference required us to undertake the detailed and lengthy research among the documents of twenty years ago, which would be needed for a full re-examination of this issue. We think it sufficient for the purpose of this Report to state that the British Government has never accepted the Arab case."

Now the particular issue here mentioned is the principal issue of all, the Arab contention that Great Britain, in the Hussein-McMahon papers of 1915-16, formally acknowledged and guaranteed Arab independence in an area which included Palestine. If this contention be true – and to the minds of most unbiased persons who have examined the papers it is true – then all the subsequent British action in contradiction to this pledge, the foundation of the "National Home," the publication of the Balfour Declaration and the insertion of it in the Mandate, all is null and illegitimate. Yet the Commission does not examine, or is not permitted to examine, this cardinal plea. It is not allowed to clarify "by the detailed and lengthy research among the documents of twenty years ago," which would appear to be its first duty, the issue upon which every other issue is dependent.

Instead of this, the Report says, as though that brought the matter an inch further, that the British Government has never accepted the Arab case. This is no excuse. In fact, it is something of an indictment. The trouble resides in this very point, that our Government has never been willing to submit the origins of the Mandate to the scrutiny of an independent party. When the Arabs declared that the Mandate was improperly constructed and – to take but one accusation – was in flat contradiction to the terms of the Covenant [of the League of Nations], all that we did was to say that in the opinion of His Majesty's Government the Mandate laid upon us the obligation of installing and furthering the progress of the "National Home." Mr Winston Churchill issued a bull on the Government's behalf, saying that he did not agree with the Arab interpretation of the dispute, and that was that. Nothing was ever referred to the Hague Court or to any independent tribunal. For twenty years we have been judges in our own quarrel.

The great defect of the Peel Report, in many ways an admirable piece of work, is that like Mr. Churchill it does not take into survey the propriety of the actions and of the general policy of successive British Governments, and particularly of the Government which assumed the Mandate. There have been too many Royal Commissions upon Palestine, none of which could or can be final because of their restricted terms of reference. What is needed to settle the imbroglio in that country, as far as it can be settled, is a Royal Commission upon Mr. Lloyd George. Lord Balfour would be included, of course, in the terms of reference. I do not mean by this that Mr. Lloyd George is to be impeached. But if the Peel Commission had merely enquired into his doings in Palestine upon the principles of scientific research, they could not have produced the Report which we have in our hands today. The Report they would have issued, whatever its findings, would have begun at the beginning of the matter. As it is, the Peel Report, like its predecessors, pretends to run a mile race and to set up its time as an example to Jew and Arab runners alike, when its drafters all started from the 440 yards mark.

That is why it must fail. That is why it is almost superfluous to deal with its ultimate scheme for Partition. I am aware that the adherents of a certain school of thought will say that I am harking back to old irreconcilable theories. They will say that this is the moment for dealing with the practical situation, and that Partition does offer a *modus vivendi*. I do not think that it does. It merely transfers the hatred between Jew and Arab, which to some extent is under Mandatory control, to the keeping of two irreconcilable States, which would have all the apparatus of governments at their disposal to foment it and to arm it.

Furthermore, I do not care for this perpetual subterfuge of the "practical solution." The way by which this solution comes to be proposed as the only possible solution is but too clear. You refuse obstinately for a period of years to consider the rights and wrongs of a question, knowing well that thereby factors are accumulating which will force a practical issue. In the present case we refused to discuss the rights and wrongs of the "National Home" but kept on introducing Jewish immigrants into Palestine, knowing that after a term of years so many would be there that their presence would form the "practical issue." This would have to be settled by methods of expediency. Thus we escape having to submit our actions in Palestine to the proper criterion of right or wrong.

Let me close on a note of hope. The Peel Report contains some contingent recommendations, in the event of Partition proving unacceptable. One of these limits Jewish immigration in the future to a figure which, allowing for the natural increase of Arabs and Jews, should maintain the Jewish percentage of population in Palestine at about the present figure. For this courageous finding, Lord Peel and his colleagues deserve the highest credit. If there is ever to be an ultimate solution of the Palestine question, the germ of it lies here. (17/7/37)

Debating the Peel Report

'How can anyone suggest that about a quarter of the Arab population should be removed by force from the land which they and theirs have occupied for untold centuries?'

On 26 July, 1937, nine days after his essay's publication, Jeffries took part in a panel discussion on the Peel Report, which included Leonard Stein, President of the Anglo-Jewish Association, and author of *Zionism* (1926), and, much later, *The Balfour Declaration* (1961). Fortunately, a transcript of the discussion, titled *The Report of the Royal Commission for Palestine: A Discussion*, appeared in the *Journal of the Royal Central Asian Society* of 4 June, 1937.[12] Jeffries' contribution reveals a man who was as good on his feet as he was with his pen:

> Let me first deal with one or two items in Mr. Stein's speech. He began by saying that a letter which appeared in *The Times* two days ago had, he hoped, disposed altogether of the McMahon papers. But this letter is by no means new. Sir Henry McMahon said the same thing fourteen years ago, and it made no difference whatsoever to the situation then. Nor does it make any difference to the situation to-day either, because in treaties, as in all legal documents, the only thing which matters is their text. If we are to be guided by the intentions people say they had or had not when writing the text, then there will never be an end in the future to any disputed issue. Every person concerned can allege intentions which no other person can corroborate. If intentions are to become the criterion of decision in international affairs, there does not seem to be much object in having written treaties at all. Why sign and countersign documents if they can be abrogated by states of mind?
>
> So with regard to the McMahon letters the fantastic plea of Sir Henry McMahon's intentions and of his belief in King Hussein's intentions governing their value cannot be entertained. Only their text is of any concern.
>
> In the second place, Mr. Stein spoke about the position of Jews elsewhere should the Jewish State envisaged in the Peel Report be

---

12. *The Report of the Royal Commission for Palestine: A Discussion, Journal of the Royal Central Asian Society*, Vol 24, Issue 4, 1937

founded in Palestine. On the whole I do not disagree with what he had to say, but I should like to mention something I encountered a good many years ago, in 1918. This was in Poland, when the war was just over. As it happened, I was the first person to enter Poland from the Allied countries.

Poland was just coming to life. Yet I found the Poles already complaining bitterly of Zionism. They had begun their renewed national life by making some sort of census, and they found that their Jewish citizens in large numbers were contracting out from it. They wrote themselves down as Zionist citizens. As early as 1918, therefore, the prospect of a Jewish State in Palestine was causing trouble. I am not defending or accusing the Poles in their relations with their Jewish subjects: I only chronicle that political Zionism was an immediate source of disaffection and bad feeling in Poland.

Mr. Stein spoke of the strategic dominance of the proposed Jewish State by the Arab State. I shall not enter into the strategic side of these future animosities. But I must observe that if you transfer the odiums which exist to-day between the Jews and the Arabs, which to-day are to some extent under the control of the Mandatory – if you transfer these odiums to a pair of States, wherein they can grow unchecked and can even be encouraged, then instead of ending the era of hatred you are merely giving it unlimited opportunity of expansion.

The most serious fallacy of the Peel Report is the assumption that separate States in Palestine would bring contentment to their populations. The Report says indeed that it is too much to hope that after Partition there would be no friction at all between Arabs and Jews, but thereon propounds the removal of minorities as a cure. But envenomed and displanted minorities, as history most often shows, fill the population they join with their own animus. Partition will give us not so much two States as two entrenched camps in Palestine.

I pass to some other considerations of the Report. No one apparently wants its recommendations much. Mr. Stein himself is dubious about them. Others of our opponents, however much they may be satisfied inwardly with Partition, are not, I think, too anxious to appear openly satisfied. The Arabs certainly do not want Partition. Parliament wishes to postpone definite discussion of it. So does the League of Nations. Mr. Ormsby-Gore has gone out to try and extract preliminary opinion from the Mandates Commission. He is much experienced in preliminary opinions, but I do not think that even he will extract one.

Not half enough attention has been paid in this matter to the League of Nations. I think there may be more obstacles at Geneva than people contemplate. Here is one of them. The Partition proposal must come eventually before a committee of the League Council. Italy, which has not quitted the League, can return to her vacant place at the Council table. Now she confirmed the Balfour Declaration, if it can be called confirmation, very differently from the other countries' way of confirmation. I speak of the old Italy, before Fascism came. She agreed to the establishment of the National Home on the understanding that no prejudice was caused to the legal and political status of the other "communities" of Palestine. She inserted in her confirmation the word "political," which, in my opinion, Lord Balfour and the other drafters so sedulously kept out of their Declaration.[13]

So the Italians are engaged to maintain the normal political rights of the Arabs throughout Palestine. They have held their hand so far, on the assumption, I presume, that the Mandate would terminate in the establishment of a National Government over all Palestine. But if a State is established in Palestine territory where the Arabs will have no political control at all, it is difficult to see how Italy can subscribe to this. Here is a source of infinite difficulty, if, of course, Italy resumes her seat at Geneva.

I come to the Peel Report itself. It is a fine Report in many ways. It contains statements which are of the highest interest. It speaks of "the door forced open for the Jews in Palestine." It says that "it is the Mandate which has created the antagonism between the Jew and Arab in Palestine." These are statements of fact which dispose of much old official fiction, such as that our Government is the victim of circumstances in having to handle an unworkable Mandate. The successive Governments which have insisted on this Mandate, of our own making, have not been the victims of circumstances, but the makers and the maintainers of these circumstances.

Then again the Report, in default of Partition, holds some valuable contingent recommendations, one in particular which amounts to keeping the present Jewish population at the level it has attained. This is for a period of years only, it is true, but as it is based on existing conditions which will not cease, it is a recommendation which will be renewed, I think, indefinitely.

Another merit of the Report is, however, a belated discovery. The members of the Commission discovered in Palestine what we

---

13. While Leonard Stein records this fact in his *The Balfour Declaration* (1961), Jonathan Schneer's 2010 book of the same title omits all mention of it.

who defend the Arabs discovered and said seventeen years ago, and have been saying ever since, when we had the opportunity. They discovered that the Arabs would not join the Jews in building up a common Palestinian State. Every child has known this in Palestine for nearly two decades. Yet we have had to wait till now for it to be acknowledged in an official document. It is held to be a great discovery, but in this respect Lord Peel, to my mind, is like a Columbus sailing out to-day and discovering modern New York.

From the Arab point of view yet another merit of the Report, and yet another belated discovery, is its confirmation that Mr. Lloyd George, General Smuts, Mr. Winston Churchill, Lord Cecil, and others from the beginning contemplated a Jewish State in Palestine. We know they did, but it is well to have the fact nailed down in the Royal Commission's own words.

But if many things are to be welcomed in the Report, its final recommendations are not. For a large Jewish State in the long run all they do is substitute a small Jewish State at once. The thesis of Jewish rule in Palestine is not dropped. The Peel Report, therefore – that is to say, the policy advocated in it – is not a change of heart, but a change of front only.

It is not surprising, therefore, that the Arabs should reject it. They reject it besides for a good many individual reasons, but I shall confine myself to speaking of three of them. The first is that Partition would grant the Jews their essential demand and refuse theirs to the Arabs. As I look at it, the essential Jewish demand is statehood in Palestine. Once this is granted the Jews, they are acknowledged to be in Palestine as by right. But the whole Arab case is that the Jews are not in Palestine by right. So that if a Jewish State were to be established and the Arabs were forced to recognize it, the Arabs would be abandoning the very basis on which every claim of theirs is built, while the Jews would have the essential basis of their claims conceded.

The second point turns on the working-out of Partition in practice. In their Report the Royal Commissioners recommend that "in the last resort the exchange (of Jews in the proposed Arab State and of Arabs in the proposed Jewish State) would be compulsory." This means that something like 225,000 Arabs are in danger of compulsory transfer.

This is an impossible proposal. It is called a transfer, but it is an eviction. How can anyone suggest that about a quarter of the Arab population should be removed by force from the land which they and theirs have occupied for untold centuries? Is it assumed that the British Army will be employed in the task of tearing families from their homes and their plots of land?[14]

In the Report an analogy is drawn on behalf of the "transfer." The example of the successful Graeco-Turkish exchange of populations after the war of 1922 is quoted. But the Graeco-Turkish transfer was the exact reverse of what is intended for Palestine. The Greeks were taken from Turkey and the Turks from Greece. In Palestine it is proposed that men, women and children shall be taken from their native soil, that they shall be removed from the fertile heart of it and from their ancient orange-groves, so that strangers may build up there an artificial State. It is a project not to be thought of.

Indeed, this transfer is so preposterous and iniquitous, there being practically no land to accommodate the evicted thousands in the hills to which they would be dispatched, that it does not ring true. I have a feeling that this scheme hs only been sponsored by the Government so that it may be withdrawn later, with lavish airs of concession to the Arabs. If it proves so, this is a familiar political gambit, and the Arabs will not be overreached by it.

The third reason is really the fundamental reason, though one does not hear much of it, largely because the Arabs have few chances of expressing their views. The Royal Central Asian Society, let me add, has shown a fine example by throwing open its tribune freely to exponents of the Arab case, and the Arabs are grateful to the Society. This, as I say, then, fundamental reason

14. Intimations of the Palestinian Nakba of 1948. Contrast this proposal to compulsorily transfer Palestinians from part of their homeland to make way for a Jewish state with the following passage in the Churchill White Paper of June 1922: 'Unauthorized statements have been made to the effect that the purpose in view [of the Balfour Declaration] is to create a wholly Jewish Palestine... His Majesty's Government... have no such aim in view. Nor have they at any time contemplated, as appears to be feared by the Arab delegation, *the disappearance or subordination of the Arabic population*... in Palestine... [I]t has been observed with satisfaction that at a meeting of the Zionist Congress... held at Carlsbad in September 1921, a resolution was passed expressing as the official statement of Zionist aims *"the determination of the Jewish people to live with the Arab people on terms of unity and mutual respect, and together with them to make the common home into a flourishing community, the up building of which may assure to each of its peoples an undisturbed national development."'* (italics mine) Now note what it is precisely that attracted Weizmann to the idea of partition: 'The Peel scheme... suggested that the restricted area offered to the Jews should be to some extent compensated by the transfer of a part at least of the Arab population at present living in that area. The possibilities offered by the Peel scheme thus become substantial, assuming that... the transfer scheme could, with the help of His Majesty's Government, be made effective, and carried out within a reasonable period of time.' (*The Letters & Papers of Chaim Weizmann: Series B.Papers, Vol II, December 1931-April 1952*, Israel Universities Press, Jerusalem, 1984, p 305)

for refusing Partition is that the establishment of a Jewish State in Palestine is not compatible with the maintenance there of Arab ways of life and of the country's native civilization.

Arab life and Jewish life, Arab aims and Jewish aims, are two irreconcilable things. They cannot continue indefinitely side by side, and there will never be any solution of any kind in Palestine till this is recognized. I have discussed this matter thoroughly with my Arab friends and that is what they feel.

The Jewish National Home, now to be turned into a Jewish State, is nothing if it is not a Westernized, industrial, urban institution. The Peel Report recognizes this readily and frequently. It says, "The remarkable urban development in Palestine has been Jewish." It speaks of the Jewish hope of yet more "new towns growing up along the sandy coast." It recognizes that out of every five hundred Jewish immigrants only thirty-two are workers on the land. "With every year that passes," says the Report, "the contrast between this intensely democratic and highly organized modern community and the old-fashioned Arab world around it grows sharper."

What till now has been falsest in our policy in Palestine has been the repeated invitation to the Arabs to take part in this essentially Jewish "development" of their country. As Palestinians they were to work hand-in-hand with the Jews at this joint task. But we never asked first of the Arabs, before issuing the invitation, whether they wished to progress after this fashion. It was assumed that they did so wish, though a modicum of thought and a modicum of enquiry would have shown that for an Arab such progress meant that he was to abandon his native culture and to assimilate himself to the culture of the Jews. There would only be a future for him if he thought like a modern Jew, acted like a modern Jew – in short, if he turned himself into a modern Jew.[15]

---

15. The Zionists and their British supporters at this time promoted their colonial project in Palestine as a necessary vector for the introduction of European industrialisation in the Middle East, a development which they claimed would ultimately benefit the Arabs whether or not they wanted it. Churchill's extraordinary speech of 4 July, 1922, in the Commons, is a classic statement of the idea: 'Left to themselves, the Arabs of Palestine would not in a thousand years have taken effective steps towards the irrigation and electrification of Palestine. They would have been quite content to dwell – a handful of philosophic people – in the wasted sun-scorched plains, letting the waters of the Jordan continue to flow unbridled and unharnessed into the Dead Sea.' Churchill's words, of course, are an immediate post-war variation on Herzl's promotion of a Jewish State in Palestine as 'a rampart of Europe against Asia, an outpost of civilization as opposed to barbarism.' Today's variation on the theme is the hyping of Israel as the original 'start-up nation,' a sort of indispensable, high-tech light unto the world.

If the Arab did this, then he would be rewarded with those "economic benefits" which figure on various pages of the Peel Report. After a great lapse of time, it was the ancient temptation of Esau renewed in more modern style, with "economic benefits" in place of pottage.

But the Esaus of Palestine have learned their lesson. The development of Palestine on Jewish lines is exactly what they will not have. A man of pre-eminent intelligence went out to Palestine some years ago and perceived that this was the kernel of the problem.[16] Dr. Weizmann had been offering the Arabs what they least desired. "The Arabs need us," said Dr. Weizmann, "with our knowledge and our experience and our money." But the celebrated visitor knew better. "There is not the slightest difficulty," he wrote, "in stating in plain words what the Arabs fear in the Jews. They fear in exact terms their knowledge and their experience and their money. The Arabs fear exactly the three things which Dr. Weizmann says they need."

That is the fundamental reason why the Arabs rejected what was called "co-operation" with the Jews under the Mandate, and it is for the very same reason that they reject Partition. What would Partition mean? It would mean, no doubt, that in their new area they might (in so far as the homeless thousands thrown upon them would permit) try to create the Palestine at which they aim, a simple country. It would be cleared of endemic diseases, of malaria and the like; it would be provided with better roads, it would inaugurate certain improvements in agriculture, it would establish a reasonable system of land-tenure. But it would remain a quiet country, free of urbanization, of intensive industrialism, of all the qualities which are the essence of the Jewish idea. It would be a country of subsistence-farming.

What would it have alongside it? A Jewish State, which, however small, yet would be highly mechanized, linked to world finance, aiming at world commerce, enmeshed with the advanced intelligentsia of every continent. Over its economic policy the Arabs would have no control, and into its orbit the Arab agricultural State must inevitably be drawn. Indeed, the Peel Report foresees this, thinks ahead and proposes that the two States should have a species of Customs-Union. How significant!

That is why the Arabs must reject Partition and must reject any scheme which does not give them general control over the economic policy of Palestine as a whole. In an Arab Palestine the Jews now present there would have their rights and could enjoy

---

16. The 'man of pre-eminent intelligence' was the British writer G.K. Chesterton.

as much of their particular kind of "development" as they have accomplished already. But there must be stop to increase of this, and the Arabs must not have forced upon them in exchange for their malaria that moral malaria of industrialism which now is devastating the West, with its class-warfare, its proletariat, its communism, its making men into mere units, and all its other attendant ills.

With Arab Palestine descending into full-scale rebellion – unsubdued until 1939 – the British government despatched yet another commission[17] to Palestine to determine the practicability of partitioning the country. For Tannous and his comrades in London, the only positive development of the time was the elevation of Colonial Secretary Ormsby-Gore to the peerage and his replacement by the more independent minded Malcolm MacDonald.

---

17. The November 1938 report of the Woodhead Commission (officially the Palestine Partition Commission) concluded that, since both Arabs and Jews were opposed to partition, it was therefore impractical. The government thereupon abandoned the idea, deciding instead to convene a conference in London for Jews and Arabs in an effort to reach a compromise of some kind.

13

Publishing Reality

'There were tears in his eyes'

Although the manuscript of *Palestine: The Reality* was ready for publication by the latter half of 1938, Jeffries found it difficult to find a publisher. Why it was not accepted by Hutchinson, the publisher of his first two books, we do not know. We can only speculate that the book, with its devastating critique of British politicians and policies, and its uncompromisingly anti-Zionist stance, was simply too hot to handle for Britain's publishers.

Tannous' account of the frustrations experienced by a joint Arab/Indian Muslim parliamentary delegation, in London at the time to lobby on behalf of Palestine's struggle for independence, sheds some light on the difficulties encountered by anyone seeking to publicise the Palestinian case:

> Upon their arrival, the delegation gave a press conference at the Arab Center which was attended by a large number of correspondents; but to our disappointment, the Jewish control of the press was able to suppress all news of the press conference [...] Because they could not get much publicity in the press, the Arab and Moslem Parliamentary Delegation decided to circulate a statement which they very carefully prepared narrating the full story of the parliamentary conference held in Cairo [in July 1938 in support of the Palestinian Arab struggle], of its resolutions,

and of their mission in the United Kingdom. By means of paid advertisements, they advertised the statement in the papers before it was circularized. However, to their great shock and astonishment they found out that there was not a single printer in London who was willing to print that statement. This made them furious and they tried again and again but in vain; and when they thought they had finally found a company who accepted the job, the statement was returned to them in its original form one day before the promised day of delivery with the company's deep regrets![1]

The above paragraph immediately precedes Tannous' account of Jeffries' own predicament at this time. It is an extraordinary story, movingly told by the Palestinian doctor, and one replete with insight into Jeffries' character and motives:

> But this was not the only case where Jewish power and influence stood in the way of such publications. The book of J.M.N. Jeffries, which took ten years to write and was ready for print, experienced the same difficulty. The book did not speak well of the Zionists and stood for rendering justice to the Arabs. But what publisher in England dares publish a book which did not praise the Zionist movement, much more to criticize it? Day after day and month after month passed by without result and poor Jeffries, indignant, reached the point of frustration. At last, one bright day, with a smile on his face, Jeffries walked into my room at the Arab Center accompanied by a gentleman. He introduced him as one of the managers of Longmans, Green & Co., a well-known publishing house with branches in New York and Toronto. Jeffries said that Longmans was willing to publish his book, which he called *Palestine: The Reality*, if I fulfilled the following conditions: 1) I had to read the manuscript and then submit to the publishers a statement to the effect that, in my opinion, the book was authentic. 2) I had to buy immediately 500 copies of the book at 20 shillings a copy, the money to be paid in advance.
>
> I asked if there were any more conditions to comply with and the manager said no. I then promised to read the manuscript and I asked the manager to be kind enough to come back for the statement and the check after the lapse of five days. Losing no time, I went straight to the Milestone Hotel and closed myself in my room for three complete days reading the manuscript. When the manager came with Jeffries on the sixth day, I handed him the

---

1. Izzat Tannous, *The Palestinians: Eyewitness History of Palestine Under British Mandate*, I.G.T. Co., New York, 1988, pp 252-54

statement and the check. Just before handing the manuscript to the manager, Jeffries wrote on the second blank page of the manuscript in his own hand: 'To my Colleagues of the "Arab Centre".' There were tears in his eyes. And when the book was published some months later, he was kind enough to present me with a copy on which he wrote: For my old friend Tannous who has helped me from milestone to milestone on the long road of this book. J.M.N. Jeffries, The Arab Centre, London, March 1939.

Jeffries thought at that time that he owed me something for helping in the publication of his book; but, alas, the contrary was the truth. Not only I, but the whole Arab world owes J.M.N. Jeffries a debt which was never paid. The ten years he spent writing that rare piece of history on Palestine were, for him, years of agony. He was of poor means, but what hurt him most was the demeanor of his Government in [relation to] the government of Palestine which he could not tolerate. Consequently, he was in pain for ten long years criticizing those in Whitehall and revealing their wrongdoings. He was the first to disclose the McMahon/Hussein Correspondence in the Daily Mail and the first to write on the collaboration between Ormsby-Gore, the Colonial Secretary, and Weizmann on the Partition Scheme of the Royal Commission. To me, Palestine: The Reality was not only the reality but the Book of Revelations.

The last time I saw J.M.N. Jeffries was in 1939, at the Arab Center. When I returned to London in 1945 to open the Arab League Centre, he was not there and I was told that he was working at the British Embassy in Madrid. But I wanted to see him again most emphatically, not only to thank him again and again for the splendid production, but to kiss the honest and noble hand which inscribed it.[2]

Apart from the 500 copies of Palestine: the Reality pre-purchased by Tannous (which presumably ended up in the Middle East), we unfortunately know nothing of the book's print run, the extent of its distribution, or its sales. No second edition appeared in Jeffries' lifetime – although a photographic reprint of the book was issued in the United States in 1976, a matter we shall return to later. (By way of contrast, my own copy of Antonius' book is a second edition, issued in December 1938, the first appearing only the month before.)

2. Tannous, pp 254-255

14

Reviewing Reality

Having at last overcome the publishing hurdle, problems seem to have arisen with regard both to the distribution and reviewing of *Palestine: The Reality*.

George Mansur, an associate of the Arab Centre, felt compelled to address an open letter on the Centre's behalf to British librarians on April 26, 1939, calling on them to stock the book. In it, he confided that 'One of the reasons which have induced this letter is that there appears to be little desire to review a book which makes unpalatable revelations, however well proved by documentary evidence.' In fact, he went on in the very next sentence of his letter to suggest that something more than a mere reluctance to review the book was involved: 'How far it is just to establish a boycott of this sort, which keeps the book from public knowledge, we must leave others to say.'

Tellingly, Mansur explained, '[*Palestine: The Reality*] has had to be issued... at a price which makes it more of a library book than one for the average private purchaser.'

We cannot say, of course, to what extent, if at all, Mansur's plea had any effect on Britain's librarians. As for reviews, however, boycott or no, several emerged from April 1939 through to October 1940. Since the focus of this work is as much, if not more, on *Palestine: The Reality* as it is on Jeffries himself, any data on how it was received by reviewers is integral to our story.

Such reviews as I have been able to find, therefore, have been included here, in whole or in large part.

Norman Bentwich
'Undisguised propaganda'

The only unfavourable review of *Palestine: The Reality*, by Norman Bentwich no less, appeared on 28 April, 1939, in the pro-Zionist *Manchester Guardian*. Predictably, given the history of antagonism between the two men dating back to 1923, not to mention the ideological gulf which separated them, Bentwich's review could perhaps be described as more an act of revenge than a review:

> This book is undisguised propaganda. It is a statement of the Arab case about Palestine by one of the principal workers of the Arab Centre in London, and it entirely fulfils its aim, "to give that case as amply as possible." Its 725 [sic] large and closely printed pages reproduce every detail of the Palestinian Arab grievances and argumentations. The book is a monument of industry and – partly – of devotion, but it is perhaps a little late in the field. It appears when the Palestine Conference is over and a few months after the Arab case has been set out more concisely and persuasively, and not less authoritatively, in the "Arab Awakening" of Mr Antonius. The elaboration of the old complaints is a bit wearisome. Thus the first chapter urges that, as Israel of the Bible did not possess the coastal plain, therefore the Jewish settlement in the plains to-day is not true Zionism. The second chapter argues that Palestine is necessary for the expansion of the Arab race and brushes aside the emptiness of Iraq. The abuse of all the statesmen who have supported the policy of the Jewish National Home is also irritating. Thus, Lord Cecil is described as "odd, eternal, inexplicable, hallucinatory." There is a gibe at Lloyd George and Balfour as "acetone and accessory," and so forth.
>
> The account on the cover innocently suggests that, if the evidence and argument are accepted, "the book alters everything in respect of Palestine." But the bias is so obvious that the book is likely only to convince the converted. An occasional slip in the facts is inevitable, but it is hard that the Bishop of Chichester should be confused with the Bishop of Rochester as the co-author of a pamphlet against the Jewish National Home.

Jeffries could hardly take such a cheap shot lying down, and replied in his usual dignified manner in the paper's issue of 13 May, 1939:

> May I be allowed a word of self defence, in relation to a book of mine, "*Palestine: The Reality*," which you were so good as to review in your number of April 28? I have nothing to say, of course, about the estimate of my book in this review, which is in nowise my affair.
>
> There is in the review, however, a misstatement of my own sentiments, and though this I am sure was unintentional, I think I am entitled to correct it.
>
> Your reviewer found irritating my "abuse of all statesmen who have supported the National Home." I am not guilty of this universal abuse. I have only abused statesmen when they passed from support of the National Home, from advocacy of the National Home that is, to the violation of the Covenant, to the installation of illegal Governments, to the falsification of the mandate, and so forth. Since I have not done this without producing my evidence, I do not see that I deserve any reprobation for it. On the evidence abuse seems to me a very minor punishment for the statesmen involved.
>
> But I went out of my way in my book to draw a distinction between these men and their successors in power who only had committed, I wrote, "sins of omission by continuing with a policy into the antecedents of which they had not inquired." Farther on I developed this point, mentioning some statesmen to whom what I said applied, and finding "moderately comforting considerations" in their attitude. This seems to me temperate enough, and very far from abuse. It is important for me that I should not be held to attack people indiscriminately for holding opinions merely, and that I should be recognised as only vituperative against improper methods of supporting opinions, and it is on these two counts that I ask leave to clear my character.

Bentwich's antipathy toward Jeffries would, in fact, continue on into the 1960s. In his 1962 autobiography, *My Seventy-seven Years: 1880-1960*, he couldn't even bring himself to name Jeffries in the following paragraph on Lord Northcliffe's visit to Palestine in 1922:

> Northcliffe brought with him the *Times* Near-East correspondent, Philip Graves, and left him to study the position and write a series of articles. By one of those ironies which

are common in Jerusalem, on the same day as Northcliffe denounced the Zionist policy a reception was given by the Jewish community to Graves, in honor of his exposure in the *Times* of the forgery of the Protocols of the Elders of Zion. The articles which Graves wrote for the *Times* were a serious but not unfriendly appreciation of the conditions in Palestine, and of the achievement both of the Jews and of the Administration. But another journalist of a different kind was sent to write up the conflict in Palestine in sensational articles for other papers owned by Northcliffe, and the campaign of abuse made the Governor's task more difficult.[1]

The remaining five reviews, all overwhelmingly positive, are quoted from in the order in which they were written.

Douglas Valder Duff
'A damning indictment of the whole of our Palestine policy'

Douglas Valder Duff was a prolific memoirist, and the author of countless tales of adventure for children. He had served as an officer in the Palestine Police in the 1920s, and had, as a consequence, (as Jeffries put it in a review of Duff's 1936 book, *Palestine Picture*)[2] a 'close knowledge of [the troubles of that land] at a crucial period.' Duff's review appeared in the *Catholic Herald* of 24 March, 1939:

> This is a damning indictment of the whole of our Palestine policy. There is no escaping the well-documented charges of perfidy and cynical breaking of promises advanced by Mr. Jeffries in this most ably written and easy-flowing book. But, and in this lies the pity, Mr. Jeffries feels so burningly the sense of shame and dishonour which we people of Britain have incurred through our toleration of things done in our name, that he has allowed his feelings to master his position as a sober historian.

---

1. Norman Bentwich, *My Seventy-seven Years 1880-1960*, Routledge & Kegan Paul Ltd, London, 1962, pp 75-76
2. *Palestinian Puzzles*, Catholic Herald, 4/12/36. Jeffries wrote of *Palestine Picture* that Duff 'quotes at every point the untouched conversations of Arabs, Jews, British and Arab police, soldiers and officers, priests and layfolk of all races, with whom he has discussed the Palestine question. All these sidelights, taken together, illumine the subject clear as the sun. The reader will be startled probably to learn how desperate is the situation.'

This is more than understandable. The whole history of our guardianship of Palestine is a wretched business. With our eyes open, with the experience of our Irish maladministration behind us, we have committed every fault, both of commission, and more especially of omission, which stained the pages of the Anglo-Irish story. If one looks back to the conquest of Palestine in 1917, across the misspent years between, it is a sorry story of the fading of the dreams of the Last Crusade into the gloom of to-day's unholy mess.

Promises were made, even when promises exactly contrary had been given a few weeks previously. Both Jew and Arab were deceived. It is hard to believe that the British Government did not realise what they were doing when they promised Palestine to the Arabs, for documents of the time other than the McMahon Correspondence fully bear out that they realised to the full they had done so.[3] In the same way the Balfour Declaration was given, after many arrangements and intrigues, when the British Cabinet were most fully aware of the previous promise to the Arabs.

But the tale does not end there – it has gone on ever since, as Mr. Jeffries' documents fully prove. But it is here that one must take leave to disagree with Mr. Jeffries. He sees the Jews as the tyrants and liars. The fact is that both Jews and Arabs are equally victims. Our own Government's mistakes and inconsistencies have had their natural consequences – we have had to go on in the same way ever since, to stifle the complaints of the Palestinians, Jews and Arabs.

People in this country hardly realise how much the question of the Holy Land is discussed by other nations. We brought the Assyrians to fight for us – they died in scores of thousands, trusting in our promise of freedom. They served us in Irak – and were left to be martyred and exiled for their Christian Faith in 1933, and since, as soon as they were of no further service to us.[4] Jews and Arabs have likewise been betrayed.

---

3. Tibawi cites 10 British documents that support the Arab case for Palestine's inclusion in the McMahon pledge. See his *Anglo-Arab Relations & the Question of Palestine: 1914-21*, pp 464-466

4. Duff refers in his autobiography to 'a shameful and callous betrayal by Britain of the Assyrians, the oldest Christian people in the world, who had shed their blood so copiously and fought so well for us, relying on our promises that they should be installed as a nation with a land of their own. The Assyrian Chaldeans, who still use, as their vernacular, the Aramaic, which was the tongue of our Lord's Ministry, suffered and died because they acted as our auxiliary troops garrisoning Iraq for us, but their betrayal was kept so quiet that few Britons realize the depth of contempt that we won for ourselves by that exceptionally shabby incident.' (*Bailing with a Teaspoon*, 1953, p 87)

If Mr. Jeffries had only restrained the journalist in himself, or rather, if his sense of injustice had not blinded him so far that his hatred and hostility of the National Home breathes from every page, his admirable book would have gained immensely in value. As it is, Mr. George Antonius's recent book has covered all the ground which Mr. Jeffries now traverses. But, if this book, *Palestine: The Reality* does something to awaken the reading public to a sense of the truth, I imagine that Mr. Jeffries will relax in his chair, conscious of work well and truly done. The book is invaluable to any student of matters Palestinian, but let that student realise that the righteous indignation breathing from every page tends to warp the values of Mr. Jeffries' conclusions.

Unfortunately, much of Duff's final paragraph is misleading.

Far from being the fire-breather he claims, Jeffries is in fact a model of controlled passion, and his barbs, though deadly, are the very model of elegant wit. Duff's aversion to what he terms Jeffries' 'hatred and hostility of the National Home' and his 'righteous indignation' tells us as much about this ex-colonial cop (with a soft spot for Zionist settlers), as it does about Jeffries. Duff's capacity for detachment, for example, evident in the following vignette from *Palestine Picture*, could be described as bordering on the callous:

Jamil, a young, fresh-faced, blue-eyed Bethlehemite came up to me, and bluntly asked me if I had returned to help the Palestine Government to suppress his people [...] I told [him] that I was a simple visitor, and, first of the Palestinians that I had met, he and his comrades believed me. "Two of our young men killed and three wounded this morning, Effendi," said Jamil. "What do you think about that?" I answered that Mustapha Effendi had said that there were no casualties. "Would you care to see the dead?" he demanded savagely. "Or to hear the groans of the wounded? You may, if you accompany us." As gently as I could I let him understand that I did not wish to mix in any of Palestine's unhappy affairs. I was a simple tourist, an onlooker, with no personal concern either way.[5]

---

5. Douglas Duff, *Palestine Picture*, Hodder & Stoughton, London, 1936, p 174

One is left wondering what Jamil said to his comrades once out of earshot.

Duff's bald assertion, moreover, that Antonius' book 'has covered all the ground which Mr Jeffries now traverses,' makes one seriously doubt whether he has actually read either in full.

Finally, the sweeping charge that Jeffries 'sees the Jews as tyrants and liars' is simply not true. One wonders whether Duff actually made it all the way to the following passage on page 711 of *Palestine: The Reality*:

> All we can do, and must do, is to see that any settlement is in accordance with the Arabs' rights. Justice, and not expediency of any kind, must guide us. We must avoid particularly false solutions based on forgiveness all round in Palestine, based on Arabs and Zionists and Britons being deemed as involved in a common misfortune and upon their all starting afresh, under some scheme which will be the old scheme disguised. Forgiveness all round is, as a doctrine, only a label for forgiving ourselves. We are no victims of circumstances in Palestine along with the Arabs and the Jews. We made the circumstances: we, by the acts of our rulers, and we alone, are primarily responsible for the state of that country, and there must be no self-absolution proposed by us.

The Tablet
'Mr Jeffries has written a book of ... permanent historical value'

Palestine: The Reality was reviewed anonymously in the Catholic weekly, *The Tablet*. The magazines' Wikipedia entry suggests that it may have been written by Douglas Woodruff: 'From 1936 to 1967, the review was edited by Douglas Woodruff, formerly of *The Times*, a historian and reputed wit whose hero was Hilaire Belloc. His wide range of contacts and his knowledge of international affairs made the paper, it was said, essential reading in embassies around the world.' The review appeared in the edition of 8 April, 1939:

> Mr. Jeffries has written a book of such permanent historical value, and at the same time of such immediate vital importance, that the reviewer's paramount task is to ensure, so far as he is able,

that the fully-documented facts contained in it should reach as large a public as possible.

The treatment of the native population of Palestine by the English Government ever since 1916 constitutes one of the blackest chapters of fraudulent diplomacy in the whole record of our dealings with other nations, and in this book every detail of the sorry business is sifted and exposed.

The succession of events may be summarized in a few words. At the end of 1915, when our failure at Gallipoli had made our position in the Near East critical, a solemn undertaking was given by the English Government to the Sherif of Mecca that, in return for his active assistance against the Turks, we should recognize and support the independence of the Arabs within the territories included in the limits and boundaries proposed by the Sherif. Palestine was an integral part of these territories. Hardly was the ink dry upon this pledge when two mutually contradictory proposals, both of which broke our word to the Sherif, emanated from our Government. These were the Petrograd Memorandum, which introduced the idea of Jewish colonization and a share for the Jews in the administration of Palestine; and the Sykes-Picot Treaty, which looked forward to the internationalization of that country. In 1917 the famous Balfour Declaration, by which the Jews were to be established in Palestine without the assent of the population, as a future Jewish State, was issued under pressure from international political Zionism.

Ever since the end of the War, in spite of the Anglo-French Proclamation to the Arabs of Palestine in 1918, that "the only care (of England and France) is to assure, by their support and efficacious assistance, the normal workings of the Governments which these populations freely shall have given themselves," political Zionism has succeeded in swaying English policy to an ever-increasing extent, and the pledged rights of the Arabs have been progressively wrested from them. The following are some of the outstanding landmarks in this anti-Arab process: the muzzling of Feisal at the Paris Peace Conference; the disregard for the just and statesmanlike "Damascus Programme" issued by the Arabs; the complete suppression of the report of the King-Crane Commission, sent out to Palestine by President Wilson, which stated that Zionism was aiming at "practically complete dispossession of the non-Jewish inhabitants," and that "nine-tenths of the population were most emphatically against the entire Zionist programme"; the decision of the Anglo-French Convention in September, 1919, to split Syria into two parts, the northern to be under French occupation and the southern (Palestine) under that of England[6]; the San Remo Conference of April, 1920, at which it was agreed that England should assume a mandate over Palestine based upon the Zionist Balfour Declaration, although, until after the Peace Treaty with Turkey and the consequent action of the League of Nations, there existed no sort of legal authority for such a mandate; the encouragement from that year onwards of an increasing volume of Jewish immigration, of Jewish influence in the government of the country, and of concessions granted exclusively to Jews – notably the Rutenberg Concession – by which Palestine should be converted into a modern industrialized State on the worst kind of Western model; and finally, the mandate itself, when at last it was authorized in 1923, which not only flagrantly transgressed the Covenant of the League of Nations governing mandates, but was demonstrably drawn up in terms dictated by the Zionists to a willingly subservient British Government, or, to put it in Mr. Jeffries' trenchant words, "the mandate represented by British Ministers to the Arab people as a behest sacredly received and dutifully observed by them was in all that mattered written by Zionists and for the rest written by themselves."

Since 1923, the date of this "gerry-mandate," which legalized (if such a term can be used) our breach of faith with the Arabs who had materially helped us to win the War, the Palestine situation, as Mr. Jeffries shows in his detailed study of all the events, both there and in England and at Geneva, has gone from bad to worse. Commission after Commission has had to be sent out from England to settle the growing violence of the feuds which Zionism has engendered, till at last the Peel Royal Commission reached Palestine in November 1936, after a year of insurrection, strikes, and extensive military measures. Its plan for the partition of the country, so soon to be negatived by the Woodhead Technical Commission, which followed it, led up within recent weeks to the London Jew-Arab Conference, which has arrived at no agreed conclusions and in its turn left things as they have been for over twenty years. This latter Conference, however, has had one beneficial effect, which the publication of Mr. Jeffries' book at so crucial a moment is likely to emphasize and greatly expand – it

---

6. With the signing of the Anglo-French Convention of 15 September, 1919, writes Jeffries, 'a provisional Franco-British frontier was arranged across the middle of Syria, by which military occupation was demarcated on Sykes-Picot lines.' (PTR, p 304) Damascus, Homs, Hama and Aleppo were evacuated by the British, but the French were to stay out of them pending an Arab appeal for 'help and advice.' The arrangement left the British with a free hand in Palestine.

has drawn public attention to the just and unanswerable claims of the Arabs, not only by causing the publication after twenty-four years of the McMahon-Hussein Correspondence which, together with their immemorial occupation of the country, is the Arabs' charter of independence in Palestine, but also by the publication of a second White Paper in which the proceedings of an Anglo-Arab enquiry into the interpretation of this correspondence are recorded, and go far to establishing the Arab contentions.

Since political Zionism appeared on the scene in 1916, the fate of Palestine, from depending upon a simple and elementary conformity with natural rights and a pledge given, is shown by Mr. Jeffries to have been wilfully complicated by a succession of English Cabinet Ministers for the express purpose of supplanting the rightful inhabitants of the country by an alien race forcibly inflicted upon it. He puts before the reader with remarkable clarity and thoroughness every detail of the Arabs' consistent and overwhelmingly convincing resistance to the contradictions and evasions of our Governments; and to the latter he applies a lens of such searching power that hardly a line in the whole picture of their subterfuges can escape notice.

This is a book in which (for all its 700-odd closely-printed pages) not a single statement is made without the production of the fullest corroborative evidence in the shape of quotation from documents and recorded speeches. It is judicial in the highest sense. But Mr. Jeffries has more to offer than even his consummate industry and conscientiousness. He has taken an important part, amongst his many other activities, in the drama of which he writes. It was he, for instance, who was responsible, as long ago as 1923, for the first publication (in the *Daily Mail*) of the McMahon-Hussein letters. He constantly visited Palestine and its neighbouring States in search of light upon the truth, and was accorded an interview by Feisal, in which the latter explained the reasons for the proclamation of Syrian independence. He is familiar, too, with many of the principal characters, English, Arab, Jewish, etc., in this absorbing chapter of history. He speaks with the authority of first-hand evidence.

But this book possesses still another quality that cannot be left without at least a brief notice. It is delightful to read. Mr. Jeffries is a master of irony, and particularly excels in the use of highly original and illuminating images. These latter appear constantly all through the book and are brilliantly apposite. For instance, speaking of [...] the "legalization" of our mandatory control after San Remo: "The status of the mandatory was legal, or it was not legal... Legalization did not creep slowly like a blush across the ivorine cheek of the Mandatory Government, nor flow like rainwater through its executive channels, so that June 1922 was rosier and more legitimate than June 1921, or February 1923 more liquidly lawful than the February of 1922. No, all was illegal and pallid and dry till, on September 29th, 1923, in one swift movement the water was turned on, or, as you like, the permanent rouge was dabbed upon the Governmental cheeks."

But had *Palestine: The Reality* been as dry as dust as it is actually exciting, it would still have been the duty of all who value justice and the integrity of England to read it.

Sir Godfrey Rolles Driver
'A serious contribution to contemporary history which deserves a place beside Mr Antonius' Arab Awakening'

Sir Godfrey Rolles Driver was a professor of Semitic Philology at Oxford University. He was an expert on the Dead Sea Scrolls, and oversaw the translation of the Old Testament for the New English Bible. According to one source, he 'was a man of ruthless honesty, but as free from malice as he was from hypocrisy.'[7] His review of *Palestine: The Reality* appeared in *The Spectator* of 30 June, 1939:

> This book, though its style and manner occasionally betray it as the work of a journalist, is a serious contribution to contemporary history and deserves a place beside Mr. Antonius' *Arab Awakening*, and it can only be hoped that the two authors will between them succeed in opening the eyes of the world to the force of the Arab claims. Both have done their work admirably, and it will not be their fault if they fail.
>
> Mr. Jeffries gives a full and detailed account of the Arab case against Zionism from a time well before the Balfour Declaration till a point just before the publication of the Woodhead Report. His work is fully documented, containing indeed many documents not generally known, which are quoted more or less *in extenso*, and his case is fully and carefully argued. Thus it becomes tragically clear how one promise could only be kept by breaking another. The defect, however, of the book is the

---

7. F.F. Bruce *Godfrey Rolles Driver, The Witness* 105, No.1255 (July 1975) pp 266-267

author's constant harping on the theme of Governmental and political dishonesty, which it is hard to associate at any rate with such a man as Lord Balfour, and this makes the new book less dignified in its statement of the case than is that of Mr. Antonius. To my mind Mr. Jeffries does not make sufficient allowance for ignorance (*e.g.*, concerning the peoples of Palestine) and opportunism (largely encouraged by the exigencies of the war), which are the common faults of politicians all the world over. Another trouble which the story reveals is the evil result of religious sentimentalism, which saw in Zionism (of whose nature it was quite unaware) the fulfilment of Biblical prophecy. Here Mr. Jeffries does good service by drawing a clear distinction between a genuine religious yearning which even before the War led pious Jews to return to the land of their fathers, pity for refugees from European persecution, and political Zionism. Inability to make these distinctions is at the bottom of much of the dangerous nonsense talked on the subject.

There is also a lesson for all governments to learn: the wisdom of not listening to the most importunate suitors. This appears to have been the besetting sin of a succession of Cabinets, from that of Mr. Lloyd George onwards, and especially of the Colonial Office; the Jews were at hand and vocal, able often to exert pressure in indirect ways, as through American Jews, while the Arabs were distant and to a large extent incapable of making themselves heard. The line of least resistance was to gratify the Jews and ignore the Arabs. The revelations, if fairly put, concerning the Foreign Office (*e.g.*, in the matter of the McMahon pledge and the Sykes-Picot agreement) and especially concerning the Colonial Office (*e.g.*, in the story of the Mavrommatis and Rutenberg concessions) can but amaze the reader. It seems clearly to emerge from the whole story that no one in the Colonial Office knew anything at first hand about Palestine: for example, no one seems to have known or, if anyone knew, to have cared, that 91% of the population is Arab, and that of the remaining 9% many of the local Jews are anti-Zionist. It is desirable that all such Civil Servants should spend a period of time every so often living in the country with which they are concerned so as to obtain knowledge of it at first hand and to keep it when acquired up to date.

Many, too, of the incidental things told by Mr. Jeffries reveal a lamentable outlook towards Palestine in every class of person: such are Lord Balfour's insolent exclamation "Who are those men in petticoats?" on seeing some Arabs in Jerusalem; Mr. Jabotinsky's ridiculous demand for the admission of six or more million Jews within ten years; and the suspicious obscurity in which the damning French Report has been shrouded.[8] This document shows that by 1935 Zionism had produced 11,000 landless Arabs and 5,000 unemployed Jews, and that it cost £72,000 in that year for the Government to buy back land to resettle a few of the dispossessed Arab families. To the absurd claim that the Zionists are conferring great benefits on the Arabs Mr. Chesterton has rightly replied that what these fear is just "their knowledge, their experience, and their money"; for they know that Western industrialisation is ruining the land, which has not enough water for both agriculture and industry, for an Eastern peasantry who have no aptitude for it. May not the Arab reply that, so far from the East wanting to be Westernised, the West may well want Easternising if its soul is to be saved? Further, Zionism, which was intended to save the War for us, has gone far towards losing the peace for us, as Sir Arnold Wilson has said. We paid for Jewish money by giving the Jews the country of our Arab allies, hypocritically deceiving ourselves into identifying the modern (largely mongrel) Jew with the ancient Hebrew, and so have forfeited the friendship of gallant allies who shed their blood in the common cause; and now Germany is making every effort to seize the chance thus offered by forming a Panislamic bureau in Munich and inviting young Arabs to Nuremberg. The only redeeming feature of a sorry situation is that the Arabs are said, despite their ungrateful treatment, still to hold individual Englishmen, especially those who administer their affairs on the spot, in honour and respect.

It is a misfortune of Mr. Jeffries' study of the Palestinian problem that it is so long that few of those who ought to read it will take the trouble to do so.

Predictably, Driver's review came under attack in a 21 July letter to the editor by Israel Cohen, General Secretary of the World

---

8. Lewis French, in Jeffries' words, 'was sent out to report on the initial steps to be taken in order to put into effect the recommendation that the whole agricultural policy of Palestine must be remodelled by the introduction of intensive development throughout its rural areas... to make a register of Arabs who had been displaced by Zionist occupation.... to draw up a scheme for the resettlement of these displaced Arab families... [and] to ascertain what State or other lands could be made available for close settlement by Jews.' This was in response to the Shaw Commission pointing out that 'a process was under way in Palestine which was creating a large landless (and discontented) class,' that is, that 'the extension of Zionist holdings was by degrees driving the Arabs out of possession of the land.' In short, the British had either to retain the present agricultural regime, and halt Zionist immigration, or change it utterly to make room for more immigrants. See PTR, pp 637-638

Zionist Organization in London. It is included here not only because, like the reviews, it is an artefact in the story of Jeffries' book (albeit, in this instance, indirectly), but because Cohen's letter perfectly illustrates Jeffries' injunction against being 'drawn into intricate discussions' with Zionists, and away from a focus on Zionism's main game, which is to 'abstract' from the Arabs 'the sole possession and control of [their] native land':

> Professor G.R. Driver, in his review of Mr. Jeffries's book, *Palestine: The Reality*, writes that the policy of the British Government concerning Palestine was "to gratify the Jews and ignore the Arabs" because "the Arabs were distant and to a large extent incapable of making themselves heard." He appears to have overlooked the fact that two official Arab delegations were heard by the Council of the Peace Conference – the first headed by the late King Feisal and the second by M. Chekri Ganem.[9] Neither of these delegations demanded independence for the Arabs of Palestine. Feisal asked for independence for various Arab territories with the exception of Palestine, which "for its universal character he left on one side for the mutual consideration of all parties interested." M. Chekri Ganem, head of the Syrian Arabs, welcomed the settlement of Jews in "an autonomous Palestine," and said: "If they form the majority there, they will be the rulers." So far were the Arabs from being ignored that they were allowed to form independent States in the Hedjaz and Iraq, Syria was promised independence after a period of mandated administration, and Transjordan was detached from Palestine and placed under the rule of Feisal's brother, Emir Abdullah.
>
> Professor Driver refers to "the suspicious obscurity in which the damning French Report has been shrouded." The Reports by Mr. Lewis French were never shrouded in any obscurity: they have always been available from the Crown Agents for the Colonies (probably also from H.M. Stationary Office) for two shillings. Since the Supplementary Report was published on April 26th, 1932, it is impossible to understand how it could have shown, according to Professor Driver, that "by 1935 Zionists

---

9. Chekri Ganem [Shukri Ghanem] was, according to Allawi, a 'French national of Syrian origin who had lived outside Syria for forty years... Ghanem made a long, flowery speech [to the Council of Ten], aimed mainly at undermining Faisal's claims to represent the Arabic speakers of the Near East. He also called for the establishment of a mandate over Syria without consultation.' (p 202)

had produced 11,000 landless Arabs and 5,000 unemployed Jews." A careful examination of the Reports fails to reveal any such figures. Mr. French wrote (p.60) that it was "impossible to forecast what numbers will eventually have to be provided for out of the 3,700 claims preferred," and that he was not prepared "to attempt at present any more precise conjecture than one which puts the figures between 1,000 and 2,000." In point of fact, the total number of claims of displaced Arabs admitted by the Government was only 644 (Report on the Administration of Palestine, 1935, pp. 62 ff.), and although the Government set aside a sum of L250,000 (out of the large surplus to which the Jews had contributed out of all proportion to their numbers) for the settlement of these Arabs upon fresh holdings, not more than £85,796 was needed for the purpose up to March, 1938 (Report on Palestine, 1938, p. 204).

Professor Driver further observes: "We paid for Jewish money by giving the Jews the country of our Arab Allies." He is utterly mistaken if he imagines that there was any sort of financial transaction or even an offer of financial assistance on the part of the Jews in connexion with the issue of the Balfour Declaration. On this point he cannot do better than refer to the Report of the Royal Commission (pp. 22-24). In any case, what does he mean by the expression "giving the Jews the country of our Arab Allies"? The British Government paid £4,000,000 for the military assistance of the Arabs outside Palestine, and that country was delivered, after 900 years under a succession of foreign rulers, by British troops, including Jewish battalions. As for "giving the Jews the country," has Professor Driver never heard of the White papers of 1922, of 1929, and of May 17th, 1939?

Nevill Barbour

'He set out, in the same sort of crusading spirit in which Emile Zola once set out to investigate the Dreyfus case, to expose what he considered to be a grave miscarriage of justice'

Nevill Barbour, a British scholar of the Arab world, reviewed *Palestine: The Reality* for the July 1939 issue of the *Journal of the Royal Central Asian Society*. Barbour would go on, in 1946, to publish his own work on Palestine, *Nisi Dominus: A Survey of the*

Palestine Controversy. Strangely, however, it contains no reference whatever to Jeffries' work[10]:

> In his book *The Arab Awakening* Mr. George Antonius wrote: "For a score of years or so the world has been looking at Palestine mainly through Zionist spectacles and has unconsciously acquired the habit of reasoning on Zionist premises." The author of *Palestine: The Reality*, having been sent to Palestine in 1920 by the late Lord Northcliffe to investigate the facts of the case on the spot, at once conceived the very gravest doubts concerning the justice and expediency of the mandatory experiment. He thereupon set out, in the same sort of crusading spirit in which Emile Zola once set out to investigate the Dreyfus case, to expose what he considered to be a grave miscarriage of justice. The result of his labours during eighteen years is now offered to the public in a volume of over 700 pages. The book is extremely readable and almost every page is adorned with felicitous and often extremely pungent epigrams. Referring to the obsession of young Zionists with various kinds of ideologies, Mr. Jeffries remarks: "Mostly these young people came from Eastern Europe, but were hardly at all Eastern. They were European in a generalized way, without territorial connections, but breathing the ideas in the European air... Theirs was a disembodied existence, with no real home save in what was thought and spoken. They had grown up in books, and they lived in speeches." The best justification for the attempt to found a National Home for the Jewish people is, of course, precisely the desirability of rooting these young people in some soil and civilization of their own. Mr. Jeffries would reply that this does not give them the right to dispossess another nation, that Palestine is in any case too small to serve the purpose, and that, since it forms an essential portion of an homogenous and hostile Arab whole, the final result is bound to be disastrous. He would claim, too, that owing to the overwhelmingly urban development of the National Home, there are, in fact, just as many *luftmenschen*, to use the Jewish phrase, in Tel Aviv as in any other city in the world which has a correspondingly large Jewish population.
>
> Those who have studied the Minutes of the Permanent Mandates Commission at Geneva will appreciate also the elements of truth in the following description: "What generally went on in Geneva... was a factitious searching of consciences in public.

---

10. Nevill Barbour is also the author of *A Survey of North West Africa (The Maghrib)*, 1959.

The Government (whichever it happened to be)... would say that it viewed 'its mission' in Palestine in such and such a fashion. Did the Mandates Commission, it would ask, feel that this point of view conformed with the obligations laid upon the Government as mandatory by the League? The Mandates Commission would anxiously ponder the point and, after a paper-deep criticism or so, would propound that the Mandatory was carrying out his obligations most satisfactorily. Proceedings always ended in exchanges of compliments, after a preliminary exhibition of virtue fearful of itself, during which Government spokesmen and members of the Mandates Commission... like mountebanks did wound/ And stab themselves with doubts profound."

Of Mr. Jeffries, at any rate, it cannot be said that he is in the habit of unconsciously "reasoning on Zionist premises." An example will make this clear. Zionists, dissatisfied at the attitude of the Military Administration, the Army and the subsequent civilian officials, have constantly complained of the haphazard way in which these administrators were selected, of their low cultural standards as compared with those of the Jews whom they had to administer – this, by the way, with regard to a body of officials of whom Sir Ronald Storrs and Mr. C.R. Ashbee were representative members! – and of their failure to comprehend Zionism ("They only half understood the Balfour Declaration" – Leonard Stein). By this means a "Zionist premise for reasoning" was established, and a succession of Colonial Secretaries and Commissions of Investigation duly devoted their time and energies to inquiring whether the difficulties of implementing the Palestine Mandate were, in fact, due to the lack of education and anti-Semitic prejudices of British officials. In the end they invariably decided that they were not; but in the meantime they had been successfully diverted from examining whether the difficulties were not due to the peculiar nature of Zionism itself. Mr. Jeffries interprets these facts in a very different manner. "The Army," he says, "was the sole large category of average British citizens which had direct access to the facts of the so-called 'Palestine problem' ... The authorities of the military administration had a knowledge of the subject which the Prime Minister and other Cabinet Ministers of Great Britain had not acquired, and indeed had steadfastly refused to obtain. So the undoubted fact that the Army in all its ranks was, with the fewest exceptions, anti-Zionist... is but the most convincing proof that officers and men were alert to what was going on around them. They reacted, more earnestly than politely, against the great wrong planned in the interests of the 'National Home' against the population in the midst of which they lived... As the Army at that time was constituted, its soldiers sprang from every class and were of every type of the British people, and the whole evidence was before them. In a way, they were empanelled by their presence upon the scene, and it was in a great trial by jury that they returned the verdict of 'Guilty' upon Zionism as practised in Palestine."

The author is very severe indeed in his criticism of Zionist diplomacy. In point of fact, however, it may be doubted whether it was any more disingenuous than that of many European powers under similar circumstances, particularly when it is realized that the Zionists had no army of their own to pull the chestnuts out of the fire for them. Mr. Jeffries is probably right in claiming that the Mandate was only a rather ill-fitting cloak, beneath which it was sought to carry out a previously planned colonizing operation entirely inconsistent with the principle which the Mandatory system had been expressly designed to embody. In many respects the project only differed by its intensity from similar operations in Algeria and Morocco, Libya and Albania. The moral justification in each case must be sought in the right of an energetic population from Europe to develop a comparatively backward land in spite of the resistance of the indigenous inhabitants. In this particular case, Jewish "need" was certainly in an altogether different category from that of either the French or the Italians. On the other hand, Palestine, owing to its very limited area and natural resources, its relatively dense existing population and the justifiable claim of its inhabitants to govern themselves, was a singularly unpromising territory for any such experiment.

Mr. Jeffries brings forth abundant evidence that the Zionists did, in fact, plan from the beginning to monopolize Palestine and its natural resources for their own exclusive benefit, while in the meantime claiming that they desired nothing more than to share with the Arabs in the task of building up a common homeland. The author quotes, for example, the following two pronouncements. They were both sponsored by Dr. Weizman, one at the end of 1916, the other early in 1917.

1) "The Jewish Chartered Company is to have power to exercise the right of pre-emption of Crown and other lands and to acquire for its own use all or any concessions which may at any time be granted by the suzerain government or governments."

2) "The Zionists are not demanding in Palestine monopolies or exclusive privileges, nor are they asking that any part of Palestine should be administered by a Chartered Company to the detriment of others."

The reader will have little difficulty in deciding which of these two statements was designed to convey Zionist aspirations in a private memorandum to the ear of the British Government and which to present them to the public in a letter to *The Times*.

How the method worked is shown by a passage from the Report of the Zionist Executive to the first Zionist Congress which was held after the war. "In quarters in which Zionist aspirations were regarded with unqualified sympathy the view was almost universally taken that it was neither possible on general grounds, nor desirable in the interests of the Zionist Movement itself, to provide in the Mandate for the conferment on the Zionist Organization of anything savouring of an economic monopoly. There could be no doubt that Zionist co-operation in the economic development of the country would, in practice, be welcomed, and that Zionists would have every opportunity of participating in it to the full extent of their resources. On the other hand, the concession, *in terms*, of far-reaching privileges, *while in itself adding little of practical value*, would excite opposition which there was no advantage in gratuitously challenging and which might even be plausibly represented as inconsistent with the Covenant of the League of Nations."

Mr. Jeffries gives detailed information of the administrative methods which were used, he maintains, to "welcome" Zionist participation, as in the case of the Rutenberg Concession, and to exclude all other participation, as in the case of the Mavrommatis Concession.

The system was rooted in the Balfour Declaration itself. The author has done a remarkable piece of research on the famous protective clauses of the Declaration "*it being clearly understood that nothing shall be done which may prejudice the civil and religious rights of existing non-Jewish communities in Palestine or the rights and political status enjoyed by Jews in any other country.*" He demonstrates that this text was drafted by the Zionists themselves, and that they utilized for their draft an earlier American-Zionist document, dealing with the demands that Jews proposed to put forward on behalf of their co-religionists at the end of the war. "This manifesto demanded for the Jews full rights wherever they lived in the world... 'It being understood,' said the manifesto, 'that the phrase full rights is deemed to include: (1) Civil, religious and political rights; (2) the securing and protecting of Jewish rights to Palestine'."

Instructed by the Foreign Office to include a clause in the Balfour Declaration, securing both Jewish rights outside Palestine and non-Jewish rights within it, the Zionist drafters carefully limited the rights to be guaranteed to the non-Jewish communities of the National Home to "civil and religious rights." These, as a Zionist advocate was later to demonstrate to the Royal Commission, meant little more than the right to hold property and to attend divine service. The late Lord Peel expressed some astonishment at this interpretation, but Mr. Stein, the advocate in question, no doubt knew the real intention of the drafters, since he had himself apparently been one of them. When, however, the drafters came to the question of the rights to be guaranteed to Jews in "all countries of the world," they dropped the limiting qualifications, "civil and religious," spoke of "rights" in general and amplified these with the new phrase "political status." In view of this evidence, there can, it would seem, be no doubt that the Zionist drafters intended to deny the Arabs in Palestine rights which they demanded for themselves in countries in which they themselves were, and expected to remain, a minority.

A short summary of the author's conclusions may be of utility. Mr. Jeffries considers that the issue of the Balfour Declaration was forced through the War Cabinet by Mr. Balfour and Mr. Lloyd George during the absence in India of Mr. Montagu, who had, on a previous occasion, succeeded in inducing the Cabinet to reject the proposal. There was no preliminary discussion of the project in Parliament, nor was any serious investigation made into conditions in Palestine. The one Near Eastern expert who had been consulted and favoured the scheme was Sir Mark Sykes. By the time of his premature death in 1919, however, he had conceived grave doubts concerning Zionism and was about to use his influence to modify the project. The text of both the Balfour Declaration and the Mandate was drafted by Zionist Jews; being modified, however, by the instructions of the Foreign Office, until they became capable of a different interpretation from that of the Zionists. No Arab representatives were ever consulted in the formulation of either the Declaration or the Mandate. The latter was forced on to the League of Nations, regardless of its inconsistency with the Covenant, by the same sort of means that it had been pushed through the Cabinet. In spite of the demand of the Assembly of the League, it was never submitted to that body for examination, discussion or approval. The Cabinet refused to allow it to be discussed by the House of Commons. The House of Lords, which did discuss it, expressed its disapproval. No independent British investigation was carried out either into the practicability of Zionism in general, as a means of solving the Jewish problem, or into the feasibility or justice of establishing a Jewish Commonwealth in Palestine. The only investigation made on the spot, that of the American King-Crane Commission, reported that "Jewish immigration should be definitely limited and that the project for making Palestine distinctly a Jewish Commonwealth should be given up." This report, for reasons which have never been fully elucidated, was not made public in time to influence the debate on the Mandate in the American House of Representatives.

The concluding chapters deal with more recent events. The documentation is here much slighter and there are demonstrable inaccuracies. Mgr. Mubarak, for example, is Maronite Archbishop of Beirut, not Patriarch.

In general, however, the book is based on the results of years of painstaking and minute research; when due allowance has been made for the element of exaggeration inherent in the author's picturesque and ironic style, his presentation of the genesis of the Mandate is deserving of the most careful consideration.

William Yale
'A book which every informed student of the Near East in general, and of the Arab lands and the Zionist movement in particular, must read with utmost care'

Finally, an American perspective from historian William Yale. Yale had been a military observer with Allenby's forces in Palestine during the war and a technical adviser to the 1919 King-Crane Commission. He had gone on to become a professor of history at New Hampshire University (1928–57), a Department of State Specialist for the Palestine area (1942–45), and a professor of history at Boston University (1957–67). His review of *Palestine: The Reality* appeared in *The American Historical Review* of October 1940:

> Mr. Jeffries's book on Palestine, like *The Awakening of the Arabs* [sic] by Antonius, is one which every informed student of the Near East in general, and of the Arab lands and the Zionist movement in particular, must read with utmost care. It deals with the intricacies of the Arab-Zionist problem from 1914 to 1938 in very considerable detail. From the very beginning to the end of his book the author makes his position absolutely clear. He is a bitter opponent of political Zionism, he believes that the Arabs

have been very unjustly treated, and he scathingly condemns the British government's policy in Palestine. Despite the polemic nature of his treatment, Mr. Jeffries's thorough knowledge of the subject, his familiarity with its many aspects known previously only to an initiated few, and his extensive documentary evidence compel respect and demand the critical attention of a wider circle of readers than the specialists in the field.

In dealing with the British commitments to the Arabs Mr. Jeffries has nothing particularly new to contribute, but his chapters on the Balfour Declaration are revealing and throw much light upon the hitherto obscure political manoeuvres which led up the historic declaration of the British foreign secretary of November 2, 1917. [...] To American readers Mr. Jeffries's analysis of the part played by Justice Louis Brandeis in framing the Balfour Declaration and in gaining the support of President Wilson is of particular interest. The author, quoting Mr. de Haas, concludes that the American Zionists, and under their influence President Wilson, were in no small degree responsible for the action of the British cabinet in supporting the Zionist movement. It may come as a surprise to many that influential members of English Jewry were profoundly opposed to political Zionism and attempted to prevent the British government from giving its endorsement to Zionism.

An interesting point made by the author is that the "Civil Government" set up in Palestine in 1920 was an unlawful government because the mandate for Palestine was not awarded to Great Britain at that time, and could not be because the peace treaty with Turkey had not then been concluded. In consequence the status of Palestine should have remained "occupied enemy's territory" under the rules of war, in which no new policies could legally be instituted which would prejudice the final disposition of conquered territory. Mr. Jeffries argues that this "illegal Civil Government" was created to get rid of a military administration which was unsympathetic to Zionism and which was obstructing the activities of the Zionist Commission in Palestine. General Bols, former chief of staff of General Allenby, the chief administrator of Palestine in 1920, in his report to the British cabinet denounced the activities of the Zionist Commission and recommended its abolition. Lloyd George is accused by the author of violating the Covenant of the League of Nations.

Considerable space is given to the Rutenberg Concessions, which are described as "monopoly grabbing," not with the aims of the usual commercial project but for the purpose of acquiring such control over the main natural resources of Palestine as to assure the Zionists of complete political power. [...]

Mr. Jeffries condemns the policy of the British government on two counts. He insists that its actions were illegal and were a repudiation of promises given to the Arabs; and he maintains that its policy has been dishonest and immoral. No one can question the sincerity of Mr. Jeffries. His book is replete with the moral indignation of a liberal idealist who feels that his ideals have been betrayed. Nevertheless, his thesis is so thoroughly supported by authoritative evidence that it cannot be disregarded. The book gives no evidence of anti-Semitism nor can it rightly be criticized as the work of a writer using his materials to forward racial antipathies. Rather, it is the work of a sincere and honest student of one of the most controversial problems of contemporary history.

15

Post-Reality Writings

With the Woodhead Report of November 1938 ruling out the partition of Palestine as impracticable, the National government of Neville Chamberlain decided to convene an all-party conference to find a solution to the Palestine problem. Known as the London (or St James Palace) Conference, it was scheduled for February 1939. Representatives of the Jewish Agency, the Palestinians' Higher Arab Committee (HAC), and the Arab states, duly arrived in the British capital, but met separately with British representatives as talks got underway.

The HAC had, in fact been proscribed by the British in September 1937, and those of its members in Palestine at the time had been exiled to the Seychelles. Its leader, the Grand Mufti, Haj Amin al-Husseini, had only escaped the same fate by fleeing to Beirut. The members of the HAC delegation had, therefore, to be released by the British in order to attend the conference. Tannous, based in London, was invited to join the delegation, and George Antonius was drafted to act as the Arab delegations' general-secretary. Haj Amin, however, was barred from attendance.

With the failure of the British and Arab delegations to reach agreement, the British government proceeded, unilaterally, to formulate a new Palestine policy. This took the form of yet another government white paper, the MacDonald White Paper. Issued in May 1939, it heralded a significant change of direction.

Jeffries wrote substantial analyses of both the conference outcome and the MacDonald White Paper for the Catholic press. These essays, along with a handful of editorial letters, should be considered as addenda to his book, extending its coverage of the Palestine problem beyond 1938, through to July 1939. They are also, unfortunately, as far as I have been able to ascertain, his last published writings on the subject of Palestine. For these reasons, therefore, they are reproduced in this chapter in full.

The Palestine Conference (February-March 1939)
'A Zionist veto upon independence, which the Arabs could not possibly accept'

The earliest of these pieces, an analysis of the reasons for the failure of the London Conference, appeared in *The Tablet* of 25 March, 1939, under the title, *The Palestine Conference*:

> The Palestine Conference ended somewhat abruptly on Friday, the 17th. It might be said to have closed earlier when the Jewish delegates refused the Government's proposals, in mid-week. There was some hope though, apparently, among the representatives of the Government that some sort of settlement or arrangement might be reached with the Arabs. The Egyptian delegates, who had been on the point of leaving then, were asked to remain a few days longer. But such proposals or explanations of the existing proposals as were produced then constituted no advance, in the opinion of the Arab bloc, upon what had been put forward already, and on the afternoon of Friday the Conference dispersed.
>
> As one of the delegates put it to me, "The Conference broke up upon a single point, but it was the all-important point." This was the question of Independence for Palestine. As far as the Arabs were concerned, they would have accepted the Government's proposals upon Jewish immigration. They did not care for them, and would have stipulated that no "right of immigration" was created by them, but in practice they would not have allowed them to become a stumbling-block to a settlement.
>
> But the Government proposals for "Independence" were found altogether inadmissible. Independence was conceded to Palestine in principle, but it was made conditional upon

"the likelihood of effective co-operation in Government" by Arabs and Zionists. The phrase "effective co-operation" was used by the Governmental draftsmen in the Government proposals no doubt because it conveyed an impression merely of mutual hard-work by Arabs and Zionists in a putative Legislative Assembly for Palestine, and this would seem an altogether proper request to make of the parties concerned.

But when the matter was debated in the Conference it was soon seen that the Government had its own ideas of what "co-operation" signified. It signified that Arabs and Zionists would have to give evidence of collaboration in a common policy for Palestine before independence could be conceded to that country. That is to say, the Arabs, two-thirds or more of the population and entirely autochthonous, must adopt a policy for their country which would secure the assent of the Zionists, one-third of the population at most, and hardly at all autochthonous.

This amounted to a Zionist veto upon independence, which the Arabs could not possibly accept. It meant government by minority. The Zionists would either rule with positive permanence, by the adoption of their policy, or with negative permanence, by barring any Administration which would not adopt their policy.

In the course of the Conference it was pointed out by Arab delegates that co-operation in Government meant that all parties in a Chamber discussed together proposed laws and the working-out of existing laws. It did not mean that a Government could only pass laws which were approved by the Opposition. But this view found no favour with Mr. MacDonald and the other official representatives, who insisted upon co-operation being interpreted in their sense.

The Arabs also pointed out that, in their opinion, the British Government when it demanded unity of policy between the Arabs and the Zionists was not facing the problems of Palestine. Palestine was an agricultural country, and they wished to maintain it as a country, apart from the citrus-fruit trade, essentially not entering into, and independent of, world-markets. The Zionist plans for Palestine were the very reverse of this. The Zionists wished to further the progress of industry in Palestine, to make it, if they could, the industrial centre of the Near East. The Arabs could not combine in a policy of this kind, which would destroy the character of their country, and was intolerable to the vast majority of its native inhabitants.

This point, the importance of which is evident, the British representatives at the Conference did not seem willing to take into discussion. They were evasive upon it, and passed to other matters.

It is not surprising, therefore, that the Conference broke up. It is felt, however, that there is some improvement of the situation as between the Arabs and this country. His Majesty's Government has shown itself for the first time willing to concede the independence of Palestine in principle, however it has negatived it in practice. That is a step forward, towards the Arabs' contention. They hold that in this matter independence is conditioned for Palestine by the Covenant of the League of Nations, that it is vested in the population of the country, for whom Great Britain is only a temporary trustee, without prerogative of sovereignty, and without right to continue the trusteeship indefinitely, or only to end it upon his own terms.

The Arab leaders now return into exile, an odd and preposterous situation, after being the guests for six weeks of the Government, and after being welcomed by Army, Navy and Air-Forces during the week-ends of the Conference.

The MacDonald White Paper (May 1939)
'The Mandate, upon which last week's White Paper is based, is entirely improper, illegal and dishonest, and till this fact is faced we shall stay in the realm of make-believe'

As we have seen, following the abortive London Conference on Palestine, the British government issued the MacDonald White Paper in May 1939. Its key features were the abandonment of the Jewish National Home policy, restrictions on Jewish immigration and land purchases, and the establishment of an independent Palestine with an Arab majority within ten years. As expected, in Tannous' words, the Zionists 'declared war on it.' More concerning, however, for Tannous and his fellow HAC delegates, was Haj Amin's implacable rejection of the White Paper, which they had been inclined to support.

Jeffries wrote an analysis of the White Paper for *The Catholic Herald* of 26 May, 1939, under the title *Mandate is a Cooked Affair*. His flawless logic, combined with the deepest possible knowledge of the issue of any British observer of his time, renders this *the* definitive critique of the document (The italics, of course, are Jeffries'.):

The Government's proposals for Palestine were issued last week in a White Paper, one more in an interminable series of White Papers, reports, statements-of-attitude, and so forth, which have trailed over Palestine for some twenty years now. Nor, unfortunately, is there much guarantee in the present document that this fantastic paper chase will come to an end.

It is true that last week's proposals contain two announcements which are of importance and have indeed been denounced by those who dislike them, the Zionists and their sympathisers, as a complete reversal of British policy. The Government will reduce Zionist immigration into Palestine to 75,000 during the next five years, and at the close of the five years will forbid it altogether. The Government also says that its objective is the establishment of an independent State in Palestine.

But the "independence" offered has no connection at all with real independence. It eradicates majority rule, declaring, though the fact is wrapped up in folds of official phraseology, that the Arabs may only govern if they adopt a policy agreeable to the Zionist minority.

This policy of enforced policy is something unheard of in any sphere of human affairs, and it was the refusal of the Arab delegates to agree to it which led to the breakdown of the Anglo-Arab negotiations at St. James's in March. Its reappearance in the White Paper cannot therefore be taken *au pied de la lettre*, and probably is no more than so much marking of time. It is of some importance, however, that the independence of Palestine should be recognised as a goal, even if no real step towards it is made.

The proposed closure of Zionist immigration is of much greater immediate moment, and it is an excellent and valuable act of justice to the Arabs. But it is not a complete reversal of policy. It is like a new flag hoisted on an old and rotten flagstaff, for the reason that the rest of the White Paper continues to expound the version of affairs in Palestine, and to expound the way of dealing with them, which by misrepresentation and misdeed respectively, created and have maintained since 1916 or so, what is known as the "Palestine Question."

The cardinal defect, the ruin, the curse of this affair is that it is only discussed upon make-believe premises, in this country at least.

The White Paper, in the way of its predecessors, treats the Mandate held by Great Britain as the source and basis of life in Palestine. By it any programme of government must be conditioned, and it is in so far as any suggested laws or decrees are consonant with the "obligations" of the Mandate, that they will or will not pass muster. Governmental spokesmen and Opposition spokesmen such as Messrs Morrison, Attlee and Noel Baker will be found to have debated in the House of Commons, during the sittings on Monday and Tuesday, upon these same lines.

All this is make-believe, the make-believe which has been going on for two decades. The true Palestine Question, which so sedulously is kept from public knowledge, is not whether Governmental proposals are in accordance with the Mandate. The true question is whether the Mandate itself is genuine or fraudulent.

The answer to this is that the Mandate for Palestine was a cooked affair, arranged in private by the British Government of the period (the Lloyd George Cabinet) and the Zionist leaders between them. The supposed "obligations" to the Zionists were mainly drafted by the Zionists themselves, and United States Zionists took a very large part in the drafting.

The Mandate thus composed, which the uninformed British public believes vaguely to have been the creation of the League of Nations, was really imposed upon the League of Nations. The then Council of the League, which did not venture to face its virtual creators, the United States and Great Britain, took the text sent to it and held its peace.

It must be remembered, too, that the approval of the League, which is the species of condonation most employed by official and Zionist advocates to justify what has been done in Palestine, is of not the slightest true legal value.

The League has not nor ever had any power over Palestine, and – this is very important – there is no legal criterion in existence for that abstraction from the people of Palestine of the ownership of their country which has been carried out under the Mandate.

It is not surprising, when its origin is considered, that the Mandate as it exists and has existed is altogether illegal, and violates the terms of the Covenant which it was allegedly created to maintain. The following are the circumstances under which it was produced.

At the close of the war Turkey ceded part of her dominions, including Palestine, not as is commonly supposed to Great Britain, but to all the Allied Powers together, to Britain, France, Italy, Japan and the United States. But these States, all and severally, before the Treaty of Peace was signed, had publicly renounced conquest.

The ceded portions of Turkey, therefore, were annexed by nobody, but were erected instead, under the Covenant, into the equivalent of what is called in private life a minority trust. Great Britain was appointed as trustee in Palestine for the native population, the members of which thereby became her wards, and automatically became the owners of the soil, albeit in wardship.

They were so much recognised as the owners of the soil – though, of course, their ownership was inherent and natural like that of the Poles of Poland and did not depend on this recognition – that in these ex-Turkish districts under Article 22 of the Covenant the Mandatory was enjoined only to offer his wards "administrative advice and assistance."

This, of course, predicted the creation of a native Government immediately, so that there might be a body to assist and to advise.

The procedure, in the case of Palestine and Irak and "Syria" was clearly differentiated by the Covenant from that to be followed by the Mandatories in Africa and in the Pacific, where the Mandatories were enjoined to set up administrations of their own.

Instead of obeying the terms of the Covenant, the ink of which was still wet from his fountain pen, Mr Lloyd George illegally set up in Palestine a ruling Administration, in order that it might in its turn set up the Zionist "National Home." This was termed a "Mandatory Government," even when at the beginning, from 1920 to 1923, the false Mandate itself was not in existence and this Administration therefore, and all that it carried out for the establishment and the development of the "National Home," were null and void twice over.

It was, of course, an additional usurpation that the Balfour Declaration (also a precious piece of Zionist collaboration) should have been inserted into the Mandate at all. Its presence there contravened Article 20 of the Covenant.[1]

The Mandate therefore, upon which last week's White Paper is based, is itself entirely improper, illegal and dishonest, and till this fact is faced we shall stay in the realm of make-believe. So long as the present Government tries to save the face of its predecessors and refuses to acknowledge their infidelities, just so

---

1. Article 20: 'The Members of the League severally agree that this Covenant is accepted as abrogating all obligations or understandings inter se which are inconsistent with the terms thereof, and solemnly undertake that they will not hereafter enter into any engagements inconsistent with the terms thereof. In case any Member of the League shall, before becoming a Member of the League, have undertaken any obligations inconsistent with the terms of this Covenant, it shall be the duty of such Member to make immediate steps to procure its release from such obligations.'

long it will be in a hopeless state. The pretence that the Mandate is honest enables the Zionist leaders quite reasonably to declare that the Government's interpretations of it are arbitrary and mean a betrayal of this country's word to them. But a Government which acknowledged the illegality of the Mandate, apart from doing its duty, would place itself in a strong position. Neither the Zionists nor their friends could raise outcries any longer, since the compacts upon which they base their claims would have been demonstrated to have been improper, and the Zionist share in them as wilful as anyone's. The necessary evidence against the Mandate is ready to hand if the Government is willing to use it, or no longer to suppress it.

The Catholic Herald
'Your issue of to-day exhales anti-Semitism'

Jeffries's association with *The Catholic Herald* at this time bears comment. From a note in the paper's *Jotter* column, in the issue of 12 May, 1939, we learn that he had been in direct contact with its editorial staff at this time. Under the heading *An Authority*, the columnist had written that,

> I had the pleasure of a chat recently with J.M.N. Jeffries, whose book, *Palestine: The Reality*, contains the detailed history of the whole sorry business. Unfortunately, the book has had to be very long and very detailed, and its cost makes it prohibitive for many. But Mr Jeffries' long experience as one of the most brilliant of modern foreign correspondents has given him a trenchant and witty style which carries the reader on. Though his health has not been too good recently he has promised me that he will himself shortly give our readers the benefit of his knowledge on this most vital and most topical question.

Since Jotter's 'chat' with Jeffries had taken place shortly before the government issued its White Paper, it seems logical to conclude that that had been the subject of their conversation.

It is worth noting that *The Catholic Herald*, then under the editorship of Michael De La Bédoyère, not only published Jeffries' analysis, but endorsed it editorially in the same issue. It is also worth noting that De La Bédoyère's statement (if in fact it was he who wrote it) arguably ranks as the most principled position ever taken on the Palestine problem by any British newspaper editor of the time.[2] The editorial reads as follows:

> In times like these anything in the nature of criticism of the British Government reads like lack of patriotism. Fearlessly to undertake the task of pointing out where and when Britain has trusted to might and expediency rather than to right and honesty is to render oneself unpopular. Yet, if we are preparing to fight for anything worthwhile today, it is surely for the democratic right to denounce those who rule us when they appear to be disregarding those very standards of truth and integrity for which we are ostensibly standing in the face of the world.
>
> In our foreign policy we have announced ourselves as acting on the very highest motives; we cannot possibly afford to let our opponents say that we cannot see the beam in our own eyes. Hitler in his Reichstag speech was not slow to mention British conduct in Palestine and Ireland. To the average Englishman, fed on a Press that is much more cleverly but scarcely less efficiently controlled than that of the totalitarian States, this sounded like nonsense. Was it nonsense? The case of Ireland is familiar enough to our readers, so many of whom have Irish blood in their veins...
>
> More immediately in the public eye at the moment is the problem of Palestine, owing to the publication of the Government plan. This plan undoubtedly makes comparatively large concessions to the Arab case, and has been denounced by the Jews in consequence. It represents a genuine attempt to abide as fairly as possible by the conflicting claims of the two parties. But there are times when the full service of truth and honesty demands, not the mediation between two existing claims, but the thorough examination of the basis of the claims. Such an examination may lead to the discovery that one of the claims is essentially unreal or even fraudulent.
>
> As it is, the present concessions to the Arabs are due to the publication of documents which the British Government has

---

2. The editorial line on Palestine taken by *The Spectator*, under the editorship (1932–53) of Henry Wilson Harris, although not in the same class as that of the *Catholic Herald*, which, as we have seen, was clearly informed by a familiarity with Jeffries' book, was nonetheless more receptive to the Arab than the Zionist case. For example, with respect to the MacDonald White Paper's proposed restrictions on Jewish immigration, the editor opined: 'But that the Arabs should be gradually reduced by a systematic and continuing immigration of Jews to the position of a minority in their own country would be intolerable. No Arab could be expected to acquiesce in that; no Englishman, if he were an Arab, would acquiesce in it.' (*The future in Palestine*, 25/5/39)

attempted to keep secret for many years, as is shown by Sir
Michael McDonnell in the current issue of *The Month*.[3] We
have now admitted that we did not exclude Palestine from our
promises to the Arabs in return for their help in "language" as
"specific or unmistakable as it was thought to be at the time."[4]
We also promised that any return of the Jews to Palestine would

---

3. Sir Michael McDonnell was Chief Justice of Palestine between 1927 and 1936.
His Wikipedia entry includes the following: 'McDonnell was forced into early
retirement in October 1936... induced by a series of clashes with Palestine's
High Commissioner, Sir Arthur Wauchope, over the role of Palestine's judiciary
in suppressing the "disturbances." This clash culminated in McDonnell's
ruling in the Qasir case. The decision pertained to house demolitions
scheduled to take place in the old city of Jaffa. Although McDonnell ruled
that the government had the authority to demolish the houses, he deemed the
government's reliance on town planning justifications, rather than military
necessity, an act of moral cowardice and accused it of "throwing dust" in
the public's eyes. After retiring from the bench and returning to London,
McDonnell took up advocacy on behalf of the Arab cause in Palestine: he
published a number of articles in which he attacked Britain's pro-Zionist
policy in Palestine, and in 1939 he was an adviser to the Arab delegation
concerning the 1915-1916 correspondence between Sir Henry McMahon and
the Sharif Hussayn of Mecca.'

4. The editorialist is referring here to the findings of a special Anglo-Arab
committee, chaired by Lord Chancellor Maugham, set up to investigate the
Correspondence and other British promissory documents. The committee
issued its report on 16 March,1939, under the title *Report of a Committee Set
Up to Consider Certain Correspondence Between Sir Henry McMahon & The
Sharif of Mecca in 1915 & 1916*. While it stated that both sides 'have been
unable to reach agreement upon an interpretation of the Correspondence,'
the British did acknowledge 'that the Arab contentions... regarding the
interpretation of the Correspondence, and especially their contentions relating
to the meaning of the phrase "portions of Syria lying to the west of the
districts of Damascus, Homs, Hama and Aleppo," have greater force than has
appeared hitherto.' They further agreed that 'Palestine was included in the area
claimed by the Sharif of Mecca in his letter of the 14th July, 1915, and that
unless Palestine was excluded from that area later in the Correspondence it
must be regarded as having been included in the area in which Great Britain
was to recognise and support the independence of the Arabs,' but maintained,
however, that 'on a proper construction of the Correspondence Palestine was
in fact excluded,' while admitting that 'the language in which its exclusion
was expressed was not so specific and unmistakable as it was thought to be at
the time.' Finally, and most significantly, they declared that 'In the opinion of
the Committee it is... evident from these statements [namely, the Sykes-Picot
Agreement, the Balfour Declaration, the Hogarth Message, the Declaration
to the Seven, various assurances of General Allenby, and the Anglo-French
Declaration] that His Majesty's Government were not free to dispose of
Palestine without regard for the wishes and interests of the inhabitants of
Palestine, and that these statements must all be taken into account in any
attempt to estimate the responsibilities which – upon any interpretation of the
Correspondence – His Majesty's Government have incurred towards those
inhabitants as a result of the Correspondence.'

be made only "in so far as was compatible with the freedom of the existing population both economic and political." On another page, Mr. Jeffries, whose book, *Palestine: The Reality*, should be read by all who wish to study the matter without prejudice, argues that the Mandate to which general appeal is made was a "cooked affair" between the Lloyd George Government and the Zionist leaders.

We do not ourselves pretend to be able to estimate the full value of the arguments put forward in defence of the Arab case, nor should we wish to see the Jews who have settled in Palestine deprived of the protection which we have guaranteed to them. But the lay reader who troubles to look personally into a case which has been kept very dark indeed will find it hard to deny that by nature and by our promises Palestine should be Arab rather than Jewish.

In some quarters there is a fear that even the White Paper is a concession to terrorists and therefore a sign of weakness. It cannot be too often repeated that recourse to violence, though it may in itself have to be deplored, cannot spoil a good case. If the Arab case is good, then the fact – for which we are indirectly responsible – that the Arabs have fought illegally for it does not render it bad. Moreover, as between primitive Arab terrorism and the persistent pressure of Jewish interests throughout the world there is no doubt that the latter is the more likely to succeed by force. No country has done more for Jewry than Britain, and this is scarcely a time for the Jews to make things more difficult for us.

If we trust to right rather than expediency we shall have no hesitation in acknowledging that Palestine is Arab and in implementing that acknowledgement, while doing everything we possibly can to see that the civil and religious rights of Jews settled in the country through our encouragement are fully protected, perhaps by some form of federation analogous to that put forward by Mr de Valera for Ireland. It may well be that in the present state of international relations this abiding by the right will also prove the wisest expediency.

The suggestion that the 'civil and religious rights of Jews settled in the country through our encouragement' be 'fully protected' is a masterstroke, such rights, of course, having been deemed quite sufficient for Palestine's 'non-Jewish communities' as per the text of the Balfour Declaration. It is a given that statements as brave as that on the matter of Palestine, whether from the 1930s or today, seldom go unchallenged, often by an accusation of anti-Semitism.

And, sure enough, in the very next edition (2 June), came this from reader Amelia Defries:

> Your issue of to-day exhales such anti-Semitism that it is very difficult to realise that this is indeed Catholicism; or that I have not been misled. To put a biased case and make wrong appear right seems to me no part of Christian teaching and cannot be acceptable to the Church. This is no time, as you say, to embarrass the Government: nor to enlarge upon what was completely summed up by Mr. Amery MP for National Conservatives, and by Mr. de Rothschild MP for Liberals, in the debate in the House. Why not, in justice, print reports of those speeches? Why not, indeed, print the very fair arguments put forward by the Government itself? Mr. MacDonald, for example, said that the problem was one of "right against right." Why not print the reasoning of Sir Thomas Inskip, who showed that the Government is giving "safeguards" to the Jews and to the Arabs; that nothing is defined yet as to the future. Why not discuss the suggestion heard in the House that the way out of the difficulty may be found if Palestine became a British Colony? But no: without any Christian charity you give in to force, and unfairly weigh the scales on the side of terrorists.

The *Herald*'s editor appended the following response to Defries' letter:

> We do not think of the matter in terms of Semitism or anti-Semitism, but in terms of history. We happen to believe on the evidence that Palestine is Arab and that the promises made by Britain pledge us to giving Arab independence to Palestine. The promises to the Jews were posterior to the Arab promises, and the Jews have been imported into the country against the wishes of its inhabitants. If this is not aggression, what is? As for not giving space to the arguments put forward by the Jews and the Government, the answer is that these have been ventilated throughout the Press and are readily accessible to all our readers. The *Catholic Herald*'s space is given over to the things that the general Press dare not emphasise, especially when they are of importance and, in our view, true. We do, however, believe that the unfortunate promises given to the Jews... throw upon Britain the duty of doing all in its power, short of injustice to the Arabs, to see that the Jews in Palestine, having entered there on our guarantee, shall receive protection and their religious and human rights.

One week later, on 9 June, Jeffries responded to Defries' gratuitous smear head on. His letter may be considered *the* definitive rebuttal of that stock-in-trade of Zionist propagandists – the false allegation of anti-Semitism:

> Defries declares in a letter that your issue of May 26 "exhales anti-Semitism." You defend yourself very easily from her charge, but since my own article in that issue of the *Catholic Herald* cannot but be involved in this accusation of hers, I think I may be allowed to defend myself, too, and not to stop at all at passive defence. These wild, and frequently wilful, charges of anti-Semitism which are constantly brought against anyone who ventures to oppose political Zionism are absolutely without excuse.
>
> Anti-Semitism is present when an attack is made upon Jews solely because they are Jews. Anti-Semites are men who accuse Jews of all manner of misdeeds, but have no evidence to offer against them but their blood, which the anti-Semite is foolish or wicked enough to think sufficient evidence.
>
> That is anti-Semitism. But when a charge is brought against the Jews responsible for the creation of the "National Home" in Palestine, not because they are Jews, but because of the illegality of the methods employed by them, and by the statesmen associated with them, in establishing the "National Home," then there is no anti-Semitism whatsoever in that charge. There is no more anti-Semitism in it than there would be in summoning a man who happened to be a Jew before a court of law. If evidence is produced and statements of fact are laid, they must be examined. It is intolerable when those who bring evidence find that it is passed over and that they are treated as though they uttered empty and unsupported allegations.

And as for Defries' suggestion that Palestine be made a British colony:

> If Miss Defries had read the issue of May 26, instead of denouncing it, she would have understood why the "suggestion heard in the House" that Palestine should become a British colony, was not discussed in your columns. It is, in fact, not a new suggestion at all, but a very old one. It only keeps cropping up in the House of Commons and in other places because those who repeat it either do not know or do not want to know the true situation of Great Britain in Palestine.
>
> Palestine does not belong to Great Britain, nor ever did. She is in Palestine as the trustee of its inhabitants, and she has no

power to seize their patrimony and turn it into a colony of her own. Nor is there any body or caucus or institution in existence which has power to sanction such an act for her. Certainly the League of Nations, which is ridiculously cited as franking every illegality which has been accomplished in Palestine, has no such power. The League of Nations has no more proprietary rights in Palestine than a Geneva sparrow.

The only relation of the League with Palestine is to supervise the behaviour there of the trustee. This duty has not been carried out properly. But even if it had been, the League thereby would not be a whit more in a position to hand over Palestine as a colony to Great Britain than a judge of the High Court is in a position to seize the estates of a minor and hand them as a present to the minor's trustee.

The correspondence did not end there. A final letter from Defries appeared in the edition of 23 June, citing a certain Fr. Vann to the effect that 'there does exist an anti-Semitic group in the Church.'

A letter from another reader on the same subject, Margaret Sutro, was published alongside that of Defries'. I reproduce it here in full, not because its content is especially germane to our subject, but simply because of the identity of the letter writer who *responded* to it in the following edition. Here, to begin with, is Sutro's letter:

As a Catholic of Jewish race, I must confess to being both perplexed and distressed by the attitude which your paper has adopted towards the Jews at this tragic moment of their history, for I cannot help feeling that it will inevitably have the effect of driving many of them further from the Church. Those of us who have come into actual contact with the refugees from Germany, both Jewish, and Catholics of Jewish descent, know that these people are suffering the very extremity of human misery; and that the fate of the "non-Aryan" Christians in Germany is particularly terrible, for they have left the Jewish community in order to follow Our Lord, and are now cast out from that of the Christians. Nevertheless, I know of cases where these people have held on to the Faith with a heroism of which we, the fortunate Catholics of England, can form no conception. These Christian outcasts deserve all the help and sympathy which their fellow Catholics can give them, even when they are unable to offer them practical support. I do not feel that the *Catholic Herald* has given them either sympathy or encouragement. A

Jew, whether baptized or unbaptized, is a child of God, a Jewish Catholic is as much a member of Christ's Mystical Body as is a Catholic of Spanish, Irish, or any other race, and should be accorded the same right of saving his immortal soul. Fortunately, the pronouncement of Pope Pius XI, that "no Christian may take part in anti-Semitism," leaves no doubt as to the official teaching of the Church on this matter, and, in my own case, the kindness of my Catholic friends, and the sympathy of the priests whom *I* have consulted over "the Jewish problem," have reassured me, and have made me feel that the Church is the home of Jew and Gentile alike; but the attitude of your paper had left me in definite need of reassurance. As I am convinced that this cannot be your intention, I feel that the most courteous and honourable course is to bring my difficulty before you.

(The editor of the *Herald* appended the following response to Sutro: 'We should be glad to have pointed out to us any editorial passage in the *Catholic Herald*, or any passage in the articles of our correspondents which can be called "anti-Semitic" in the sense that we advocate discriminating against Jews on the ground that they are Jews.')

On 7 July came this response to Sutro's letter – not from Jeffries, but from his sister, Marie N. Jeffries (of Easthayes, Cullompton, Devon):

It is not perhaps, for one of your humblest readers to rush in defence of the *Catholic Herald*'s attitude towards the Jews, or rather the Jewish question in Palestine or elsewhere, but your correspondent, Margaret Sutro, possibly fails to recognise the importance of Catholics having a lay paper which does not distort the truth in news and views of world affairs and politics. Based upon the fundamental teaching of Christian Doctrine, the *Catholic Herald* is at pains to give its lay readers the well informed truth in its news and policy. We cannot get this in the daily press, which on the whole has had a great share in the suppression of the truth sufficient to bring about the chaos in Europe which we are now experiencing.

The Catholic Church, whose ideals permeate the *Catholic Herald*'s, is the merciful Mother of all persecuted humanity: but she does not single out the Jews to be defended more than the persecuted of other races and nations. On the other hand, the vast and powerful press of America and England and other countries do keep silence over – and suppress the defence of – the persecuted Christians, particularly Catholics, in Spain, Mexico, Russia and elsewhere, and their testimonies of the truth.

Since the same address as that given by Marie N. Jeffries – Easthayes, Cullompton, Devon – appears on most of Jeffries' public correspondence we may safely assume that, throughout the period from 1933 to 1939, the period during which, save for visits to the Arab Centre in London, he was working on *Palestine: The Reality*, Jeffries resided, for the most part, with his sister, Marie.

Hatay
'The democratic countries, whose policies in the international area are linked to-day, are not practicing in Asia Minor that respect of treaty and League obligations which they champion in Europe'

The last editorial letter from Jeffries that I have been able to find appeared in *The Times* of 20 July, 1939, and pertains to a familiar theme of his: the hypocrisy inherent in criticising fascist Italy's international lawlessness while remaining silent about that of the democracies, in this instance France's illegal cession of the Syrian province of Hatay to Turkey. Since the issue will be unfamiliar to most of us today, however, the following backgrounder is in order:

> The Hatay region, located on the coast north of Latakia, was originally part of Syria according to the French Mandate for Syria and the Lebanon… but Turkey showed interest in the area and its large Turkish-speaking community. In 1936, the Turkish government began to push for Hatay's "reunification" with Turkey. The French decision to hand it over to Ankara three years later came in tandem with a Turkish-French treaty guaranteeing Turkish "friendship" during the Second World War. It was a blunt violation of the Treaty of Lausanne that partitioned the former Ottoman Empire and the text of the French mandate, both written in 1923, but the move was defended by France before the League of Nations as necessary in order to avoid a Turkish attack on Syria. The 1939 annexation met with heavy protests in Syria, which was then still struggling for its own independence from

France. Even if the French decision was accepted in practice (at least on the decisionmaking level) as a necessary concession to secure Syrian independence, this didn't mean that Syria would let the issue go. After independence, the country staunchly refused to recognize the border that now separates Hatay from Syria. Official Syrian maps continued to include Hatay as part of the country's national territory. But at the same time, public discussion of the matter was discouraged, and Syrian governments rarely raised the issue for fear of openly provoking new conflicts with Turkey. The Hatay issue therefore remained largely unknown to the international community, but it didn't go away.[5]

Jeffries' letter, which turns yet again on the subject of the proper exercise of League mandates by the Mandatory powers, reads as follows. (It also contains, in its final paragraph, the only thoughts we have of his on the tensions that immediately preceded the outbreak of war in September.):

Has not the Italian Note to France on the cession of Hatay to Turkey been misconstrued in the brief comments which have appeared upon it in this country? It draws attention to a transaction which certainly needs explanation. France may have a full answer to the Note, in which case she certainly should give it, for Britain's sake as much as for her own. It would be unwise, to say the least of it, to pass over any complaint that the democratic countries, whose policies in the international area are linked to-day, are not practising in Asia Minor that respect of treaty and League obligations which they champion in Europe.

Most of us are entirely satisfied that there should be an agreement binding Turkey to the democratic *bloc*, but I fancy nobody would consider that this praiseworthy and indeed necessary end was a justification for any means taken to secure it which were not legal.

There is fortunately no need to enter into the intricacies of the Hatay question in order to reach the kernel of the matter. France made the cession of the Hatay to Turkey in one of two capacities, either as a Mandatory or as one of the Powers which defeated Turkey in the War.

If she acted as Mandatory, she could not cede territory in which she exerted only the powers of a temporary adviser, under

5. Emma Lundgren Jorum, *Syria's 'Lost Province': The Hatay question returns*, Carnegie Endowment, 28/1/14

Article 22 of the Mandate. She has no territorial rights over the Hatay. Nor could the Council of the League frank her action, since the League also has no territorial rights, either in the Hatay or anywhere else. The League was never put into possession of any soil, and its role in the mandatory areas is merely to see that the Mandate is carried out in accordance with the Mandate's own terms.

On the other hand, if France made the cession of Hatay to Turkey as one of the Powers which defeated Turkey, she would seem to be arrogating to herself rights which she only held in common with all those other Powers. Turkey in fact made no cession of territory to any individual Power of the 1914-18 Allies, but to all of them together.

On this point, therefore, the Italian claim that Italy should have been consulted seems not without foundation. The departure of Italy from the League would have no effect upon it, for it is as a member of the Alliance and not as a member of the League that the claim, in this eventuality, would be made.

For these reasons surely the Italian Note merits an answer. What is most needed too at the present moment is the reintroduction of discussion and of reasoned argument between the Axis and the Democratic Powers. I do not see that we of the latter group, who sincerely desire peace, should mind if the preliminary topic of discussion even is likely to turn unfavourably to us. Our action would offer proof to the populations of the totalitarian States, particularly in this case to the Italians, of the genuineness of our aims. The principal weapon of our opponents in those States has ever been to present them as suspect.

16

September 1939 'The Dark Days That Were to Come'

'Jeffries was allowed to kick his heels in unemployment for a long period and is now employed in a very different quarter of the world'

The outbreak of war on 3 September, 1939, led eventually to the breakup of the Higher Arab Committee, and in its wake, the closure of London's Arab Centre. As Tannous relates,

Despite the declaration of war, I did not want to shut down the Arab Center. It was too dear to my heart. I, therefore, asked Mrs. Erskine, J.M.N. Jeffries and George Mansour to continue the work as usual while I went to Beirut to make arrangements for the new situation. On my arrival in Beirut, I found the whole Middle East in nervous tension and I found those who had survived the horrors of the First World War in a state of shock. It was not strange, therefore, to have found the Arab Higher Committee in distress and at a loss what to do. Having refrained from accepting the White Paper, the ban on its members to enter Palestine was not lifted. And amid this perplexity and bewilderment, Haj Ameen showed no indication that he was reconsidering his position with regard to the White Paper. Evidently, his mind was quite set on another plan which, even the declaration of a Second World War, could not alter.

Unable to convince Haj Ameen by any means to alter his position and thus start a new life in Palestine, the remaining members of the Arab Higher Committee had no other resort but to dismiss themselves and disperse. The other alternative was to confront Haj Ameen and declare their acceptance of the White Paper, but, unfortunately, they did not have the courage to do that because of the state of mind of the Palestinian masses. Consequently, unable to operate as heretofore, the only way left open to them was to dismantle, each to go his own way, seeking sanctuary against the dark days that were to come... This sudden disruption of the A.H.C. made me immediately decide to close down the Arab Center in London for which I could not solely bear responsibility. I therefore, with tears in my eyes, cabled Mrs. Erskine and George Mansour in London to settle accounts, dispose of the furniture and place all documents at the Saudi Arabian Legation to whose Minister, Sheikh Hafez Wahba, I had cabled.[1]

With the closure of the Arab Centre, Jeffries disappears from view. We know nothing of his thoughts or movements at this time. Nor do we know how *Palestine: The Reality* had fared since its publication. Certainly, nothing could be more guaranteed than a *second* European war to shift the focus of the British public away from the Palestine problem and the book that had uncovered its deepest roots. With Fascist Italy and Nazi Germany concluding their Pact of Steel in May; with Prime Minister Chamberlain reaffirming his support for Poland in July; with the Soviet Union and Nazi Germany signing the Molotov-Ribbentrop Pact in August (giving the Germans a free hand in Poland); and, finally, with the German invasion of Poland in September, distant Palestine could not hope to compete for the attention of Britons.

The only reference to Jeffries in the British media that I have been able to find between the closure of the Arab Centre (presumably not long after Britain's declaration of war on 3 September) and the end of the war in 1945, appeared in *The Catholic Herald* of 4 July, 1941, quite indirectly, by way of an editorial reflection on the inapplicability of the term 'Quisling' to describe the abortive pro-German coup of Rashid Ali in Iraq in April 1941. (Vidkun Quisling, of course, was the war-time leader of Norway whose collaboration with the Nazis has led to his name becoming a synonym for collaborator.):

---

1. Izzat Tannous, *The Palestinians: Eyewitness History of Palestine Under the Mandate*, I.G.T Company, New York, 1988, pp 323-324

Another field where the Quisling terminology can only be applied with inaccuracy and danger is the Middle East. In three remarkable articles, Miss Freya Stark, an authority on the East and herself imprisoned in the Baghdad Legation during the recent troubles, has explained the root causes of the Iraqi revolt. In this war we are standing in the Arab world for age against youth, for vested interests against future hopes, for inefficiency against a new Arab world. Moreover we have been held down by our difficult Palestinian commitments and our association with the blind French military rule in Syria. Our lazy policy, ignorantly run from Whitehall and too often administered by men with insufficient experience of the countries involved, has enabled the Germans to race ahead and command loyalties that could and should have been ours. Now we are given a last-minute opportunity to act firmly and generously and in dissociation from the French colonial rule. Britain must show herself ready to foster all that is most alive in the Arab world in the realisation that it is only in genuine Arab friendship that the legitimate interests of the British Empire in the Middle East can possibly be preserved. If we put ourselves – and still more our sectional interests – first and the realities of the Arab world second, we shall lose all. Many a warning has been given us, notably by the Catholic journalist, J.M.N. Jeffries, who was allowed to kick his heels in unemployment for a long period and is even now employed, we believe, in a very different quarter of the world. To avoid such problems by finding refuge in the term "Quislingism" is madness.[2]

That 'very different quarter of the world' was, in fact, Spain, where (as Tannous had indicated) Jeffries was employed as a press attaché at the British Embassy in Madrid. We know nothing, however, of the circumstances or the timing of his employment there.

Britain's policy with respect to Spain at this time was aimed at keeping its dictator, General Franco, from entering the war on the side of the Axis powers. Central to this effort was the embassy's press section, led by Tom Burns, a former employee of Longmans, Green & Co, the publisher of *Palestine: The Reality*[3]. It is tempting to speculate that Burns, like Jeffries, a graduate of Stonyhurst, may have been responsible for his employment in Spain, possibly through the agency of Britain's revived (September 1939) Ministry

---

2. *Catholic Herald*, 'Quislings' in the Arab World, 4/7/41
3. Burns became the publisher and part owner of *The Tablet* in 1967.

of Information. (And even that he may have been the anonymous Longmans' manager who agreed to the publication of *Palestine: The Reality*.) Having said that, there is no mention of Jeffries in Burns' 1993 memoir,[4] a somewhat curious state of affairs given the following reference to Jeffries in a recent MA thesis on Britain's propaganda campaign in wartime Spain:

> Burns' second assistant was J. Walter, who was originally responsible for the publication of the Embassy bulletin, BBC bulletins in Spanish and English, the *British Official News*, the *Liberation News*, and the *Northern Bulletin*... Walter was later replaced by J.M.N. Jeffries at the bulletins section and became Burns' deputy 'in all matters concerning general administration except those specifically covered by Malley and Stordy' [Burns' other assistants].[5]

Nor, unfortunately, does Jeffries figure in the 1946 memoir of Sir Samuel Hoare, Britain's ambassador in Madrid, although some idea of the nature of his work at the embassy may nevertheless be gleaned from the following passage in that work:

> The difficulties of the press department were typical of the troubles that crowded upon us. When we started our work, the Germans were in complete possession of the field. [Falangist leader] Serrano Suner, who controlled the press and propaganda of the Spanish Government, publicly boasted that they were parts of Goebbel's master machine. Every kind of obstacle was put in the way of our activities. A decree was passed prohibiting all propaganda by foreign agencies. Although never carried into effect against the Germans, it was rigidly enforced against us. The press department was frequently surrounded by police and visitors interrogated, assaulted or imprisoned. Our messengers were attacked in the streets, our books and papers from the Ministry of Information intercepted and confiscated, our correspondence with the Consulates never delivered...
>
> The most protracted battle took place over a sheet that was known as our *Bulletin*. Under the decree, no propaganda was

---

4. Tom Burns, *The Use of Memory: Publishing & Further Pursuits*, Sheed & Ward, London, 1993

5. Pedro Correa Martin Arroyo, *Propaganda Wars in Wartime Spain: Sir Samuel Hoare, the British Embassy and the British Campaign for 'Neutral' Spain, 1940-1945*, MA Thesis, Oxford, 27/6/14, open access.leidenuniv.nl, p 25

permitted to be sent to any but a limited and approved list of Spanish Ministers and senior officials. The fact that the Germans turned this official list into a general circulation that ran into hundreds of thousands, made no difference to the restrictions imposed on us. We were not, however, to be defeated by this flagrant differentiation. We accordingly drew a clear distinction between our propaganda and our news. So far as direct propaganda was concerned, we husbanded our resources for great occasions and for better opportunities of making use of it. For the straight news, however, we made every effort to spread it from one end of Spain to the other. It was the news that chiefly mattered. Propaganda had been so overdone by the Germans that it was already discredited. The news, particularly when our fortunes took a turn for the better, was far more effective than pamphlets and leaflets with an obviously ulterior motive under every line. The method that we adopted was to produce twice daily a bulletin of the B.B.C. news and to circulate it widely in Madrid and the principal cities. The demand for the sheet was unlimited. Crowds, sometimes embarrassingly great, gathered round the press department at the hours of distribution. The copies, once distributed, passed from hand to hand, and sold for sums as high as twenty pesetas each in the black market. The result was an effective circulation far greater than that of any Spanish newspaper, and a reading public that at last had the opportunity of believing what it read. Our military communiqués, in particular, that hitherto had been mutilated or suppressed in the Spanish press, were eagerly read from one end of Spain to the other.[6]

Jeffries absence from both Burns' and Hoare's books may in part be accounted for, however, by the sheer size of the press department as indicated in a biography of Burns: 'By 1942, Burns's 'press office' had mushroomed into the British embassy's biggest section with its own separate building and more than 120 British and local permanent and part-time employees.'[7]

One other reference in that biography sheds further light on Jeffries' story:

The guilt that Burns sometimes felt at leaving London for Madrid was accentuated by the German aerial offensive on the capital

---

6. Rt. Hon. Sir Samuel Hoare, *Ambassador on Special Mission*, Collins, London, 1946, pp 134-135

7. Jimmy Burns, *Papa Spy*, Bloomsbury, London, 2009, p 211

which began on 7 September, 1940, and continued every night until 2 November that year. The horror of the Blitz was brought home to those who had shared the vigorous literary life of the 1930s by news of a heavy air raid on a publishing house in Paternoster Row, near St. Paul's.[8]

The publishing house referred to, of course, was Burns' former employer (and the publisher of *Palestine: The Reality*), Longmans, Green & Co. The Wikipedia entry for Longmans further informs us that 'In December 1940, Longmans' Paternoster Row offices were destroyed in the Blitz along with most of the company's stock.'

Just how many copies of *Palestine: The Reality*, if any, were among that stock we cannot say, but it is possible to speculate that the event may have had something to do with the current scarcity of second-hand copies of the book. The question arises as to whether, as seems likely, Jeffries sought to interest his publisher in producing a second edition after the war. The following reference in Ghada Karmi's introduction to the 2017 edition suggests that he may, in fact, have been turned down:

> When in 1959 Rabbi Elmer Berger's [anti-Zionist] American Council for Judaism was considering a republication of *Palestine: The Reality*, and contacted Longmans about the book, they were informed that Longmans would by then have formally returned the rights to the author who was said to be living in Spain at the time. But they had no contact details for him, and, curiously, they added that they did 'not want to be associated further' with it.[9]

We will return to the question of the book's disappearance in Chapter 19.

---

8. Burns, p 111
9. *Palestine: The Reality,* reprint, 2017, Skyscraper Publications, p. XXVI

17

Jeffries Resurfaces

'Goldbeck. There you are!'

Apart from trips to Britain, Jeffries remained in Spain for much of the rest of his life. We do not know at which point in the final decade of his life he left Spain permanently – only that he died in England in 1960. Nor do we know why he stayed on in Spain after the war. He was, of course, accustomed to living 'Europeanly,' as he once put it, but whether life in Spain was to his liking, as later evidence suggests, or economic circumstances compelled him to continue working for the embassy, or a combination of the two, we simply do not know.[1]

The idea of republishing *Palestine: The Reality*, however, was never far from his mind, as a letter he wrote to Lesley Frost Ballantine, director of the US Information Library in Madrid from 1945–47 (and daughter of the American poet, Robert Frost), indicates. Dated 29 August, 1947, it reads in part,

> This reached me today from Habib Katibah (of the Arab American Institute, 160 Broadway) 'Dear Mr Katibah, I regret to say that we think it would not be wise for us to take on the book submitted: Palestine: The Reality by J.M.N.J. We are

---

1. See the *ABC* obituary at the end of this narrative.

holding the copy per your instructions. Signed, Cecil Goldbeck, Editor, Coward-McCann.' Goldbeck. There you are! Alas, your poor friend Coward continues ill, so he hasn't read it.

The Arabs, or rather Katibah, speaks of submitting the book to other publishers. He says the size of the work militates against it: I fancy the subject of it militates more. It's all very depressing. The Arab Higher Committee sent me a cable asking me to go to NY to assist them in drafting their case but I'm held here in Spain. Unless when I get back to Madrid I find some economic axe at work.[2]

Tellingly, Jeffries had underlined the name 'Goldbeck.'

Habib I. Katibah was a Syrian-American activist and writer, involved with New York's Institute of Arab-American Affairs in the 40s. In the preface to his 1940 book, *The New Spirit in Arab Lands*, he had written that 'The facts of Arab nationalism, particularly those relating to what is known as the *Palestine question*, have now become quite accessible, thanks to the indefatigable works of research and penetrating studies of such authors as Hans Kohn, George Antonius, J.M.N. Jeffries, Philip Willard Ireland, Miss Elizabeth MacCallum and many others.'[3]

A second letter, dated 26 September, 1947 (and sent from HBM's Embassy, Madrid) was written to Frost following her return to the United States. Jeffries' trademark wit and charm are much in evidence, as are his intimations of a post-war Pax Americana:

Dear L.F. (for I observe the friendly signing of your letter, and correspond *emocianado* with those initials which those who know us know we invest with more value than lopped Christian names. When Jack writes to Jill nowadays, in G.B., there may or may not be a centimeter of esteem there, but when J. writes to J., deep calls to deep. [Extract from my unpublished 'Psychology of the British, or Solving the Insoluble'])...

I am so glad that you've had that lecture-tour offer, and that you'll be able to tell lots of people necessary truths. I've always

---

2. Lesley Frost Ballantine Papers, 1890-1980, University of New Hampshire Library, Durham, NH

3. Habib I. Katibah, *The New Spirit in Arab Lands*, Published Privately by the Author, New York, 1940, p 315. In a bibliographical appendix to his book, Katibah had described *Palestine: The Reality* as 'An able, full and authoritative account of the Palestine question, containing valuable documents and revelations.'

understood your public was responsive. You'll take especial care of the Press no doubt: lean on the local Press's arm as you would on a small man's, and make the reporters think they are 'escorting' you. Anything you get across on foreign policy will be inestimable to this Continent.

Foreign policy was a sort of luxury before in the US. The country left its everyday business and family life and went to the club. Europe was just an unreal atmosphere, a club atmosphere. There the country relaxed and ordered a Dry Martini foreign-policy or a Horse's Neck foreign-policy or whatever you like. That's all over. U.S. foreign policy is a necessity now.

Revesz of 'A.B.C.' made a good point – or borrowed it – about the U.S. this week. He said that her policy had been formed for her by her frontiers. (It struck me at once that this was a logical sequence of what Adams has to say of the interior frontiers in that book of his I got from the Casa.) She had had Canada on one side and Mexico on the other. The latter was no menace ever, and the former hardly was a frontier at all. She could not understand what danger meant therefore, and could not understand European countries which had not got Canada on one side and Mexico on the other.

That's a correct view, I think. Now of course the world's gone in like a concertina and the United States have got frontiers at last, frontiers 'what are frontiers'. Russia is the new frontier, and on more sides than the geography shows. The era of mock and peaceful frontiers is over for you and yours.

The 'American Library' theme is very necessary. People say to me what they wouldn't say to you and that is that "the Americans are full of deeds but empty of thoughts. They are wonderful, and inspiring even in their way, but they're children. Now you English etc. etc."

That's the notion, in the present condition of things, which it is more important to counteract than anything else – for you. And USers should understand that it will never be counteracted by even the most marvellous physical accomplishments. You may build a house in an hour, or freeze hens so magically that they squawk when the receptacle is opened by the housewife in ten months' time, or produce a 'plane which gets so fast to one place that it doesn't need to leave the other one. But nothing of that, not a thousand Kaysers (the ship man) or other great industrials, will make Europeans think that Americans are not children. It is only men like your father who can make it clear to Europe that Americans can think, and therefore can be trusted not merely as moulders of tools and tubes, but as moulders of destiny.

As always, however, there was the book:

> How I appreciate all you offer to do about my book. The
> Arabs of the Broadway bureau seem baffled, poor chaps. The
> book would need a new introduction, I think, and the last two
> or three chapters have not got the importance they had at the
> time of writing, and could be reduced. But after all the book's a
> history, and as such it should appear; history not knowing what
> back-matter means.
>
> If you can ever get in touch with (Professor) Hocking of
> Harvard, he was a great stalwart of the cause in the pre-war
> days. I've asked him to lend his copy of the book – as I believe
> he who wrote that article in the 'Atlantic' and deserves to have
> knowledge of the whole affair, Larry Rue of the 'Chicago Tribune'
> (who bless his heart is a 'fan' of the book), wrote to me that
> 'Bill Bullitt is very anxious to read it.' If B.B. could see it, and
> reacted as I hope, do you think him a promising factor? Rue's in
> Germany, but Bullitt is in the States.[4]

---

4. Ibid

18

Glimpses of Reality

'I have seen Jeffries' book, but my eyes are sufficiently weak so as not to read all of Jeffries. I have read some of it'

While, in the post-World War II period, we get only glimpses of Jeffries, much the same can be said with regard to his book. These rare 'sightings' are as follows:

- In an essay, the great Palestinian historian Walid Khalidi recalls a 'small "ecumenical" circle of friends which met regularly in Jerusalem at its "headquarters," the bar of the King David Hotel' in the 40s. One of these, he notes, was Freddie Blenkinsop, 'a senior official in the Secretariat (Executive) who unfailingly, on 2 November of each year, circulated to his British colleagues a refutation of the Balfour Declaration on the anniversary of its issuance. Freddie died in the rubble of the Secretariat wing of the King David Hotel when it was blown up by Menachem Begin's Irgun in July 1946.'[1]

---

1. Walid Khalidi, *On Albert Hourani, the Arab Office, & the Anglo-Arab Committee of 1946*, Journal of Palestine Studies, 2005

While it cannot be proven, it is hard to imagine Freddie Blenkinsop's 'refutation' of the Balfour Declaration being anything other than the forensic Chapter 11 of *Palestine: The Reality*, the one chapter of Jeffries' book which, as we have noted, Khalidi included in his monumental 1971 anthology, *From Haven to Conquest: Readings in Zionism & the Palestine Problem Until 1948*. Certainly, the opening paragraph of a six-page memorandum on the Palestine problem, written by Blenkinsop and dated 2 November, 1944, has Jeffries written all over it:

> Twenty-seven years ago to-day the Palestine problem began with that fateful mental aberration known to history as the Balfour Declaration. We shall perhaps never know for certain all the motives and intentions of the statesmen who endorsed that Declaration. But the Zionists have never doubted that it was the first step towards the establishment in Palestine of a Jewish State. The Arabs not unnaturally have placed upon it the same interpretation and have consistently and unanimously opposed it almost from the very beginning. But the warnings of the King-Crane Commission were disregarded by our politicians who, while they laboured to make the world safe for democracy, ignored the public opposition of the Arabs, and withheld the truth from their own people.[2]

- One particularly fascinating reference to *Palestine: The Reality* arose in the context of a public hearing in Jerusalem of the United Nations Special Committee on Palestine (UNSCOP) on 8 July, 1947. Weizmann was being questioned by a member of the Committee, the Indian lawyer and diplomat, Sir Abdur Rahman. At one point, he began asking Weizmann about his role in securing the Balfour Declaration:

Sir Abdur Rahman: Well... since you were really responsible, or at least one of the gentlemen responsible for the Balfour Declaration, I could get better information from you than from anyone else just now. A number of drafts of these declarations came into existence before this one came out, is that correct?

Mr Weizmann: Yes.

---

2. F.W.G. Blenkinsop, *Memorandum*: 2/11/44, GB165-0030, Archive, Middle East Centre, St Anthony's College, Oxford

Sir Abdur Rahman: And some of them were considered by the Zionist Congress?

Mr Weizmann: I would like to correct you, sir.

Sir Abdur Rahman: By its Political Committee?

Mr Weizmann: There was no Congress at that time.

Sir Abdur Rahman: The Zionist Political Committee?

Mr Weizmann: There was a Zionist group which helped. We all cooperated. Of course, all the drafts were considered by them.

Sir Abdur Rahman: Have you, by any chance, seen those drafts printed in Jeffries' book?

Mr Weizmann: No. I have seen Jeffries' book, but my eyes are sufficiently weak so as not to read all of Jeffries. I have read some of it.

Sir Abdur Rahman: I just wanted to know if you had seen them?

Mr Weizmann: I know exactly what you want to know.

Sir Abdur Rahman: Are those drafts, as printed there, more or less correctly printed? That is all I was trying to find out.

Mr Weizmann: I know that there is one draft. I do not know whether it is printed in Jeffries. There was one draft which was submitted to Mr Balfour and to Lloyd George, which said that His Majesty's Government favours the establishment of Palestine as a Jewish National Home. Is that all you want to know?

Sir Abdur Rahman: That is all I wanted to know.[3]

Weizmann, it will be recalled, would go on to complain in his autobiography about the *Daily Mail*'s 'virulent campaign against us. In particular, a certain J.M.N. Jeffries succeeded, in a series of savage articles, in presenting a wholly distorted picture of Jewish life in Palestine.' But of *Palestine: The Reality*, Weizmann makes no mention. Perhaps this is one of those cases where silence speaks louder than words.

---

3. unispal.un.org?UNISPAL NSF/0/364A6ACODC52ADA7852...

- The following reference to *Palestine: The Reality* appears in an important Arabic language primary source covering the period of the great Palestinian Revolt of 1936-1939, *Yaumiyat Akram Zu'aytir: al-harakat al-wataniya al-filastiniya 1935-1939 (The Diaries of Akram Zu'aytir: The Palestinian National Movement: 1935-1939)*. The reference occurs in Zu'aytir's final diary entry (13 November, 1939), which records the very warm welcome accorded Palestinian political exiles, including the leader of the HAC, Haj Amin al-Husseini, by the Iraqi government of Nuri as-Said in November 1939:

> The most important English-language book on the issue of Palestine, by the most impartial of authors, was published at this time – *Palestine: The Reality*, by Jeffries. Salih Jabr, the minister of education, instructed the ministry to purchase copies of it using all available funds.[4]

- In *Palestine: The Reality*, Jeffries points out that the British army in Palestine 'was the sole large category of average British citizens which had direct access to the facts of the so-called "Palestine problem," the sole such category which had encountered Zionism in Palestine, and had experienced what it meant. It was the sole such category which was aware of the Arabs' true situation, which knew that they were not the fantastically dubbed "non-Jewish community" which the home politicians called them. But the people of the land of Palestine, whose native rights had been guaranteed and now were about to be betrayed.'[5]

In light of the above, the following 'sighting' of *Palestine: The Reality* would surely have delighted Jeffries and confirmed his faith in the British Tommy. It comes in a story posted online in 2016:

> It was back in London [after my last trip abroad] that my father visited me in hospital. He had brought me a book, *Palestine:*

---

4. Akram Zu'ayter, *yaumiyat akram zu'aytir: al-harakat al-wataniya al-filastiniya 1935-1939*, mu'assasat ad-dirasat al-filastiniya, Beirut, 1980, pp 611-612

5. . PTR, p 369

The Reality and said, 'Here Bob, get a real education.' I didn't read it. I was educated enough – or so I thought.

Let me explain a little about my father. Dad had served in Palestine with British forces from 1938 to 1943. At the time, British and Aussie troops were manning the port of Jaffa and other places as Jewish refugees were flooding in. He was a dispatch rider who loved his motorbike and delivered mail from British military HQ in Jerusalem's King David Hotel to HQ in Gaza, a place he particularly enjoyed. Like many other British soldiers in Palestine he'd witnessed acts of injustice against the Arabs. And once, he'd found himself in jail, although he never really told me why or for how long.

It had to do with a shooting incident he'd witnessed, and him supporting the testimony of a Palestinian over that of a Jew, and refusing to change his story, and ending up in jail for his honesty. To tell you the truth, I was not much interested at the time, and I regret it now. He died in 2012 at the age of 91, and it wasn't until his funeral that I thought again of the book he'd given me. The preacher was telling the story of his life, about how he'd served in Palestine and his happiest days had been in Gaza... And so I began reading *Palestine: The Reality*, and trust me, it isn't an easy read. So much invaluable information. But I got the gist of it and was really quite shaken up. Then I read it again, and the names of those tyrants, Lloyd George, Balfour, Churchill, Smuts and Milner started to hit home. They were all respected names in the UK... and then it all became clear – 'Lord' Balfour and his knights had sold both Palestine and Britain to the Zionists, and *Palestine: The Reality* was *the legal case for Palestine*.

As Jeffries would have exclaimed: Exactly!

- Finally, it should be noted that *Palestine: The Reality* was translated into Arabic in 1971 by Ahmad Khalil al-Haj as *Filastin: Ilaykum Al-Haqiqah*, a work commissioned by Sultan bin Mohamed al-Qassim, the ruler of Sharjah.[6]

---

6. How it rose from the dead, Bob Smith, 7/1/16, http://www.thelibertybeacon. com/thank-you. Note that Smith's piece has been edited for clarity.

19

Reality Goes Missing

In the introduction to this book, I quoted a reference to Jeffries in Karl Sabbagh's memoir of 2007, *Palestine: A Personal History*, in which he wrote that 'unlike most books that have fallen out of print because they were of interest at a particular time and have been superseded, [*Palestine: The Reality*] has disappeared from view in the second-hand market and is only obtainable from a few libraries.'[1]

It is to that 'disappearance' that we now turn. We have already, at various points in this narrative, touched on possible reasons for the book's *extreme* scarcity. Unfortunately, apart from the 500 copies pre-purchased by Tannous (and presumably taken to the Middle East at the end of 1939), we do not know whether the size of the book's print run or the extent of its distribution to bookshops had anything to do with the matter. Certainly, any undistributed copies remaining in Longmans' Paternoster Row premises at the time of their destruction in the Blitz would have been destroyed. (See Chapter 16.) But could there have been an altogether different reason for the book's rarity? Could *Palestine: The Reality*, perhaps, have been the victim of a deliberate Zionist 'disappearance' campaign?

---

1. Karl Sabbagh, *Palestine: A Personal History*, Grove Press, New York, 2007, p 328

Although it has not been possible to verify it, I have it on good authority that a 1947 publication of the New York-based Institute of Arab American Affairs (1945–50), *Papers on Palestine*, contains the following statement: 'One, notably, *Palestine: The Reality* (London, 1939) by J.M.N. Jeffries, which told the whole truth about Zionism and the betrayal of the Arabs after World War I, has disappeared completely from all the libraries and book shops in the United States.'[2]

Further support for the thesis may be gleaned from Ghada Karmi's introduction to the 2017 edition of *Palestine: The Reality*, where she writes that 'By the time of the present edition, copies of the book had become very rare. No more than 20 or so remained in various libraries, and some of them had gone missing. Longmans' own archives at the University of Reading library included a folder about the author (MS1393 2/290/12), but whose contents had also gone missing.'

Karmi adds, significantly, that,

> One is almost tempted to wonder if there is something sinister in this, that a well-documented, contemporary expose of a particularly ignoble period in Britain's recent history whose disastrous results live on to this day might not have been worth suppressing, or at least making inaccessible. Perhaps what the *Western Morning News* of 30 March, 1939 said in its review of the book: it 'puts the case in a fair and exhaustive manner… We have heard the other side often enough, and it is time we heard the other,' was not welcome in a situation where ensuring the success of the Zionist project was paramount to government policy.

Certainly, allegations that Zionists have engaged in the practice of disappearing books have been made in relation to at least two other Palestine-related books:

- 'The definitive word [on the King-Crane Commission of 1919] is Harry N. Howard's book, *The King-Crane Mission*, Beirut, 1967, of which I hope you have a copy, secured. William Yale is well reported there. Zionists have sought to "disappear" it from public view.'[3]

---

2. The Institute for Arab American Affairs, *Papers on Palestine*, 1947, p 75
3. Ernestine E. King, *Guide to the William Yale Papers*, library.unh.edu, 25/2/10

- '*Assault on the Liberty* [1980] is routinely removed from bookshelves... when area spokesmen for Israel complain to booksellers that they have stocked a book that is "anti-Israel" and "offensive to Jewish people everywhere".'[4]

Whatever the reason, however, in 1976 (16 years after Jeffries' death), Hyperion Press, a US publisher based in Westport, Connecticut, issued photographic reprints of a number of pre-World War II books on the Palestine problem under the series title, *The Rise of Jewish Nationalism & the Middle East*. One was Philip Graves' *Palestine, the Land of Three Faiths*. Another was *Palestine: The Reality*. How many copies of the latter were printed, however, is not known.

As a final aside on the matter of 'disappeared books,' it is worth keeping in mind the following statement:

> Just how free is free speech in the United States? Even though the First Amendment protects freedom of speech and freedom of the press, government authorities and other powerful interests still find ways to suppress the truth. "Open societies are also no strangers to the censorship of contentious novels and historical accounts of controversial events," Abby Martin said last year on her show "Breaking the Set." "Now, of course, the First Amendment prohibits the outright banning of books by the federal government, but there are many less insidious ways that 'dangerous content' is kept off American bookshelves.'
>
> Martin interviewed Mark Crispin Miller, a Professor of Media Studies at New York University to mark the launch of the "Forbidden Bookshelf," Millers' curated collection of suppressed literature. Beginning with five books last June, the collection has grown to 14 titles. "Hundreds of books on crucial subjects, indispensable subjects, have been undone in one way or other," Miller told Martin. "Threats of litigation by powerful interests, reviewers freezing out certain titles, or what happens most often is books are written off as conspiracy theory."[5]

---

4. James M. Ennes Jr., *The Wisconsin Library Wars*, ussliberty.org

5. *US still bans, suppresses books despite the First Amendment*, Kit O'Connell, http://www.mintpressnews.com/us--still-bans-suppresses-books-despite-the-forbidden-bookshelf/207064/print/ 29/6/15.

20

Death of a Country

The final twelve years of Jeffries' life – 1948–60 – remain something of a mystery. It is obvious from his letters to Frost Ballantine in 1947 that his failure to find an American publisher for *Palestine: The Reality* weighed heavily on his mind. It was not the size of the book, as he ruefully explained to her, but the subject that militated against it. Zionism, after all, was on a roll, both in the US and in Palestine at the time, and, for those such as Jeffries, who stood in opposition to it, there was invariably a price to pay.

George Orwell described the consequences faced by those who seek to challenge a prevailing orthodoxy in 1945:

> At any given moment there is an orthodoxy, a body of ideas which it is assumed that all right-thinking people will accept without question. It is not exactly forbidden to say this, that or the other, but it is 'not done' to say it... Anyone who challenges the prevailing orthodoxy finds himself silenced with surprising effectiveness. A genuinely unfashionable opinion is almost never given a fair hearing, either in the popular press or in the highbrow periodicals. At this moment what is demanded by the prevailing orthodoxy is an uncritical admiration of Soviet Russia. Everyone knows this, nearly everyone acts on it. Any serious criticism of the Soviet regime, any disclosure of facts which the Soviet government would prefer to keep hidden, is next door to unprintable.[1]

---

1. George Orwell, *The Freedom of the Press: Orwell's Proposed Preface to Animal Farm*, orwell.ru/library/novels/Animal_Farm. This preface was omitted by the publisher from the first edition of *Animal Farm* (1945) and not republished until 1972.

The prospects for anyone seeking to challenge the prevailing orthodoxy of uncritical admiration for Zionist project in Palestine, however, were infinitely worse, as Tannous has testified:

> The Zionists, led by the Jewish Agency, covered up their evil deeds in Palestine by misinformation and distortion. Their propaganda machinery, the most efficient in the world, obscured the truth, and whenever they found themselves in trouble and the truth was leaking out, they used their sharpest weapon which they had carefully made up. The word "anti-Semitic," which was made to sound so inhuman and sinful, surrounded the Zionist Jews with a "Halo of Safety" against all attacks against whatever crimes they had committed. The threat of the use of this word against many an honest historian, reporter, government official, politician or businessman, made their victims kneel before them, pleading for mercy.[2]

In addition to the frustration at not being able to find another publisher for his book in 1947, there can be no doubt that Jeffries was also deeply troubled by the turn of events in Palestine at this time. A Zionist rebellion against the Mandate government had forced the British to refer their self-created Palestine problem to the United Nations. Worse still, on 29 November, 1947, the UN General Assembly had voted, in violation of its Charter and against the wishes of the majority of Palestine's population, for a resolution recommending that Palestine be partitioned into Jewish and Arab states.

In June 1939, Jeffries had exclaimed, in his editorial letter to Amelia Defries, that 'The League of Nations has no more proprietary rights in Palestine than a Geneva Sparrow.' He may well have exclaimed to any willing ear at this time that 'The United Nations has no more proprietary rights in Palestine than a New York Sparrow.'

Following the UNGA vote, the Arab Palestine which Jeffries had defended so tenaciously for two decades came under a sustained military offensive by an array of Zionist militias, bent on driving the indigenous Arab population into exile, in order to establish a majority Jewish state in as much of the country as its forces could overrun.

---

2. Izzat Tannous, *The Palestinians: Eyewitness History of Palestine Under British Mandate*, I.G.T. Company, New York, 1988, pp 744-745

Given his emotional and intellectual investment in the cause of the Palestinian Arabs, we can only assume that Jeffries, at this time, was in a state akin to grief. While we cannot, thus far, document this, we can at least extrapolate from the testimonies of others on whom Palestine had left its mark. One of these was the British journalist, Owen Tweedy. The following epitaph by Tweedy on the passing away of the old Palestine would surely have resonated with Jeffries:

> My mother kept a diary. It was a Victorian diary, and the last pages of each year had the funeral heading: "Deaths within the year"; and there, with the date of each demise, "Uncle Chambers," "Joseph Clarke" (the coachman) and "Rook" (her dog) rubbed shoulders with Disraeli and the Emperor Napoleon III. From her I inherited the fun of keeping a diary. But modern diaries have no special pages for "Deaths within the year." So I've always made one for myself; and with 1950 now passing into history, I've just been reading my obituary list for the twelve months.
>
> This is the entry for April 24th. "Palestine. Ave atque Vale." For on that day Palestine died. It was a geographical death after a long illness. Already, two years before, on May 15th, 1948, part of Palestine had become the new sovereign State of Israel. On April 24th this year the remainder of the country was annexed by the new Hashemite Kingdom of Jordan. And, with that, the Palestine so many of us had known and loved became no more. (Indeed – who knows – in another hundred years our Palestine may be remembered only as we remember Phrygia and Pamphilia and Jerome Napoleon's ephemeral kingdom of Westphalia.) To me the passing of Palestine was, as it were, the death of an old friend. And my feelings are, I am sure, those of many like myself who, in fair weather or foul, maybe as soldiers, maybe as civilians, knew Palestine as a home. None of us will ever forget her.[3]

Given the turmoil in Palestine from 1947–49, the absence of editorial commentary of any kind by Jeffries is striking. One reason for this silence may have been that the conditions of his employment prevented it. (Since his letters to Frost Ballantine carry the address of the British embassy in Madrid, we can infer that he remained in government service until at least the end of 1947.) The idea that he kept entirely silent on the issue for the remainder of his life, however, hardly seems credible.

---

3. Owen Tweedy, *Farewell Palestine*, *The Spectator*, 22/12/50

Simply reading about developments in Palestine in 1948 in the pages of *The Spectator*, to take but one example, would have given him ample opportunity for letters on the subject. How, for example, could he have read Edward Hodgkin's critical commentary of 13 February, 1948, *The Unholy Land*, without the desire to respond with, among other things, a bitter reflection on the culpability of Lloyd George, Balfour and Churchill for the situation described therein? Here it is in part:

> Latest news from Palestine is entirely of violence. Large uniformed Arab bands have more than once crossed the frontiers from Syria and Transjordan to attack Jewish settlements; Haganah, the Zionist militia, is engaged in offensive as well as defensive operations. Both Jews and Arabs boast of the extensive destruction they have already achieved in the life and property of the rival community. Both communities have descended into a state of war which is only partially circumscribed by the British troops and police still in the country. Soon these will have left, and we shall be occupying the unfamiliar role of spectators. Perhaps we shall be able to use our new detachment to rid ourselves of some of the illusions – about Zionism, the Arabs, their attitude towards each other and towards ourselves – which we have too often liked to foster while we still held the mandate. These illusions have been many, and it is impossible here to do more than indicate the outlines of a few of them.
>
> First, Zionism. When assessing its potentialities we must not forget that it is today a very different creature from the comparatively unknown child which received encouragement from the British Cabinet 30 years ago. It has grown greatly in the interval in wealth, power and self-confidence. In Zionism is expressed the nationalism of the Jewish people, and like other forms of nationalism it is self-centred, impatient and always prepared to justify the means by the end. The end, of course, is to convert Palestine into a Jewish State. Let us forget the text of the Balfour Declaration, for Zionists only remember it in so far as it supports their claims, and it is, after all, only an incident in the history of Zionism. With or without Balfour and the British, and in spite of the Arabs, the Zionists are set on making Palestine Jewish. Partition is accepted only as a step to wider rule, and sooner or later Jewish authority must be made effective in Jerusalem. Zionism without Zion is a meaningless faith. The leaders of a Jewish State which does not include Jerusalem will feel their work as incomplete as did Cavour and

Victor Emmanuel when they ruled a united Italy whose writ stopped at the gates of Rome.

Does this mean that Zionist protestations of friendship towards the Arabs are hypocrisy? To a large extent it does. Inasmuch as the Arabs of Palestine are the greatest obstacle to a Jewish Palestine, they can only be treated as enemies – and are now being so treated. As a docile and inferior population they would probably receive reasonably benevolent treatment. But in their present temper they can only expect the fate of the Jebusites or Gibeonites. It is right that we should use these Old Testament analogies, for they are always present to the minds of Zionists. It is not to be supposed that the Jews in their time of bitterest persecution have supported their faith with a programme based on post-war compromise. On the contrary, the more desperate their present state the more passionate has been their memory of past glories; Zionists today are the heirs of Joshua and the Maccabees. Palestine has been won before by Jewish arms, and Zionist youth can consider no more glorious service than to take part in another – perhaps a final – conquest. It is no use arguing the risks involved. Exclusive nationalism has never anywhere calculated the risks as the outside observer calculates them.

In dealing with this ebullient nationalism we must also remember that most of its adherents cordially dislike us. Many of the older generation may recall with gratitude the help which the Zionist movement has received in the past from British Governments and individuals, but the youth of Zionism sees nothing to quarrel with in the slogan of the Irgun Zwei Leumi: "Britain is the enemy." We are the bruised reed on which the Jewish people have lent and which has pierced their hand. When we go, we shall not leave behind us in Palestine "a legacy of goodwill." Goodwill could only have been maintained if our co-operation had kept pace with the fullest demands of the Zionists. By not being with them we have placed ourselves in the camp of their enemies. Zionist youth, either reared in Palestine or for Palestine, considers Britain as a more subtle and therefore a more dangerous enemy than the Nazis [...]

As the British troops withdraw from Palestine and the familiar realities of war are more plainly apparent, we must banish any hope of "moderate opinion" on either side influencing the conduct or aims of the struggle to any noticeable degree. Moderation is already treason in both communities. Are we to be surprised if they both mean to win, and are not particular how they win? War between these two wholly incompatible nationalisms was inevitable because neither has ever taken any account of the other.

Zionists, from Herzl onwards, have allowed no place for the Arabs in the new dispensation. To the self-conscious Arab world, still flushed with its recent self-discovery, Zionism is an impudent intrusion. For either side to refuse the challenge of war would be to admit that the basis of its modern existence is a delusion.[4]

Even if Jeffries had not felt inclined to comment on Hodgkin's analysis, it is difficult to imagine him forgoing an opportunity to expose the deceptions and/or self-deceptions in the following response to Hodgkin, written by Jeffries' old foe, Norman Bentwich:

Mr Hodgkin's article on *The Unholy Land* gives the gloomy prospect of war as the only way out of the conflict [...] Mr Hodgkin's statements about "two wholly incompatible nationalisms," and there being no place for the Arabs in the new dispensation of the Jewish State, are too sweeping [...] Nor are the Jews regardless of the Arabs in their prospective State. At the outset there will be 300,000 Arabs, constituting some 40% of the population in the State... Circumstance as well as principle will compel the Jews to pursue a way of understanding with the Arabs. It is a disservice to exaggerate the hostility and distrust which have been engendered by despair, fomented by extremists, and fed by reckless partisanship. It is time for the peacemakers to rally their forces in Jerusalem, which may be again 'the threshold of peace.'[5]

Moving on to the issue of 6 August, 1948, Jeffries would have read with horror the following letter by 'Middle East Observer' quoted here in part:

Hundreds of thousands of Arabs have been driven by Jewish military and political action from their homes and farms, and have made a pitiful trek to Transjordan, to Syria, to the Lebanon, to Egypt and even as far afield as to Iraq. It is surely ironical that the attempt to solve the Jewish refugee problem in Europe has produced an equally grievous Arab refugee problem in the Orient. A few weeks ago I was in Amman, the capital of Transjordan, and spent an evening driving round the town with an official of the Ministry of the Interior. The town was packed with these refugee Arabs, crouching in doorways, lying in the gutters, sleeping in the provincial buses, in schools, in hospitals, in the fields – even in the

---

4. Edward Hodgkin, *The Unholy Land*, *The Spectator*, 13/2/48. Hodgkin was the director of Palestine's Near East Broadcasting Station from 1945-1947.

5. Norman Bentwich, Letter to *The Spectator*, 20/2/48

graveyards. Many of their faces were already gaunt with hunger. For years there has been no begging in this town, but at this time one could not walk ten yards down the street without being accosted for alms […] It was inevitable that, as soon as the British left Palestine, the Jews should attempt to undertake the elimination of the Arab minority from the predominantly Jewish area of Palestine. This they have accomplished with a ruthlessness and efficiency which was born of their fear of a Fifth Column in their midst…[6]

And likewise this response to it:

Your correspondent, "Middle East Observer", highlights one of the most unfair aspects of the Palestine problem – the driving away of Arabs from their own land. A friend of mine, recently returned from this area, confirms everything that your correspondent writes. He points out that the Jewish Agency has steadfastly refused to allow any Arab to work on Jewish land, thus depriving the refugees of any chance to earn a living. One thing that impressed my friend very forcibly was the utter ruthlessness displayed by the Israeli authorities towards the Arab minorities. One Jewish Agency spokesman just tapped his revolver when my acquaintance asked him how the Israeli State would deal with any Arab pockets of population should the Zionists obtain the upper hand in the dispute. Asked if he did not consider the massacre of Arab women and children at Deir Yassin a shameful episode, this spokesman only laughed and said that such things were the price that the Arabs must pay for obstructing the new Zion in the "fulfilment of its ordained destiny."

That fear of massacre is very present amidst the Arab villagers, my friend tells me, can be seen from the way in which they run in terror from any strange party approaching their villages. In company with several other Britons, my informant drove up to a village and the result was a frantic flight of all the inhabitants. When finally reassured, they explained that they had mistaken the party for a Zionist raiding party. A village only a few miles away, they said, had lately been burned to the ground with loss of many lives. Although it is hard to form a clear picture of the position in Palestine from the conflicting newspaper reports appearing in the world's Press, one cannot help noticing how almost every person who has had the opportunity of visiting the Middle East and of judging first-hand for himself seems to support the Arab case.[7]

---

6. "Middle East Observer", Letter to *The Spectator*, 6/8/48
7. W.J. Harris, Letter to *The Spectator*, 13/8/48

In response to such an account of Zionist cruelty and Arab flight, Jeffries could have taken the opportunity to remind *The Spectator*'s readers of the following utterly deceitful and/or deluded words of Churchill, taken from his June 1922 White Paper on Palestine:

> Phrases have been used such as that Palestine is to become "as Jewish as England is English." His Majesty's Government regard any such expectation as impracticable and have no such aim in view. Nor have they at any time contemplated, as appears to be feared by the Arab Delegation, the disappearance or subordination of the Arabic population, language or culture in Palestine... It has been observed with satisfaction that at the meeting of the Zionist Congress... held at Carlsbad in September 1921, a resolution was passed expressing as the official statement of Zionist aims "the determination of the Jewish people to live with the Arab people on terms of mutual respect, and together with them to make the common home into a flourishing community, the upbuilding of which may assure to each of its peoples an undisturbed national development".

In any case, whether or not Jeffries took up his pen to write on the subject of the Palestinian Nakba and its aftermath, we do have some personal reflections from him on life in Spain, in Spanish, for the Madrid newspaper *ABC*. There may well be more, but I am only aware of the following three pieces: *Pruebe Usted A Ser Extranjero* (Just try being a foreigner) 6/3/55; *Espana Y Las Horas* (Spain & the hours) 22/5/55; *El Nuevo Ruido* (The new noise) 27/5/56.

21

Obituaries

'Jeffries was a formidable journalist, a great writer, and one of the most perfect gentlemen I have ever met'

I have been able to find only three obituaries for Jeffries; two in the British press (*The Catholic Herald* & *The Times*), the first with an underestimate of his age, and one in the Spanish (*ABC*). While woefully inadequate as epitaphs for Jeffries, they may, sadly, be all we have:

The Catholic Herald:
A veteran of the First World War (16/12/60)

The recent death of J.M.N. Jeffries at the age of 75 brings back after many years of silence a name that was once familiar to all readers of the British press. As war correspondent of the *Daily Mail* during the 1914-1918 war, Jeffries showed a bravery, initiative, and effectiveness of writing that links his name with that other Catholic veteran, Sir Philip Gibbs.

Joseph Mary Nagle Jeffries was born in Cork of an Irish father and an Irish-American mother. He was educated at Stonyhurst and tried his religious vocation, but without success. Many stories are told of the ingenuity with which he obtained exclusive stories and reports for the *Daily Mail*, even from enemy-occupied country. The same ingenuity and courage was shown by Jeffries during the post-treaty Irish troubles.

During the last war, he served as assistant press attaché in the British Embassy in Spain, where he continued to live. Among his writings was *Palestine: The Reality* in support of the Arab cause.

The Times:

Mr J.M.N. Jeffries: Distinguished dispatches from the front (13/12/60)

Mr. J.M.N. Jeffries, whose war reports were a distinguished feature of the *Daily Mail* in the years of the First World War, has died in Surrey while on a visit from Spain, where he was Press Attaché during the Second World War and where he had lived for the past 15 years. He was 80.

He came of a Cork family, the first of three generations not to enter the medical profession. At Stonyhurst he did extremely well and with the priesthood in mind went to study in Rome. Later, finding himself unsuited for holy orders, he went to Paris, taught a little English and learnt a lot of French. The necessity of earning a living brought him to London. His entry into the ranks of professional journalism removed a serious rival to those who took part in the literary competitions of the *Westminster Gazette*. The *Gazette* could not use him but Thomas Marlowe, editor of the *Daily Mail*, to whom he sent a batch of his prize-winning pieces, saw his promise and engaged him. The war of 1914-18 became his oyster: he got into Liege during the siege and got the news out; he was at the Marne retreat and at the siege of Antwerp. As J.L. Hodson wrote, his great asset – apart from his professional skill – was that he telegraphed in French. Quite early in the war he crossed the Dutch frontier into occupied Belgium to attend a German flag-raising ceremony – slipping away just before the Germans could arrest him.

To traverse all his ground would not be easy, for he visited almost every country involved directly or indirectly in hostilities, with permission and without it. It was said that Northcliffe was so delighted with his war reports that on his return he was given an immediate bonus of £100, a lot of money in those days. He drew the money in sovereigns, went straight home, and poured them all into his mother's lap.

In the Irish troubles of 1922 Jeffries with courage and penetration was reporting what was going on, not from Ulster but from the Free State. His messages, which daily took to task the more extreme Republicans, might have earned him physical violence or death at any time, and in fact he did not get off scot free. He was arrested as a spy by "irregulars," who held him prisoner for five hours. They were debating whether to shoot him – although he was an Irishman himself – when he was saved by the arrival of someone who recognized him.[1]

His wartime reminiscences were published under the title *Front Everywhere* (1935), and he wrote also *London and Better* (1936); and, a firm supporter of the Arab cause, *Palestine: The Reality* (1939). He was unmarried.

Jeffries' old friend, Sir Compton Mackenzie, was moved to respond with the following letter to *The Times*:

May I offer a footnote to your obituary of J.M.N. Jeffries? All through the difficult days of 1916 in Athens Jeffries gave invaluable help to our Intelligence. In 1917 a careerist British General in Athens who found the shrewd eye of Jeffries a handicap to his intrigues managed to get him recalled to be examined for active service. In a letter to my Chief in London I wrote:

"This plot has been worked by General --- in conjunction with --- the correspondent of the *Daily* --- who is by no means to be trusted. Jeffries has never shirked exposing himself on every occasion. He has never taken advantage of his position to send any message that complicated the situation, even when such a message would have redounded to his credit in Fleet Street: he is nearly 40 and extremely fragile and delicate. It would be a great scandal and injustice if he were recalled, and I do hope you will put this point of view before his Editor."

Jeffries was not recalled and came to see me in Syra in the spring of 1917. During that visit Jeffries leapt up on the sill in my office to open the window and gashed the top of his head on a nail. I thought for a moment we had killed the best newspaper correspondent in Europe, but "as a lily among thorns" he stood serene and his hurt was tended.[2]

A lily among thorns indeed!

---

1. See *Correspondent tells of being held as spy: English writer was well treated by rebels – tried to interview de Valera, The New York Times,* 5/7/22
2. Compton Mackenzie, *Letter to The Times,* 16/12/60

ABC:

Mr. J.M.N. Jeffries (14/12/60)

The illustrious writer and journalist, J.M.N. Jeffries, well known to readers of the *ABC* for his entertaining stories and articles, has passed away at his home in Surrey, England.

He was born in the south of Ireland into one of those families known to the native Irish as the "English garrison," and educated at the Jesuit college, Stonyhurst, in the north of England.

Jeffries was for a long time the *Daily Mail*'s Middle East correspondent. His brilliant work there contributed to the cordial relations that have always existed between those countries and Great Britain. He also spent much time in France, which he knew well, and described shrewdly and warmly.[3]

He did important work in the British Embassy in Madrid for a time which enabled him to get to know the different regions and customs of Spain. Jeffries was a fervent admirer of ours. Some of his pieces, devoted to his impressions of the country as he travelled around it, earned him such epithets as "Hispanist," and "Illustrious Hispanophile." His death is deeply regretted by those whom he honoured with his friendship. He was a true gentleman.[4]

Finally, a brief and heartfelt tribute to Jeffries by the *ABC*'s Paris correspondent ('J.M.') appeared in its edition of 7/1/61 under the title *J.M.N. Jeffries, El Curioso Amigo Impertinente De Los Españoles* ('J.M.N. Jeffries, *A Curious, Cheeky Friend of the Spanish*').

Unfortunately, while J.M.'s tribute speaks to the esteem in which he held his friend, it yields little hard information about Jeffries' remaining years. The subject of Palestine is conspicuous by its absence. Still, it is all we have at this point in time. Here it is in part:

> If I know something about England, it is not because of the many times I have been there during the reigns of Edward VII, George V, Edward VIII, George VI and Elizabeth II, but because I was

---

3. Jeffries, of course, was a *DM* foreign correspondent, not a ME correspondent, a journalistic designation not in existence at the time. As for that second sentence, make of it what you will.

4. We can assume that this obituary was written by the *ABC*'s Paris correspondent, J.M.

a friend of J.M.N. Jeffries. We had maintained, you see, a long-running correspondence. And so, on the occasion of his death – *The Times* remembered him as the best correspondent the British press had ever had – I find myself re-reading his letters. In truth, my friend, the Lord has reserved a place for you by His side, in the company of only the truest and wittiest of men.[5]

He came to Madrid about 25 years ago as a special correspondent for the *Daily Mail*[6], and we had enjoyed an uninterrupted relationship since that time. He criticised us and I criticised his people. We were united in open rebellion against false patriots and pseudo intellectuals... We met once or twice every year, almost always in London. He would invite me to lunch at the St. James Club, and I would invite him to the Spanish Centre in Cavendish Square, once the residence of [Emma] Hamilton... and Admiral Horatio Nelson.

Jeffries lived in Madrid, albeit with innumerable reservations about his 25 years there. Although he lived there, he didn't particularly like the place. One day he confessed to me that he'd come to terms with Madrid only "because it was close to Spain and because its founders had chosen the location because of its proximity to the most impressive golf club in the world." [...]

I've never known a person to ask for forgiveness with such grace for something which was quite unavoidable. On one occasion, for example, he excused himself for not sending me a book with these words: "A criminal and persistent gripe has impeded my work for much of the month. Huge mountains of paper had accumulated on my table. The worst part of a sickness, as you know perfectly well, is that your work isn't sick at the same time. You return to your post in that awful 'post-flu' state, and there it is, everything you'd hoped to avoid, in insultingly good health, challenging you to action." [...]

Occasionally, consumed with nostalgia, he'd leave Madrid behind and seek out the home of Brigadier W.T. Jeffries' of Sunningdale, Berkshire.

Jeffries was a formidable journalist, a great writer, and one of the most perfect gentlemen I have ever met. Spain cannot

---

5. What, I wonder, has become of this correspondence?

6. 'He came to Madrid about 25 years ago as a special correspondent for the *Daily Mail*.' If J.M.'s 25 years is correct, that would mean that Jeffries had visited Madrid in 1935. If so, we know nothing of the circumstances or the reason. As J.M. refers later in his piece to Jeffries having *lived* in Madrid (*Jeffries vivio en Madrid*) for 25 years, I can only assume that his timing is out. If we reckon Jeffries' living in Madrid began in 1940, it would make his residence there 20 years in duration.

thank him enough. He was as tall, thin and energetic as Alonso
Quijano el Bueno.[7]

The reference to Brigadier W.T. Jeffries is interesting.[8] In *Front
Everywhere*, Jeffries refers to a 'cousin, W.F. (the only other Jeffries
of our ilk, who was up at Trinity).' In an online archive, we find
"W.F." profiled thus:

> General Staff, Special Employment, War Office, 1939-1940; Col,
> 1940; Commandant, Intelligence Corps, 1940-1942; Deputy-
> Head of psychological warfare department, Middle East, and
> Central Mediterranean Forces, 1943-1945; Brig, 1943.[9]

One simply cannot imagine the subject of Palestine *not* being
discussed by these two in Brigadier Jeffries' home, Broomfield
House, Sunningdale, Berkshire. Oh to have been a fly on the wall
at the time...

---

7. Alonso Quijano el Bueno (the Good) was the name Cervantes' Don Quixote
    assumed on his deathbed: '"My good friends," said he, "I have happy news to
    tell you; I am no longer Don Quixote de la Mancha, but Alonso Quixano, the
    same whom the world for his fair behaviour has been formerly pleased to call
    the Good."' (Wordsworth Classics edition, 1993, p 764)

8. FE, p 14

9. archives hub.ac.uk/data/gb99-kclmajeffries. Re the name Brigadier W.T.
    Jeffries, there is an entry in the publication *Who Was Who, 1961-1970* (Adam
    & Charles Black, 1972) for a Brigadier William Francis Jeffries (1891-1969),
    the only son of W. Carey Jeffries, M.D., of Coolcarron, Co. Cork. We have,
    therefore, two Jeffries on our hands, a W.T. and a W.F., who appear to be one
    and the same man. To complicate matters still further, in that entry, William
    Francis is cited as the author of a 1914 travel memoir, *Two Undergraduates in
    the East*. That book, however, carries the author's name as W. Carey Jeffries,
    B.A., and, curiously, nowhere in it are the titular 'undergraduates' mentioned
    by name. My guess is that the two 'undergraduates' are, in fact, father
    (W. Carey Jeffries, M.D.) and son (W.F/W.T. Jeffries, B.A.). In which case,
    considering that there is a chapter on Palestine in the book, Jeffries' cousin, the
    Brigadier, would have been twice to that country – 1913 and 1943–44.

APPENDIX 1:
Contemporary 'Scholarship' & the Hussein-McMahon Correspondence

Both Jeffries and Antonius were emphatic as to the significance of the Hussein-McMahon Correspondence, with Jeffries, as we have seen, declaring Hussein's opening letter 'one of the great salient events in the history of the [Palestine] question,'[1] and Antonius asserting that McMahon's fourth letter 'may perhaps be regarded as the most important international document in the history of the Arab national movement.'[2]

And yet, despite the weight of such judgments, the Correspondence has all but faded from contemporary scholarly memory. Two classic works on the Palestine problem from the late 1970s, for example, David Hirst's *The Gun & the Olive Branch: The Roots of Violence in the Middle East* (1977), and Edward Said's *The Question of Palestine* (1979), make no reference to it at all. But even if the Correspondence *is* mentioned by scholars, misconceptions and errors often occur. We shall examine here three cases in point.

Greg Philo and Mike Berry's *Bad News from Israel* (2004), a study of how the mainstream media covers the Palestine-Israel conflict, contains the following reference in its lengthy introduction, *Histories of the Conflict*:

---

1. PTR, p 63
2. Antonius, p 169

> British assurances of Arab independence after the defeat of the
> Axis Powers (which had been pledged as a reward for Arab support
> during the First World War) can be found in the correspondence
> between Sir Henry McMahon... and Sharif Hussein... However,
> these pledges by European Powers... conflicted with British
> assurances given, at the time, to Zionist leaders that Britain
> would seek the establishment of a Jewish homeland in Palestine.[3]

To begin with there were no 'pledges by European powers' to the
Arabs, only a *British* pledge. Moreover, on reading this, one could
be forgiven for thinking that the Balfour Declaration *preceded* the
Hussein-McMahon Correspondence, with all that that implies by
way of which should take priority.

Philo and Berry's lack of clarity on the subject of the Hussein-
McMahon Correspondence, however, pales into insignificance
when compared to the distortions encountered in Jeremy Paxman's
account of the Correspondence in his book, *Empire* (2012):

> McMahon wrote to the leader of the Hashemite clan, the Sharif,
> or religious leader, of Mecca, Hussein bin Ali, suggesting that
> an uprising would herald the arrival of that eternal will o' the
> wisp, an Arab nation. Hussein claimed descent from the prophet
> Muhammad, and was not to be bought cheaply. In return for
> rising against the Ottoman Empire, he expected money, guns and
> the title 'King of the Arabs'. The first two commodities presented
> no problem to the British, and to appease Hussein's vanity the
> British letters opened with eighty-two words of fawning honorifics
> including describing this romantic yet ineffectual man as 'him of
> the Exalted Presence and the Lofty Rank' and 'the Lodestar of the
> Faithful and the cynosure of all devout Believers'. Had the 'King
> of the Arabs' bothered with the details of the offer being made
> by the British, he might have wondered precisely what some of
> the small print about the promised Arab state meant, for example
> the condition that 'the districts of Mersin and Alexandretta, and
> portions of Syria lying to the west of the districts of Damascus,
> Homs, Hama and Aleppo, cannot be said to be purely Arab, and
> must on that account be excepted'. But he did not hesitate.[4]

---

3. Greg Philo & Mike Berry, *Bad News from Israel*, Pluto Press, London, 2004,
   pp 5-6
4. Jeremy Paxman, *Empire*, Penguin Books, London, 2012, pp 226-227

While highly entertaining, Paxman's sketch plays havoc with
the historical record in several respects:

1) As we have seen, it was Hussein, not McMahon, who initiated
   the Correspondence.

2) Paxman's facile quip about the 'Arab nation' being an 'eternal
   will o' the wisp' may ring true if we look at today's balkanised
   Middle East, but the prospects for Arab unity at the time were
   far from unreal. The Anglo-French machinations which cruelled
   those prospects were still to come. But for these, a viable Arab
   union of sorts may well have emerged – with, needless to say,
   direct implications for a stable, peaceful and prosperous Middle
   East today.

3) Paxman's portrait of the Sharif is an appalling caricature. He
   is completely misrepresented as a stereotypical Middle Eastern
   potentate, motivated solely by greed and vanity. The charge that
   'in return for rising against the Ottoman Empire he expected
   money, guns and the title "King of the Arabs"' from the British
   is simply not true. If Paxman had actually taken the trouble to
   read the Correspondence, he would have discovered that the
   realisation of Arab independence and nationhood was all that
   mattered to Hussein. As Hussein told McMahon in his third
   letter: 'Were it not for the determination shown by the Arabs to
   realise their aspirations, I would have elected to retire to some
   mountain-top.' (Antonius' translation) Note also the following
   declaration in his fourth letter: 'You will have satisfied yourself
   that our attitude was not prompted by personal desires, which
   would have been foolish, but was the result of the decisions
   taken and the desires expressed by our people; and that our
   role in the matter was confined to conveying and putting into
   effect those desires and decisions, thus merely discharging a duty
   with which our people had invested us. It is, in my view, most
   important that Your Excellency should realise that. But they
   pressed me to lead the movement to its goal.'

There is, as we have seen, reference to an Arab caliphate in the Correspondence, but no mention of kingship. The circumstances in which the Sharif Hussein later became King Hussein are described by Tibawi as follows:

> Apart from the shortage of arms the Sharif was disappointed by the lack of British formal recognition of his declaration of Arab independence... The Turks were quick to exploit the lack of British recognition by representing the Sharif to the Arabs and Muslims as a British stooge. Abdullah [Hussein's second son] sought to counteract the Turkish propaganda... From personal experience he anticipated a British negative... to his secret plan of proclaiming his father as king. Accordingly he convened an assembly of ulema, officials and notables at the palace on... 29 October 1916. Previous soundings and briefings prepared the gathering... The meeting was opened by an oration delivered by the editor of *al-Qibla* in which he eulogised the Arab nation and sang the praise of the Sharif. At the end he handed to Abdullah a packet of letters from notables in the Arab provinces still under Turkish rule, notably Syria and Iraq in which they recognise the Sharif as the sovereign of the Arab nation. Thereupon the assembly acclaimed him as such and also as 'the final religious authority' pending the decision of the Muslim world regarding the caliphate. Then Shaikh Abdullah Siraj, the Chief Qadi of Mecca, went to the private apartment and submitted to the Sharif the assembly's plea for him to accept their decision... He never thought their decision was necessary... The revolt he proclaimed was to avert danger and calamity to the Hijaz and the Arab nation as a whole. But he never entertained any desire to be king 'when you and I started our blessed movement'... 'If you make it imperative for me to accept what you are offering me,' he said, 'I must ask you to help me and support me... in the service of the Arabs in particular and the Muslims in general'.[5]

The extent to which Paxman misrepresents Hussein's character becomes apparent when we consider the following account of his refusal to accept the terms of a draft treaty which T.E. Lawrence, by then a Colonial Office official, presented to him in Jedda, in August 1921:

5. A.L. Tibawi, *Anglo-Arab Relations & The Question of Palestine 1914-1921*, Luzac & Company Ltd, London, 1977, pp 151-152 *The Question of Palestine*, p 245

Briefly the British proposals were that Hussein should wash his
hands of Arab affairs and direct all his attention to Hejaz, content
that Feisal had ascended the throne of Iraq and Abdullah had
become Emir of Transjordan. The King was further urged that he
might do well to be content with an alliance with Great Britain,
in the hope that she would curb his ambitious neighbours...
Furthermore, Britain would continue paying the monthly subsidy
into the Hejaz treasury. Hussein had no eye for personal gain.
He looked on himself rather as a keeper of a sacred trust and
a representative of the spirit of the Arab nation, who could not
possibly condone imperialistic designs on Arab countries. The
seventy-year-old King held obstinately to his convictions for
the safeguarding of his nation's destiny, and he did not hide his
contempt for Lawrence and the offers he brought.

Lawrence on his part acted on the suggestion of the King's
family. On 12 October, he reached Amman, where he discussed
with Emir Abdullah the articles of the draft treaty... Making
further amendments, the Emir signed the draft treaty and sent
it on to his father with a letter asking for permission to sign the
treaty in the King's name. But Hussein refused to receive the
letter, which he returned sealed to his son. Thus the negotiations
came to nothing...[6]

4) As for those 'fawning honorifics,' Jeffries refers merely to
'customary compliments,' while Antonius explains that these
were 'a medley of Turco-Persian toadyisms, which someone
on McMahon's staff had thought appropriate.' Antonius adds,
moreover, that 'This flummery served only to annoy Hussein,
who showed irritation in his reply.'[7] It should be noted here that
Hussein's exact words, in his second letter to McMahon, read,
'For our aim... is to ensure that the conditions which are essential
to our future shall be secured on a foundation of reality, and not
on highly-decorated phrases and titles.' (Antonius' translation)

5) Finally, it should be pointed out that Hussein did not so much
overlook the 'fine print' of McMahon's letters as take too
seriously the expression that an Englishman's word is his honour.

---

6. Suleiman Moussa, *T.E. Lawrence: An Arab View*, Oxford University Press,
    London, 1966, p 243

7. George Antonius, *The Arab Awakening*, Hamish Hamilton, London, 1938, pp
    166-167

Sean McMeekin's *The Ottoman Endgame: War, Revolution & the Making of the Modern Middle East, 1908-1923* (2015) is yet another account of the Correspondence that has one reaching for correctives such as those of Jeffries, Antonius and Tibawi. After portraying Hussein as a traitor to the Ottoman cause motivated solely by greed, McMeekin goes on to write:

> Then there were the ill-fated negotiations between Hussein and Sir Henry McMahon... over the future disposition of Palestine, Syria, and Mesopotamia, in which McMahon so elegantly sidestepped making direct promises that diplomatic historians... still argue today about who, exactly, the British promised would get to rule each area after the war... Only in retrospect was the "McMahon-Hussein correspondence," conducted in equally bad faith on both sides, invested with earnestness and epochal significance.[8]

To begin with, McMahon did make a direct promise, namely: 'Subject to the above modifications [the districts of Mersina and Alexandretta and portions of Syria lying to the west of the districts of Damascus, Homs, Hama and Allepo], Great Britain is prepared to recognise and support the independence of the Arabs within the territories included within the limits and boundaries proposed by the Shereef of Mecca.'

Moreover, the negotiations had nothing whatever to do with the future of Palestine and Syria as discrete entities within those boundaries. Nor was the Correspondence 'conducted equally in bad faith' on both sides. While one may well harbour doubts about McMahon in this respect, there is certainly no evidence of bad faith on Hussein's part.

Needless to say, McMeekin's grasp of the contemporary Middle East is equally problematic. For example:

> Britain's backing of Zionism in the Balfour Declaration of 1917 was... a step too far, which awakened Arabs from a centuries-long slumber to rise up against the latter-day Crusaders – Europeans and Israelis alike – who had seized their lands. The more recent rise of pan-Islamic movements such as the Muslim Brotherhood,

---

8. Sean McMeekin, *The Ottoman Endgame: War, Revolution & the Making of the Modern Middle East, 1908-1923*, 2015, pp 303-304

Hamas, Hezbollah, al-Qaeda, and the Islamic State – groups that all strive to erase artificial, European-imposed state boundaries – now appears to be putting the final nails in the coffin of Sykes-Picot.[9]

His conflation here of regional Islamic resistance movements such as Hamas and Hezbollah with pan-Islamic movements is nothing less than a gross misrepresentation.

---

9. McMeekin, p xvi

APPENDIX 2:
Contemporary 'Scholarship' and the Balfour Declaration

A s with the Hussein-McMahon Correspondence, many of the more recent scholarly treatments of the Balfour Declaration hardly do it justice. In general, considering the Declaration's lasting impact on the Palestinian and other Arab peoples, they either (at best) lack depth, or (at worst) embody an underlying Zionist or British imperial perspective.

While hardly an exhaustive survey, the following five texts illustrate the problem.

If Jeffries subjects the Declaration to the ultimate scrutiny, David Fromkin's widely read and cited, *A Peace to End All Peace: Creating the Modern Middle East 1914-1922* (1989), simply avoids it altogether. To do so would only detract from his basically Zionist perspective. The words of American historian Charles D. Smith are apposite here:

> The aim of this scholarship, to legitimize Zionism at the expense of Arab, especially Palestinian, national claims, is still current and popular, especially in the United States, as seen in the works of David Fromkin and Efraim Karsh.[1]

---

1.   Charles D. Smith, *The Historiography of World War I & the Emergence of the Contemporary Middle East, in Middle Eastern Historiographies: Narrating the Twentieth Century*, ed. By Israel Gershoni, Amy Singer & Y. Hakan Erdem, University of Washington Press, Washington, 2006, p 43

Niall Ferguson's *Empire: How Britain Made the Modern World*, manages, incredibly, to relegate the Balfour Declaration to a mere footnote, which simply informs us that 'the terms of the 1917 Balfour Declaration had turned out to contain a hopeless contradiction.'[2]

The reference to the Declaration in Jeremy Paxman's *Empire* is on surer ground, but one would never guess from it, however, that the Zionists had a direct hand in its formulation:

> The tortuous form of words has the stamp of a committee all over it, and, moreover, a British committee – sophisticated, ponderous and, on contentious points, oblique. What *was* a 'national home'? What would the British actually *do* if the 'civil and religious rights of existing non-Jewish communities' were compromised or violated? The cabinet wasn't much bothered: the document which Jews claimed gave the state of Israel its founding legitimacy was just one of several agreements knocked out in the region. Cynical doesn't really seem to do justice to the British behaviour.[3]

Walter Reid's *Empire of Sand: How Britain Made the Middle East* is very much an apologia for imperial Britain:

> My conclusion is that British policy was formulated in good faith, the outcome of a desperate and uncoordinated series of attempts to stave off defeat... Some policy initiatives – the Balfour Declaration is the most egregious – were subsequently assumed to have a significance greater than their authors had intended.[4]

His assessment – that the British Government was too distracted by the war to really know what it was doing when it drafted and issued the Balfour Declaration - could hardly be more at odds with that of Jeffries:

> The Government on its own part did mean to give as much of the Zionists' sense to the Declaration as was safe, from the very start. As the margin of safety grew, as its own hold on the land

---

2. Niall Ferguson, *Empire: How Britain Made the Modern World*, Allen Lane, London, 2003, p 357. Ferguson is Professor of International History at Harvard University.

3. Jeremy Paxman, *Empire*, Penguin Books, London, 2012, pp 229-230

4. Walter Reid, *Empire of Sand: How Britain Made the Middle East*, Birlinn Limited, Edinburgh, 2011, p 349

became stronger, as a menial prosperity enticed the mass of Arabs, and the opposition of the remainder had been measured and met, then the Government would increase its support of the Zionist establishment in widening degrees, till the Jewish State at last arose. On the other hand, the Government kept a way of retreat open in case some formidable opposition... might make headway against official alliance with political Zionism.[5]

Then there is this particular oddity of Reid's:

It can be argued... that the declaration served British interests tolerably well for 40 years. But that is not to say that the declaration may not have been a tragedy for the rest of the world.[6]

'Tolerably well for 40 years,' but 'a tragedy for the rest of the world' hardly amounts to a ringing endorsement. And what does he mean by 'tolerably well'? Apparently, control of Iraqi oil, the creation of Jordan, and keeping the French and Germans out of Palestine.[7] Finally, one is left to ponder exactly what he means by 'a tragedy for the rest of the world.' The tragedy, first and foremost, was for the Palestinian people.

Reid's clearest disclaimer that Britain was *not in any* way responsible for the ensuing conflict in Palestine which followed its promotion of the Zionist project simply defies reality:

The Balfour Declaration... did not commit Arabs and Jews to conflict. They chose that conflict for themselves. The Arabs exacerbated the problems inherent in Palestine by their sulky non-cooperation and obstructiveness, the Jews by their desire for much more than amicable coexistence.[8]

This pox-on-both-your-houses approach is extraordinarily naïve, and ignores completely settler-colonial logic; if only the colonised had embraced their colonisers, and the latter renounced their colonisation!

The following shockingly ignorant sentence alone is enough to discredit Reid's book. (italics mine):

---

5. PTR, p 176
6. Reid, p 92
7. Reid, p 351-352
8. Reid p 352

> The Balfour Declaration was based on the idea that Jewry dispersed throughout the world by persecution and cruelty was entitled to consideration *along with the wishes of the largely nomadic peoples who happened to be in Palestine in 1917.*[9]

This portrayal of the Palestinian Arabs is, if anything, even worse than the Balfour Declaration's 'existing non-Jewish communities in Palestine.'

Reid, incidentally, is described on his book's dust jacket as the author of 'a number of highly acclaimed works of military and political history.'

Jonathan Schneer's *The Balfour Declaration*, while not overtly Zionist in orientation, makes no attempt to come to grips with the appalling crime against humanity set in motion by the Declaration:

> Zionists and many others have viewed [the Declaration] ever since as a terrific achievement, a foundation stone along the way to the establishment of modern Israel. Many Arabs, on the other hand, have seen it as a terrible setback, the real starting point of their dispossession and misery.[10]

The suggestion here is that *only* Arabs could possibly have seen the Declaration as a 'terrible setback,' and even then only 'many' of them. Moreover, the term 'setback' hardly does justice to the Palestinian Nakba (catastrophe) of 1948 and all that has followed since then.

Then there is this:

> As for the majority of Palestinian Arabs, they directed their resentment against Jews (whom [sic] they thought were stealing their land) and against British officials (whom [sic, again] they thought were protecting the Jews).[11]

Schneer comes perilously close here to suggesting that the Zionist purchase and alienation of Arab land, and the protection of British bayonets under which it proceeded, were merely figments of the Arab imagination.

---

9. Reid, p 353

10. Jonathan Schneer, *The Balfour Declaration*, Random House, New York, 2010 p 374

11. Schneer, p 375

Index

PUBLISHER'S NOTE

A reprint of *Palestine: The Reality* by J.M.N. Jeffries,
with additional material, is available from
Skyscraper Publications in the U.K. (ISBN 9781911072225,
price £25.00) and from Olive Branch Press in the
U.S.A. (ISBN 9781566560245, price $30.00).

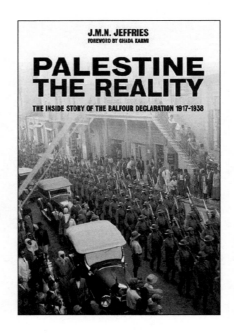